Expository Thoughts on
The Gospel of John

Expository Thoughts on
The Gospel of John

J. C. Ryle

We love hearing from our readers. Please contact us
at www.anekopress.com/questions-comments with
any questions, comments, or suggestions.

Expository Thoughts on the Gospel of John – J. C. Ryle
Revised Edition Copyright © 2019
First edition published 1869

Scripture quotations marked JUB are taken from the Jubilee Bible,
copyright © 2000, 2001, 2010, 2013 by Russell M. Stendal.
Used by permission of Russell M. Stendal, Bogota, Colombia.
All rights reserved.

Cover Design: J. Martin

Cover Background: ilolab/Shutterstock

Editors: Sheila Wilkinson; Jeremiah Zeiset

Printed in the United States of America

Aneko Press

www.anekopress.com

Aneko Press, Life Sentence Publishing, and our logos are trademarks of
Life Sentence Publishing, Inc.
203 E. Birch Street
P.O. Box 652
Abbotsford, WI 54405

RELIGION / Biblical Commentary / New Testament / Jesus, the Gospels & Acts

Paperback ISBN: 978-1-62245-627-7
eBook ISBN: 978-1-62245-628-4

10 9 8 7 6 5 4 3 2 1

Available where books are sold

Contents

Preface

I send forth the volume now in the reader's hands with much reserve and a very deep sense of responsibility. It is no light matter to publish an exposition of any book in the Bible. It is a peculiarly serious undertaking to attempt a Commentary on the Gospel of John.

I do not forget that we are all apt to exaggerate the difficulties of our own particular department of literary labor. But I think every intelligent student of Scripture will bear me out when I say that John's Gospel is pre-eminently full of things "hard to be understood" (2 Peter 3:16). It contains a large portion of our Lord Jesus Christ's doctrinal teaching. It abounds in "deep things of God," and "sayings of the King," which we instinctively feel we have no *line* to fully fathom, no *mind* to fully comprehend, no *words* to fully explain. It must needs be that such a book of Scripture should be difficult. I can truly say that I have commented on many a verse in this Gospel with fear and trembling. I have often said to myself, "Who is sufficient for these things?" (2 Corinthians 2:16) – "The place whereon thou standest is holy ground" (Exodus 3:5).

The nature of the work now published requires a few words of explanation. It is a continuation of the "Expository Thoughts on the Gospels," of which the first three Gospels have been already sent forth. Like the previous volumes, the composition of this book is a continuous series of short expositions, intended for family or private reading or for the use of those who visit the sick and the poor.

We live in a day of abounding vagueness and indistinctness on doctrinal subjects in religion. Now, if ever, it is the duty of all advocates of clear, well-defined, sharply cut theology to supply proof that their views are thoroughly borne out by Scripture. I have endeavored to do so in this Commentary. I hold that the Gospel of John, rightly interpreted, is the best and simplest answer to those who profess to admire a vague and indistinct Christianity.

The theological standpoint which the writer of this Commentary occupies will be obvious to any intelligent reader. Such a one will see at a glance that I belong to that school in the Church of England which, rightly or wrongly, is called "Evangelical." He will see that I have no sympathy whatever with either Romish or Neologian tendencies. He will see that I hold firmly the distinctive theological views of the Reformers and doctrinal Puritans, and that I totally disapprove the loose and broad theology of some modern schools of divines. But while I say all this, I must be allowed to add that in interpreting Scripture, I "call no man master or father." I abhor the idea of twisting and warping God's Word in order to make it support party views. Throughout this Commentary I have endeavored honestly and conscientiously to find out the real meaning of every sentence on which I have commented. I have evaded no difficulty and shrunk from no inference. I have simply followed Scripture wherever its words seemed to point and accepted whatever they seemed to mean. I have never hesitated to express my disagreement from the views of other commentators if occasion required, but when I have done so, I have tried to do it with courtesy and respect.

On one point of vast importance in the present day, the reader will see that I hold very decided opinions. That point is *inspiration*. I feel no hesitation in avowing that I believe in the "plenary inspiration" of every word of the original text of Holy Scripture. I hold not only that the Bible *contains* the Word of God, but that every jot of it was written or brought together by Divine inspiration and is the Word of God. I entirely disagree with those who maintain that the writers of the Bible were partially inspired or inspired to such a limited extent that discrepancies, inaccuracies, and contradictions to the facts of science and history must be expected and do exist in their writings. I utterly repudiate such a theory. I consider that it practically destroys the whole value of God's Word, puts a sword in the hand of infidels and sceptics, and raises far more serious difficulties than it pretends to solve. . . .

For my own part, I believe that the whole Bible, as it came originally from the hands of the inspired writers, was verbally perfect and without flaw. I believe that the inspired writers were infallibly guided by the Holy Spirit, both in their selection of matter and their choice of words. I believe that even now, when we cannot explain alleged difficulties in Holy Scripture, the wisest course is to blame the interpreter and not the text, to suspect our own ignorance to be in fault, and not any defect in God's Word. The theological system of modern days, which delights in magnifying the so-called mistakes of the Bible, in explaining away its miraculous narratives and in making as little as possible of its Divine character and supernatural element, is a system that I cannot away with. It seems to me to take a rock from beneath our feet and plant us on a quicksand. It robs us of bread and does not give us in its place so much as a stone. . . .

I now conclude this preface with an earnest prayer that it may please God to pardon the many deficiencies of this volume and to use it for His own glory and the good of souls. It has cost me a large amount of time and thought and labor. But if the Holy Spirit shall make it useful to the Church of Christ, I shall feel abundantly repaid.

Ignorance of Scripture is the root of every error in religion and the source of every heresy. To be allowed to remove a few grains of ignorance and to throw a few rays of light on God's precious word is, in my opinion, the greatest honor that can be put on a Christian.

Introduction

The following prefatory remarks on John's Gospel may prove useful to some readers:

Firstly, there is no doubt that this Gospel was written by John, the Apostle, the son of Zebedee, and brother of James, once a fisherman on the sea of Galilee, and afterwards called to be a disciple of the Lord Jesus, an eyewitness of all Christ's ministry, and a pillar of the church. John, be it remembered, is specially called "the disciple whom Jesus loved." He was one of the chosen three who alone saw the daughter of Jairus raised – were eyewitnesses of the transfiguration – and were bystanders during our Lord's agony in the garden. He was the one who leaned on Christ's breast at the last supper, and to whom our Lord committed the care of the Virgin Mary, when He was dying on the cross. It is an interesting fact, that he was the disciple who was specially inspired to write the deepest things concerning Christ.

Secondly, there is little doubt that this Gospel was written at a much later date than the other three Gospels. How much later and at what precise time, we do not know. It is commonly supposed that it was written after the rise of heresies about the Person and natures of Christ. It is not likely that it was written at so late a period as the destruction of Jerusalem. If this had been the case, John would hardly have spoken of the "sheep-market" at Jerusalem as still standing (John 5:2).

Thirdly, the substance of this Gospel is, for the most part, peculiar to itself. With the exception of the crucifixion and a few other matters, the things which John was inspired to record concerning our Lord are only found in his gospel. He says nothing about our Lord's birth and infancy, His temptation, the Sermon on the Mount, the transfiguration, the prophecy about Jerusalem, and the appointment of the Lord's Supper. He gives us very few miracles, and even fewer parables. But the things which John does relate are among the most precious treasures which Christians possess. The chapters about Nicodemus – the woman of Samaria – the raising of Lazarus – and our Lord's appearance to Peter after His resurrection at the sea of Galilee – the public discourses of the fifth, sixth, seventh, eighth, and tenth chapters – the private discourses of the thirteenth, fourteenth, fifteenth, and sixteenth chapters – and, above all, the prayer of the seventeenth chapter are some of the most valuable portions of the Bible. All these chapters, be it remembered, we owe to John.

Fourthly, the style of this Gospel is no less peculiar than its substance. There appears extraordinary simplicity in many of its statements, and yet there is a depth about them, which no man can entirely fathom. It contains many expressions which are used in a profound and spiritual sense, such as "light," "darkness," "world," "life," "truth," "to abide," "to know." It contains two names of the second and third Persons of the Trinity, not found in the other Gospels. These are "the Word," as a name of our Lord, and "the Comforter," as a name of the Holy Spirit. It contains, from time to time, explanatory comments and remarks on our Lord's words. Moreover, it contains frequent short explanations of Jewish customs and terms, which serve to show that it was not written so much for Jewish readers as for the whole church throughout the world.

Lastly, the preface of this Gospel is one of the most striking peculiarities about the whole book. Under the term preface, I include the first eighteen verses of the first chapter. This preface forms the quintessence of the whole book and is composed of simple, short, condensed propositions. Nowhere in the Bible shall we find such clear and distinct statements about our Lord Jesus Christ's divine nature. Nowhere shall we find so many expressions, which for want of mental power, no mortal man can fully grasp or explain. In no portion of Scripture is it so deeply important to notice each word and even each tense employed in each sentence. In no portion of Scripture do the perfect grammatical accuracy and verbal precision of an inspired composition shine out so brightly. It is not, perhaps, too much to say that not a single word could be altered in the first five verses of John's Gospel without opening the door to some heresy.

John Chapter 1

John 1:1-5

*In the beginning was the Word, and the Word was with the
God, and the Word was God. The same was in the beginning
with the God. All things were made by him, and without him
was not any thing made that was made. In him was life, and
the life was the light of men. And the light shines in the darkness, and the darkness apprehended it not.*

THE GOSPEL OF JOHN, which begins with these verses, is in many
respects very unlike the other three Gospels. It contains many things,
which they omit. It omits many things, which they contain. Good
reason might easily be shown for this unlikeness. But it is enough to
remember that Matthew, Mark, Luke, and John wrote under the direct
inspiration of God. In the general plan of their respective Gospels and
in the particular details – in everything that they record and in everything that they do not record – they were all four equally and entirely
guided by the Holy Spirit.

About the matters, which John was specially inspired to relate in his
Gospel, one general remark will suffice. The things which are peculiar
to his Gospel are among the most precious possessions of the Church
of Christ. No one of the four Gospel writers has given us such full
statements about the divinity of Christ, about justification by faith,
about the offices of Christ, about the work of the Holy Spirit, and about
the privileges of believers as we read in the pages of John. On none of
these great subjects, undoubtedly, have Matthew, Mark, and Luke been
silent. But in John's Gospel, they stand out prominently on the surface,
unmistakable in meaning.

The five verses now before us contain a statement of matchless sublimity concerning the divine nature of our Lord Jesus Christ. He it is, beyond all question, whom John means when he speaks of "the Word." No doubt there are heights and depths in that statement which are far beyond man's understanding. And yet there are plain lessons in it, which every Christian would do well to treasure up in his mind.

We learn, firstly, that our Lord Jesus Christ is *eternal*. John tells us that "in the *beginning* was the Word." He did not begin to exist when the heavens and the earth were made. Much less did He begin to exist when the Gospel was brought into the world. He had glory with the Father "before the world was" (John 17:5). He was existing when matter was first created and before time began. He was "before all things" (Colossians 1:17). He was from all eternity.

We learn, secondly, that our Lord Jesus Christ is *a Person distinct from God the Father, and yet one with Him*. John tells us that "the Word was with God."[1] The Father and the Word, though two persons, are joined by an ineffable union. Where God the Father was from all eternity, there also was the Word, even God the Son – their glory equal, their majesty co-eternal, and yet their Godhead one. This is a great mystery! Happy is he who can receive it as a little child without attempting to explain it.

We learn, thirdly, that the Lord Jesus Christ is *very God*. John tells us that "the Word was God." He is not merely a created angel, or a being inferior to God the Father, and invested by Him with power to redeem sinners. He is nothing less than perfect God – equal to the Father as touching His Godhead – God of the substance of the Father, begotten before the worlds.

We learn, fourthly, that the Lord Jesus Christ is the *Creator of all things*. John tells us that "by Him were all things made, and without Him was not any thing made that was made." So far from being a

---

1   The expression, "the Word," is a very difficult one and is peculiar to John. I see no clear proof that it is used by any other New Testament writer. The texts, Acts 20:32 and Hebrews 4:12, are, to say the least, doubtful proofs. That it here signifies a "person," and not a spoken word, and that it is applied to our Lord Jesus Christ, is clear from the after sentence, "The Word was made flesh, and dwelt among us." That it was a term familiar to the Jews is undeniable. But why this particular name is used by John, both here and in his other writings, is a point on which commentators have differed greatly. . . . This sentence means that the Lord Jesus Christ, the eternal Word, was in nature, essence and substance, very God, and that "as the Father is God, so also the Son is God."

creature of God, as some heretics have falsely asserted, He is the Being who made the worlds and all that they contain. "He commanded and they were created" (Psalm 148:5).

We learn, lastly, that the Lord Jesus Christ is the *source of all spiritual life and light*. John tells us that "in Him was life, and the life was the light of men." He is the eternal fountain from which alone the sons of men have ever derived life. Whatever spiritual life and light Adam and Eve possessed before the fall was from Christ. Whatever deliverance from sin and spiritual death any child of Adam has ever enjoyed since the fall, whatever light of conscience or understanding any one has obtained – all has flowed from Christ. The vast majority of mankind in every age have refused to know Him, have forgotten the fall and their own need of a Savior. The light has been constantly shining "in darkness." Most have "not comprehended the light." But if any men and women out of the countless millions of mankind have ever had spiritual life and light, they have owed all to Christ.

Such is a brief summary of the leading lessons, which these wonderful verses appear to contain. There is much in them without controversy, which is above our reason, but there is nothing contrary to it. There is much that we cannot explain and must be content humbly to believe. Let us however never forget that there are plain practical consequences flowing from the passage, which we can never grasp too firmly or know too well.

Would we know, for one thing, the exceeding sinfulness of sin? Let us often read these first five verses of John's Gospel. Let us mark what kind of Being the Redeemer of mankind must needs be, in order to provide eternal redemption for sinners. If no one less than the Eternal God, the Creator and Preserver of all things, could take away the sin of the world, sin must be a far more abominable thing in the sight of God than most men suppose. The right measure of sin's sinfulness is the dignity of Him who came into the world to save sinners. If Christ is so great, then sin must indeed be sinful!

Would we know, for another thing, the strength of a true Christian's foundation for hope? Let us often read these first five verses of John's Gospel. Let us mark that the Savior in whom the believer is bid to trust

3

is nothing less than the Eternal God, One able to save to the uttermost all that come to the Father by Him. He that was "with God" and "was God" is also "Emmanuel, God with us." Let us thank God that our help is laid on One that is mighty (Psalm 89:19). In ourselves we are great sinners. But in Jesus Christ we have a great Savior. He is a strong foundation stone, able to bear the weight of a world's sin. He that believes on Him shall not be confounded (1 Peter 2:6).

John 1:6-13

There was a man sent from God, whose name was John. The same came for a witness, to bear witness of the Light, that all men through him might believe. He was not the Light, but was sent to bear witness of the Light. That Word was the true Light, which lightens every man that comes into this world. He was in the world, and the world was made by him, and the world knew him not. He came unto his own, and his own received him not. But as many as received him, to them gave he power to become sons of God, even to them that believe on his name, who are not born of blood, nor of the will of flesh, nor of the will of man, but of God.

John, after beginning his gospel with a statement of our Lord's nature as God, proceeds to speak of His forerunner, John the Baptist.[2] The contrast between the language used about the Savior and that used about His forerunner ought not to be overlooked. Of Christ we are told that He was the eternal God – the Creator of all things – the source of life and light. Of John the Baptist we are told simply that "there was a man sent from God, whose name was John."

We see, firstly, in these verses, *the true nature of a Christian minister's office.* We have it in the description of John the Baptist – "He

---

2 Verses 6 and 7 are a short and striking description of John the Baptist. He was the messenger whom God promised to send before Messiah's face. He was born when his parents were aged, by God's miraculous interposition. He was filled with the Holy Spirit from his mother's womb. He received a special commission from God to preach the baptism of repentance and to proclaim the immediate coming of Christ. In short, he was specially raised up by God to prepare the way for the Messiah. For all these reasons he is here called "a man sent from God."

came for a witness to bear witness of the light that all men through him might believe."

Christian ministers are not priests, nor mediators between God and man. They are not agents into whose hands men may commit their souls and carry on their religion by deputy. They are witnesses. They are intended to bear testimony to God's truth and especially to the great truth that Christ is the only Savior and light of the world. This was Peter's ministry on the day of Pentecost. "With many other words did he *testify*" (Acts 2:40). This was the whole tenor of Paul's ministry. "He *testified* both to the Jews and Greeks repentance towards God, and faith towards our Lord Jesus Christ" (Acts 20:21). Unless a Christian minister bears a full testimony to Christ, he is not faithful to his office. So long as he does testify of Christ, he has done his part and will receive his reward, although his hearers may not believe his testimony. Until a minister's hearers believe on that Christ, of whom they are told, they receive no benefit from the ministry. They may be pleased and interested; but they are not profited until they believe. The great end of a minister's testimony is "that through him, men may believe."

We see, secondly, in these verses, *one principal position, which our Lord Jesus Christ occupies towards mankind.* We have it in the words, "He was the true light which lighteth every man that cometh into the world."

Christ is to the souls of men what the sun is to the world. He is the center and source of all spiritual light, warmth, life, health, growth, beauty, and fertility. Like the sun, He shines for the common benefit of all mankind – for high and for low, for rich and for poor, for Jew and for Greek. Like the sun, He is free to all. All may look at Him and drink health out of His light. If millions of mankind were mad enough to dwell in caves underground or to bandage their eyes, their darkness would be their own fault and not the fault of the sun. So, likewise, if millions of men and women love spiritual "darkness rather than light," the blame must be laid on their blind hearts and not on Christ (John 3:19). "Their foolish hearts are darkened" (Romans 1:21). But whether men will see or not, Christ is the true sun and the light of the world. There is no light for sinners except in the Lord Jesus.

We see, thirdly, in these verses, *the desperate wickedness of man's natural heart.* We have it in the words – Christ "was in the world, and the world was made by Him, and the world knew Him not. He came unto His own, and His own received Him not."

Christ was in the world *invisibly,* long before He was born of the Virgin Mary. He was there from the very beginning – ruling, ordering, and governing the whole creation. By Him all things are held together (Colossians 1:17). He gave to all life and breath, rain from heaven, and fruitful seasons. By Him kings reigned, and nations were increased or diminished. Yet men knew Him not and honored Him not. They "worshiped and served the creature more than the Creator" (Romans 1:25). Well may the natural heart be called "wicked!"

But Christ came visibly into the world when He was born at Bethlehem and fared no better. He came to the very people whom He had brought out from Egypt and purchased for His own. He came to the Jews, whom He had separated from other nations and to whom He had revealed Himself by the prophets. He came to those very Jews who had read of Him in the Old Testament Scriptures – seen Him under types and figures in their temple services – and professed to be waiting for His coming. And yet, when He came, those very Jews received Him not. They even rejected Him, despised Him, and slew Him. Well may the natural heart be called "desperately wicked!"

We see, lastly, in these verses, *the vast privileges of all who receive Christ and believe on Him.* We are told that "as many as received Him, to them gave He power to become the sons of God, even to those who believe on His name."

Christ will never be without some servants. If the vast majority of the Jews did not receive Him as the Messiah, there were, at any rate, a few who did. To them He gave the privilege of being God's children. He reckoned them His own brethren and sisters, bone of His bone and flesh of His flesh. He conferred on them a dignity, which was ample recompense for the cross which they had to carry for His sake. He made them sons and daughters of the Lord Almighty.

Privileges like these, be it remembered, are the possession of all, in every age, who receive Christ by faith and follow Him as their Savior.

They are "children of God by faith in Christ Jesus" (Galatians 3:26). They are born again by a new and heavenly birth and adopted into the family of the King of kings. Few in number and despised by the world as they are, they are cared for with infinite love by a Father in heaven who, for His Son's sake, is well pleased with them. In time He provides them with everything that is for their good. In eternity He will give them a crown of glory that fades not away. These are great things! But faith in Christ gives men an ample title to them. Good masters care for their servants, and Christ cares for His.

Are we ourselves sons of God? Have we been born again? Have we the marks, which always accompany the new birth – sense of sin, faith in Jesus, love of others, righteous living, separation from the world? Let us never be content until we can give a satisfactory answer to these questions.

Do we desire to be sons of God? Then let us "receive Christ" as our Savior and believe on Him with the heart. To every one that so receives Him, He will give the privilege of becoming a son of God.

John 1:14

And the Word was made flesh and dwelt among us (and we beheld his glory, the glory as of the only begotten of the Father), full of grace and truth.

The passage of Scripture now before us is very short, if we measure it by words. But it is very long, if we measure it by the nature of its contents. The substance of it is so immensely important that we shall do well to give it separate and distinct consideration. This single verse contains more than enough matter for a whole exposition.

The main truth, which this verse teaches is *the reality of our Lord Jesus Christ's incarnation, or being made man.* John tells us that "the Word was made flesh, and dwelt among us."[3]

The plain meaning of these words is that our divine Savior really took

---

3   The expression "the Word," shows clearly the "the Word" who "was with God and was God," must be a Person. It could not reasonably be said of any one but a Person, that He became "flesh and dwelt among us."

human nature upon Him in order to save sinners. He really became a man like ourselves in all things, sin only excepted. Like ourselves, he was born of a woman, though born in a miraculous manner. Like ourselves, He grew from infancy to boyhood and from boyhood to man's estate, both in wisdom and in stature (Luke 2:52). Like ourselves, he hungered, thirsted, ate, drank, slept, was wearied, felt pain, wept, rejoiced, marveled, and was moved to anger and compassion. Having become flesh and taken a body, He prayed, read the Scriptures, suffered being tempted, and submitted His human will to the will of God the Father. And finally, in the same body, He really suffered and shed His blood, really died, was really buried, really rose again, and really ascended up into heaven. And yet all this time He was God as well as man!

This union of two natures in Christ's one Person is doubtless one of the greatest mysteries of the Christian religion. It needs to be carefully stated. It is just one of those great truths, which are not meant to be curiously pried into but to be reverently believed. Nowhere, perhaps, shall we find a more wise and judicious statement than in the second article of the Church of England. "The Son, which is the Word of the Father, begotten from everlasting of the Father, the very and eternal God, and of one substance with the Father, took man's nature in the womb of the blessed Virgin of her substance – so that two whole and perfect natures, that is to say, the Godhead and the manhood, were joined together in one Person, never to be divided, whereof is one Christ, truly God and truly man." This is a most valuable declaration. This is "sound speech, which cannot be condemned."

But while we do not pretend to explain the union of two natures in our Lord Jesus Christ's Person, we must not hesitate to fence the subject with well-defined cautions. While we state most carefully what we *do* believe, we must not shrink from declaring boldly what we do *not* believe. We must never forget that though our Lord was God and man at the same time, the divine and human natures in Him were never confounded. One nature did not swallow up the other. The two natures remained perfect and distinct. The divinity of Christ was never for a moment laid aside, although veiled. The manhood of Christ, during His lifetime, was never for a moment unlike our own, though by union with the Godhead, greatly dignified. Though perfect God, Christ has always been perfect man from the first moment of His incarnation. He who is gone into heaven and is sitting at the Father's right hand to intercede for sinners is man as well as God. Though perfect man, Christ never ceased to be perfect God. He that suffered for sin on the cross, and was made sin for us, was "God manifest in the flesh." The blood with which the Church was purchased is called the blood "of God" (Acts 20:28). Though He became "flesh" in the fullest sense, when He was born of the Virgin Mary, He never at any period ceased to be the Eternal Word. To say that He constantly manifested His divine nature during His earthly ministry would, of course, be contrary to plain facts. To attempt to explain why His Godhead was sometimes veiled and at other times unveiled, while He was on earth, would be venturing on ground, which we had better leave alone. But to say that at any instant of His earthly ministry He was not fully and entirely God is nothing less than heresy.

The cautions just given may seem at first sight needless, wearisome, and hair-splitting. It is precisely the neglect of such cautions which ruins many souls. This constant undivided union of two perfect natures in Christ's Person is exactly that which gives infinite value to His mediation, and qualifies Him to be the very Mediator that sinners need. Our Mediator is One who can sympathize with us, because He is very man. And yet, at the same time, He is One who can deal with the Father for us on equal terms, because He is very God. It is the same union which gives infinite value to His righteousness when imputed to believers. It is the righteousness of One who was God as well as man. It is the same union which gives infinite value to the atoning blood which He shed for sinners on the cross. It is the blood of One who was God as well as man. It is the same union which gives infinite value to His resurrection. When He rose again, as the Head of the body of believers, He rose not as a mere man, but as God. Let these things sink deeply into our hearts. The second Adam is far greater than the first Adam was. The first Adam was only man, and so he fell. The second Adam was God as well as man, and so He completely conquered.

Let us leave the subject with feelings of deep gratitude and thankfulness.

It is full of abounding consolation for all who know Christ by faith and believe on Him.

Did the Word become flesh? Then He is One who can be touched with the feeling of His people's infirmities, because He has suffered Himself, being tempted. He is almighty because He is God, and yet He can sympathize with us, because He is man.

Did the Word become flesh? Then He can supply us with a perfect pattern and example for our daily life. Had he walked among us as an angel or a spirit, we could never have copied Him. But having dwelt among us as a man, we know that the true standard of holiness is to "walk even as He walked" (1 John 2:6). He is a perfect pattern, because He is God. But He is also a pattern exactly suited to our needs, because He is man.

Finally, did the Word become flesh? Then let us see in our mortal bodies a real, true dignity and not defile them by sin. Vile and weak as our body may seem, it is a body which the Eternal Son of God was not ashamed to take upon Himself, and to take up to heaven. That simple fact is a pledge that He will raise our bodies at the last day and glorify them together with His own.

John 1:15-18

John bore witness of him and cried, saying, This is he of whom I spoke, He that comes after me is preferred before me, for he was before me. And of his fullness we have all received, and grace for grace. For the law was given through Moses, but the grace and the truth of God came through Jesus, the Christ. No man has seen God at any time; the only begotten Son, which is in the bosom of the Father, he has declared him.

The passage before us contains three great declarations about our Lord Jesus Christ. Each of the three is among the foundation principles of Christianity.

We are taught, firstly, that *it is Christ alone who supplies all the spiritual needs of all believers.* It is written that "of his fullness have we all received, and grace for grace."

There is an infinite fullness in Jesus Christ. As Paul says, "It pleased the Father that in him should all fullness dwell" (Colossians 1:19). "In Him are hid all the treasures of wisdom and knowledge" (Colossians 2:3). There is laid up in Him, as in a treasury, a boundless supply of all that any sinner can need, either in time or eternity. The Spirit of Life is His special gift to the Church, and conveys from Him, as from a great root, sap and vigor to all the believing branches. He is rich in mercy, grace, wisdom, righteousness, sanctification, and redemption. Out of Christ's fullness, all believers in every age of the world have been supplied. They did not clearly understand the fountain from which their supplies flowed in Old Testament times. The Old Testament saints only saw Christ afar off and not face to face. But from Abel downwards, all saved souls have received all they have had from Jesus Christ alone. Every saint in glory will at last acknowledge that he is Christ's debtor for all he is. Jesus will prove to have been all in all.

We are taught, secondly, *the vast superiority of Christ to Moses, and of the Gospel to the Law.* It is written that "the law was given by Moses, but grace and truth came by Jesus Christ."

Moses was employed by God "as a servant" to convey to Israel the moral and ceremonial law (Hebrews 3:5). As a servant, he was faithful to Him who appointed him, but he was only a servant. The moral law, which he brought down from Mount Sinai, was holy and just and good. But it could not justify. It had no healing power. It could wound, but it could not bind up. It "worked wrath" (Romans 4:15). It pronounced a curse against any imperfect obedience. The ceremonial law, which he was commanded to impose on Israel, was full of deep meaning and typical instruction. Its ordinances and ceremonies made it an excellent schoolmaster to guide men toward Christ (Galatians 3:24). But the ceremonial law was only a schoolmaster. It could not make him that kept it perfect, as pertaining to the conscience (Hebrews 9:9). It laid a grievous yoke on men's hearts, which they were not able to bear. It was a ministration of death and condemnation (2 Corinthians 3:7-9). The light which men got from Moses and the law was at best only starlight compared to noonday.

Christ, on the other hand, came into the world "as a Son" with the keys of God's treasury of grace and truth entirely in His hands (Hebrews 3:6). Grace came by Him when He made fully known God's gracious plan of salvation by faith in His own blood and opened the fountain of mercy to all the world. Truth came by Him, when He fulfilled in His own Person the types of the Old Testament and revealed Himself as the true Sacrifice, the true mercy seat, and the true Priest. No doubt there was much of "grace and truth" under the law of Moses. But the whole of God's grace and the whole truth about redemption were never known until Jesus came into the world and died for sinners.

We are taught, thirdly, that *it is Christ alone who has revealed God the Father to man.* It is written that "no man has seen God at any time – the only begotten Son, who is in the bosom of the Father, he has declared him."

The eye of mortal man has never beheld God the Father. No man could bear the sight. Even to Moses it was said, "Thou canst not see my face: for no man shall see me and live" (Exodus 33:20). Yet all that mortal man is capable of knowing about God the Father is fully revealed to us by God the Son. He, who was in the bosom of the Father from all eternity, has been pleased to take our nature upon Him and to exhibit to us in the form of man all that our minds can comprehend of the Father's perfections. In Christ's words, and deeds, and life, and death, we learn as much concerning God the Father as our feeble minds can at present bear. His perfect wisdom – His almighty power – His unspeakable love to sinners – His incomparable holiness – His hatred of sin, could never be represented to our eyes more clearly than we see them in Christ's life and death. In truth, "God was manifest in the flesh" (1 Timothy 3:16) when the Word took on Him a body. "He was the brightness of the Father's glory, and the express image of His person" (Hebrews 1:3). He says Himself, "I and my Father are one" (John 10:30). "He that has seen me has seen the Father" (John 14:9). "In Him dwelleth all the fullness of the Godhead bodily" (Colossians 2:9). These are deep and mysterious things. But they are true.

And now, after reading this passage, can we ever give too much honor to Christ? Can we ever think too highly of Him? Let us banish the unworthy thought from our minds forever. Let us learn to exalt Him more in our hearts, and to rest more confidingly the whole weight of our souls in His hands. Men may easily fall into error about the three Persons in the holy Trinity if they do not carefully adhere to the teaching of Scripture. But no man ever errs on the side of giving too much honor to the Son. Christ is the meeting point between the Trinity and the sinner's soul. "He that does not honour the Son does not honour the Father who has sent him" (John 5:23).

John 1:19-28

And this is the testimony of John, when the Jews sent priests and Levites from Jerusalem to ask him, Who art thou? And he confessed and denied not, but confessed, I am not the Christ. And they asked him, What then? Art thou Elijah? And he said, I am not. Art thou the prophet? And he answered, No. Then said they unto him, Who art thou? that we may give an answer to those that sent us. What sayest thou of thyself? He said, I am the voice of one crying in the wilderness, Make straight the way of the Lord, as said the prophet Isaiah. And those who were sent were of the Pharisees. And they asked him and said unto him, Why dost thou baptize then if thou art not the Christ, nor Elijah, nor the prophet? John answered them, saying, I baptize with water, but there stands one among you, whom ye know not; he it is, who coming after me is preferred before me, whose shoe's latchet I am not worthy to unloose. These things were done in Bethabara beyond Jordan, where John was baptizing.

The verses we have now read begin the properly historical part of John's Gospel. Hitherto we have been reading deep and weighty statements about Christ's divine nature, incarnation, and dignity. Now we come to the plain narrative of the days of Christ's earthly ministry and the plain story of Christ's doings and sayings among men. And here, like the other Gospel writers, John begins at once with "the record" or testimony of John the Baptist (Matthew 3:1; Mark 1:2; Luke 3:2).

We have, for one thing, in these verses, *an instructive example of true humility*. That example is supplied by John the Baptist himself.

John the Baptist was an eminent saint of God. There are few names which stand higher than his in the Bible calendar of great and good men. The Lord Jesus Himself declared that "Among those that are born of women there has not risen a greater than John the Baptist" (Matthew 11:11). The Lord Jesus Himself declared that he was "a burning and a shining light" (John 5:35). Yet here in this passage we see this eminent saint lowly, self-abased, and full of humility. He puts away from himself the honor, which the Jews from Jerusalem were ready to pay him. He declines all flattering titles. He speaks of himself as nothing more than the "voice of one crying in the wilderness" and as one who "baptized with water." He proclaims loudly that there is One standing among the Jews far greater than himself, One whose shoe latchet he is not worthy to unloose. He claims honor not for himself but for Christ. To exalt Christ was his mission, and to that mission he steadfastly adheres.

The greatest saints of God in every age of the Church have always been men of John the Baptist's spirit. In gifts, and knowledge, and general character, they have often differed widely. But in one respect, they have always been alike – they have been "clothed with humility" (1 Peter 5:5). They have not sought their own honor. They have thought little of themselves. They have been ever willing to decrease if Christ might only increase, to be nothing if Christ might be all. And here has been the secret of the honor God has put upon them. "He that humbles himself shall be exalted" (Luke 14:11).

If we profess to have any real Christianity, let us strive to be of John the Baptist's spirit. Let us study humility. This is the grace with which all must begin, who would be saved. We have no true religion about us, until we cast away our high thoughts, and feel ourselves sinners. This is the grace which all saints may follow after, and which none have any excuse for neglecting. All God's children have not gifts, or money, or time to work, or a wide sphere of usefulness; but all may be humble.

This is the grace, above all, which will appear most beautiful in our latter end. Never shall we feel the need of humility so deeply, as when we lie on our deathbeds and stand before the judgment seat of Christ. Our whole lives will then appear a long catalogue of imperfections, ourselves nothing and Christ all.

We have, for another thing, in these verses, *a mournful example of the blindness of unconverted men.* That example is supplied by the state of the Jews who came to question John the Baptist.

These Jews professed to be waiting for the appearance of Messiah. Like all the Pharisees, they prided themselves on being children of Abraham and possessors of the covenants. They rested in the law and made their boast of God. They professed to know God's will and to believe God's promises. They were confident that they themselves were guides of the blind and lights of those who sat in darkness (Romans 2:17-19). And yet at this very moment their souls were utterly in the dark. "There was standing among them," as John the Baptist told them, "One whom they knew not." Christ Himself, the promised Messiah, was in the midst of them, and yet they neither knew Him, nor saw Him, nor received Him, nor acknowledged Him, nor believed Him. And worse than this, the vast majority of them never would know Him! The words of John the Baptist are a prophetic description of a state of things, which lasted during the whole of our Lord's earthly ministry. Christ "stood among the Jews," and yet the Jews knew Him not, and the greater part of them died in their sins.

It is a solemn thought that John the Baptist's words in this place apply strictly to thousands in the present day. Christ is still standing among many who neither see, nor know, nor believe. Christ is passing by in many a parish and many a congregation, and the vast majority have neither an eye to see Him, nor an ear to hear Him. The spirit of slumber seems poured out upon them. Money, and pleasure, and the world they know; but they know not Christ. The kingdom of God is close to them; but they sleep. Salvation is within their reach; but they sleep. Mercy, grace, peace, heaven, and eternal life are so near that they might touch them; and yet they sleep. "Christ standeth among them and they know him not." These are sorrowful things to write down.

But every faithful minister of Christ can testify, like John the Baptist, that they are true.

What are we doing ourselves? This, after all, is the great question that concerns us. Do we know the extent of our religious privileges in this country and in these times? Are we aware that Christ is going to and fro in our land, inviting souls to join Him and to be His disciples? Do we know that the time is short and that the door of mercy will soon be closed for evermore? Do we know that Christ rejected will soon be Christ withdrawn? Happy are they who can give a good account of these inquiries and who "know the day of their visitation!" (Luke 19:44). It will be better at the last day never to have been born than to have had Christ "standing among us" and not to have known Him.

John 1:29-34

The next day John saw Jesus coming unto him and said, Behold the Lamb of God, who takes away the sin of the world. This is he of whom I said, After me comes a man who is pre-ferred before me, for he was before me. And I knew him not; but that he should be made manifest to Israel, therefore am I come baptizing with water. And John gave testimony, saying, I saw the Spirit descending from heaven like a dove, and it abode upon him. And I knew him not; but he that sent me to baptize with water, the same said unto me, Upon whom thou shalt see the Spirit descending and abiding on him, the same is he who baptizes with the Holy Spirit. And I have seen and have given testimony that this is the Son of God

This passage contains a verse which ought to be printed in great letters in the memory of every reader of the Bible. All the stars in heaven are bright and beautiful, and yet one star exceeds another star in glory. So also all texts of Scripture are inspired and profitable, and yet some texts are richer than others. Of such texts the first verse before us is preeminently one. Never was there a fuller testimony borne to Christ upon earth, than that which is here borne by John the Baptist.

Let us notice, firstly, in this passage, *the peculiar name which John the Baptist gives to Christ.* He calls Him "The Lamb of God."

This name did not merely mean, as some have supposed, that Christ was meek and gentle as a lamb. This would be truth no doubt, but only a very small portion of the truth. There are greater things here than this! It meant that Christ was the great sacrifice for sin, who was come to make atonement for transgression by His own death upon the cross. He was the true Lamb which Abraham told Isaac at Moriah God would provide (Genesis 22:8). He was the true Lamb to which every morning and evening sacrifice in the temple had daily pointed. He was the Lamb of which Isaiah had prophesied, that He would be "brought to the slaughter" (Isaiah 53:7). He was the true Lamb of which the Passover lamb in Egypt had been a vivid type. In short, He was the great propitiation for sin, which God had covenanted from all eternity to send into the world. He was God's Lamb.

Let us take heed that in all our thoughts of Christ, we first think of Him as John the Baptist here represents Him. Let us serve him faithfully as our *Master.* Let us obey Him loyally as our *King.* Let us study His teaching as our *Prophet.* Let us walk diligently after Him as our *Example.* Let us look anxiously for Him as our coming *Redeemer* of body as well as soul. But above all, let us prize Him as our *Sacrifice* and rest our whole weight on His death as an atonement for sin. Let His blood be more precious in our eyes every year we live. Whatever else we glory in about Christ, let us glory above all things in His cross. This is the cornerstone, this is the citadel, this is the rule of true Christian theology. We know nothing rightly about Christ, until we see him with John the Baptist's eyes and can rejoice in Him as "the Lamb that was slain."

Let us notice, secondly, in this passage, *the peculiar work which John the Baptist describes Christ as doing.* He says that "he taketh away the sin of the world."

Christ is a Savior. He did not come on earth to be a conqueror, or a philosopher, or a mere teacher of morality. He came to save sinners. He came to do that which man could never do for himself – to do that which money and learning can never obtain – to do that which is essential to man's real happiness; He came to "take away sin."

Christ is a complete Savior. He "taketh away sin." He did not merely make vague proclamations of pardon, mercy, and forgiveness. He "took" our sins upon Himself and carried them away. He allowed them to be laid upon Himself and "bore them in His own body on the tree" (1 Peter 2:24). The sins of every one that believes on Jesus are made as though they had never been sinned at all. The Lamb of God has taken them clean away.

Christ is an almighty Savior, and a Savior for all mankind. He "taketh away the sin of the world." He did not die for the Jews only, but for the Gentile as well as the Jew. He did not suffer for a few people only, but for all mankind. The payment that He made on the cross was more than enough to make satisfaction for the debts of all. The blood that He shed was precious enough to wash away the sins of all. His atonement on the cross was sufficient for all mankind, though *efficient* only to those who believe. The sin that He took up and bore on the cross was the sin of the whole world.

Last, but not least, Christ is a perpetual and unwearied Savior. He "taketh away" sin. He is daily taking it away from every one that believes on Him – daily purging, daily cleansing, daily washing the souls of His people, daily granting and applying fresh supplies of mercy. He did not cease to work for His saints, when He died for them on the cross. He lives in heaven as a Priest to present His sacrifice continually before God. In grace as well as is providence, Christ works still. He is ever taking away sin.

These are golden truths indeed. Well would it be for the Church of Christ, if they were used by all who know them! Our very familiarity with texts like these is one of our greatest dangers. Blessed are they who not only keep this text in their memories, but feed upon it in their hearts!

Let us notice, lastly, in this passage, *the peculiar office which John the Baptist attributes to Christ.* He speaks of Him as Him "who baptizes with the Holy Spirit."

The baptism here spoken of is not the baptism of water. It does not consist either of dipping or sprinkling. It does not belong exclusively either to infants or to grown up people. It is not a baptism, which any man can give, Episcopalian or Presbyterian, Independent or Methodist, layman or minister. It is a baptism, which the great Head of the Church keeps exclusively in His own hands. It consists of the implanting of grace into the inward man. It is the same thing with the new birth. It is a baptism, not of the body, but of the heart. It is a baptism, which the penitent thief received, though neither dipped nor sprinkled by the hand of man. It is a baptism, which Ananias and Sapphira did not receive, though admitted into church communion by apostolic men.

Let it be a settled principle in our religion that the baptism of which John the Baptist speaks here is the baptism which is absolutely necessary to salvation. It is well to be baptized into the visible Church; but it is far better to be baptized into that Church which is made up of true believers. The baptism of water is a most blessed and profitable ordinance and cannot be neglected without great sin. But the baptism of the Holy Spirit is of far greater importance. The man who dies with his heart not baptized by Christ can never be saved.

Let us ask ourselves, as we leave this passage, whether we are baptized with the Holy Spirit and whether we have any real interest in the Lamb of God? Thousands, unhappily, are wasting their time in controversy about water baptism but are neglecting the baptism of the heart. Thousands more are content with a head knowledge of the Lamb of God or have never sought Him by faith that their own sins may be actually taken away. Let us take heed that we ourselves have new hearts, and believe to the saving of our souls.

John 1:35-42

And again the next day John stood, and two of his disciples, and looking upon Jesus as he walked, he said, Behold the Lamb of God! And the two disciples heard him speak and followed Jesus. Then Jesus turned and saw them following and said unto them, What seek ye? They said unto him, Rabbi (which is to say, being interpreted, Master), where dwellest thou? He said unto them, Come and see. They came and saw where he dwelt and abode with him that day, for it was about the tenth hour. One of the two who heard John

speak and followed him was Andrew, brother of Simon Peter.
He first found his own brother Simon and said unto him,
We have found the Messias, which is, being interpreted, the
Christ. And he brought him to Jesus. And when Jesus beheld
him, he said, Thou art Simon the son of Jonah: thou shalt be
called Cephas, which is by interpretation, A stone.

These verses ought always to be interesting to every true Christian. They describe the first beginnings of the Christian Church. Vast as that church is now, there was a time when it consisted of only two weak members. The calling of those two members is described in the passage, which is now before our eyes.

We see, for one thing, in these verses, *what good is done by continually testifying of Christ.*

The first time that John the Baptist cried, "Behold the Lamb of God," no result appears to have followed. We are not told of any who heard, inquired, and believed. But when he repeated the same words the next day, we read that two of his disciples "heard him speak and followed Jesus." They were received most graciously by Him whom they followed. "They came and saw where he dwelt, and abode with him that day." Truly it was a day in their lives most eventful and most blessed! From that day they became fast and firm disciples of the new-found Messiah. They took up the cross. They continued with Him in His temptations. They followed Him wherever He went. One of them at least, if not both, became a chosen apostle and a master builder in the Christian temple. And all was owing to John the Baptist's testimony, "Behold the Lamb of God." That testimony was a little seed. But it bore mighty fruits.

This simple story is a pattern of the way in which good has been done to souls in every age of the Christian Church. By such testimony as that before us, and by none else, men and women are converted and saved. It is by exalting Christ, not the church – Christ, not the sacraments – Christ, not the ministry – it is by this means that hearts are moved, and sinners are turned to God. To the world such testimony may seem weakness and foolishness. Yet, like the ram's horns, before whose blast the walls of Jericho fell down, this testimony is mighty to the pulling down of strongholds. The story of the crucified Lamb of God has proved in every age, the power of God unto salvation. Those who have done most for Christ's cause in every part of the world have been men like John the Baptist. They have not cried, Behold me, or Behold the church, or Behold the ordinances, but "Behold the Lamb." If souls are to be saved, men must be pointed directly to Christ.

One thing, however, must never be forgotten. There must be patient continuance in preaching and teaching the truth, if we want good to be done. Christ must be set forth again and again, as the "Lamb of God which taketh away the sin of the world." The story of grace must be told repeatedly – line upon line, and precept upon precept. It is the constant dropping, which wears away the stone. The promise shall never be broken, that "God's word shall not return unto him void" (Isaiah 55:11). But it is nowhere said that it shall do good the very first time that it is preached. It was not the first proclamation of John the Baptist, but the second, which made Andrew and his companion follow Jesus.

We see, for another thing, *what good a believer may do to others, by speaking to them about Christ.*

No sooner does Andrew become a disciple than he tells his brother Simon what a discovery he has made. Like one who has unexpectedly heard good tidings, he hastens to impart it to the one nearest and dearest to him. He says to his brother, "We have found the Messiah," and he "brings him to Jesus." Who can tell what might have happened if Andrew had been of a silent, reserved, and uncommunicative spirit, like many a Christian in the present day? Who can tell but his brother might have lived and died a fisherman on the Galilean lake? But happily for Simon, Andrew was not a man of this sort. He was one whose heart was so full that he must speak.

And to Andrew's outspoken testimony, under God, the great apostle Peter owed the first beginning of light in his soul.

The fact before us is most striking and instructive. Out of the three first members of the Christian Church, one at least was brought to Jesus by the private, quiet word of a relative. He seems to have heard no public preaching. He saw no mighty miracle wrought. He was not convinced by any powerful reasoning. He only heard his brother telling him that he had found a Savior himself, and at once the work began in his soul.

The simple testimony of a warm-hearted brother was the first link in the chain by which Peter was drawn out of the world and joined to Christ. The first blow in that mighty work by which Peter was made a pillar of the Church was struck by Andrew's words, "We have found the Christ."

Well would it be for the Church of Christ if all believers were more like Andrew! Well would it be for souls if all men and women who have been converted themselves would speak to their friends and relatives on spiritual subjects and tell them what they have found! How much good might be done! How many might be led to Jesus, who now live and die in unbelief! The work of testifying the Gospel of the grace of God ought not to be left to ministers alone. All who have received mercy ought to find a tongue and to declare what God has done for their souls. All who have been delivered from the power of the devil ought to "go home and tell their friends what great things God has done for them" (Mark 5:19). Thousands, humanly speaking, would listen to a word from a friend, who will not listen to a sermon. Every believer ought to be a home-missionary, a missionary to his family, children, servants, neighbors, and friends. Surely, if we can find nothing to say to others about Jesus, we may well doubt whether we are savingly acquainted with Him ourselves.

Let us take heed that we are among those who really follow Christ and abide with Him. It is not enough to hear Him preached from the pulpit and to read of Him as described in books. We must actually follow Him, pour out our hearts before Him, and hold personal communion with Him. Then, and not until then, we shall feel constrained to speak of Him to others. The man who only knows Christ by the hearing of the ear will never do much for the spread of Christ's cause in the earth.

John 1:43-51

The day following Jesus desired to go forth into Galilee and found Philip and said unto him, Follow me. Now Philip was of Bethsaida, the city of Andrew and Peter. Philip found Nathanael and said unto him, We have found him of whom Moses in the law and the prophets wrote: Jesus of Nazareth, the son of Joseph. And Nathanael said unto him, Can any good thing come out of Nazareth? Philip said unto him, Come and see. Jesus saw Nathanael coming to him and said of him, Behold a true Israelite, in whom is no guile! Nathanael said unto him, From where dost thou know me? Jesus answered and said unto him, Before Philip called thee, when thou wast under the fig tree, I saw thee. Nathanael answered and said unto him, Rabbi, thou art the Son of God; thou art the King of Israel. Jesus answered and said unto him, Because I said unto thee, I saw thee under the fig tree, believest thou? thou shalt see greater things than these. And he said unto him, Verily, verily, I say unto you, Hereafter ye shall see the heaven open and the angels of God ascending and descending upon the Son of man.

Let us observe, as we read these verses, *how various are the paths by which souls are led into the narrow way of life.*

We are told of a man, named Philip, being added to the little company of Christ's disciples. He does not appear to have been moved, like Andrew and his companions, by the testimony of John the Baptist. He was not drawn, like Simon Peter, by the outspoken declaration of a brother. He seems to have been called directly by Christ Himself, and the agency of man seems not to have been used in his calling. Yet in faith and life, he became one with those who were disciples before him. Though led by different paths, they all entered the same road, embraced the same truths, served the same Master, and at length reached the same home.

The fact before us is a deeply important one. It throws light on the history of all God's people in every age and of every tongue. There are diversities of operations in the saving of souls. All true Christians are led by one Spirit, washed in one blood, serve one Lord, lean on one Savior, believe one truth, and walk by one general rule. But all are not converted in one and the same manner. All do not pass through the same experience. In conversion, the Holy Spirit acts as a sovereign. He calls every one severally as He will.

A careful recollection of this point may save us much trouble. We must beware of making the experience of other believers the measure of our own. We must beware of denying another's grace, because he has not been led by the same way as ourselves. Has a man got the real grace of God? This is the only question that concerns us. Is he a penitent man? Is he a believer? Does he live a holy life? Provided these inquiries can be answered satisfactorily, we may well be content. It matters nothing by what path a man has been led, if he has only been led at last into the right way.

Let us observe, secondly, in these verses, *how much of Christ there is in the Old Testament Scriptures.* We read that when Philip described Christ to Nathanael, he says, "We have found Him of whom Moses in the law and the prophets did write."

Christ is the sum and substance of the Old Testament. To Him the earliest promises pointed in the days of Adam, and Enoch, and Noah, and Abraham, and Isaac, and Jacob. To Him every sacrifice pointed in the ceremonial worship appointed at Mount Sinai. Of Him every high priest was a type, and every part of the tabernacle was a shadow, and every judge and deliverer of Israel was a figure. He was the prophet like unto Moses, whom the Lord God promised to send, and the King of the house of David, who came to be David's Lord as well as son. He was the Son of the virgin, and the Lamb, foretold by Isaiah – the righteous Branch mentioned by Jeremiah – the true Shepherd, foreseen by Ezekiel – the Messenger of the Covenant, promised by Malachi – and the Messiah, who, according to Daniel, was to be cut off, though not for Himself. The further we read in the volume of the Old Testament, the clearer do we find the testimony about Christ. The light, which the inspired writers enjoyed in ancient days, was at best, but dim compared to that of the Gospel. But the coming Person they all saw afar off, and on whom they all fixed their eyes, was one and the same. The Spirit, which was in them, testified of Christ (1 Peter 1:11).

Do we stumble at this saying? Do we find it hard to see Christ in the Old Testament, because we do not see His name? Let us be sure that the fault is all our own. It is our spiritual vision, which is to blame and not the book. The eyes of our understanding need to be enlightened. The veil has yet to be taken away. Let us pray for a more humble, childlike, and teachable spirit, and let us take up "Moses and the prophets" again. Christ is there, though our eyes may not yet have seen Him. May we never rest until we can subscribe to our Lord's words about the Old Testament Scriptures, "They are they which testify of me" (John 5:39).

Let us observe, thirdly, in these verses, *the good advice which Philip gave to Nathanael.* The mind of Nathanael was full of doubts about the Savior, of whom Philip told Him. "Can there any good thing," he said, "come out of Nazareth?" And what did Philip reply? He said, "Come and see."

Wiser counsel than this it would be impossible to conceive! If Philip had reproved Nathanael's unbelief, he might have driven him back for many a day and given offence. If he had reasoned with him, he might have failed to convince him or might have confirmed him in his doubts. But by inviting him to prove the matter for himself, he showed his entire confidence in the truth of his own assertion and his willingness to have it tested and proved. And the result shows the wisdom of Philip's words. Nathanael owed his early acquaintance with Christ to that frank invitation, "Come and see."

If we call ourselves true Christians, let us never be afraid to deal with people about their souls as Philip dealt with Nathanael. Let us invite them boldly to make proof of our religion. Let us tell them confidently that they cannot know its real value until they have tried it. Let us assure them that vital Christianity courts every possible inquiry. It has no secrets. It has nothing to conceal. Its faith and practice are spoken against, just because they are not known. Its enemies speak evil of things with which they are not acquainted. They understand neither what they say nor whereof they affirm. Philip's mode of dealing, we may be sure, is one principal way to do good. Few are ever moved by reasoning and argument. Still fewer are frightened into repentance. The man who does most good to souls is often the simple believer who says to his friends, "I have found a Savior; come and see Him."

Let us observe, lastly, in these verses, *the high character which Jesus gives of Nathanael.* He calls him "an Israelite indeed, in whom is no guile."

Nathanael, there can be no doubt, was a true child of God, and a child of God in difficult times. He was one of a very little flock. Like Simeon and Anna, and other pious Jews, he was living by faith and waiting prayerfully for the promised Redeemer, when our Lord's ministry began. He had that which grace alone can give, an honest heart, a heart without guile. His knowledge was probably small. His spiritual eyesight was dim. But he was one who had lived carefully up to his light. He had diligently used such knowledge as he possessed. His eye had been single, though his vision had not been strong. His spiritual judgment had been honest, though it had not been powerful. What he saw in Scripture, he had held firmly, in spite of Pharisees and Sadducees, and all the fashionable religion of the day. He was an honest Old Testament believer, who had stood alone. And here was the secret of our Lord's peculiar commendation! He declared Nathanael to be a true son of Abraham – a Jew inwardly, possessing circumcision in the spirit as well as in the letter – an Israelite in heart, as well as a son of Jacob in the flesh.[4]

Let us pray that we may be of the same spirit as Nathanael. An honest, unprejudiced mind – a child-like willingness to follow the truth, wherever the truth may lead us – a simple, hearty desire to be guided, taught, and led by the Spirit – a thorough determination to use every spark of light which we have – are a possession of priceless value. A man of this spirit may live in the midst of much darkness and be surrounded by every possible disadvantage to his soul. But the Lord Jesus will take care that such a man does not miss the way to heaven. "The meek will he guide in judgment: and the meek will he teach his way" (Psalm 25:9).

---

4   Who was Nathanael? . . . The most probable opinion to my own mind is that Nathanael was the apostle who is called elsewhere Bartholomew, and who, like others of the apostles, had two names. In favor of this opinion there are three remarkable facts. The first is, that in three lists of the twelve apostles out of four, the names of Philip and Bartholomew are always found together (Matthew 10:3; Mark 3:18; Luke 6:14). The second is that Nathanael is specially mentioned after our Lord's ascension as a companion of Peter, Thomas, James, John, and two other disciples. The third is that John never once mentions the name of Bartholomew in his Gospel. The objection that Nathanael's name is never mentioned by Matthew, Mark, or Luke is of no weight. No one of the three, it may be replied, tells us that Peter was called Cephas. Only Matthew gives Jude, the brother of James, the name of Lebbaeus. The point happily is not one of any particular importance. I only say that the conjectural probability that Nathanael was an apostle and was the same as Bartholomew seems to me very strong and well founded.

John Chapter 2

John 2:1-11

And the third day there was a marriage in Cana of Galilee, and the mother of Jesus was there, and Jesus and his disciples were also called to the marriage. And being short of wine, the mother of Jesus said unto him, They have no wine. Jesus said unto her, Woman, what have I to do with thee? My hour is not yet come. His mother said unto the servants, Whatsoever he saith unto you, do it. And there were set there six waterpots of stone, after the manner of the purifying of the Jews, containing two or three firkins apiece. Jesus said unto them, Fill the waterpots with water. And they filled them up to the brim. And he said unto them, Draw out now and bear unto the butler. And they bore it. When the butler had tasted the water that was made wine and knew not where it was from (but the servants who drew the water knew), the butler called the bridegroom and said unto him, Every man at the beginning sets forth the good wine, and when they are well satisfied, then that which is worse; but thou hast kept the good wine until now. This beginning of the signs Jesus did in Cana of Galilee and manifested forth his glory, and his disciples believed on him.

THESE VERSES DESCRIBE A miracle, which should always possess a special interest in the eyes of a true Christian. It is the first, in order of time, of the many mighty works, which Jesus did when He was upon earth. We are distinctly told, "This beginning of miracles did Jesus in Cana of Galilee." Like every other miracle, which John was inspired to record, it is related with great minuteness and particularity. And, like every other miracle in John's Gospel, it is rich in spiritual lessons.

We learn, firstly, from these verses, *how honorable in the sight of Christ is the estate of matrimony.* To be present at a "marriage" was almost the first public act of our Lord's earthly ministry.

Marriage is not a sacrament, as the Church of Rome asserts. It is simply a state of life ordained by God for man's benefit. But it is a state which ought never to be spoken of with levity or regarded with disrespect. The Prayerbook service has well described it as "an honorable estate, instituted of God in the time of man's innocence and signifying unto us the mystical union that is between Christ and his Church." Society is never in a healthy condition, and true religion never flourishes in that land where the marriage tie is lightly esteemed. They who lightly esteem it have not the mind of Christ. He who "beautified and adorned the estate of matrimony by His presence and first miracle that He wrought in Cana of Galilee" is One who is always of one mind. "Marriage," says the Holy Spirit by Paul, "is honorable in all" (Hebrews 13:4).

One thing, however, ought not to be forgotten. Marriage is a step which so seriously affects the temporal happiness and spiritual welfare of two immortal souls that it ought never to be taken in hand "unadvisedly, lightly, wantonly, and without due consideration." To be truly happy, it should be undertaken "reverently, discreetly, soberly, and in the fear of God." Christ's blessing and presence are essential to a happy wedding. The marriage at which there is no place for Christ and His disciples is not one that can justly be expected to prosper.

We learn, secondly, from these verses, that *there are times when it is lawful to be merry and rejoice.* Our Lord Himself sanctioned a wedding feast by His own presence. He did not refuse to be a guest at "a marriage in Cana of Galilee." "A feast," it is written, "is made for laughter, and wine makes merry" (Ecclesiastes 10:19). Our Lord, in the passage before us, approves both the feast and the use of wine.

True religion was never meant to make men melancholy. On the contrary, it was intended to increase real joy and happiness among men. The servant of Christ unquestionably ought to have nothing to do with races, balls, theaters, and such-like amusements, which tend to frivolity and indulgence, if not to sin. But he has no right to hand over innocent recreations and family gatherings to the devil and the world. The Christian who withdraws entirely from the society of his fellow-men and walks the earth with a face as melancholy as if he was always attending a funeral does injury to the cause of the Gospel. A cheerful, kindly spirit is a great recommendation to a believer. It is a real misfortune to Christianity when a Christian cannot smile. A merry heart and a readiness to take part in all innocent mirth are gifts of inestimable value. They go far to soften prejudices, to take up stumbling blocks out of the way, and to make way for Christ and the Gospel.

The subject no doubt is a difficult and delicate one. On no point of Christian practice is it so hard to hit the balance between that which is lawful and that which is unlawful, between that which is right and that which is wrong. It is very hard indeed to be both merry and wise. High spirits soon degenerate into levity. Acceptance of many invitations to feasts soon leads to waste of time and begets leanness of soul. Frequent eating and drinking at other men's tables soon lowers a Christian's tone of religion. Going often into company is a heavy strain on spirituality of heart. Here, if anywhere, God's children have need to be on their guard. Each must know his own strength and natural temperament, and must act accordingly. One believer can go without risk where another cannot. Happy is he who can use his Christian liberty without abusing it! It is possible to be sorely wounded in soul at marriage feasts and the tables of friends.

One golden rule on the subject may be laid down, the use of which will save us much trouble. Let us take care that we always go to feasts in the spirit of our divine Master, and that we never go where He would not have gone. Like Him, let us endeavor to be always "about our Father's business" (Luke 2:49). Like Him, let us willingly promote joy and gladness, but let us strive that it may be sinless joy, if not joy in the Lord. Let us endeavor to bring the salt of grace into every company and to drop the word in season in every ear we address. Much good may be done in society by giving a healthy tone to conversation. Let us never be ashamed to show our colors and to make men see whose we are and whom we serve. We may well say, "Who is sufficient for these things?" But if Christ went to a marriage feast in Cana, there is surely something that Christians can do on similar occasions. Let them only remember that if they go where their Master went, they must go in their Master's spirit.

We learn lastly, from these verses, *the Almighty power of our Lord Jesus Christ.* We are told of a miracle, which He wrought at the marriage feast, when the wine failed. By a mere act of will, He changed water into wine and so supplied the need of all the guests.

The manner in which the miracle was worked deserves especial notice. We are not told of any outward visible action, which preceded or accompanied it. It is not said that He touched the waterpots containing the water that was made wine. It is not said that He commanded the water to change its qualities, or that He prayed to His Father in Heaven. He simply willed the change, and it took place. We read of no prophet or apostle in the Bible who ever worked a miracle after this fashion. He who could do such a mighty work, in such a manner, was nothing less than very God.

It is a comfortable thought that the same almighty power of will, which our Lord here displayed, is still exercised on behalf of His believing people. They have no need of His bodily presence to maintain their cause. They have no reason to be cast down because they cannot see Him with their eyes interceding for them, or touch Him with their hands that they may cling to Him for safety. If He "wills" their salvation and the daily supply of all their spiritual need, they are as safe and well provided for as if they saw Him standing by them. Christ's *will* is as mighty and effectual as Christ's *deed.* The will of Him who could say to the Father, "I will that they whom thou hast given me be with me where I am" is a will that has all power in heaven and earth and must prevail (John 17:24).

Happy are those who, like the disciples, believe on Him by whom this miracle was wrought. A greater marriage feast than that of Cana will one day be held, when Christ Himself will be the bridegroom, and believers will be the bride. A greater glory will one day be manifested, when Jesus shall take to Himself His great power and reign. Blessed will they be in that day who are called to the marriage supper of the Lamb! (Revelation 19:9).

John 2:12-25

After this he went down to Capernaum, he and his mother and his brethren and his disciples, and they continued there not many days. And passover of the Jews was at hand, and Jesus went up to Jerusalem and found in the temple those that sold oxen and sheep and doves, and the money changers seated; and when he had made a scourge of small cords, he drove them all out of the temple, and the sheep and the oxen, and poured out the changers' money and overthrew the tables and said unto those that sold the doves, Take these things away from here; do not make my Father's house a house of merchandise. Then his disciples remembered that it was written, The zeal of thine house has consumed me. Then the Jews answered and said unto him, What sign showest thou unto us, seeing that thou doest these things? Jesus answered and said unto them, Dissolve this temple, and in three days I will raise it up. Then said the Jews, This temple was forty-six years in building, and wilt thou raise it up in three days? But he spoke of the temple of his body. Therefore when he was risen from the dead, his disciples remembered that he had said this unto them; and they believed the scripture and the word which Jesus had said. Now when he was in Jerusalem at the passover, in the feast day, many believed in his name, seeing the signs which he did. But Jesus did not trust himself unto them because he knew all men and needed not that any man should give testimony, for he knew what was in man.

The second miracle which our Lord is recorded to have wrought demands our attention in these verses. Like the first miracle at Cana, it is eminently typical and significant of things yet to come. To attend a marriage feast and cleanse the temple from profanation were among the first acts of our Lord's ministry at His first coming. To purify the whole visible Church and hold a marriage supper will be among His first acts, when He comes again.

We see, for one thing, in this passage, *how much Christ disapproves all irreverent behavior in the house of God.*

We are told that He drove out of the temple those whom He found selling oxen and sheep and doves within its walls – that He poured out the changers' money and overthrew their tables – and that He said to those who sold doves, "Take these things hence; make not my Father's house an house of merchandise." On no occasion in our Lord's earthly ministry do we find Him acting so energetically and exhibiting such righteous indignation as on the occasion now before us. Nothing seems to have called from Him such a marked display of holy wrath as the gross irreverence, which the priests permitted in the temple, notwithstanding all their boasted zeal for God's law. Twice, it will be remembered, He discovered the same profanation of His Father's house going on within three years, once at the beginning of His ministry and once at the end. Twice we see Him expressing his displeasure in the strongest terms. "The thing is doubled" in order to impress a lesson more strongly on our minds.

The passage is one that ought to raise deep searchings of heart in many quarters. Are there none who profess and call themselves Christians, behaving every Sunday just as badly as these Jews? Are there none who secretly bring into the house of God their money, their lands, their houses, their cattle, and a whole train of worldly affairs? Are there none who bring their bodies only into the place of worship and allow their hearts to wander into the ends of the earth? Are there none who are "almost in all evil, in the midst of the congregation?" (Proverbs 5:14). These are serious questions! Multitudes, it may be feared, could not give them a satisfactory answer. Christian churches and chapels, no doubt, are very unlike the Jewish temple. They are not built after a divine pattern. They have no altars or holy places. Their furniture has no typical meaning. But they are places where God's word is read, and where Christ is specially present. The man who professes to worship in them should surely behave with reverence and respect. The man who brings his worldly matters with him when he professes to worship is doing that which is evidently most offensive to Christ. The words which Solomon wrote by the Holy Spirit are applicable to all times, "Watch thy feet when thou goest to the house of God" (Ecclesiastes 5:1).

We see, for another thing, in this passage, *how men may remember words of religious truth long after they are spoken, and may one day see a meaning in those who at first they did not see.*

We are told that our Lord said to the Jews, "Destroy this temple and in three days I will raise it up." John informs us distinctly that "He spoke of the temple of His body," that he referred to His own resurrection. Yet the meaning of the sentence was not understood by our Lord's disciples at the time that it was spoken. It was not until "He was risen from the dead," three years after the events here described, that the full significance of the sentence flashed on their hearts. For three years it was a dark and useless saying to them. For three years it lay sleeping in their minds, like a seed in a tomb, and bore no fruit. But at the end of that time, the darkness passed away. They saw the application of their Master's words, and as they saw it were confirmed in their faith. "They remembered that He had said this," and as they remembered "they believed."

It is a comfortable and cheering thought that the same kind of thing that happened to the disciples is often going on at the present day. The sermons that are preached to apparently heedless ears in churches are not all lost and thrown away. The instruction that is given in schools and pastoral visits is not all wasted and forgotten. The texts that are taught by parents to children are not all taught in vain. There is often a resurrection of sermons, and texts, and instruction, after an interval of many years. The good seed sometimes springs up after he that sowed it has been long dead and gone. Let preachers go on preaching, and teachers go on teaching, and parents go on training up children in the way they should go. Let them sow the good seed of Bible truth in faith and patience. Their labor is not in vain in the Lord. Their words are remembered far more than they think and will yet spring up "after many days" (1 Corinthians 15:58; Ecclesiastes 11:1).

We see, lastly, in this passage, *how perfect is our Lord Jesus Christ's knowledge of the human heart.*

We are told that when our Lord was at Jerusalem the first time, He "did not commit Himself" to those who professed belief in Him. He knew that they were not to be depended on. They were astonished at the miracles, which they saw Him work. They were even intellectually convinced that He was the Messiah whom they had long expected. But they were not "disciples indeed" (John 8:31). They were not converted and true believers. Their hearts were not right in the sight of God, though their feelings were excited. Their inward man was not renewed, whatever they might profess with their lips. Our Lord knew that nearly all of them were stony-ground hearers (Luke 8:13). As soon as tribulation or persecution arose because of the word, their so-called faith would probably wither away and come to an end. All this our Lord saw clearly, if others around Him did not. Andrew, and Peter, and John, and Philip, and Nathanael perhaps wondered that their Master did not receive these seeming believers with open arms. But they could only judge things by the outward appearance. Their Master could read hearts. "He knew what was in man."

The truth now before us is one which ought to make hypocrites and false professors tremble. They may deceive men, but they cannot deceive Christ. They may wear a cloak of religion and appear, like whited sepulchers, beautiful in the eyes of men. But the eyes of Christ see their inward rottenness, and the judgment of Christ will surely overtake them, except they repent. Christ is already reading their hearts, and as He reads, He is displeased. They are known in heaven, if they are not known on earth, and they will be known at length to their shame, before assembled worlds, if they die unchanged. It is written, "I know thy works, that thou hast a name that thou livest, and art dead" (Revelation 3:1).

But the truth before us has two sides like the pillar of cloud and fire at the Red Sea (Exodus 13:21-22; 14:20). If it looks darkly on hypocrites, it looks brightly on true believers. If it threatens wrath to false professors, it speaks peace to all who love the Lord Jesus Christ in sincerity. A real Christian may be weak, but he is true. One thing, at any rate, the servant of Christ can say, when cast down by a sense of his own infirmity or pained by the slander of a lying world. He can say, "Lord, I am a poor sinner, but I am in earnest, I am true. You know all things – you know that I love you. You know all hearts, and you know that weak as my heart is, it is a heart that cleaves to you." The false Christian shrinks from the eye of an all-seeing Savior. The true Christian desires his Lord's eye to be on him morning, noon, and night. He has nothing to hide.

John Chapter 3

John 3:1-8

*There was a man of the Pharisees, named Nicodemus, a
prince of the Jews; the same came to Jesus by night and said
unto him, Rabbi, we know that thou art a teacher come from
God, for no one can do these signs that thou doest unless
God is with him. Jesus answered and said unto him, Verily,
verily, I say unto thee, Except a person be born again from
above, he cannot see the kingdom of God. Nicodemus said
unto him, How can a man be born when he is old? Can he
enter the second time into his mother's womb and be born?
Jesus answered, Verily, verily, I say unto thee, Unless a man
is born of water and of the Spirit, he cannot enter into the
kingdom of God. That which is born of the flesh is flesh, and
that which is born of the Spirit is spirit. Marvel not that I
said unto thee, Ye must be born again from above. The wind
blows where it desires, and thou hearest the sound of it,
but canst not tell from where it comes or where it goes; so is
every one that is born of the Spirit.*

THE CONVERSATION BETWEEN CHRIST and Nicodemus, which
begins with these verses, is one of the most important passages in the
whole Bible. Nowhere else do we find stronger statements about those
two mighty subjects, the new birth and salvation by faith in the Son
of God. The servant of Christ will do well to make himself thoroughly
acquainted with this chapter. A man may be ignorant of many things
in religion and yet be saved. But to be ignorant of the matters handled
in this chapter is to be in the broad way which leads to destruction.

We should notice, firstly, in these verses, *what a weak and feeble beginning a man may make in religion and yet finally prove a strong Christian.* We are told of a certain Pharisee named Nicodemus who, feeling concerned about his soul, "came to Jesus by night."

There can be little doubt that Nicodemus acted as he did on this occasion from the fear of man. He was afraid of what man would think, or say, or do, if his visit to Jesus was known. He came "by night," because he had not faith and courage enough to come by day. And yet there was a time afterwards when this very Nicodemus took our Lord's part in open day in the council of the Jews. "Does our law judge any man," he said, "before it hears him, and knows what he does?" (John 7:51). Nor was this all. There came a time when this same Nicodemus was one of the only two men who did honor to our Lord's dead body. He helped Joseph of Arimathea to bury Jesus, when even the apostles had forsaken their Master and fled. His last things were more than his first. Though he began weakly, he ended well.

The history of Nicodemus is meant to teach us that we should never "despise the day of small things" in religion (Zechariah 4:10).We must not set down a man as having no grace, because his first steps towards God are timid and wavering, and the first movements of his soul are uncertain, hesitating, and stamped with much imperfection. We must remember our Lord's reception of Nicodemus. He did not "break the bruised reed, or quench the smoking flax," which He saw before Him (Matthew 12:20). Like Him, let us take inquirers by the hand and deal with them gently and lovingly. In everything there must be a beginning. It is not those who make the most flaming profession of religion at first, who endure the longest and prove the most steadfast. Judas Iscariot was an apostle when Nicodemus was just groping his way slowly into full light. Yet afterwards, when Nicodemus was boldly helping to bury his crucified Savior, Judas Iscariot had betrayed Him and hanged himself! This is a fact which ought not to be forgotten.

We should notice, secondly, in these verses, *what a mighty change our Lord declares to be needful to salvation, and what a remarkable expression He uses in describing it.* He speaks of a new birth. He says to Nicodemus, "Except a man be born again, he cannot see the kingdom of God." He announces the same truth in other words, in order to make it more plain to his hearer's mind – "Except a man be born of water and of the Spirit, he cannot enter into the kingdom of God." By this expression He meant Nicodemus to understand that "no one could become His disciple, unless his inward man was as thoroughly cleansed and renewed by the Spirit as the outward man is cleansed by water." To possess the privileges of Judaism a man only needed to be born of the seed of Abraham after the flesh. To possess the privileges of Christ's kingdom, a man must be born again of the Holy Spirit.

The change which our Lord here declares needful to salvation is evidently no slight or superficial one. It is not merely reformation, or amendment, or moral change, or outward alteration of life. It is a thorough change of heart, will, and character. It is a resurrection. It is a new creation. It is a passing from death to life. It is the implanting in our dead hearts of a new principle from above. It is the calling into existence of a new creature, with a new nature, new habits of life, new tastes, new desires, new appetites, new judgments, new opinions, new hopes, and new fears. All this, and nothing less than this is implied, when our Lord declares that we all need a "new birth."

This change of heart is rendered absolutely necessary to salvation by the corrupt condition in which we are all, without exception, born. "That which is born of the flesh is flesh." Our nature is thoroughly fallen. The carnal mind is enmity against God (Romans 8:7). We come into the world without faith, or love, or fear toward God. We have no natural inclination to serve Him or obey Him, and no natural pleasure in doing His will. Left to himself, no child of Adam would ever turn to God. The truest description of the change which we all need in order to make us real Christians is the expression "new birth."

This mighty change, it must never be forgotten, we cannot give to ourselves. The very name which our Lord gives to it is a convincing proof of this. He calls it "a birth." No man is the author of his own existence, and no man can quicken his own soul. We might as well expect a dead man to give himself life as expect a natural man to make himself spiritual. A power *from above* must be put in exercise, even that same power which created the world (2 Corinthians 4:6). Man can do many

39

things, but he cannot give life either to himself or to others. To give life is the peculiar prerogative of God. Well may our Lord declare that we need to be "born again!"

This mighty change, we must, above all, remember, is a thing without which we cannot go to heaven and could not enjoy heaven if we went there. Our Lord's words on this point are distinct and express. "Except a man be born again, he can neither *see* nor *enter* the kingdom of God." Heaven may be reached without money, or rank, or learning. But it is clear as daylight, if words have any meaning, that nobody can enter heaven without a "new birth."

We should notice, lastly, in these verses, *the instructive comparison which our Lord uses in explaining the new birth.* He saw Nicodemus perplexed and astonished by the things he had just heard. He graciously helped his wondering mind by an illustration drawn from "the wind." A more beautiful and fitting illustration of the work of the Spirit it is impossible to conceive.

There is much about the wind that is mysterious and inexplicable. "You cannot tell," says our Lord, "whence it comes and where it goes." We cannot handle it with our hands, or see it with our eyes. When the wind blows, we cannot point out the exact spot where its breath first began to be felt, and the exact distance to which its influence shall extend. But we do not on that account deny its presence. It is just the same with the operations of the Spirit in the new birth of man. They may be mysterious, sovereign, and incomprehensible to us in many ways. But it is foolish to stumble at them because there is much about those who we cannot explain.

But whatever mystery there may be about the wind, its presence may always be known by its sound and effects. "You hear the sound thereof," says our Lord. When our ears hear it whistling in the windows, and our eyes see the clouds driving before it, we do not hesitate to say, "There is wind." It is just the same with the operations of the Holy Spirit in the new birth of man. Marvelous and incomprehensible as His work may be, it is work that can always be seen and known. The new birth is a thing that "cannot be hidden." There will always be visible "fruits of the Spirit" in every one that is born of the Spirit.

Would we know what the marks of the new birth are? We shall find them already written for our learning in the First Epistle of John. The man born of God "believes that Jesus is the Christ" – "does not commit sin" – "does righteousness" – "loves the brethren" – "overcomes the world" – "keeps himself from the wicked one." This is the man born of the Spirit! Where these fruits are to be seen, there is the new birth of which our Lord is speaking. He that lacks these marks is yet dead in trespasses and sins (1 John 5:1; 3:9; 2:29; 3:14; 5:4; 5:18).

And now let us solemnly ask ourselves whether we know anything of the mighty change of which we have been reading? Have we been born again? Can any marks of the new birth be seen in us? Can the sound of the Spirit be heard in our daily conversation? Is the image and superscription of the Spirit to be discerned in our lives? Happy is the man who can give satisfactory answers to these questions! A day will come when those who are not born again will wish that they had never been born at all.

John 3:9-21

Nicodemus answered and said unto him, How can this be done? Jesus answered and said unto him, Art thou a teacher of Israel and knowest not this? Verily, verily, I say unto thee that we speak what we know and testify that which we have seen, and ye do not receive our witness. If I have told you earthly things and ye do not believe, how shall ye believe if I tell you of heavenly things? And no one has ascended up to the heaven but he that came down from the heaven, even the Son of man, who is in the heaven. And as Moses lifted up the serpent in the wilderness, even so must the Son of man be lifted up, that whosoever believes in him should not perish but have eternal life. For God so loved the world that he gave his only begotten Son, that whosoever believes in him should not perish but have eternal life. For God did not send his Son into the world to condemn the world, but that the world through him might be saved. He that believes on him is not condemned, but he that does not believe is condemned already because he has not believed in the name of the only begotten Son of God. And this is the condemnation, that the light is come into the world, and men loved darkness more than the light because their deeds were evil. For every one that does evil hates the light, and does not come to the light, lest his deeds should be reproved. But he that does truth comes to the light, that his deeds may be made manifest, that they are wrought in God.

We have in these verses the second part of the conversation between our Lord Jesus Christ and Nicodemus. A lesson about regeneration is closely followed by a lesson about justification! The whole passage ought always to be read with affectionate reverence. It contains words which have brought eternal life to myriads of souls.

These verses show us, firstly, *what gross spiritual ignorance there may be in the mind of a great and learned man.* We see a "master of Israel" unacquainted with the first elements of saving religion. Nicodemus is told about the new birth and at once exclaims, "How can these things be?" When such was the darkness of a Jewish teacher, what must have been the state of the Jewish people? It was indeed due time for Christ to appear! The pastors of Israel had ceased to feed the people with knowledge. The blind were leading the blind, and both were falling into the ditch (Matthew 15:14).

Ignorance like that of Nicodemus is unhappily far too common in the Church of Christ. We must never be surprised if we find it in quarters where we might reasonably expect knowledge. Learning, and rank, and high ecclesiastical office are no proof that a minister is taught by the Spirit. The successors of Nicodemus, in every age, are far more numerous than the successors of Peter. On no point is religious ignorance so common as on the work of the Holy Spirit. That old stumbling block, at which Nicodemus stumbled, is as much an offence to thousands in the present day as it was in the days of Christ. "The natural man does not perceive the things of the Spirit of God" (1 Corinthians 2:14). Happy is he who has been taught to prove all things by Scripture and to call no man master upon earth (1 Thessalonians 5:21; Matthew 23:9).

These verses show us, secondly, *the original source from which man's salvation springs*. That source is the love of God the Father. Our Lord says to Nicodemus, "God so [in such a way] loved the world that He gave His only begotten Son, that whosoever believeth in Him should not perish, but have everlasting life."

Let us take heed that our views of the love of God are scriptural and well-defined. The subject is one on which error abounds on either side. On the one hand, we must beware of vague and exaggerated opinions. We must maintain firmly that God hates wickedness, and that the end of all who persist in wickedness will be destruction. It is not true that God's love is "lower than hell." It is not true that God so loved the world that all mankind will be finally saved, but that He so loved the world that He gave His Son to be the Savior of all who believe. His love is offered to all men freely, fully, honestly, and unreservedly, but it is only through the one channel of Christ's redemption. He that rejects Christ cuts himself off from God's love and will perish everlastingly.

On the other hand, we must beware of narrow and contracted opinions. There is a "kindness and love" in God towards mankind. It was in consequence of that love that Christ came into the world and died upon the cross. Let us not be wise above that which is written or more systematic in our statements than Scripture itself. God has no pleasure in the death of the wicked. God would have all men to be saved. God loves the world (John 6:32; Titus 3:4; 1 John 4:10; 2 Peter 3:9; 1 Timothy 2:4; Ezekiel 33:11).

These verses show us, thirdly, *the peculiar plan by which the love of God has provided salvation for sinners*. That plan is the atoning death of Christ on the cross. Our Lord says to Nicodemus, "As Moses lifted up the serpent in the wilderness, even so must the Son of man be *lifted up*, that whoever believes in Him should not perish, but have eternal life."

By being "lifted up," our Lord meant nothing less than His own death upon the cross. That death, He would have us know, was appointed by God to be "the life of the world" (John 6:51). It was ordained from all eternity to be the great propitiation and satisfaction for man's sin. It was the payment, by an Almighty Substitute and Representative of man's enormous debt to God. When Christ died upon the cross, our many sins were laid upon Him. He was made "sin" for us. He was made "a curse" for us (2 Corinthians 5:21; Galatians 3:13). By His death He purchased pardon and complete redemption for sinners.

The bronze serpent, lifted up in the camp of Israel, brought health and cure within the reach of all who were bitten by the snakes. Christ crucified, in like manner, brought eternal life within reach of lost mankind. Christ has been lifted up on the cross, and man looking to Him by faith may be saved.

The truth before us is the very foundation stone of the Christian religion. Christ's death is the Christian's life. Christ's cross is the Christian's title to heaven. Christ "lifted up" and put to shame on Calvary is the ladder by which Christians "enter into the holiest" and are at length landed in glory. It is true that we are sinners – but Christ has suffered for us. It is true that we deserve death – but Christ has died for us. It is true that we are guilty debtors – but Christ has paid our debts with His own blood. This is the real Gospel! This is the good news! On this let us lean while we live. To this let us cling when we die. Christ has been "lifted up" on the cross and has thrown open the gates of heaven to all believers.

These verses show us, fourthly, *the way in which the benefits of Christ's death are made our own.* That way is simply to put faith and trust in Christ. Faith is the same thing as believing. Three times our Lord repeats this glorious truth to Nicodemus. Twice He proclaims that "whosoever believeth shall not perish." Once He says, "He that believeth on the Son of God is not condemned."

Faith in the Lord Jesus is the very key of salvation. He that has it has life, and he that has it not has not life. Nothing whatever *beside* this faith is necessary to our complete justification; but nothing whatever *except* this faith will give us an interest in Christ. We may fast and mourn for sin, and do many things that are right, and use religious ordinances, and give all our goods to feed the poor, and yet remain unpardoned and lose our souls. But if we will only come to Christ as guilty sinners and believe on Him, our sins shall at once be forgiven, and our iniquities shall be entirely put away. Without faith there is no salvation; but through faith in Jesus, the vilest sinner may be saved.

If we would have a peaceful conscience in our religion, let us see that our views of saving faith are distinct and clear. Let us beware of supposing that justifying faith is anything more than a sinner's simple trust in a Savior, the grasp of a drowning man on the hand held out for his relief. Let us beware of mingling anything else with faith in the matter of *justification*. Here we must always remember faith stands entirely alone. A justified man, no doubt, will always be a holy man. True believing will always be accompanied by godly living. But that which gives a man a saving interest in Christ is not his *living* but his *faith*. If we would know whether our faith is genuine, we do well to ask ourselves how we are living. But if we would know whether we are justified by Christ, there is but one question to be asked. That question is "Do we believe?"

These verses show us, lastly, *the true cause of the loss of man's soul*. Our Lord says to Nicodemus, "This is the condemnation, that light is come into the world, and *men loved darkness* rather than light, because their deeds were evil."

The words before us form a suitable conclusion to the glorious tidings which we have just been considering. They completely clear God of injustice in the condemnation of sinners. They show in simple and unmistakable terms that although man's salvation is entirely of God, his ruin, if he is lost, will be entirely from himself. He will reap the fruit of his own sowing.

The doctrine here laid down ought to be carefully remembered. It supplies an answer to a common cavil of the enemies of God's truth. There is no decreed reprobation, excluding any one from heaven. "God sent not His Son into the world to condemn the world, but that the world through Him might be saved." There is no unwillingness on God's part to receive any sinner, however great his sins. God has sent "light" into the world, and if man will not come to the light, the fault is entirely on man's side. His blood will be on his own head, if he makes shipwreck of his soul. The blame will be at his own door, if he misses heaven. His eternal misery will be the result of his own choice. His destruction will be the work of his own hand. God loved him and was willing to save him; but he "loved darkness," and therefore darkness must be his everlasting portion. He would not come to Christ, and therefore he could not have life (John 5:40).

The truths we have been considering are peculiarly weighty and solemn. Do we live as if we believed them? Salvation by Christ's death is close to us today. Have we embraced it by faith, and made it our own? Let us never rest until we know Christ as our own Savior. Let us look to Him without delay for pardon and peace, if we have never looked before. Let us go on believing on Him, if we have already believed. "Whosoever," is His own gracious word – "whosoever believeth on Him, shall not perish, but have eternal life."

John 3:22-36

After these things Jesus and his disciples came into the land of Judaea, and he tarried there with them and baptized. And John also was baptizing in Aenon near to Salim because there was much water there, and they came and were baptized. For John was not yet cast into prison. Then there arose a question between the disciples of John and the Jews about purifying. And they came unto John and said unto him, Rabbi, he that was with thee beyond Jordan of whom thou gave witness, behold, the same baptizes, and all men come to him. John answered and said, A man can receive nothing except it is given him from the heaven. Ye yourselves are my witnesses that I said, I am not the Christ, but that I am sent before him. He that has the bride is the bridegroom, but the friend of the bridegroom, who stands and hears him, rejoices greatly because of the bridegroom's voice; this my joy therefore is fulfilled. It is expedient unto him to increase, but unto me, to decrease. He that comes from above is above all; he that is of the earth is earthly and speaks earthly things: he that comes from heaven is above all. And what he has seen and heard, that he testifies; and no one receives his testimony. He that has received his testimony has set to his seal that God is true. For he whom God has sent speaks the

*words of God; for God does not give the Spirit by measure
unto him. The Father loves the Son and has given all things
into his hand. He that believes in the Son has eternal life,
and he that does not obey the Son shall not see life, but the
wrath of God abides on him.*

On one account, this passage deserves the special attention of all devout
readers of the Bible. It contains the last testimony of John the Baptist
concerning our Lord Jesus Christ. That faithful man of God was the
same at the end of his ministry that he was at the beginning – the same
in his views of self – the same in his views of Christ. Happy is that
church whose ministers are as steady, bold, and constant to one thing,
as John the Baptist!

We have, firstly, in these verses, *a humbling example of the petty
jealousies and party spirit which may exist among professors of religion.*
We are told that the disciples of John the Baptist were offended, because
the ministry of Jesus began to attract more attention than that of their
master. "They came unto John, and said unto him, Rabbi, he that was
with thee beyond Jordan, to whom thou barest witness, behold the same
baptizeth, and all men come to him."

The spirit exhibited in this complaint is unhappily too common in
the Churches of Christ. The succession of these complainers has never
failed. There are never lacking religious professors who care far more for
the increase of their own party than for the increase of true Christianity;
and who cannot rejoice in the spread of religion, if it spreads anywhere
except within their own denomination. There is a generation which can
see no good being done except in the ranks of its own congregations;
and which seems ready to shut men out of heaven, if they will not enter
therein under their banner.

The true Christian must watch and pray against the spirit here manifested by John's disciples. It is very insidious, very contagious, and very
injurious to the cause of religion. Nothing so defiles Christianity and
gives the enemies of truth such occasion to blaspheme as jealousy and
party spirit among Christians. Wherever there is real grace, we should
be ready and willing to acknowledge it, even though it may be outside
our own pale. We should strive to say with the apostle, "If Christ be

preached, I rejoice, yes! and will rejoice" (Philippians 1:18). If good is done, we ought to be thankful, though it even may not be done in what we think the best way. If souls are saved, we ought to be glad, whatever be the means that God may think fit to employ.

We have, secondly, in these verses, *a splendid pattern of true and godly humility.* We see in John the Baptist a very different spirit from that displayed by his disciples. He begins by laying down the great principle that acceptance with man is a special gift of God and that we must therefore not presume to find fault, when others have more acceptance than ourselves. "A man can receive nothing except it be given him from heaven." He goes on to remind his followers of his repeated declaration, that one greater than himself was coming – "I said, I am not the Christ." He tells them that his office, compared to that of Christ, is that of the bridegroom's friend, compared to the bridegroom. And finally, he solemnly affirms that Christ must and will become greater and greater, and that he himself must become less and less important until, like a star eclipsed by the rising sun, he has completely disappeared.

A frame of mind like this is the highest degree of grace to which mortal man can attain. The greatest saint in the sight of God is the man who is most thoroughly "clothed with humility" (1 Peter 5:5). Would we know the prime secret of being men of the stamp of Abraham, and Moses, and Job, and David, and Daniel, and Paul, and John the Baptist? They were all eminently humble men. Living at different ages and enjoying very different degrees of light, in this matter at least they were all agreed. In themselves they saw nothing but sin and weakness. To God they gave all the praise of what they were. Let us walk in their steps. Let us covet earnestly the best gifts, but above all, let us covet humility. The way to true honor is to be humble. No man ever was so praised by Christ as the very man who says here, "I must decrease," the humble John the Baptist.

We have, thirdly, in these verses, *an instructive declaration of Christ's honor and dignity.* John the Baptist teaches his disciples once more, the true greatness of the Person whose growing popularity offended them. Once more, and perhaps for the last time, he proclaims Him as one worthy of all honor and praise. He uses one striking expression after another to convey a correct idea of the majesty of Christ. He speaks of Him as "the bridegroom" of the Church – as "him that comes from above" – as "him whom God has sent" – as "him to whom the Spirit is given without measure" – as Him "whom the Father loves" and into "whose hands all things are given" – to believe in whom is life everlasting and to reject whom is eternal ruin. Each of these phrases is full of deep meaning and would supply matter for a long sermon. All show the depth and height of John's spiritual attainments. More honorable things are nowhere written concerning Jesus than these verses recorded as spoken by John the Baptist.

Let us endeavor in life and death to hold the same views of the Lord Jesus to which John here gives expression. We can never make too much of Christ. Our thoughts about the Church, the ministry, and the sacraments may easily become too high and extravagant. We can never have too high thoughts about Christ, can never love Him too much, trust Him too implicitly, lay too much weight upon Him, and speak too highly in His praise. He is worthy of all the honor that we can give Him. He will be all in heaven. Let us see to it, that He is all in our hearts on earth.

We have, lastly, in these verses, *a broad assertion of the nearness and presentness of the salvation of true Christians.* John the Baptist declares, "He that believes in the Son has eternal life." He is not intended to look forward with a sick heart to a far distant privilege. He "has" eternal life as soon as he believes. Pardon, peace, and a complete title to Heaven are an immediate possession. They become a believer's own from the very moment he puts faith in Christ. They will not be more completely his own, if he lives to the age of Methuselah.

The truth before us is one of the most glorious privileges of the Gospel. There are no works to be done, no conditions to be fulfilled, no price to be paid, no wearing years of probation to be passed, before a sinner can be accepted with God. Let him only believe on Christ, and he is at once forgiven. Salvation is close to the chief of sinners. Let him only repent and believe, and this day it is his own. By Christ, all that believe are at once justified from all things.

Let us leave the whole passage with one grave and heart-searching thought. If faith in Christ brings with it present and immediate privileges, to remain unbelieving is to be in a state of tremendous peril. If heaven is very near to the believer, hell must be very near to the unbeliever. The greater the mercy that the Lord Jesus offers, the greater will be the guilt of those who neglect and reject it. "He that does not obey the Son shall not see life, but the wrath of God abides on him."

John Chapter 4

John 4:1-6

When therefore the Lord knew how the Pharisees had heard that Jesus made and baptized more disciples than John (though Jesus himself baptized not, but his disciples), he left Judaea and departed again into Galilee. And it was necessary that he go through Samaria. Then he came to a city of Samaria, which is called Sychar, near to the parcel of ground that Jacob gave to his son Joseph. Now Jacob's well was there. Jesus, therefore, being wearied with his journey, sat thus on the well; and it was about the sixth hour.

THERE ARE TWO SAYINGS in these verses, which deserve particular notice. They throw light on two subjects in religion, on which clear and well-defined opinions are of great importance.

We should observe, for one thing, *what is said about baptism*. We read that "Jesus himself baptized not, but his disciples."

The expression here used is a very remarkable one. In reading it we seem irresistibly led to one instructive conclusion. That conclusion is that baptism is not the principal part of Christianity, and that to baptize is not the principal work for which Christian ministers are ordained. Frequently we read of our Lord preaching and praying. Once we read of His administering the Lord's Supper. But we have not a single instance recorded of His ever baptizing any one. And here we are distinctly told that it was a *subordinate* work, which He left to others. Jesus "himself baptized not, but his disciples."

The lesson is one of peculiar importance in the present day. Baptism, as a sacrament ordained by Christ Himself, is an honorable ordinance and ought never to be lightly esteemed in the churches. It cannot be neglected or despised without great sin. When rightly used, with faith and prayer, it is calculated to convey the highest blessings. But baptism was never meant to be exalted to the position which many now-a-days assign to it in religion. It does not act as a *charm*. It does not necessarily convey the grace of the Holy Spirit. The benefit of it depends greatly on the manner in which it is used. The doctrine taught, and the language employed about it, in some quarters are utterly inconsistent with the fact announced in the text. If baptism was all that some say it is, we would never have been told that "Jesus himself baptized not."

Let it be a settled principle in our minds that the first and chief business of the Church of Christ is to preach the Gospel. The words of Paul ought to be constantly remembered – "Christ sent me not to baptize, but to preach the Gospel" (1 Corinthians 1:17). When the Gospel of Christ is faithfully and fully preached, we need not fear that the sacraments will be undervalued. Baptism and the Lord's Supper will always be most truly reverenced in those churches where the truth as it is in Jesus is most fully taught and known.

We should observe, for another thing, in this passage, *what is said about our Lord's human nature*. We read that Jesus was "wearied with his journey."

We learn from this, as well as many other expressions in the Gospels that our Lord had a body exactly like our own. When "the Word became flesh," He took on Him a nature like our own in all things, sin only excepted. Like ourselves, He grew from infancy to youth, and from youth to man. Like ourselves, He hungered, thirsted, felt pain, and needed sleep. He was liable to every sinless infirmity to which we are liable. In all things His body was framed like our own.

The truth before us is full of comfort for all who are true Christians. He to whom sinners are bid to come for pardon and peace is one who is man as well as God. He had a real human nature when He was upon earth. He took a real human nature with Him, when He ascended up into heaven. We have at the right hand of God a High Priest who can be touched with the feeling of our infirmities, because He has suffered Himself being tempted. When we cry to Him in the hour of bodily pain and weakness, He knows well what we mean. When our prayers and praises are feeble through bodily weariness, He can understand our condition. He knows our frame. He has learned by experience what it is to be a man. To say that the Virgin Mary or any one else can feel more sympathy for us than Christ is ignorance no less than blasphemy. The man Christ Jesus can enter fully into everything that belongs to man's condition. The poor, the sick, and the suffering, have in heaven One who is not only an almighty Savior, but a most sympathetic Friend.

The servant of Christ should grasp firmly this great truth, that there are two perfect and complete natures in the one Person whom he serves. The Lord Jesus, in whom the Gospel bids us believe, is without doubt almighty God – equal to the Father in all things and able to save to the uttermost all those that come unto God by Him. But that same Jesus is no less certainly perfect man – able to sympathize with man in all his bodily sufferings, and acquainted by experience with all that man's body has to endure. Power and sympathy are marvelously combined in Him who died for us on the cross. Because He is God, we may repose the weight of our souls upon Him with unhesitating confidence. He is mighty to save. Because He is man, we may speak to Him with freedom about the many trials to which flesh is heir. He knows the heart of a man. Here is rest for the weary! Here is good news! Our Redeemer is man as well as God, and God as well as man. He that believes on Him has everything that a child of Adam can possibly require, either for safety or for peace.

John 4:7-26

There came a woman of Samaria to draw water; Jesus said unto her, Give me to drink. (For his disciples were gone away unto the city to buy food.) Then said the Samaritan woman unto him, How is it that thou, being a Jew, askest drink of me, who am a woman of Samaria? for the Jews have no dealings with the Samaritans. Jesus answered and said unto her, If thou knewest the gift of God and who it is that saith to thee, Give me to drink, thou wouldest have asked of him, and he would have given thee living water. The woman said unto him, Sir, thou hast nothing to draw with, and the well is deep; from where then hast thou that living water? Art thou greater than our father Jacob, who gave us the well and drank thereof himself, and his sons and his cattle? Jesus answered and said unto her, Whosoever drinks of this water shall thirst again, but whosoever drinks of the water that I shall give him shall never thirst, but the water that I shall give him shall be in him a fountain of water springing up into eternal life. The woman said unto him, Lord, give me this water, that I not thirst, neither come here to draw. Jesus said unto her, Go, call thy husband and come here. The woman answered and said, I have no husband. Jesus said unto her, Thou hast well said, I have no husband; for thou hast had five husbands, and he whom thou now hast is not thy husband; this hast thou said with truth. The woman said unto him, Lord, I perceive that thou art a prophet. Our fathers worshipped in this mountain, and ye say that in Jerusalem is the place where it is necessary to worship. Jesus said unto her, Woman, believe me, the hour comes when neither in this mountain nor in Jerusalem shall ye wor-ship the Father. Ye worship what ye know not; we worship what we know, for saving health is of the Jews. But the hour comes, and now is, when the true worshippers shall wor-ship the Father in spirit and in truth, for the Father seeks such to worship him. God is a Spirit and those that worship him must worship him in spirit and in truth. The woman said unto him, I know that the Messiah is to come, who is called the Christ; when he is come, he will declare unto us all things. Jesus said unto her, I AM that speak unto thee.

The history of the Samaritan woman, contained in these verses, is one of the most interesting and instructive passages in John's Gospel.[5]

---

5   The enmity between the Jews and Samaritans no doubt originated in the separation of the ten tribes under Jeroboam and the establishment of the kingdom of Israel. It was exceed-ingly increased after the ten tribes were carried into captivity by the Assyrians, by the fact that the Samaritans became mingled with foreigners, whom the king of Assyria sent

John has shown us in the case of Nicodemus how our Lord dealt with a self-righteous formalist. He now shows us how our Lord dealt with an ignorant, carnal-minded woman, whose moral character was more than ordinarily bad. There are lessons in the passage for ministers and teachers, which they would do well to ponder.

We should mark, firstly, *the mingled tact and humility of Christ in dealing with a careless sinner.*

Our Lord was sitting by Jacob's well when a woman of Samaria came there to draw water. At once He says to her, "Give me to drink." He does not wait for her to speak to Him. He does not begin by reproving her sins, though He doubtless knew them. He opens communication by asking a favor. He approaches the woman's mind by the subject of "water," which was naturally uppermost in her thoughts. Simple as this request may seem, it opened a door to spiritual conversation. It threw a bridge across the gulf, which lay between her and Him. It led to the conversion of her soul.

Our Lord's conduct in this place should be carefully remembered by all who want to do good to the thoughtless and spiritually ignorant. It is vain to expect that such people will voluntarily come to us and begin to seek knowledge. We must begin with them and go down to them in the spirit of courteous and friendly offensive. It is vain to expect that such people will be prepared for our instruction, and will at once see and acknowledge the wisdom of all we are doing. We must go to work wisely. We must study the best avenues to their hearts and the most likely way of arresting their attention. There is a handle to every mind, and our chief aim must be to get hold of it. Above all, we must be kind in manner and beware of showing that we feel conscious of our own superiority. If we let ignorant people fancy that we think we are doing

---

to Samaria from Babylon and other places, and so lost their right to be called pure Jews (2 Kings 17). It was further aggravated by the opposition, which the inhabitants of Samaria made to the rebuilding of Jerusalem, after the return from the captivity of Babylon in the days of Ezra (Ezra 4). In the days of our Lord the Jews seem to have gone into the extreme of regarding the Samaritans as entirely foreigners and aliens from the commonwealth of Israel. When they told our Lord that He was "a Samaritan and had a devil," they meant the expression to convey the bitterest scorn and reproach (John 8:48). It is clear, however, from the conversation in this chapter that the Samaritans, however mistaken on many points, were not ignorant heathens. They regarded themselves as descended from Jacob. They had a kind of Old Testament religion. They expected the coming of Messias.

them a great favor in talking to them about religion, there is little hope of doing good to their souls.

We should mark, secondly, *Christ's readiness to give mercies to careless sinners.* He tells the Samaritan woman that if she had asked, "He would have given her living water." He knew the character of the person before Him perfectly well. Yet He says, "If she had asked, He would have given" – He would have given the living water of grace, mercy, and peace.

The infinite willingness of Christ to receive sinners is a golden truth, which ought to be treasured up in our hearts and diligently impressed on others. The Lord Jesus is far more ready to hear than we are to pray and far more ready to give favors than we are to ask them. All day long He stretches out His hands to the disobedient and gainsaying. He has thoughts of pity and compassion towards the vilest of sinners, even when they have no thoughts of Him. He stands waiting to bestow mercy and grace on the worst and most unworthy, if they will only cry to Him. He will never draw back from that well-known promise, "Ask and you shall receive – seek and you shall find." The lost will discover at the last day that they *had* not, because they *asked* not.

We should mark, thirdly, *the priceless excellence of Christ's gifts when compared with the things of this world.* Our Lord tells the Samaritan woman, "He that drinks of this water shall thirst again, but he that drinks of the water that I shall give him shall never thirst."[6]

The truth of the principle here laid down may be seen on every side by all who are not blinded by prejudice or love of the world. Thousands of men have every temporal good thing that heart could wish and are yet weary and dissatisfied. It is now as it was in David's time – "There be many that say, Who will show us any good" (Psalm 4:6). Riches, and rank, and place, and power, and learning, and amusements, are utterly unable to fill the soul. He that only drinks of these waters is sure to thirst again. Every Ahab finds a Naboth's vineyard nearby his palace,

---

6   Some have thought that there is a tacit reference in these words to the woman's insatiable love of sin. The similarity ought to be noticed between our Lord's line of argument in this verse and the line He adopts in recommending to the Jews the bread of life in the sixth chapter. He showed the Jews the superiority of the bread of life over the manna by the words "your fathers did eat manna and are dead" (John 6:49). Just so in this place, He shows the inferiority of the water of Jacob's well to the living water by saying "He that drinks of this water shall thirst again." The two passages deserve a careful comparison.

and every Haman sees a Mordecai at the gate. There is no heart satisfaction in this world, until we believe on Christ. Jesus alone can fill up the empty places of our inward man. Jesus alone can give solid, lasting, enduring happiness. The peace that He imparts is a fountain, which once set flowing within the soul, flows on to all eternity. Its waters may have their ebbing seasons; but they are living waters, and they shall never be completely dried.

We should mark, fourthly, *the absolute necessity of conviction of sin before a soul can be converted to God.* The Samaritan woman seems to have been comparatively unmoved until our Lord exposed her breach of the seventh commandment. Those heart-searching words, "Go, call your husband," appear to have pierced her conscience like an arrow. From that moment, however ignorant, she speaks like an earnest, sincere inquirer after truth. And the reason is evident. She felt that her spiritual disease was discovered. For the first time in her life, she saw herself.

To bring thoughtless people to this state of mind should be the principal aim of all teachers and ministers of the Gospel. They should carefully copy their Master's example in this place. Until men and women are brought to feel their sinfulness and need, no real good is ever done to their souls. Until a sinner sees himself as God sees him, he will continue careless, trifling, and unmoved. By all means we must labor to convince the unconverted man of sin, to pierce his conscience, to open his eyes, to show him himself. To this end we must expound the length and breadth of God's holy law. To this end we must denounce every practice contrary to that law, however fashionable and customary. This is the only way to do good. Never does a soul value the Gospel medicine until it feels its disease. Never does a man see any beauty in Christ as a Savior, until he discovers that he is himself a lost and ruined sinner. Ignorance of sin is invariably attended by neglect of Christ.

We should mark, fifthly, *the utter uselessness of any religion which only consists of formality.* The Samaritan woman, when awakened to spiritual concern, started questions about the comparative merits of the Samaritan and Jewish modes of worshiping God. Our Lord tells her that true and acceptable worship depends not on the place in which it is offered, but on the state of the worshiper's heart. He declares, "The hour comes when ye shall neither in this place nor at Jerusalem worship the Father." He adds that "the true worshipers shall worship in spirit and in truth."

The principle contained in these sentences can never be too strongly impressed on professing Christians. We are all naturally inclined to make religion a mere matter of outward forms and ceremonies and to attach an excessive importance to our own particular manner of worshiping God. We must beware of this spirit, and especially when we first begin to think seriously about our souls. The heart is the principal thing in all our approaches to God. "The Lord looks on the heart" (1 Samuel 16:7). The most gorgeous cathedral service is offensive in God's sight, if all is gone through coldly, heartlessly, and without grace. The feeblest gathering of three or four poor believers in a lowly cottage to read the Bible and pray is a more acceptable sight to Him who searches the heart than the fullest congregation which is ever gathered in St. Peter's at Rome.

We should mark, lastly, *Christ's gracious willingness to reveal Himself to the chief of sinners.* He concludes His conversation with the Samaritan woman by telling her openly and unreservedly that He is the Savior of the world. "I that speak to you," He says, "am the Messiah." Nowhere in all the Gospels do we find our Lord making such a full avowal of His nature and office as He does in this place. And this avowal, be it remembered, was made not to learned Scribes, or moral Pharisees, but to one who up to that day had been an ignorant, thoughtless, and immoral person!

Dealings with sinners, such as these, form one of the grand peculiarities of the Gospel. Whatever a man's past life may have been, there is hope and a remedy for him in Christ. If he is only willing to hear Christ's voice and follow Him, Christ is willing to receive him at once as a friend and to bestow on him the fullest measure of mercy and grace. The Samaritan woman, the penitent thief, the Philippian jailor, the tax collector Zacchaeus, are all patterns of Christ's readiness to show mercy and to confer full and immediate pardons. It is His glory that, like a great physician, He will undertake to cure those who are apparently incurable, and that none are too bad for Him to love and heal. Let these things sink down into our hearts. Whatever else we doubt, let us never doubt that Christ's love to sinners passes knowledge, and that Christ is as willing to receive as He is almighty to save.

What are we ourselves? This is the question, after all, which demands our attention. We may have been up to this day careless, thoughtless, sinful as the woman whose story we have been reading. But yet there is hope – He who talked with the Samaritan woman at the well is yet living at God's right hand, and never changes. Let us only ask, and He will "give us living water."

John 4:27-30

And upon this came his disciples and marvelled that he talked with that woman; yet no one said, What askest thou? or, What talkest thou with her? The woman then left her waterpot and went into the city and said to those men, Come, see a man who told me all that I have done; is perchance this the Christ? Then they went out of the city and came unto him.

These verses continue the well-known story of the Samaritan woman's conversion. Short as the passage may appear, it contains points of deep interest and importance. The mere worldling, who cares nothing about experimental religion, may see nothing particular in these verses. To all who desire to know something of the experience of a converted person, they will be found full of food for thought.

We see, firstly, in this passage, *how marvelous in the eyes of man are Christ's dealings with souls.* We are told that the disciples "marveled that he talked with the woman." That their Master should take the trouble to talk to a woman at all, and to a *Samaritan* woman, and to an *adulterous* woman at a well, when He was wearied with His journey – all this was amazing to the disciples. It was a sort of thing which they did not expect. It was contrary to their idea of what a religious teacher should do. It startled them and filled them with surprise.

The feeling displayed by the disciples on this occasion does not stand alone in the Bible. When our Lord allowed publicans and sinners to draw near to Him and be in His company, the Pharisees marveled. They exclaimed, "This man receives sinners and eats with them" (Luke 15:2). When Saul came back from Damascus, a converted man and a new creature, the Christians at Jerusalem were astonished. "They believed not that he was a disciple" (Acts 9:26). When Peter was delivered from Herod's prison by an angel and brought to the door of the house where disciples were praying for his deliverance, they were so taken by surprise that they could not believe it was Peter. "When they saw him they were astonished" (Acts 12:16).

But why should we stop short in Bible instances? The true Christian has only to look around him in this world in order to see abundant illustrations of the truth before us. How much astonishment every fresh conversion occasions. What surprise is expressed at the change in the heart, life, tastes, and habits of the converted person! What wonder is felt at the power, the mercy, the patience, the compassion of Christ! It is now as it was eighteen hundred years ago. The dealings of Christ are still *a marvel* both to the Church and to the world.

If there was more real faith on the earth, there would be less surprise felt at the conversion of souls. If Christians believed more, they would expect more, and if they understood Christ better, they would be less startled and astonished when He calls and saves the chief of sinners. We should consider nothing impossible and regard no sinner as beyond the reach of the grace of God. The astonishment expressed at conversions is a proof of the weak faith and ignorance of these latter days. The thing that ought to fill us with surprise is the obstinate unbelief of the ungodly and their determined perseverance in the way to ruin. This was the mind of Christ. It is written that He thanked the Father for *conversions*. But He marveled at unbelief (Matthew 11:25; Mark 6:6).

We see, secondly, in this passage, *how absorbing is the influence of grace, when it first comes into a believer's heart.* We are told that after our Lord had told the woman He was the Messiah, "She left her water-pot and went her way into the city and said to the men, Come, see a man which told me all things that ever I did." She had left her home for the express purpose of drawing water. She had carried a large vessel to the well, intending to bring it back filled. But she found at the well a new heart and new objects of interest. She became a new creature. Old things passed away. All things became new. At once everything else was forgotten for the time. She could think of nothing but the truths she had heard, and the Savior she had found. In the fullness of her heart she "left her waterpot" and hastened away to tell others.

We see here the expulsive power of the grace of the Holy Spirit. Grace once introduced into the heart drives out old tastes and interests. A converted person no longer cares for what he once cared for. A new tenant is in the house. A new pilot is at the helm. The whole world looks different. All things have become new. It was so with Matthew the tax-collector. The moment that grace came into his heart, he left the receipt of custom (Matthew 9:9). It was so with Peter, James, and John, and Andrew. As soon as they were converted, they forsook their nets and fishing boats (Mark 1:19-20). It was so with Saul the Pharisee. As soon as he became a Christian, he gave up all his brilliant prospects as a Jew in order to preach the faith he had once despised (Acts 9:20). The conduct of the Samaritan woman was precisely of the same kind. For the time present, the salvation she had found completely filled her mind. That she never returned for her waterpot would be more than we have a right to say. But under the first impressions of new spiritual life, she went away and "left her waterpot" behind.

Conduct like that here described is doubtless uncommon in the present day. Rarely do we see a person so entirely taken up with spiritual matters that attention to this world's affairs is made a secondary matter or postponed. And why is it so? Simply because true conversions to God are uncommon. Few really feel their sins and flee to Christ by faith. Few really pass from death to life and become new creatures. Yet these few are the real Christians of the world. These are the people whose religion, like the Samaritan woman's, tells on others. Happy are they who know something by experience of this woman's feelings and can say with Paul, "I count all things but loss for the excellency of the knowledge of Christ" (Philippians 3:8). Happy are they who have given up everything for Christ's sake or at any rate have altered the relative importance of all things in their minds! "If thine eye is sincere, thy whole body shall be full of light" (Matthew 6:22).

We see, lastly, in this passage, *how zealous a truly converted person is to do good to others.* We are told that the Samaritan woman "went into the city, and said to the men, Come, see a man which told me all things that ever I did: is not this the Christ?" In the day of her conversion she became a missionary! She felt so deeply the amazing benefit she had received from Christ that she could not hold her peace about Him. Just as Andrew told his brother Peter about Jesus, and Philip told Nathanael that he had found Messiah, and Saul, when converted, immediately preached Christ, so in the same way, the Samaritan woman said, "Come and see Christ." She used no abstruse arguments. She attempted no deep reasoning about our Lord's claim to be the Messiah. She only said, "Come and see." Out of the abundance of her heart, her mouth spoke.

That which the Samaritan woman here did, all true Christians ought to do likewise. The Church needs it. The state of the world demands it. Common sense points out that it is right. Every one who has received the grace of God, and tasted that Christ is gracious ought to find words to testify of Christ to others. Where is our faith, if we believe that souls around us are perishing, and that Christ alone can save them, and yet remain silent? Where is our charity if we can see others going down to hell, and yet say nothing to them about Christ and salvation? We may well doubt our own love to Christ, if our hearts are never moved to speak of Him. We may well doubt the safety of our own souls, if we feel no concern about the souls of others.

What are we ourselves? This is the question, after all, which demands our notice. Do we feel the supreme importance of spiritual things and the comparative nothingness of the things of the world? Do we ever talk to others about God, and Christ, and eternity, and the soul, and heaven, and hell? If not, what is the value of our faith? Where is the reality of our Christianity? Let us take heed lest we awake too late and find that we are lost forever, a wonder to angels and devils, and above all, a wonder to ourselves, because of our own obstinate blindness and folly.

John 4:31-42

In the meanwhile his disciples entreated him, saying, Rabbi,

*eat. But he said unto them, I have a food to eat that ye
know not of. Therefore said the disciples one to another, Has
anyone brought him anything to eat? Jesus said unto them,
My food is to do the will of him that sent me and to finish
his work. Do ye not say, There are yet four months and then
comes harvest? Behold, I say unto you, Lift up your eyes
and look on the fields, for they are white already to harvest.
And he that reaps receives wages and gathers fruit unto
eternal life, that both he that sows and he that reaps may
rejoice together. And herein is that saying true, One sows
and another reaps. I have sent you to reap that upon which
ye bestowed no labour; others laboured, and ye have entered
into their labours. And many of the Samaritans of that city
believed in him by the word of the woman, who testified, He
told me all that I have done. So when the Samaritans were
come unto him, they asked him to abide with them; and he
abode there two days. And many more believed by his own
word and said unto the woman, Now we believe, not because
of thy speech; for we have heard him ourselves and know
that this is indeed the Christ, the Saviour of the world.*

We have, for one thing, in these verses, *an instructive pattern of zeal
for the good of others*. We read that our Lord Jesus Christ declares, "My
meat is to do the will of him who sent me, and to finish his work." To
do good was not merely duty and pleasure to Him. He counted it as His
food and drink. Job, one of the holiest Old Testament saints, could say
that he esteemed God's *word* "more than his necessary food" (Job 23:12).
The Great Head of the New Testament Church went even further. He
could say the same of God's *work*.

Do we do any work for God? Do we try, however feebly, to set forward His cause on earth – to check that which is evil, to promote that
which is good? If we do, let us never be ashamed of doing it with all our
heart, and soul, and mind, and strength. Whatever our hand finds to
do for the souls of others, let us do it with our might (Ecclesiastes 9:10).
The world may mock and sneer, and call us enthusiasts. The world can
admire zeal in any service but that of God and can praise enthusiasm on

any subject but that of religion. Let us work on unmoved. Whatever men may say and think, we are walking in the steps of our Lord Jesus Christ.

Let us, beside this, take comfort in the thought that Jesus Christ never changes. High in heaven at God's right hand, He still delights to save sinners and still approves zeal and labor in the cause of God. The work of the missionary and the evangelist may be despised and ridiculed in many quarters. But while man is mocking, Christ is well pleased! Thanks be to God, Jesus is the same yesterday, and today, and forever.

We have, for another thing, in these verses, strong encouragement held out to those who *labor for the Lord.* We read that our Lord described the world as a "field white for the harvest;" and then said to His disciples, "He that reaps, receives wages, and gathers fruit unto life eternal."

Work for the souls of men is undoubtedly attended by great discouragements. The heart of natural man is very hard and unbelieving. The blindness of unsaved men to their own lost condition and peril of ruin is something past description. "The carnal mind is enmity against God" (Romans 8:7). No one can have any just idea of the desperate hardness of men and women, until he has tried to do good. No one can have any conception of the small number of those who repent and believe, until he has personally endeavored to "save some" (1 Corinthians 9:22). To suppose that everybody will become a true Christian who is told about Christ and entreated to believe is mere childish ignorance. "Few there be that find the narrow way!" The laborer for Christ will find the vast majority of those among whom he labors, unbelieving and impenitent, in spite of all that he can do. "The many" will not turn to Christ. These are discouraging facts. But they are facts, and facts that ought to be known.

The true antidote against despondency in God's work is an abiding recollection of such promises as that before us. There are "wages" laid up for faithful reapers. They shall receive a reward at the last day, far exceeding anything they have done for Christ – a reward proportioned not to their success, but to the quantity of their work. They are gathering "fruit," which shall endure when this world has passed away – fruit in some souls saved, if many will not believe, and fruit in evidences of their own faithfulness to be brought out before assembled worlds. Do our hands ever hang down, and our knees wax faint? Do we feel disposed to say, "my labor is in vain and my words without profit." Let us lean back at such seasons on this glorious promise. There are "wages" yet to be paid. There is "fruit" yet to be exhibited. "We are a sweet savor of Christ, both in them who are saved and in them that perish" (2 Corinthians 2:15). Let us work on. "He that goes forth and weeps, bearing the precious seed, shall doubtless come again with rejoicing, bringing his sheaves with him" (Psalm 126:6). One single soul saved shall outlive and outweigh all the kingdoms of the world.

We have, lastly, in these verses, *a most teaching instance of the variety of ways by which men are led to believe Christ.* We read that "many of the Samaritans believed on Christ for the saying of the woman." But this is not all. We read again, "Many more believed because of Christ's own word." In short, some were converted through the means of the woman's testimony, and some were converted by hearing Christ Himself.

The words of Paul should never be forgotten, "There is dispersal of operations, but it is the same God who works all in each one" (1 Corinthians 12:6). The *way* in which the Spirit leads all God's people is always one and the same. But the paths by which they are severally brought into that road are often widely different. There are some in whom the work of conversion is sudden and instantaneous. There are others in whom it goes on slowly, quietly, and by imperceptible degrees. Some have their hearts gently opened, like Lydia. Others are aroused by violent alarm, like the jailor at Philippi. All are finally brought to repentance toward God, faith toward our Lord Jesus Christ, and holiness of conversation. But all do not begin with the same experience. The weapon which carries conviction to one believer's soul is not the one which first pierces another. The arrows of the Holy Spirit are all drawn from the same quiver. But He uses sometimes one and sometimes another, according to His own sovereign will.

Are we converted ourselves? This is the one point to which our attention ought to be directed. Our experience may not tally with that of other believers. But that is not the question. Do we feel sin, hate it, and flee from it? Do we love Christ, and rest solely on Him for salvation? Are we bringing forth fruits of the Spirit in righteousness and true holiness? If these things are so, we may thank God and take courage.

John 4:43-54

*Now after two days he departed from that place and went
into Galilee. For Jesus himself testified that a prophet has
no honour in his own country. Then when he was come into
Galilee, the Galilaeans received him, having seen all the
things that he had done in Jerusalem at the feast, for they
had also gone to the feast. So Jesus came again into Cana of
Galilee, where he had made the water wine. And there was a
certain nobleman whose son was sick at Capernaum. When
he heard that Jesus was come out of Judaea into Galilee, he
went unto him and besought him that he would come down
and heal his son, for he was at the point of death. Then Jesus
said unto him, Except ye see signs and wonders, ye will not
believe. The nobleman said unto him, Sir, come down before
my child dies. Jesus said unto him, Go; thy son lives. And
the man believed the word that Jesus spoke unto him, and
he went. And as he was now going down, his slaves met
him and told him, saying, Thy son lives. Then he enquired
of them the hour when he began to get better. And they said
unto him, Yesterday at the seventh hour the fever left him. So
the father knew that it was at the same hour in which Jesus
said unto him, Thy son lives; and he believed, and his whole
house. This again is the second sign that Jesus did when he
was come out of Judaea into Galilee.*

Four great lessons stand out boldly on the face of this passage. Let us
fix them in our memories and use them continually as we journey
through life.

We learn, firstly, *that the rich have afflictions as well as the poor.* We
read of a nobleman in deep anxiety because his son was sick. We need
not doubt that every means of restoration was used that money could
procure. But money is not almighty. The sickness increased, and the
nobleman's son lay at the point of death.

The lesson is one which needs to be constantly impressed on the
minds of men. There is no more common or more mischievous error
than to suppose that the rich have no cares. The rich are as liable to

sickness as the poor, and have a hundred anxieties beside, of which the poor know nothing at all. Silks and satins often cover very heavy hearts. The dwellers in palaces often sleep more uneasily than the dwellers in poor cottages. Gold and silver can lift no man beyond the reach of trouble. They may shut out debt and rags, but they cannot shut out care, disease, and death. The higher the tree, the more it is shaken by storms. The broader its branches, the greater is the mark which it exposes to the tempest. David was a happier man when he kept his father's sheep at Bethlehem than when he dwelt as a king at Jerusalem and governed the twelve tribes of Israel.

Let the servant of Christ beware of desiring riches. They are certain cares, and uncertain comforts. Let him pray for the rich and not envy them. How hardly shall a rich man enter the kingdom of God! Above all, let him learn to be content with such things as he has. He only is truly rich who has treasure in heaven.

We learn, secondly, in this passage that *sickness and death come to the young as well as to the old*. We read of a son sick unto death and a father in trouble about him. We see the natural order of things inverted. The elder is obliged to minister to the younger, and not the younger to the elder. The child draws near to the grave before the parent, and not the parent before the child.

The lesson is one which we are all slow to learn. We are apt to shut our eyes to plain facts and to speak and act as if young people, as a matter of course, never died when young. And yet the gravestones in every churchyard would tell us that few people out of a hundred ever live to be fifty years old, while many never grow up to man's estate at all. The first grave that ever was dug on this earth was that of a young man. The first person who ever died was not a father but a son. Aaron lost two sons at a stroke. David, the man after God's own heart, lived long enough to see three children buried. Job was deprived of all his children in one day. These things were carefully recorded for our learning.

He that is wise, will never consider long life as a certainty. We never know what a day may bring forth. The strongest and fairest are often cut down and hurried away in a few hours, while the old and feeble linger on for many years. The only true wisdom is to be always prepared to meet God, to put nothing off which concerns eternity, and to live like men ready to depart at any moment. So living, it matters little whether we die young or old. Joined to the Lord Jesus, we are safe in any event.

We learn, thirdly, from this passage, *what benefits affliction can confer on the soul.* We read that anxiety about a son led the nobleman to Christ in order to obtain help in time of need. Once brought into Christ's company, he learned a lesson of priceless value. In the end, "he believed, and his whole house." All this, be it remembered, hinged upon the son's sickness. If the nobleman's son had never been ill, his father might have lived and died in his sins!

Affliction is one of God's medicines. By it He often teaches lessons which would be learned in no other way. By it He often draws souls away from sin and the world, which would otherwise have perished everlastingly. Health is a great blessing, but sanctified disease is a greater. Prosperity and worldly comfort are what all naturally desire, but losses and crosses are far better for us, if they lead us to Christ. Thousands at the last day, will testify with David and the nobleman before us, "It is good for me that I have been afflicted" (Psalm. 119:71).

Let us beware of murmuring in the time of trouble. Let us settle it firmly in our minds that there is a meaning, a needs-be, and a message from God in every sorrow that falls upon us. There are no lessons so useful as those learned in the school of affliction. There is no commentary that opens up the Bible so much as sickness and sorrow. "No chastening at present seems to be cause for joy, but rather for grief; nevertheless, afterward it yields the peaceable fruit" (Hebrews 12:11). The resurrection morning will prove that many of the losses of God's people were in reality eternal gains.

We learn, lastly, from this passage *that Christ's word is as good as Christ's presence.* We read that Jesus did not come down to Capernaum to see the sick young man but only spoke the word, "Thy son liveth." Almighty power went with that little sentence. That very hour the patient began to amend. Christ only spoke, and the cure was done. Christ only commanded, and the deadly disease stood fast.

The fact before us is singularly full of comfort. It gives enormous value to every promise of mercy, grace, and peace, which ever fell from

Christ's lips. He that by faith has laid bold on some word of Christ has placed his feet upon a rock. What Christ has said, He is able to do; and what He has undertaken, He will never fail to make good. The sinner who has really reposed his soul on the word of the Lord Jesus is safe to all eternity. He could not be safer, if he saw the book of life and his own name written in it. If Christ has said, "Him that cometh to me, I will in no wise cast out," and our hearts can testify, "I have come," we need not doubt that we are saved. In the things of this world, we say that seeing is believing. But in the things of the Gospel, believing is as good as seeing. Christ's word is as good as man's deed. He of whom Jesus says in the Gospel, "He liveth," is alive for evermore and shall never die.

And now let us remember that afflictions, like that of the nobleman, are very common. They will probably come to our door one day. Have we known anything of bearing affliction? Would we know where to turn for help and comfort when our time comes? Let us fill our minds and memories betimes with Christ's words. They are not the words of man only, but of God. The words that he speaks are spirit and life (John 6:63).

John Chapter 5

John 5:1-15

*After these things there was a feast of the Jews, and Jesus
went up to Jerusalem. Now in Jerusalem there is a pool by
the sheep gate, which in Hebrew is called, Bethesda, having five porches. In these lay a great multitude of those who
were sick, blind, halt, withered, waiting for the moving of
the water. For an angel went down at a certain time into the
pool and troubled the water; whosoever then first after the
troubling of the water stepped in was made whole of whatever disease he had. And a certain man was there who had
an infirmity thirty-eight years. When Jesus saw him lying
there and knew that he had been now a long time in that
case, he said unto him, Dost thou desire to be made whole?
The impotent man answered him, Sir, I have no man when
the water is troubled to put me into the pool, but while I
am coming, another steps down before me. Jesus said unto
him, Rise, take up thy bed, and walk. And immediately the
man was made whole and took up his bed and walked, and
on that day was the sabbath. The Jews therefore said unto
him that was cured, It is the sabbath day; it is not lawful for
thee to carry thy bed. He answered them, He that made me
whole, the same said unto me, Take up thy bed and walk.
Then they asked him, Who is the man that said unto thee,
Take up thy bed and walk? And he that was healed did not
know who it was; for Jesus had conveyed himself away, a
multitude being in that place. Afterward Jesus found him in
the temple and said unto him, Behold, thou art made whole;
sin no more, lest a worse thing come unto thee. The man*

departed and told the Jews that it was Jesus who had made him whole.

We have in this passage one of the few miracles of Christ, which John records. Like every other miracle in this Gospel, it is described with great minuteness and particularity. And like more than one other miracle, it leads on to a discourse full of singularly deep instruction.[7]

We are taught, for one thing, in this passage, *what misery sin has brought into the world.* We read of a man who had been ill for no less than thirty-eight years! For thirty-eight weary summers and winters, he had endured pain and infirmity. He had seen others healed at the waters of Bethesda and going to their homes rejoicing. But for him there had been no healing. Friendless, helpless, and hopeless, he lay near the wonder-working waters but derived no benefit from them. Year after year passed away and left him still uncured. No relief or change for the better seemed likely to come, except from the grave.

When we read of cases of sickness like this, we should remember how deeply we ought to hate sin! Sin was the original root, and cause, and fountain of every disease in the world. God did not create man to be full of aches, and pains, and infirmities. These things are the fruits of the Fall. There would have been no sickness, if there had been no sin.

No greater proof can be shown of man's inbred unbelief than his carelessness about sin. "Fools," says the wise man, "make a mock at sin" (Proverbs 14:9). Thousands delight in things which are explicitly evil and run greedily after that which is downright poison. They love that which God abhors and dislike that which God loves. They are like the madman, who loves his enemies and hates his friends. Their eyes are blinded. Surely if men would only look at hospitals and infirmaries and think what havoc sin has made on this earth, they would never take pleasure in sin as they do.

Well may we be told to pray for the coming of God's kingdom! Well

---

7   The simplest view of this is that it was a standing miracle wrought once every year, or at any rate at some special season only, by God's appointment, to keep the Jews in mind of the wonderful works that had been done for them in time past, and to remind them that the God of miracles was unchanged – But when this singular miracle first began, on what occasion it began, why we never hear anything else about it, in what way the angel came down – are questions which cannot be answered. . . . The wisest course is to take the passage as we find it, and to believe though we cannot explain.

may we be told to long for the second advent of Jesus Christ! Then, and not until then, shall there be no more curse on the earth, no more suffering, no more sorrow, and no more sin. Tears shall be wiped from the faces of all who love Christ's appearing, when their Master returns. Weakness and infirmity shall all pass away. Hope deferred shall no longer make hearts sick. There will be no chronic invalids and incurable cases, when Christ has renewed this earth.

We are taught, for another thing, in this passage, *how great is the mercy and compassion of Christ.* He "saw" the poor sufferer lying in the crowd. Neglected, overlooked, and forgotten in the great multitude, he was observed by the all-seeing eye of Christ. "He knew" full well, by His Divine knowledge, how long he had been "in that case," and pitied him. He spoke to him unexpectedly, with words of gracious sympathy.[8] He healed him by miraculous power, at once and without tedious delay and sent him home rejoicing.

This is just one among many examples of our Lord Jesus Christ's kindness and compassion. He is full of undeserved, unexpected, abounding love towards man. "He delighteth in mercy" (Micah 7:18). He is far more ready to save than man is to be saved, far more willing to do good than man is to receive it.

No one ever need be afraid of beginning the life of a true Christian, if he feels disposed to begin. Let him not hang back and delay, under the vain idea that Christ is not willing to receive him. Let him come boldly and trust confidently. He who healed the cripple at Bethesda is still the same.

We are taught, lastly, the lesson that *recovery from sickness ought to impress upon us.* That lesson is contained in the solemn words which our Savior addressed to the man He had cured – "Sin no more, lest a worse thing come unto you."

Every sickness and sorrow is the voice of God speaking to us. Each has its peculiar message. Happy are they who have an eye to see God's

---

8   *Wilt thou be made whole?* . . . Is not this, to take a spiritual view, the very language that Christ is continually addressing to every man and woman who hears His Gospel? He sees us in a wretched, miserable, sin-sick condition. The one thing He asks us is, "Hast thou any wish to be saved?"

hand and an ear to hear His voice in all that happens to them. Nothing in this world happens by chance.

And as it is with sickness, so it is with recovery. Renewed health should send us back to our post in the world with a deeper hatred of sin, a more thorough watchfulness over our own ways and a more constant purpose of mind to live for God. Far too often the excitement and novelty of returning health tempt us to forget the vows and intentions of the sick room. There are spiritual dangers attending a recovery! Well would it be for us all after illness to grave these words on our hearts, "Let me sin no more, lest a worse thing come unto me."

Let us leave the passage with grateful hearts, and bless God that we have such a Gospel and such a Savior as the Bible reveals. Are we ever sick and ill? Let us remember that Christ sees, and knows, and can heal as He thinks fit. Are we ever in trouble? Let us hear in our trouble the voice of God and learn to hate sin more.

John 5:16-23

And for this reason the Jews persecuted Jesus and sought to kill him: because he had done these things on a sabbath. But Jesus answered them, My Father works until now, and I work. Therefore the Jews sought the more to kill him, because he not only had broken the sabbath but also called God his own Father, making himself equal with God. Then Jesus answered and said unto them, Verily, verily, I say unto you, The Son can do nothing of himself but what he sees the Father do; for all that he does, this also the Son does together with him. For the Father loves the Son and shows him all the things that he does, and he will show him greater works than these that ye may marvel. For as the Father raises up the dead and gives them life; even so the Son gives life unto whom he will. For the Father judges no man but has committed all judgment unto the Son that everyone should honour the Son, even as they honour the Father. He that does not honour the Son does not honour the Father who has sent him.

These verses begin one of the most deep and solemn passages in the four Gospels. They show us the Lord Jesus asserting His own Divine nature, His unity with God the Father, and the high dignity of His office. No where does our Lord dwell so fully on these subjects as in the chapter before us. And no where, we must confess, do we find out so thoroughly the weakness of man's understanding! There is much, we must all feel, that is far beyond our comprehension in our Lord's account of Himself. Such knowledge, in short, is too astonishing for us. "It is high – we cannot attain unto it" (Psalm 139:6). How often men say that they want clear explanations of such doctrines as the Trinity. Yet here we have our Lord handling the subject of His own Person, and, behold, we cannot follow Him. We seem only to touch His meaning with the tip of our fingers.

We learn, for one thing, from the verses before us, *that there are some works which it is lawful to do on the Sabbath day.*

The Jews, as on many other occasions, found fault because Jesus healed a man, who had been ill for thirty-eight years, on the Sabbath. They charged our Lord with a breach of the fourth commandment.

Our Lord's reply to the Jews is very remarkable. "My Father," he says, "worketh hitherto, and I also work."[9] It is as though He said – "Though my Father rested on the seventh day from His work of creation, He has never rested for a moment from His providential government of the world and from His merciful work of supplying the daily needs of all His creatures. Were He to rest from such work, the whole frame of nature would stand still. And I also work works of mercy on the Sabbath day. I do not break the fourth commandment when I heal the sick, any more than my Father breaks it when He causes the sun to rise and the grass to grow on the Sabbath."

We must distinctly understand that neither here nor elsewhere does

---

9   Two things should be observed in this sentence. One is the plain practical lesson that the Sabbath was not meant to be a day of total idleness and of entire cessation from all kinds and sorts of work. "The Sabbath was made for man," – for his benefit, comfort, and advantage. Works of mercy and of real necessity to man's life and animal existence on the Sabbath day were never intended to be forbidden. The other thing to be observed is our Lord's assertion of His own Divinity and equality with God the Father.

the Lord Jesus overthrow the obligation of the fourth commandment. Neither here nor elsewhere is there a word to justify the vague assertions of some modern teachers that "Christians ought not to keep a Sabbath" and that it is "a Jewish institution which has passed away." The utmost that our Lord does is to place the claims of the Sabbath on the right foundation. He clears the day of rest from the false and superstitious teaching of the Jews about the right way of observing it. He shows us clearly that works of necessity and works of mercy are no breach of the fourth commandment.

After all, the errors of Christians on this subject, in these latter days, are of a very different kind from those of the Jews. There is little danger of men keeping the Sabbath too strictly. The thing to be feared is the disposition to keep it loosely and partially, or not to keep it at all. The tendency of the age is not to exaggerate the fourth commandment but to cut it out of the Decalogue and throw it aside altogether. Against this tendency it becomes us all to be on our guard. The experience of eighteen centuries supplies abundant proofs that vital religion never flourishes when the Sabbath is not well kept.

We learn, for another thing, from these verses, *the dignity and greatness of our Lord Jesus Christ.*

The Jews, we are told, sought to kill Jesus because He said "that God was his Father, making himself equal with God." Our Lord, in reply, on this special occasion, enters very fully into the question of His own Divine nature. In reading His words, we must all feel that we are reading mysterious things, and treading on very holy ground. But we must feel a deep conviction, however little we may understand, that the things He says could never have been said by one who was only man. The Speaker is nothing less than "God manifest in the flesh" (1 Timothy 3:16).

He asserts His own unity with God the Father. No other reasonable meaning can be put on the expressions – "The Son can do nothing of himself, but what he seeth the Father do: for what things soever he doeth, these also doeth the Son likewise. The Father loveth the Son, and showeth him all things that himself doeth." Such language, however deep and high, appears to mean that in operation, and knowledge, and heart, and will, the Father and the Son are One – two Persons, but one

God. Truths such as these are of course beyond man's power to explain particularly. Enough for us to believe and rest upon them.

He asserts, in the next place, His own Divine power to give life. He tells us, "The Son quickeneth whom he will." Life is the highest and greatest gift that can be bestowed. It is precisely that thing that man, with all his cleverness, can neither give to the work of his hands nor restore when taken away. But life, we are told, is in the hands of the Lord Jesus, to bestow and give at His discretion. Dead bodies and dead souls are both alike under His dominion. He has the keys of death and hell. In Him is life. He is the life (John 1:4; Revelation 1:18).

He asserts, in the last place, His own authority to judge the world. "The Father," we are told, "has committed all judgment unto the Son." All power and authority over the world is committed to Christ's hands. He is the King and the Judge of mankind. Before Him every knee shall bow, and every tongue shall confess that he is Lord. He that was once despised and rejected of man, condemned and crucified as a malefactor, shall one day hold a great judgment and judge all the world. "God shall judge the secrets of man by Jesus Christ" (Romans 2:16).

And now let us think whether it is possible to make too much of Christ in our religion. If we have ever thought so, let us cast aside the thought forever. Both in His Own nature as God and in His office as commissioned Mediator, He is worthy of all honor. He that is one with the Father – the Giver of life – the King of kings – the coming Judge – can never be too much exalted. "He that honoureth not the Son, honoureth not the Father that sent him."

If we desire salvation, let us lean our whole weight on this mighty Savior. So leaning, we never need be afraid. Christ is the rock of ages, and he that builds on Him shall never be confounded – neither in sickness, nor in death, nor in the judgment day. The hand that was nailed to the cross is almighty! The Savior of sinners is "mighty to save" (Isaiah 63:1).

John 5:24-29

Verily, verily, I say unto you, He that hears my word and believes him that sent me has eternal life and shall not come into judgment but has passed from death unto life. Verily, verily, I say unto you, The hour shall come, and now is, when the dead shall hear the voice of the Son of God, and they that hear shall live. For as the Father has life in himself, so has he given to the Son to have life in himself and has also given him power and authority to execute judgment because he is the Son of man. Marvel not at this, for an hour shall come when all that are in the graves shall hear his voice, and those that have done good shall come forth unto the resurrection of life; but those that have done evil, unto the resurrection of judgment.

The passage before us is singularly rich in weighty truths. To the minds of Jews, who were familiar with the writings of Moses and Daniel, it would come home with peculiar power. In the words of our Lord, they would not fail to see fresh assertions of His claim to be received as the promised Messiah.

We see in these verses that *the salvation of our soul depends on hearing Christ.* It is the man, we are told, who "hears Christ's word," and believes that God the Father sent Him to save sinners, who "has everlasting life." Such "hearing" of course is something more than mere listening. It is hearing as a humble learner – hearing as an obedient disciple – hearing with faith and love – hearing with a heart ready to do Christ's will – this is the hearing that saves. It is the very hearing of which God spoke in the famous prediction of a "prophet like unto Moses" – "Unto him shall you hearken." – "Whosoever will not hearken unto my words which he shall speak in my name, I will require it of him" (Deuteronomy 18:15-19).

To "hear" Christ in this way, we must never forget, is just as needful now as it was eighteen hundred years ago. It is not enough to hear sermons and run after preachers, though some people seem to think this makes up the whole of religion. We must go much further than this – we must "hear Christ." To submit our hearts to Christ's teaching – to sit humbly at His feet by faith and learn of Him – to enter His school as penitents and become His believing scholars – to hear His voice and follow Him – this is the way to heaven. Until we know something experimentally of these things, there is no life in us.

We see, secondly, in these verses, *how rich and full are the privileges of the true hearer and believer.* Such a man enjoys a present salvation. Even now, at this present time, he "has everlasting life." Such a man is completely justified and forgiven. There remains no more condemnation for him. His sins are put away. "He shall not come into condemnation." Such a man is in an entirely new position before God. He is like one who has moved from one side of a gulf to another; "He is passed from death unto life."

The privileges of a true Christian are greatly underrated by many. Chiefly from deplorable ignorance of Scripture, they have little idea of the spiritual treasures of every believer in Jesus. These treasures are brought together here in beautiful order, if we will only look at them. One of a true Christian's treasures is the "presentness" of his salvation. It is not a far distant thing which he is to have at last, if he does his duty and is good. It is his own in title the moment he believes. He is already pardoned, forgiven, and saved, though not in heaven. Another of a true Christian's treasures is the "completeness" of his justification. His sins are entirely removed, taken away, and blotted out of God's book by Christ's blood. He may look forward to judgment without fear and say, "who is he that condemns them?" (Romans 8:34). He shall stand without fault before the throne of God. The last, but not the least, of a true Christian's treasures, is the entire change in his relation and position toward God. He is no longer as one dead before Him – dead, legally, like a man sentenced to die and dead in heart. He is "alive unto God" (Romans 6:11). "He is a new creature. Old things are passed away, and all things are become new" (2 Corinthians 5:17). Well would it be for Christians if these things were better known! It is lack of knowledge in many cases that is the secret of lack of peace.

We see, thirdly, in these verses, *a striking declaration of Christ's power to give life to dead souls.* Our Lord tells us that "the hour is coming and now is, when the dead shall hear the voice of the Son of God; and they that hear shall live." It seems most unlikely that these words were meant to be confined to the rising of men's bodies and were fulfilled by such miracles as that of raising Lazarus from the grave. It appears far more probable that what our Lord had in view was the quickening of souls, the resurrection of conversion (Ephesians 2:1; Colossians 2:13).

The words were fulfilled in not a few cases during our Lord's own ministry. They were fulfilled far more completely after the day of Pentecost through the ministry of the Apostles. The myriads of converts at Jerusalem, at Antioch, at Ephesus, at Corinth, and elsewhere were all examples of their fulfillment. In all these cases, "the voice of the Son of God" awakened dead hearts to spiritual life and made them feel their need of salvation, repent, and believe. They are fulfilled at this very day in every instance of true conversion. Whenever any men or women among ourselves awaken to a sense of their soul's value and become alive to God, the words are made good before our eyes. It is Christ who has spoken to their hearts by His Spirit. It is "the dead hearing Christ's voice, and living."[10]

We see, lastly, in these verses, *a most solemn prophecy of the final resurrection of all the dead.* Our Lord tells us that "the hour is coming when all that are in the grave shall hear his voice, and shall come forth; they that have done good to the resurrection of life, and they that have done evil to the resurrection of damnation."

The passage is one of those that ought to sink down very deeply into our hearts and never be forgotten. All is not over when men die. Whether they like it or not, they will have to come forth from their graves at the last day and to stand at Christ's judgment bar.[11] None can escape His summons. When His voice calls them before Him, all must obey. When men rise again, they will not all rise in the same condition. There will be two classes – two parties – two groups of people. Not all

---

10　Let it be noted that it is only those who "hear" or "have heard" with faith the voice of Christ that live. Spiritual life turns on believing. "Ye also trusted, after that ye heard the word of truth" (Ephesians 1:13).

11　In virtue of His Mediatorial office the Second Person of the Trinity is specially appointed to be the Judge of all mankind. In the counsels of God concerning man, "judgment" is assigned to the Son, and not to the Father, or to the Holy Spirit. It is undoubtedly true that God is "the Judge of all" (Hebrews 12:23). But it is also true that it is God the Son who will execute judgment and sit on the throne at the last day. Verse 27 seems to imply that there is a connection between our Lord's incarnation and His filling the office of the Judge. It is because He humbled Himself to take our nature on Him and be born of the Virgin Mary that he will at length be exalted to execute judgment at the last day. It appears to be the same thought that Paul expresses when he tells the Philippians that because of Christ's humiliation, "God also hath highly exalted him, and given him a name which is above every name" (Philippians 2:9).

will go to heaven. Not all will be saved. Some will rise again to inherit eternal life, but some will rise again only to be condemned. These are alarming things! But the words of Christ are plain and unmistakable. Thus it is written, and thus it must be.

Let us make sure that we hear Christ's quickening voice now, and are numbered among His true disciples. Let us know the privileges of true believers, while we have life and health. Then, when His voice shakes heaven and earth and is calling the dead from their graves, we shall feel confidence and not be "ashamed before Him at his coming" (1 John 2:28).

John 5:30-39

I can of my own self do nothing; as I hear, I judge, and my judgment is just because I seek not my own will, but the will of the Father who has sent me. If I bear witness of myself, my witness is not true. There is another that bears witness of me, and I know that the witness which he witnesses of me is true. Ye sent unto John, and he bore witness unto the truth. But I receive not testimony from man, but I say these things that ye might be saved. He was a burning and a shining light, and ye were willing to rejoice for one hour in his light. But I have greater testimony than that of John; for the works which the Father has given me to finish, the same works that I do, bear witness of me that the Father has sent me. And the Father himself, who has sent me, has borne witness of me. Ye have neither heard his voice at any time nor seen his appearance. And ye do not have his word abiding in you; for whom he has sent, him ye do not believe. Search the scriptures, for in them ye think ye have eternal life; and they are those who testify of me.

In these verses we see the proof of our Lord Jesus Christ being the promised Messiah set forth before the Jews in one view. Four different witnesses are brought forward. Four kinds of evidence are offered.

His Father in heaven – His forerunner, John the Baptist – the miraculous works He had done – the Scriptures, which the Jews professed to honor – each and all are named by our Lord as testifying that He was the Christ, the Son of God. Hard must those hearts have been which could hear such testimony and yet remain unmoved! But it only proves the truth of the old saying – that unbelief does not arise so much from lack of evidence as from lack of will to believe.

Let us observe for one thing in this passage *the honor Christ puts on His faithful servants.* See how He speaks of John the Baptist. "He bore witness of the truth" – "He was a burning and a shining light." John had probably passed away from his earthly labors when these words were spoken. He had been persecuted, imprisoned, and put to death by Herod – none interfering, none trying to prevent his murder. But this murdered disciple was not forgotten by his Divine Master. If no one else remembered him, Jesus did. He had honored Christ, and Christ honored him.

These things ought not to be overlooked. They are written to teach us that Christ cares for all His believing people and never forgets them. Forgotten and despised by the world, perhaps, they are never forgotten by their Savior. He knows where they dwell, and what their trials are. A book of remembrance is written for them. "Their tears are all in His bottle" (Psalm 56:8). Their names are engraved on the palms of His hands. He notices all they do for Him in this evil world, though they think it not worth notice, and He will confess it one day publicly before His Father and the holy angels. He that bore witness to John the Baptist never changes. Let believers remember this. In their worst estate they may boldly say with David – "I am poor and needy; yet the Lord will remember me" (Psalm 40:17).

Let us observe, for another thing, *the honor Christ puts upon miracles, as an evidence of His being the Messiah.* He says – "The works which the Father hath given me to finish, the same works that I do, bear witness of me that the Father has sent me."

The miracles of the Lord receive far less attention in the present day as proofs of His Divine mission than they ought to do. Too many regard them with a silent incredulity as things which, not having seen, they cannot be expected to care for. Not a few openly avow that they do not believe in the possibility of such things as miracles and would like to strike them out of the Bible as weak stories, which, like burdensome lumber, should be cast overboard to lighten the ship.

But, after all, there is no getting over the fact that in the days when our Lord was upon earth, His miracles produced an immense effect on the minds of men. They aroused attention to Him who worked them. They excited inquiry, if they did not convert. They were so many, so public, and so incapable of being explained away that our Lord's enemies could only say that they were done by satanic agency. That they were done, they could not deny. "This man," they said, "does many signs" (John 11:47). The facts, which wise men pretend to deny now, no one pretended to deny eighteen hundred years ago.[12]

Let the enemies of the Bible take our Lord's last and greatest miracle – His own resurrection from the dead – and disprove it if they can. When they have done that, it will be time to consider what they say about miracles in general. They have never answered the evidence of it yet, and they never will. Let the friends of the Bible not be moved by objections against miracles, until that one miracle has been fairly disposed of. If that is proved unassailable, they need not care much for quibbling arguments against other miracles. If Christ did really rise from the dead by His own power, there is none of His mighty works which man need hesitate to believe.

Let us observe, lastly, in these verses, *the honor that Christ puts upon the Scriptures*. He refers to them in concluding His list of evidences, as the great witnesses to Him. "Search the Scriptures," He says – "they are they which testify of me."

The "Scriptures" of which our Lord speaks are of course the Old Testament. And His words show the important truth which too many

---

12 Five things should always be noted about our Lord's miracles. (1) Their *number*: they were not a few only, but very many indeed. (2) Their *greatness*: they were not little, but mighty interferences with the ordinary course of nature. (3) Their *publicity*: they were generally not done in a corner, but in open day, and before many witnesses, and often before enemies. (4) Their *character*: they were almost always works of love, mercy, and compassion, helpful and beneficial to man, and not mere barren exhibitions of power. (5) Their *direct appeal to men's senses*: they were visible, and would bear any examination. The difference between them and the boasted miracles of the Church of Rome, on all these points, is striking and instructive.

are apt to overlook – that every part of our Bibles is meant to teach us about Christ. Christ is not merely in the Gospels and Epistles. Christ is to be found directly and indirectly in the Law, the Psalms, and the Prophets. In the promises to Adam, Abraham, Moses, and David – in the types and emblems of the ceremonial law – in the predictions of Isaiah and the other prophets – Jesus, the Messiah, is everywhere to be found in the Old Testament.

How is it that men see these things so little? The answer is plain. They do not "search the Scriptures." They do not dig into that wondrous mine of wisdom and knowledge and seek to become acquainted with its contents. Simple, regular reading of our Bibles is the grand secret of establishment in the faith. Ignorance of the Scriptures is the root of all error.

And now what will men believe, if they do not believe the Divine mission of Christ? Great indeed is the obstinacy of infidelity. A cloud of witnesses testify that Jesus was the Son of God. To talk of lacking evidence is childish folly. The plain truth is that the chief seat of unbelief is the heart. Many do not wish to believe and therefore remain unbelievers.

John 5:40-47

And ye will not come to me, that ye might have life. I do not receive glory from men. But I know you that ye have not the love of God in you. I have come in my Father's name, and ye receive me not; if another shall come in his own name, him ye will receive. How can ye believe, who take glory one from another, and seek not the glory that comes only from God? Do not think that I will accuse you to the Father; there is one that accuses you, even Moses, in whom ye trust. For had ye believed Moses, ye would have believed me, for he wrote of me. But if ye do not believe his writings, how shall ye believe my words?

This passage concludes our Lord Jesus Christ's wondrous defense of His own divine mission. It is a conclusion worthy of the defense, full of heart-searching appeals to the consciences of His enemies and rich in deep truths. A mighty sermon is followed by a mighty application.

Let us mark, in this passage, *the reason why many souls are lost.* The Lord Jesus says to the unbelieving Jews – "Ye will not come to me that ye might have life."

These words are a golden sentence, which ought to be engraved in our memories and treasured up in our minds. It is lack of will to come to Christ for salvation that will be found, at last, to have shut the many out of heaven. It is not any limit in Christ's work of redemption. He has paid a price sufficient for all mankind. It is something far more than this. It is man's own innate unwillingness to come to Christ, repent, and believe. Either from pride, or laziness, or love of sin, or love of the world, the many have no mind, or wish, or heart, or desire to seek life in Christ. "God has given to us eternal life, and this life is in his Son" (1 John 5:11). But men stand still and will not stir hand or foot to get life. And this is the whole reason why many of the lost are not saved.

This is a painful and solemn truth, but one that we can never know too well. It contains a first principle in Christian theology. Thousands in every age are constantly laboring to shift the blame of their condition from off themselves. They talk of their inability to change. They tell you complacently that they cannot help being what they are! They know undeniably that they are wrong, but they cannot be different! It will not do. Such talk will not stand the test of the Word of Christ before us. "Light is come into the world, and men love darkness rather than light" (John 3:19). The words of the Lord Jesus will silence many – "I would have gathered you, and ye would not be gathered" (Matthew 23:37).

Let us mark, secondly, in this passage, *one principal cause of unbelief.* The Lord Jesus says to the Jews, "How can ye believe which receive honour one of another, and seek not the honour that comes of God only?" He meant by that saying that they were not honest in their religion. With all their apparent desire to hear and learn, they cared more in reality for pleasing man than God. In this state of mind they were never likely to believe.

A deep principle is contained in this saying of our Lord's, and one that deserves special attention. True faith does not depend merely on the state of man's head and understanding, but on the state of his heart. His mind may be convinced. His conscience may be pierced. But so long as there is anything the man is secretly loving more than God, there will be no true faith. The man himself may be puzzled and wonder why he does not believe. He does not see that he is like a child sitting on the lid of his box and wishing to open it, but not considering that his own weight keeps it shut. Let a man make sure that he honestly and really desires first the praise of God. It is the lack of an honest heart which makes many stick fast in their false religion all their days and die at length without peace. Those who complain that they hear, and approve, and assent, but make no progress and cannot get any hold on Christ should ask themselves this simple question – "Am I honest? Am I sincere? Do I really desire first the praise of God?"

Let us mark, lastly, in this passage, *the manner in which Christ speaks of Moses.* He says to the Jews, "Had ye believed Moses ye would have believed me – for he wrote of me."

These words demand our special attention in these latter days. That there really was such a person as Moses – that he really was the author of the writings commonly ascribed to him – on both these points our Lord's testimony is distinct. "He wrote of me." Can we suppose for a moment that our Lord was only accommodating Himself to the prejudices and traditions of His hearers, and that He spoke of Moses as a writer, though He knew in His heart that Moses never wrote at all? Such an idea is profane. It would make out our Lord to have been dishonest. Can we suppose for a moment that our Lord was ignorant about Moses and did not know the wonderful discoveries which learned men, falsely so called, have made in the nineteenth century? Such an idea is ridiculous blasphemy. To imagine the Lord Jesus speaking ignorantly in such a chapter as the one before us is to strike at the root of all Christianity. There is but one conclusion about the matter. There was such a person as Moses. The writings commonly ascribed to him were written by him. The facts recorded in them are worthy of all credit. Our Lord's testimony is an unanswerable argument. The skeptical writers against Moses and the Pentateuch have greatly erred.

Let us beware of handling the Old Testament irreverently, and allowing our minds to doubt the truth of any part of it, because of alleged diffi-culties. The simple fact that the writers of the New Testament continu-ally refer to the Old Testament and speak even of the most miraculous events recorded in it as undoubtedly true should silence our doubts. Is it at all likely, probable, or credible that we of the nineteenth century are better informed about Moses than Jesus and His Apostles? God forbid that we should think so! Then let us stand fast and not doubt that every word in the Old Testament, as well as in the New, was given by inspiration of God.

John Chapter 6

John 6:1-14

After these things Jesus went over the sea of Galilee, which is the sea of Tiberias. And a great multitude followed him because they saw his signs which he did on the sick. And Jesus went up into a mountain, and he sat there with his disciples. And the passover, the feast of the Jews, was near. Then Jesus lifted up his eyes and saw a great company come unto him; he said unto Philip, From where shall we buy bread that these may eat? But he said this to prove him, for he knew what he would do. Philip answered him, Two hundred denarius of bread is not sufficient for them, that each one of them may take a little. One of his disciples, Andrew, Simon Peter's brother, said unto him, There is a lad here, who has five barley loaves and two small fishes, but what are they among so many? Then Jesus said, Make the men sit down. Now there was much grass in the place. So the men sat down, in number about five thousand. And Jesus took the loaves, and when he had given thanks, he distributed to the disciples and the disciples to those that were sitting down; and likewise of the fishes as much as they desired. When they were filled, he said unto his disciples, Gather up the fragments that remain that nothing be lost. Therefore they gathered them together and filled twelve baskets with the fragments of the five barley loaves which were left over from those that had eaten. Then those men, as they had seen the sign that Jesus did, said, This is of a truth the prophet that was to come into the world.

THESE VERSES DESCRIBE ONE of our Lord's most remarkable miracles. Of all the great works that He did, none was done so publicly as this and before so many witnesses. Of all the miracles related in the Gospels, this is the only one which all the four Gospel writers alike record. This fact alone (like the four times repeated account of the crucifixion and resurrection) is enough to show that it is a miracle demanding special attention.

We have, for one thing, in this miracle, *a lesson about Christ's almighty power.* We see our Lord feeding five thousand men with "five barley loaves and two small fishes." We see clear proof that a miraculous event took place in the "twelve baskets of fragments" that remained after all had eaten. Creative power was manifestly exercised.[13] Food was called into existence that did not exist before. In healing the sick and raising the dead, something was amended or restored that had already existed. In feeding five thousand men with five loaves, something must have been created which before had no existence.

Such a history as this ought to be specially instructive and encouraging to all who endeavor to do good to souls. It shows us the Lord Jesus "able to save to the uttermost." He is One who has all power over dead hearts. Not only can He mend that which is broken – build up that which is ruined – heal that which is sick – strengthen that which is weak. He can do even greater things than these. He can call into being that which was not before and call it out of nothing. We must never despair of any one being saved. So long as there is life, there is hope. Reason and sense may say that some poor sinner is too hardened or too old to be converted. Faith will reply – "Our Master can create as well as renew. With a Savior who, by His Spirit, can create a new heart, nothing is impossible."

We have, for another thing, in this miracle, *a lesson about the office of ministers.* We see the apostles receiving the bread from our Lord's hands, after He had blessed it, and distributing it to the multitude. It was

---

13   It is certain that on no other occasion did our Lord manifest so clearly His creative power. No doubt it was as easy to Him to cause bread to be, as to say "let there be light" or to make the earth bring forth herbs and corn at the creation of the world. But the miracle was clearly intended to be one which Christians should hold in special remembrance. It is at any rate noteworthy that this is the only passage in Christ's life which all the four Gospel writers alike record. In this respect the miracle stands alone.

not their hands that made it increase and multiply but their Master's. It was His almighty power that provided an unfailing supply. It was their work to receive humbly and distribute faithfully.

Now here is a lively emblem of the work which a true minister of the New Testament is meant to do. He is not a mediator between God and man. He has no power to put away sin or impart grace. His whole business is to receive the bread of life which his Master provides and to distribute it among the souls among whom he labors. He cannot make men value the bread or receive it. He cannot make it soul-saving or life-giving to any one. This is not his work. For this he is not responsible. His whole business is to be a faithful distributor of the food which his Divine Master has provided; and that done, his office is discharged.

We have, lastly, in this miracle, *a lesson about the sufficiency of the Gospel for the needs of all mankind.* We see the Lord Jesus supplying the hunger of a huge multitude of five thousand men. The provision seemed, at first sight, utterly inadequate for the occasion. To satisfy so many craving mouths with such scanty fare in such a wilderness seemed impossible. But the event showed that there was enough and to spare. There was not one who could complain that he was not filled.

There can be no doubt that this was meant to teach the adequacy of Christ's Gospel to supply the necessities of the whole world. Weak, and feeble, and foolish as it may seem to man, the simple story of the Cross is enough for all the children of Adam in every part of the globe. The tidings of Christ's death for sinners and the atonement made by that death is able to meet the hearts and satisfy the consciences of all nations, and peoples, and kindreds, and tongues. Carried by faithful messengers, it feeds and supplies all ranks and classes. "The preaching of the cross is to them that perish foolishness, but to us who are saved it is the power of God" (1 Corinthians 1:18). Five barley loaves and two small fishes seemed scanty provision for a hungry crowd. But blessed by Christ and distributed by His disciples, they were more than sufficient.

Let us never doubt for a moment, that the preaching of Christ cruci-fied – the old story of His blood, and righteousness, and substitution – is enough for all the spiritual necessities of all mankind. It is not worn out. It is not obsolete. It has not lost its power. We need nothing new

– nothing more broad and kind – nothing more intellectual – nothing more effectual. We need nothing but the true bread of life, distributed faithfully among starving souls. Let men sneer or ridicule as they will. Nothing else can do good in this sinful world. No other teaching can fill hungry consciences and give them peace. We are all in a wilderness. We must feed on Christ crucified and the atonement made by His death, or we shall die in our sins.

John 6:15-21

Jesus therefore knowing that they would come and take him by force to make him king, he departed again into a mountain himself alone. And when evening was come, his disciples went down unto the sea and entered into a ship and were crossing the sea toward Capernaum. And it was now dark, and Jesus had not come to them. And the sea arose by reason of a great wind that blew. So when they had rowed about twenty-five or thirty furlongs, they saw Jesus walking upon the sea and drawing nigh unto the ship, and they were afraid. But he said unto them, I AM; be not afraid. Then they willingly received him into the ship, and immediately the ship was at the land where they went.

We should notice, in these verses, *our Lord Jesus Christ's humility.* We are told that, after feeding the multitude, He "perceived that they would come and take him by force to make him a king." At once He departed and left them. He wanted no such honors as these. He had come, "not to be ministered unto, but, to minister and to give his life a ransom for many" (Matthew 20:28).

We see the same spirit and frame of mind all through our Lord's earthly ministry. From His cradle to His grave, He was "clothed with humility" (1 Peter 5:5). He was born of a poor woman and spent the first thirty years of His life in a carpenter's house at Nazareth. He was followed by poor companions – many of them no better than fishermen. He was poor in his manner of living – "The foxes had holes, and the birds of the air their nests: but the Son of man had not where to lay his head" (Matthew 8:20). When He went on the Sea of Galilee, it was in a borrowed boat. When He rode into Jerusalem, it was on a borrowed donkey. When He was buried, it was in a borrowed tomb. "Though he was rich, yet for our sakes he became poor" (2 Corinthians 8:9).

The example is one which ought to be far more remembered than it is. How common are pride, and ambition, and high-mindedness! How rare are humility and lowly-mindedness! How few ever refuse greatness when offered to them! How many are continually seeking great things for themselves and forgetting the injunction – "Seek them not!" (Jeremiah 45:5). Surely it was not for nothing that our Lord, after washing the disciples' feet, said – "I have given you an example that ye should do as I have done" (John 13:15). There is little, it may be feared, of that feet-washing spirit among Christians. But whether men will hear or forbear, humility is the queen of the graces. "Tell me," it has been said, "how much humility a man has, and I will tell you how much religion he has." Humility is the first step toward heaven, and the true way to honor. "He that humbles himself shall be exalted" (Luke 18:14).

We should notice, secondly, in these verses, *the trials through which Christ's disciples had to pass.* We are told that they were sent over the lake by themselves, while their Master tarried behind. And then we see them alone in a dark night, tossed about by a great wind on stormy waters, and worst of all, Christ not with them. It was a strange transition. From witnessing a mighty miracle and helping it instrumentally amid an admiring crowd, to solitude, darkness, winds, waves, storm, anxiety, and danger, the change was very great! But Christ knew it, and Christ appointed it, and it was working for their good.

Trial, we must distinctly understand, is part of the diet which all true Christians must expect. It is one of the means by which their grace is proved and by which they find out what there is in themselves. Winter as well as summer – cold as well as heat – clouds as well as sunshine – are all necessary to bring the fruit of the Spirit to ripeness and maturity. We do not naturally like this. We would rather cross the lake with calm weather and favorable winds, with Christ always by our side and the sun shining down on our faces. But it may not be. It is not in this way that God's children are made "partakers of His holiness" (Hebrews

12:10). Abraham, and Jacob, and Moses, and David, and Job were all men of many trials. Let us be content to walk in their footsteps and to drink of their cup. In our darkest hours we may seem to be left – but we are never really alone.

Let us notice, in the last place, *our Lord Jesus Christ's power over the waves of the sea.* He came to His disciples as they were rowing on the stormy lake, "walking on" the waters. He walked on them as easily as we walk on dry land. They bore Him as firmly as the pavement of the Temple or the hills around Nazareth. That which is contrary to all natural reason was perfectly possible to Christ.

The Lord Jesus, we must remember, is not only the Lord but the Maker of all creation. "All things were made by him; and without him was not anything made that was made" (John 1:3). It was just as easy for Him to walk on the sea as to form the sea at the beginning – just as easy to suspend the common laws of nature, as they are called, as to impose those laws at the first. Learned men talk solemn nonsense sometimes about the eternal fixity of the "laws of nature," as if they were above God Himself and could never be suspended. It is well to be reminded sometimes by such miracles as that before us, that these so-called "laws of nature" are neither immutable nor eternal. They had a beginning and will one day have an end.

Let all true Christians take comfort in the thought that their Savior is Lord of waves and winds, of storms and tempests, and can come to them in the darkest hour, "walking upon the sea." There are waves of trouble far heavier than any on the Lake of Galilee. There are days of darkness which test the faith of the holiest Christian. But let us never despair if Christ is our Friend. He can come to our aid in an hour when we do not think and in ways that we did not expect. And when He comes, all will be calm.

John 6:22-27

The day following when the multitude which was on the other side of the sea saw that there was no other boat there except the one in which his disciples had entered and that

Jesus had not gone with his disciples into the boat, but that
his disciples had gone away alone (but other boats came
from Tiberias near unto the place where they ate bread after
the Lord had given thanks); when the people therefore saw
that Jesus was not there, nor his disciples, they also entered
into the boats and came to Capernaum, seeking for Jesus.
And when they had found him on the other side of the sea,
they said unto him, Rabbi, when didst thou come here? Jesus
answered them and said, Verily, verily, I say unto you, Ye
seek me, not because ye have seen the signs, but because ye
ate of the loaves and were filled. Labour not for the food
which perishes, but for the food which abides unto eternal
life, which the Son of man shall give unto you, for him has
God the Father sealed.

We should mark first, in this passage, *what knowledge of man's heart our Lord Jesus Christ possesses.* We see Him exposing the false motives of those who followed Him for the sake of the loaves and fishes. They had followed Him across the Lake of Galilee. They seemed at first sight ready to believe in Him and do Him honor. But He knew the inward springs of their conduct and was not deceived. "Ye seek me," He said, "not because ye saw the miracles, but because ye did eat of the loaves, and were filled."

The Lord Jesus, we should never forget, is still the same. He never changes. He reads the secret motives of all who profess and call themselves Christians. He knows exactly why they do all they do in their religion. The reasons why they go to Church and why they receive the sacrament – why they attend family prayers and why they keep Sunday holy – all are naked and opened to the eyes of the great Head of the Church. By Him actions are weighed as well as seen. "Man looks on the outward appearance, but the LORD looks on the heart" (1 Samuel 16:7).

Let us be real, true, and sincere in our religion, whatever else we are. The sinfulness of hypocrisy is very great, but its folly is greater still. It is not hard to deceive ministers, relatives, and friends. A little decent outward profession will often go a long way. But it is impossible to deceive Christ. "His eyes are as a flame of fire" (Revelation 1:14). He sees us through and through. Happy are those who can say – "Thou, Lord, who knowest all things, knowest that we love thee" (John 21:17).

We should mark, secondly, in this passage, *what Christ forbids.* He told the crowds who followed Him so diligently for the loaves and fishes, "not to labor for the meat that perisheth." It was a remarkable saying and demands explanation.

Our Lord, we may be sure, did not mean to encourage idleness. It would be a great mistake to suppose this hard labor was the appointed lot of Adam in Paradise. Labor was ordained to be man's occupation *after* the fall. Labor is honorable in all men. No one need be ashamed of belonging to "the working classes." Our Lord himself worked in the carpenter's shop at Nazareth. Paul worked as a tentmaker with his own hands.

What our Lord did mean to rebuke was that excessive attention to labor for the body while the soul is neglected, which prevails everywhere in the world. What He reproved was the common habit of laboring only for the things of time and letting alone the things of eternity – of minding only the life that now is and disregarding the life to come. Against this habit He delivers a solemn warning.

Surely, we must all feel our Lord did not say the words before us without good cause. They are a startling caution which should ring in the ears of many in these latter days. How many in every rank of life are doing the very thing against which Jesus warns us! They are laboring night and day for "the food that perisheth" and doing nothing for their immortal souls. Happy are those who early learn the respective value of soul and body and give the first and best place in their thoughts to salvation. One thing is needful. He that seeks first the kingdom of God will never fail to find "all other things added to him" (Matthew 6:33).

We should mark, thirdly, in this passage, *what Christ advises.* He tells us to "labor for the meat that endureth to everlasting life." He would have us take pains to find food and satisfaction for our souls. That food is provided in rich abundance in Him. But he that would have it must diligently seek it.

How are we to labor? There is but one answer. We must labor in the use of all appointed means. We must read our Bibles like men digging for hidden treasure. We must wrestle earnestly in prayer like men contending with a deadly enemy for life. We must take our whole heart to the house of God and worship and hear like those who listen to the reading of a benefactor's will. We must fight daily against sin, the world, and the devil, like those who fight for liberty, and must conquer or be slaves. These are the ways we must walk in if we would find Christ and be found of Him. This is "laboring." This is the secret of getting on about our souls.

Labor like this no doubt is very uncommon. In carrying it on we shall have little encouragement from man and shall often be told that we are "extreme" and go too far. Strange and absurd as it is, the natural man is always fancying that we may take too much thought about religion, and refusing to see that we are far more likely to take too much thought about the world. But whatever man may say, the soul will never get spiritual food without labor. We must "strive," we must "run," we must "fight," we must throw our whole heart into our soul's affairs. It is "the violent" who take the kingdom (Matthew 11:12).

We should mark, lastly, in this passage, *what a promise Christ holds out.* He tells us that He himself will give eternal food to all who seek it – "The Son of man shall give you the meat that endureth unto everlasting life."

How gracious and encouraging these words are! Whatever we need for the relief of our hungering souls, Christ is ready and willing to bestow. Whatever mercy, grace, peace, strength we require, the Son of man will give freely, immediately, abundantly, and eternally. He is "sealed," and appointed, and commissioned by God the Father for this very purpose.[14] Like Joseph in the Egyptian famine, it is His office to be the Friend, and Benefactor, and Reliever of a sinful world. He is far

---

14   When our Lord says, "Him hath God the Father sealed," He probably refers to the custom of setting apart for any specific purpose and marking for any peculiar use by a seal. So also deeds and public documents were sealed to testify their execution and validity and give them authority. So it is said in Esther: "The writing that is written in the king's name and sealed with the king's ring may no man reverse" (Esther 8:8). The expression applied to our Lord in this place certainly stands alone, but I think there can be little doubt as to its meaning. It signifies that in the eternal counsels of God the Father, He has sealed, commissioned, designated, and appointed the Son of man, the Incarnate Word, to be the Giver of everlasting life to man. It is an office for which He has been solemnly set apart by the Father.

more willing to give than man is to receive. The more sinners apply to Him, the better He is pleased.

And now, as we leave this rich passage, let us ask ourselves, what use we make of it? For what are we laboring ourselves? What do we know of lasting food and satisfaction for our inward man? Never let us rest until we have eaten of the food which Christ alone can give. Those who are content with any other spiritual food will sooner or later "lie down in sorrow" (Isaiah 50:11).

John 6:28-34

Then they said unto him, What shall we do that we might work the works of God? Jesus answered and said unto them, This is the work of God, that ye believe in him whom he has sent. They said therefore unto him, What sign showest thou then that we may see and believe thee? what dost thou work? Our fathers ate manna in the desert, as it is written, He gave them of the bread from the heaven to eat. Then Jesus said unto them, Verily, verily, I say unto you, Moses gave you not that bread from the heaven, but my Father gives you the true bread from the heaven. For the bread of God is he who descended from heaven and gives life unto the world. Then said they unto him, Lord, always give us this bread.

These verses form the beginning of one of the most remarkable passages in the Gospels. None, perhaps, of our Lord's discourses has occasioned more controversy and been more misunderstood than that which we find in the Sixth Chapter of John.

We should observe, for one thing, in these verses, *the spiritual ignorance and unbelief of the natural man.* Twice over we see this brought out and exemplified. When our Lord instructed his hearers to "labor for the meat which endureth to eternal life," they immediately began to think of works to be done and a goodness of their own to be established.

"What shall we do that we might work the works of God?"[15] Doing, doing, doing was their only idea of the way to heaven. Again, when our Lord spoke of Himself as One sent of God and the need of believing on Him at once, they turn round with the question "What sign showest thou? what dost thou work?" Fresh from the mighty miracle of the loaves and fishes, one might have thought they had had a sign sufficient to convince them. Taught by our Lord Jesus Christ himself, one might have expected a greater readiness to believe. But alas! there are no limits to man's dullness, prejudice, and unbelief in spiritual matters. It is a striking fact that the only thing which our Lord is said to have "marvelled" at during His earthly ministry was man's "unbelief" (Mark 6:6).

We shall do well to remember this, if we ever try to do good to others in the matter of religion. We must not be cast down because our words are not believed and our efforts seem thrown away. We must not complain of it as a strange thing and suppose that the people we have to deal with are peculiarly stubborn and hard. We must recollect that this is the very cup of which our Lord had to drink, and like Him we must patiently work on. If even He, so perfect and so plain a Teacher, was not believed, what right have we to wonder if men do not believe us? Happy are the ministers, and missionaries, and teachers who keep these things in mind! It will save them much bitter disappointment. In working for God, it is of first importance to understand what we must expect in man. Few things are so little realized as the extent of human unbelief.

We should observe, for another thing, in these verses, *the high honor Christ puts on faith in Himself.* The Jews had asked Him – "What shall we do, that we might work the works of God?" In reply He says – "This is the work of God, that ye believe on him whom he hath sent."[16] A truly

---

15   Many no doubt content themselves with saying, "What shall we do?" and like those of whom we are reading, never get any further. But, on the other hand, in many cases, "what shall I do?" is the beginning of eternal life, the first step toward heaven, the first breath of grace, the first spiritual pulsation. The Jews on the day of Pentecost said, "what must we do?" Saul, when the Lord met him near Damascus, said, "Lord, what wilt thou have me to do?" The Philippian jailor said, "What must I do to be saved?" Whenever therefore we hear a person ask the question about his soul, "what shall I do?" we must try to help him and put him in the right way. We never know what it may lead to. It may perhaps end in nothing and prove a mere temporary feeling. But it may also come to something, and end in the conversion of a soul.

16   In this verse our Lord takes hold of the expression used by the Jews about "work" and answers them according to their state of mind. Did they ask what work they should do?

striking and remarkable expression! If any two things are put in strong contrast in the New Testament, they are faith and works. Not working, but believing, not of works, but through faith – are words familiar to all careful Bible-readers. Yet here the great Head of the Church declares that believing on Him is the highest and greatest of all "works!" It is "the work of God."

Doubtless our Lord did not mean that there is anything meritorious in believing. Man's faith, at the very best, is feeble and defective. Regarded as a "work," it cannot stand the severity of God's judgment, deserve pardon, or purchase heaven. But our Lord did mean that faith in Himself, as the only Savior, is the first act of the soul which God requires at a sinner's hands. Until a man believes on Jesus and rests on Jesus as a lost sinner, he is nothing. Our Lord did mean that faith in Himself is that act of the soul which specially pleases God. When the Father sees a sinner casting aside his own righteousness and simply trusting in His dear Son, He is well pleased. Without such faith it is impossible to please God. Our Lord did mean that faith in Himself is the root of all saving religion. There is no life in a man until he believes. Above all, our Lord did mean that faith in Himself is the hardest of all spiritual acts to the natural man. Did the Jews want something to do in religion? Let them know that the greatest thing they had to do was to cast aside their pride, confess their guilt and need, and humbly believe.

Let all who know anything of true faith thank God and rejoice. Blessed are those who believe! It is an attainment which many of the wise of this world have never yet reached. We may feel ourselves to be poor, weak sinners. But do we believe? We may fail and come short in many things. But do we believe? He that has learned to feel his sins and to trust Christ as a Savior has learned the two hardest and greatest

---

Let them know that the first thing God called them to do was to believe in His Son, the Messiah whom He had sent and whom they saw before them. When our Lord calls faith "the work of God," we must not suppose He means here that it is the work of His Spirit and His gift. This is undoubtedly true, but not the truth of the text. He only means that believing is "the work that pleases God" and is most agreeable to God's will and mind. Of course every well-instructed Bible reader will remember that, strictly speaking, believing is so far from being a "work" that it is the very opposite of working. "To him that worketh not, but believeth on Him that justifieth the ungodly, his faith is counted to him for righteousness" (Romans 4:5). But it is evident that our Lord accommodates His manner of speaking to the ignorant minds with which He had to deal. Thus Paul calls the doctrine of faith the "law of faith" (Romans 3:27).

lessons in Christianity. He has been in the best of schools. He has been taught by the Holy Spirit.

We shall observe, lastly, in these verses, *the far greater privileges of Christ's hearers than of those who lived in the times of Moses.* Wonderful and miraculous as the manna was which fell from heaven, it was nothing in comparison to the true bread which Christ had to bestow on His disciples. He himself was the bread of God, who had come down from heaven to give life to the world. The bread which fell in the days of Moses could only feed and satisfy the body. The Son of man had come to feed the soul. The bread which fell in the days of Moses was only for the benefit of Israel. The Son of man had come to offer eternal life to the world. Those who ate the manna died and were buried, and many of them were lost forever. But those who ate the bread which the Son of man provided would be eternally saved.[17]

And now let us take heed to ourselves and make sure that we are among those who eat the bread of God and live. Let us not be content with lazy waiting, but let us actually come to Christ and eat the bread of life and believe to the saving of our souls. The Jews could say – "Evermore give us this bread." But it may be feared they went no further. Let us never rest until, by faith, we have eaten this bread and can say, "Christ is mine. I have tasted that the Lord is gracious. I know and feel that I am His."

John 6:35-40

And Jesus said unto them, I AM the bread of life; he that comes to me shall never hunger, and he that believes in me

---

17   The use of the present tense should be noticed in verse 31. The idea seems to be "What Moses could not give you, even the true bread which feeds the soul, My Father does give you and is actually giving you at this moment, in that He gives you myself." The expression "giveth you" must not be supposed to imply actual reception on the part of the Jews. It rather means 'giving" in the sense of "offering" for acceptance a thing which those to whom it is offered may not receive. – It is a very remarkable saying and one of those which seems to me to prove unanswerably that Christ is God's gift to the whole world – that His redemption was made for all mankind – that He died for all – and is offered to all. It is like the famous texts "God so love the world that he gave his only begotten Son" (John 3:16) and "God hath given to us eternal life, and this life is in his Son" (1 John 5:11). It is a gift no doubt which is utterly thrown away like many other gifts of God to man, and is profitable to none but those that believe.

shall never thirst. But I said unto you, That even though ye have seen me, ye do not believe. All that the Father gives me shall come to me, and he that comes to me I will in no wise cast out. For I came down from the heaven, not to do my own will, but the will of him that sent me. And this is the Father's will who has sent me, that of all whom he has given me I should lose nothing but should raise it up again in the last day. And this is the will of him that sent me, That every one who sees the Son and believes in him may have eternal life, and I will raise him up in the last day.

Three of our Lord Jesus Christ's great sayings are strung together like pearls in this passage. Each of them ought to be precious to every true Christian. All taken together, they form a mine of truth, into which he that searches need never search in vain.

We have, first, in these verses, *a saying of Christ about Himself.* We read that Jesus said – "I am the bread of life – he that comes to me shall never hunger, and he that believes in me shall never thirst."

Our Lord would have us know that He himself is the appointed food of man's soul. The soul of every man is naturally starving and famishing through sin. Christ is given by God the Father to be the Satisfier, the Reliever, and the Physician of man's spiritual need. In Him and His mediatorial office – in Him and His atoning death – in Him and His priesthood – in Him and His grace, love, and power – in Him alone will empty souls find their needs supplied. In Him there is life. He is "the bread of life."

With what divine and perfect wisdom this name is chosen! Bread is necessary food. We can manage tolerably well without many things on our table, but not without bread. So is it with Christ. We must have Christ or die in our own sins. Bread is food that suits all. Some cannot eat meat, and some cannot eat vegetables. But all like bread. It is food both for the Queen and the pauper. So is it with Christ. He is just the Savior that meets the needs of every class. Bread is food that we need daily. Other kinds of food we take, perhaps, only occasionally. But we need bread every morning and evening in our lives. So is it with Christ.

There is no day in our lives but we need His blood, His righteousness, His intercession, and His grace. Well may He be called, "The bread of life!"

Do we know anything of spiritual hunger? Do we feel anything of craving and emptiness in conscience, heart, and affections? Let us distinctly understand that Christ alone can relieve and supply us, and that it is His office to relieve. We must come to Him by faith. We must believe on Him and commit our souls into His hands. So coming, He pledges His royal word we shall find lasting satisfaction both for time and eternity. It is written – "He that comes unto me shall never hunger, and he that believes in me shall never thirst."

We have, secondly, in these verses, *a saying of Christ about those who come to Him.* We read that Jesus said – "Him that cometh to me I will in no wise cast out."[18]

What does "coming to Christ" mean? It means that movement of the soul which takes place when a man, feeling his sins and finding out that he cannot save himself, hears of Christ, applies to Christ, trusts in Christ, lays hold on Christ, and leans all his weight on Christ for salvation. When this happens, a man is said, in Scripture language, to "come" to Christ.

What did our Lord mean by saying – "I will in no wise cast him out"? He meant that He will not refuse to save any one who comes to Him, no matter what he may have been. His past sins may have been very great. His present weakness and infirmity may be very great. But does he come to Christ by faith? Then Christ will receive him graciously, pardon him freely, place him in the number of His dear children, and give him everlasting life.

These are golden words indeed! They have smoothed down many a dying pillow and calmed many a troubled conscience. Let them sink down deeply into our memories and abide there continually. A day will come when flesh and heart shall fail, and the world can help us no

---

18 The words "coming" and "believing" in this verse appear to mean very nearly one and the same thing. To "come" to Christ is to "believe" on Him and to "believe" on Him is to "come to Him – both expressions mean that act of the soul whereby, under a sense of its sins and necessity, it applies to Christ, lays hold on Christ, trusts itself to Christ, casts itself on Christ – "Coming" is the soul's movement towards Christ. "Believing" is the soul's venture on Christ. – If there is any difference, it is that "coming" is the first act of the soul when it is taught by the Holy Spirit, and that "believing" is a continued act or habit which never ends.

more. Happy shall we be in that day, if the Spirit witnesses with our spirit that we have really come to Christ!

We have, lastly, in these verses, *a saying of Christ about the will of His Father*. Twice over come the solemn words – "This is the will of him that sent me." Once we are told it is His will, "that every one that seeth the Son may have everlasting life." Once we are told it is His will that, "of all which he hath given to Christ he shall lose nothing."

We are taught by these words that Christ has brought into the world a salvation open and free to everyone. Our Lord draws a picture of it from the story of the bronze serpent, by which bitten Israelites in the wilderness were healed. Every one that chose to "look" at the bronze serpent might live. Just in the same way, every one who desires eternal life may "look" at Christ by faith and have it freely. There is no barrier, no limit, no restriction. The terms of the Gospel are wide and simple. Every one may "look and live."

We are taught, furthermore, that *Christ will never allow any soul that is committed to Him to be lost and cast away*. He will keep it safe from grace to glory, in spite of the world, the flesh, and the devil. Not one bone of His mystical body shall ever be broken. Not one lamb of His flock shall ever be left behind in the wilderness. He will raise to glory, in the last day, the whole flock entrusted to His charge and not one shall be found missing.

Let the true Christian feed on the truths contained in this passage and thank God for them. Christ the Bread of life – Christ the Receiver of all who come to Him – Christ the Preserver of all believers – Christ is for every man who is willing to believe on Him, and Christ is the eternal possession of all who so believe. Surely this is glad tidings and good news!

John 6:41-51

The Jews then murmured of him because he said, I AM the bread which descended from the heaven. And they said, Is not this Jesus, the son of Joseph, whose father and mother we know? How is it then that he says, I descended from heaven?

Jesus therefore answered and said unto them, Murmur not among yourselves. No one can come to me unless the Father who has sent me draws him, and I will raise him up in the last day. It is written in the prophets, And they shall all be taught of God. Every man therefore that has heard from the Father and has learned comes unto me. Not that anyone has seen the Father, except he who is of God, he has seen the Father. Verily, verily, I say unto you, He that believes in me has eternal life. I AM the bread of life. Your fathers ate manna in the wilderness and are dead. This is the bread which comes down from heaven, that anyone may eat of it and not die. I AM the living bread which came down from heaven; if anyone eats of this bread, they shall live for ever; and the bread that I will give is my flesh, which I will give for the life of the world.

Truths of the weightiest importance follow each other in rapid succession in the chapter we are now reading. There are probably very few parts of the Bible which contain so many "deep things" as the Sixth Chapter of John. Of this the passage before us is a signal example.

We learn, for one thing, from this passage, that *Christ's lowly condition, when He was upon earth, is a stumbling block to the natural man.* We read that "the Jews murmured, because Jesus said, I am the bread that came down from heaven. And they said, Is not this Jesus, the son of Joseph, whose father and mother we know? How is it then that he saith, I came down from heaven?" Had our Lord come as a conquering king with wealth and honors to bestow on His followers and mighty armies in His train, they would have been willing enough to receive Him. But a poor, and lowly, and suffering Messiah was an offence to them. Their pride refused to believe that such an one was sent from God.

There is nothing that need surprise us in this. It is human nature showing itself in its true colors. We see the same thing in the days of the Apostles. Christ crucified was "to the Jews a stumbling block, and to the Greeks foolishness" (1 Corinthians 1:23). The cross was an offence to many wherever the Gospel was preached. We may see the same thing in our own times. There are thousands around us who loathe

the distinctive doctrines of the Gospel on account of their humbling character. They cannot tolerate the atonement, and the sacrifice, and the substitution of Christ. His moral teaching they approve. His example and self-denial they admire. But speak to them of Christ's blood – of Christ being made sin for us – of Christ's death being the cornerstone of our hope – of Christ's poverty being our riches – and you will find they hate these things with a deadly hatred. Truly the offence of the cross is not yet ceased!

We learn, for another thing, from this passage, *man's natural helplessness and inability to repent or believe.* We find our Lord saying – "No man can come unto me, except the Father which hath sent me draw him." Until the Father draws the heart of man by His grace, man will not believe.

The solemn truth contained in these words is one that needs careful weighing. It is vain to deny that without the grace of God no one ever can become a true Christian. We are spiritually dead and have no power to give ourselves life. We need a new principle put in us from above. Facts prove it. Preachers see it. The Tenth Article of our own Church expressly declares it – "The condition of man after the fall of Adam is such that he cannot turn and prepare himself, by his own natural strength and good works, to faith and calling upon God." This witness is true.

But after all, of what does this inability of man consist? In what part of our inward nature does this impotence reside? Here is a point on which many mistakes arise. Forever let us remember that the will of man is the part of him which is in fault. His inability is not physical, but moral. It would not be true to say that a man has a real wish and desire to come to Christ but no power to come. It would be far more true to say that a man has no power to come because he has no desire or wish. It is not true that he would come if he could. It is true that he could come if he would. The corrupt will – the secret disinclination – the lack of heart are the real causes of unbelief. It is here the mischief lies. The power that we lack is a new will. It is precisely at this point that we need the "drawing" of the Father.

These things, no doubt, are deep and mysterious. By truths like these

God proves the faith and patience of His people. Can they believe Him? Can they wait for a fuller explanation at the last day? What they see not now they shall see hereafter. One thing at any rate is abundantly clear, and that is – man's responsibility for his own soul. His inability to come to Christ does not make an end of his accountableness. Both things are equally true. If lost at last, it will prove to have been his own fault. His blood will be on his own head. Christ would have saved him, but he would not be saved. He would not come to Christ that he might have life.

We learn, lastly, in this passage, that *the salvation of a believer is a present thing.* Our Lord Jesus Christ says – "Verily, verily, I say unto you, he that believeth on me hath everlasting life." Life, we should observe, is a present possession. It is not said that he shall have it at last in the judgment day. It is now, even now, in this world, his property. He has it the very day that he believes.

The subject is one which much concerns our peace to understand, and one about which errors abound. How many seem to think that forgiveness and acceptance with God are things which we cannot attain in this life – that they are things which are to be earned by a long course of repentance and faith and holiness – things which we may receive at the bar of God at last but must never pretend to touch while we are in this world! It is a complete mistake to think so. The very moment a sinner believes on Christ he is justified and accepted. There is no condemnation for him. He has peace with God, and that immediately and without delay. His name is in the book of life, however little he may be aware of it. He has a title to heaven, which death and hell and Satan can not overthrow. Happy are those who know this truth! It is an essential part of the good news of the Gospel.

After all, the great point we have to consider is whether we believe. What shall it profit us that Christ has died for sinners, if we do not believe on Him? "He that believes in the Son has eternal life, and he that does not obey the Son shall not see life, but the wrath of God abides on him" (John 3:36).

John 6:52-59

The Jews therefore contended among themselves, saying,
How is he able to give us his flesh to eat? Then Jesus said
unto them, Verily, verily, I say unto you, Unless ye eat the
flesh of the Son of man and drink his blood, ye shall have no
life in you. Whosoever eats my flesh and drinks my blood
has eternal life, and I will raise him up at the last day. For
my flesh is food indeed, and my blood is drink indeed. He
that eats my flesh and drinks my blood abides in me, and
I in him. As the living Father has sent me, and I live by the
Father, so he that eats me, he shall also live by me. This is the
bread which came down from heaven; not as your fathers
ate manna and are dead; he that eats of this bread shall live
eternally. He said these things in the synagogue as he taught
in Capernaum.

Few passages of Scripture have been so painfully twisted and perverted as that which we have now read. The Jews are not the only people who have striven about its meaning. A sense has been put upon it, which it was never intended to bear. Fallen man, in interpreting the Bible, has an unhappy aptitude for turning food into poison. The things that were written for his benefit, he often makes an occasion for falling.

Let us first consider carefully, *what these verses do not mean.* The "eating and drinking" of which Christ speaks do not mean any literal eating and drinking. Above all, the words were not spoken with any reference to the Sacrament of the Lord's Supper. We may eat the Lord's Supper, and yet not eat and drink Christ's body and blood. We may eat and drink Christ's body and blood, and yet not eat the Lord's Supper. Let this never be forgotten.

The opinion here expressed may startle some who have not looked closely into the subject. But it is an opinion which is supported by three weighty reasons. For one thing, a literal "eating and drinking" of Christ's body and blood would have been an idea utterly revolting to all Jews and flatly contradictory to an often repeated precept of their law. For another thing, to take a literal view of "eating and drinking" is to interpose a bodily act between the soul of man and salvation. This is a thing for which there is no precedent in Scripture. The only things without which we cannot be saved are repentance and faith. Last, but not least, to take a literal view of "eating and drinking" would involve most blasphemous and profane consequences. It would shut out of heaven the penitent thief. He died long after these words were spoken without any literal eating and drinking. Will any dare to say he had "no life" in Him? It would admit to heaven thousands of ignorant, godless communicants in the present day. They literally eat and drink, no doubt! But they have no eternal life and will not be raised to glory at the last day. Let these reasons be carefully pondered.

The plain truth is, there is a melancholic anxiety in fallen man to put a carnal sense on Scriptural expressions, wherever he possibly can. He struggles hard to make religion a matter of forms and ceremonies – of doing and performing – of sacraments and ordinances – of sense and of sight. He secretly dislikes that system of Christianity which makes the state of the heart the principal thing and labors to keep sacraments and ordinances in the second place. Happy is that Christian who remembers these things and stands on his guard! Baptism and the Lord's Supper, no doubt, are holy sacraments and mighty blessings when rightly used. But it is worse than useless to drag them in everywhere, and to see them everywhere in God's Word.

Let us next consider carefully, *what these verses do mean.* The expressions they contain are, no doubt, very remarkable. Let us try to get some clear notion of their meaning.

The "flesh and blood of the Son of man" means that sacrifice of His own body, which Christ offered up on the cross, when He died for sinners. The atonement made by His death, the satisfaction made by his sufferings as our Substitute, the redemption effected by His enduring the penalty of our sins in His own body on the tree – this seems to be the true idea that we should set before our minds.

The "eating and drinking," without which there is no life in us, means that reception of Christ's sacrifice which takes place when a man believes on Christ crucified for salvation.[19] It is an inward and spiritual

---

19 "Except ye eat the flesh . . . " When our Lord uses this phrase "except . . . " at the beginning of a sentence, we generally find something of more than ordinary importance in it. Thus,

act of the heart and has nothing to do with the body. Whenever a man, feeling his own guilt and sinfulness, lays hold on Christ and trusts in the atonement made for him by Christ's death, at once he "eats the flesh of the Son of man, and drinks His blood." His soul feeds on Christ's sacrifice by faith, just as his body would feed on bread. Believing, he is said to "eat." Believing, he is said to "drink." And the special thing that he eats, and drinks, and gets benefit from is the atonement made for his sins by Christ's death for him on Calvary.

The practical lessons which may be gathered from the whole passage are weighty and important. The point being once settled, that "the flesh and blood" in these verses means Christ's atonement, and the "eating and drinking" means faith, we may find in these verses great principles of truth, which lie at the very root of Christianity.

We may learn that faith in Christ's atonement is a thing of absolute necessity to salvation. Just as there was no safety for the Israelite in Egypt who did not eat the Passover lamb in the night when the first-born were slain, so there is no life for the sinner who does not eat the flesh of Christ and drink His blood.

We may learn that faith in Christ's atonement unites us by the closest possible bonds to our Savior and entitles us to the highest privileges. Our souls shall find full satisfaction for all their needs – "His flesh is meat indeed, and His blood is drink indeed." All things are secured to us that we can need for time and eternity – "Whoso eateth my flesh and drinketh my blood hath eternal life, and I will raise him up at the last day."[20]

Last, but not least, we may learn that *faith in Christ's atonement is*

"Except a man be born again," "except ye be converted and become as little children," "except ye repent" (John 3:3; Matthew 18:3; Luke 13:3). Here he tells the Jews that they "have no life," no title to eternal life – no spiritual life . . . if they do not "eat the flesh and drink the blood" of the Son of man . . . Considering that the Jewish passover was nigh at hand, and that many of our Lord's hearers were probably on their way to Jerusalem to attend it, it seems highly probable that our Lord desired to direct the minds of those He addressed to Himself as the true Passover and sacrifice for sin.

20 I believe His meaning to be "Except ye believe on me as the one sacrifice for sin, and by faith receive into your hearts the redemption purchased by my blood, ye have no spiritual life and will not be saved." The atonement of Christ, His vicarious death and sacrifice, and faith in it – these things are the key to the whole passage. I believe this must be kept steadily in view. . . . My own impression is that both "flesh and blood" are mentioned here by our Lord to make it certain to the Jews that He spoke of His death and of the offering of His whole body in sacrifice on the cross. The body of the sin offering was just as essential a part of the sacrifice as the blood (Leviticus 4:1-12).

a personal act, a daily act, and an act that can be felt. No one can eat and drink for us, and no one, in like manner, can believe for us. We need food every day and not once a week or once a month – and, in like manner, we need to employ faith every day. We feel benefit when we have eaten and drunk, we feel strengthened, nourished, and refreshed; and, in like manner, if we believe truly, we shall feel the better for it by sensible hope and peace in our inward man.

Let us take heed that we use these truths, as well as know them. The food of this world, for which so many take thought, will perish in the using and not feed our souls. He only that eats of "the bread that came down from heaven" shall live forever.

John 6:60-65

Many therefore of his disciples when they had heard this said, This is a hard word; who can hear it? But Jesus, knowing in himself that his disciples murmured at it, said unto them, Does this offend you? What if ye shall see the Son of man ascend up where he was before? The Spirit is he that gives life; the flesh profits nothing; the words that I have spoken unto you, they are Spirit and they are life. But there are some of you that do not believe. For Jesus knew from the beginning who they were that did not believe and who should betray him. And he said, Therefore I said unto you that no one can come unto me unless it is given unto them of my Father.

We learn from these verses that *some of Christ's sayings seem hard to flesh and blood.* We are told that "many" who had followed our Lord for a season, were offended when He spoke of "eating his flesh and drinking his blood." They murmured and said, "This is a hard saying; who can accept it?"

Murmurs and complaints of this kind are very common. It must never surprise us to hear them. They have been, they are, they will be as long as the world stands. To some Christ's sayings appear hard to

111

understand. To others, as in the present case, they appear hard to believe and harder still to obey. It is just one of the many ways in which the natural corruption of man shows itself. So long as the heart is naturally proud, worldly, unbelieving, and fond of self-indulgence, if not of sin, so long there will never be lacking people who will say of Christian doctrines and precepts, "These are hard sayings; who can hear them?"

Humility is the frame of mind which we should labor and pray for, if we would not be offended by scriptural teaching. If we find any of Christ's sayings hard to understand, we should humbly remember our present ignorance and believe that we shall know more by and by. If we find any of His sayings difficult to obey, we should humbly recollect that He will never require of us impossibilities, and that what He bids us do, He will give us grace to perform.

We learn, secondly, from these verses, that *we must beware of putting a carnal meaning on spiritual words.* We read that our Lord said to the murmuring Jews who stumbled at the idea of eating His flesh and drinking His blood, "It is the Spirit that quickeneth; the flesh profiteth nothing: the words that I speak unto you, they are spirit and they are life."

It is useless to deny that this verse is full of difficulties. It contains expressions "hard to be understood." It is far more easy to have a general impression of the meaning of the whole sentence than to explain it word by word. Some things nevertheless we can see clearly and grasp firmly. Let us consider what they are.

Our Lord says, "It is the Spirit that quickeneth." By this He means that it is the Holy Spirit who is the special author of spiritual life in man's soul. By His agency it is first imparted and afterwards sustained and kept up. If the Jews thought He meant that man could have spiritual life by bodily eating or drinking, they were greatly mistaken.

Our Lord says, "The flesh profiteth nothing." By this He means that neither His flesh nor any other flesh, literally eaten, can do good to the soul. Spiritual benefit is not to be had through the mouth but through the heart. The soul is not a material thing, and cannot therefore be nourished by material food.

Our Lord says, "the words that I speak unto you, they are spirit and they are life." By this He signifies that His words and teachings, applied to the heart by the Holy Spirit, are the true means of producing spiritual influence and conveying spiritual life. By words, thoughts are begotten and aroused. By words, mind and conscience are stirred. And Christ's words especially are spirit-stirring and life-giving.

The principle contained in this verse, however faintly we may grasp its full meaning, deserves peculiar attention in these times. There is a tendency in many minds to attach an excessive importance to the outward and visible or "doing" part of religion. They seem to think that the sum and substance of Christianity consists in Baptism and the Supper of the Lord in public ceremonies and forms, in appeals to the eye and ear and bodily excitement. Surely they forget that it is "the Spirit that quickeneth," and that the "flesh profiteth nothing." It is not so much by noisy public demonstrations, as by the still quiet work of the Holy Spirit on hearts that God's cause prospers. It is Christ's words entering into consciences, which "are spirit and life."

We learn, lastly, from these verses, that *Christ has a perfect knowledge of the hearts of men.* We read that "He knew from the beginning who they were that believed not, and who should betray him."

Sentences like this are found so frequently in the Gospels that we are apt to underrate their importance. Yet there are few truths which we shall find it so good for our souls to remember as that which is contained in the sentence before us. The Savior with whom we have to do is one who knows all things!

What light this throws on the marvelous patience of the Lord Jesus in the days of His earthly ministry! He knew the sorrow and humiliation before Him and the manner of His death. He knew the unbelief and treachery of some who professed to be His familiar friends. But "for the joy that was set before Him," he endured it all (Hebrews 12:2).

What light this throws on the folly of hypocrisy and false profession in religion! Let those who are guilty of it recollect that they cannot deceive Christ. He sees them, knows them, and will expose them at the last day, except they repent. Whatever we are as Christians and however weak, let us be real, true, and sincere.

Finally, what light this throws on the daily pilgrimage of all true Christians! Let them take comfort in the thought that their Master knows them. However much unknown and misunderstood by the world, their Master knows their hearts and will comfort them at the last day. Happy is he who, in spite of many infirmities, can say with Peter – "Lord, Thou knowest all things; thou knowest that I love thee" (John 21:17).

John 6:66-71

After this, many of his disciples went back and walked no more with him. Then Jesus said unto the twelve, Will ye also go away? Then Simon Peter answered him, Lord, to whom shall we go? thou hast the words of eternal life. And we believe and know that thou art the Christ, the Son of the living God. Jesus answered them, Have not I chosen you twelve, and one of you is a devil? He spoke of Judas Iscariot the son of Simon, for it was he that should betray him, being one of the twelve.

These verses form a sorrowful conclusion to the famous discourse of Christ which occupies the greater part of the sixth chapter. They supply a melancholy proof of the hardness and corruption of man's heart. Even when the Son of God was the preacher, many seem to have heard in vain.

Let us mark in this passage *what an old sin backsliding is.* We read that when our Lord had explained what He meant by "eating and drinking his flesh and blood," – "From that time, many went back and walked no more with him."

The true grace of God no doubt is an everlasting possession. From this men never fall away entirely, when they have once received it. "The foundation of God standeth sure" (2 Timothy 2:19). "My sheep shall never perish" (John 10:28). But like the stony ground hearers in the parable of the sower, many "have no root in themselves, and so in time of temptation fall away." All is not gold that glitters. All blossoms do not come to fruit. All are not Israel which are called Israel. Men may have feelings, desires, convictions, resolutions, hopes, joys, sorrows in religion, and yet never have the grace of God. They may run well for a season and bid fair to reach heaven, and yet break down entirely after a time, go back to the world, and end like Demas, Judas Iscariot, and Lot's wife.

It must never surprise us to see and hear of such cases in our own days. If it happened in our Lord's time and under our Lord's teaching, much more may we expect it to happen now. Above all, it must never shake our faith and discourage us in our course. On the contrary, we must make up our minds that there will be backsliders in the Church as long as the world stands. The sneering infidel, who defends his unbelief by pointing at them, must find some better argument than their example. He forgets that there will always be counterfeit coin where there is true money.

Let us mark, secondly, in this passage, *the noble declaration of faith which the Apostle Peter made.* Our Lord had said to the twelve, when many went back, "Will ye also go away?" At once Peter replied with characteristic zeal and fervor, "Lord, to whom shall we go? thou hast the words of eternal life. And we believe and art sure that thou art that Christ, the Son of the living God."

The confession contained in these words is a very remarkable one. Living in a professedly Christian land and surrounded by Christian privileges, we can hardly form an adequate idea of its real value. For a humble Jew to say of one whom Scribes, and Pharisees, and Sadducees agreed in rejecting, "Thou hast the words of eternal life; thou art the Christ," was an act of mighty faith.[21] No wonder that our Lord said, in another place, "Blessed art thou, Simon Bar-jona: for flesh and blood hath not revealed it unto thee, but my Father which is heaven" (Matthew 16:17).

But the question with which Peter begins is just as remarkable as his confession. "To whom shall we go?" said the noble-hearted Apostle. "Whom shall we follow? To what teacher shall we betake ourselves? Where shall we find any guide to heaven to compare with thee? What shall we gain by forsaking thee? What Scribe, what Pharisee, what

---

21   We must not, however, misunderstand the extent of Peter's confession. He declared his faith that our Lord was the Anointed Messiah, the Son of the living God. The Messiahship and divinity of Christ were the points on which he and the other apostles laid firm hold. But the sacrifice and death of Christ and His substitution for us on the cross were not things which he either saw or understood at present (Matthew 16:22, 23).

Sadducee, what Priest, what Rabbi can show us such words of eternal life as thou showest?"

The question is one which every true Christian may boldly ask, when urged and tempted to give up his religion and go back to the world. It is easy for those who hate religion to pick holes in our conduct, to make objections to our doctrines, to find fault with our practices. It may be hard sometimes to give them any answer. But after all, "To whom shall we go," if we give up our religion? Where shall we find such peace, and hope, and solid comfort as in serving Christ, however poorly we serve Him? Can we better ourselves by turning our back on Christ and going back to our old ways? We cannot. Then let us hold on our way and persevere.

Let us mark, lastly, in this passage, *what little benefit some men get from religious privileges.* We read that our Lord said, "Have not I chosen you twelve, and one of you is a devil." And it goes on, "He spoke of Judas Iscariot, the son of Simon."

If ever there was a man who had great privileges and opportunities, that man was Judas Iscariot. A chosen disciple,[22] a constant companion of Christ, a witness of His miracles, a hearer of His sermons, a commissioned preacher of His kingdom, a fellow and friend of Peter, James, and John – it would be impossible to imagine a more favorable position for a man's soul. Yet if anyone ever fell hopelessly into hell and made shipwreck at last for eternity, that man was Judas Iscariot. The character of that man must have been black indeed, of whom our Lord could say he is "a devil."

Let us settle it firmly in our minds that the possession of religious privileges alone is not enough to save our souls. It is neither place, nor light, nor company, nor opportunities but grace that man needs to make him a Christian. With grace we may serve God in the most difficult position – like Daniel in Babylon, Obadiah in Ahab's court, and the saints in Nero's household. Without grace we may live in the full

---

22 I do not think that the "choosing" here spoken of means anything more than selection for office. The word is evidently used in this simple sense in Luke 6:13 – "Of them he chose twelve, whom he called apostles"; Acts 6:5 – "They chose Stephen, a man full of faith"; Acts 15:22 – "It pleased the apostles to send chosen men of their own company to Antioch." I say confidently that in each one of these cases, the Greek word rendered "chosen," the very same word that is used here, can mean nothing more than "chosen or selected for an office."

sunshine of Christ's countenance, and yet, like Judas, be miserably cast away. Then let us never rest until we have grace reigning in our souls. Grace is to be had for the asking. There is One sitting at the right hand of God who has said – "Ask, and it shall be given you" (Matthew 7:7). The Lord Jesus is more willing to give grace than man is to seek it. If men have it not, it is because they do not ask it.

John Chapter 7

John 7:1-13

After these things Jesus walked in Galilee, for he would not walk in Judea because the Jews sought to kill him. Now the feast of the Jews, of the tabernacles, was at hand. His brethren therefore said unto him, Depart from this place and go into Judea that thy disciples also may see the works that thou doest. For no one who seeks to be clearly known does anything in secret. If thou doest these things, show thyself to the world. For not even his brethren believed in him. Then Jesus said unto them, My time is not yet come, but your time is always ready. The world cannot hate you, but it hates me because I testify of it that its works are evil. Go ye up unto this feast; I go not up yet unto this feast, for my time is not yet fulfilled. And having said these things unto them, he abode still in Galilee. But when his brethren were gone up, then he also went up unto the feast, not openly, but as it were in secret. Then the Jews sought him at the feast and said, Where is he? And there was much murmuring among the people concerning him, for some said, He is a good man; others said, No, but he deceives the people. But no one spoke openly of him for fear of the Jews.

THE CHAPTER WE NOW begin is divided from the preceding one by a wide interval of time.[23] The many miracles which our Lord wrought,

---

23   The events of the last chapter took place about the time of the Passover, in spring. The events of the chapter we now begin took place in autumn, at the feast of tabernacles. . . . The feast of tabernacles was one of the three great feasts in the Jewish year, when, by God's command, all pious Jews went up to Jerusalem (Deuteronomy 16:16). . . . There are several things peculiar to the feast of tabernacles, which ought to be remembered in reading this chapter, because some of them throw light on it. (1) It was an occasion of special mirth and rejoicing with the Jews. They were ordered to dwell in booths or tabernacles made

while He "walked in Galilee," are passed over by John in comparative silence. The events which he was specially inspired to record are those which took place in or near Jerusalem.

We should observe in this passage *the desperate hardness and unbelief of human nature.* We are told that even our Lord's "brethren did not believe in Him." Holy and harmless and blameless as He was in life, some of his nearest relatives, according to the flesh, did not receive Him as the Messiah. It was bad enough that His own people, "the Jews sought to kill Him."[24] But it was even worse that "His brethren did not believe."

That great Scriptural doctrine, man's need of preventing and converting grace, stands out here, as if written with a sunbeam. It becomes all who question that doctrine to look at this passage and consider. Let them observe that seeing Christ's miracles, hearing Christ's teaching, living in Christ's own company were not enough to make men believers. The mere possession of spiritual privileges never yet made any one a Christian. All is useless without the effectual and applying work of God the Holy Spirit. No wonder that our Lord said in another place, "No one can come to me unless the Father who has sent me draws him" (John 6:44).

The true servants of Christ in every age will do well to remember this. They are often surprised and troubled to find that in religion they stand alone. They are apt to fancy that it must be their own fault that all around them are not converted like themselves. They are ready to blame themselves because their families remain worldly and unbelieving. But let them look at the verse before us. In our Lord Jesus Christ there was no fault either in temper, word, or deed. Yet even Christ's own "brethren did not believe in Him."

---

of branches for seven days in remembrance of their dwelling in temporary booths when they came out of Egypt and to "rejoice before the Lord" (Leviticus 23:39-43). (2) It was a feast at which more sacrifices were offered up than at any of the Jewish feasts (Numbers 29:12-34). (3) It was a feast at which, once every seven years, the law was publicly read to the whole people. (4) It was a feast at which water was drawn from the pool of Siloam every day with great solemnity and poured upon the altar, while the people sung the 12th chapter of Isaiah. (5) It was a feast which followed close on the great day of atonement, when the peculiarly typical ordinances of the scapegoat, and the High Priest going once in the year into the holy of holies were fresh in the minds of the people. These things should be carefully noted and remembered as we read through the chapter.

24 By "the Jews" we must understand the leaders and rulers of the Jewish nation. There is no proof that the lower orders felt the same enmity that the upper classes did against our Lord. "The common people heard Him gladly" (Mark 12:37).

Our blessed Master has truly learned by experience how to sympathize with all his people who stand alone. This is a thought "full of sweet, pleasant, and unspeakable comfort." He knows the heart of every isolated believer, and can be touched with the feeling of his trials. He has drunk this bitter cup. He has passed through this fire. Let all who are fainting and cast down, because brothers and sisters despise their religion, turn to Christ for comfort and pour out their hearts before Him. He "has suffered Himself being tempted" in this way, and He can help as well as feel (Hebrews 2:18).

We should observe, for another thing, in this passage, *one principal reason why many hate Christ.* We are told that our Lord said to His unbelieving brethren, "The world cannot hate you; but me it hateth, because I testify of it, that the works thereof are evil."

These words reveal one of those secret principles which influence men in their treatment of Christ. They help to explain that deadly enmity with which many during our Lord's earthly ministry regarded Him and His Gospel. It was not so much the high doctrines which He preached as the high standard of practice which He proclaimed, which gave offence. It was not even His claim to be received the Messiah which men disliked so much, as His witness against the wickedness of their lives. In short, they could have tolerated His opinions if He would only have spared their sins.

The principle, we may be sure, is one of universal application. It is at work now just as much as it was eighteen hundred years ago. The real cause of many people's dislike to the Gospel is the holiness of living which it demands. Teach abstract doctrines only, and few will find any fault. Denounce the fashionable sins of the day and call on men to repent and walk consistently with God, and thousands at once will be offended. The true reason why many profess to be infidels and abuse Christianity is the witness that Christianity bears against their own bad lives. Like Ahab, they hate it, "because it does not prophesy good concerning them, but evil" (1 Kings 22:8).

We should observe, lastly, in this passage, *the strange variety of opinions about Christ, which were current from the beginning.* We are told that "there was much murmuring among the people concerning him:

for some said, He is a good man: others said, Nay, but he deceiveth the people." The words which old Simeon had spoken thirty years before were here accomplished in a striking manner. He had said to our Lord's mother, "This child is set for the fall and rising again of many in Israel: and for a sign which shall be spoken against – that the thoughts of many hearts may be revealed" (Luke 2:34, 35). In the diversities of opinion about our Lord which arose among the Jews, we see the good old man's saying fulfilled.

In the face of such a passage as this, the endless differences and divisions about religion, which we see on all sides in the present day, ought never to surprise us. The open hatred of some toward Christ – the carping, faultfinding, prejudiced spirit of others – the bold confession of the few faithful ones – the timid, man-fearing temperament of the many faithless ones – the unceasing war of words and strife of tongues with which the Churches of Christ are so sadly familiar – are only modern symptoms of an old disease. Such is the corruption of human nature, that Christ is the cause of division among men wherever He is preached. So long as the world stands, some, when they hear of Him, will love, and some will hate – some will believe, and some will believe not. That deep, prophetical saying of His will be continually verified – "Think not that I have come to introduce peace into the land; I came not to introduce peace, but a sword" (Matthew 10:34).

What do we think of Christ ourselves? This is the one question with which we have to do. Let us never be ashamed to be of that little number who believe on Him, hear His voice, follow Him, and confess Him before men. While others waste their time in vain jangling and unprofitable controversy, let us take up the cross and give all diligence to make our calling and election sure. The children of this world may hate us, as it hated our Master, because our religion is a standing witness against them. But the last day will show that we chose wisely, lost nothing, and gained a crown of glory that fades not away.

John 7:14-24

Now about the midst of the feast Jesus went up into the temple and taught. And the Jews marvelled, saying, How does this man know letters, having never learned? Jesus answered them and said, My doctrine is not mine, but his that sent me. If anyone desires to do his will, he shall know of the doctrine, whether it is of God or whether I speak of myself. He that speaks of himself seeks his own glory, but he that seeks the glory of him that sent him, the same is true, and no unrighteousness is in him. Did not Moses give you the law, and yet none of you keeps the law? Why do ye go about to kill me? The people answered and said, Thou hast a demon; who goes about to kill thee? Jesus answered and said unto them, I have done one work, and ye all marvel. Moses therefore gave unto you circumcision (not because it is of Moses, but of the fathers), and ye on the sabbath day circumcise a man. If a man on the sabbath day receives circumcision without the law of Moses being broken, are ye angry at me because I have made a man entirely whole on the sabbath day? Judge not according to the appearance, but judge with righteous judgment.

We learn first in this passage, that *honest obedience to God's will is one way to obtain clear spiritual knowledge.* Our Lord says, "If any man will do His will, he shall know of the doctrine, whether it be of God, or whether I speak of myself."

The difficulty of finding out "what is truth" in religion is a common subject of complaint among men. They point to the many differences which prevail among Christians on matters of doctrine and profess to be unable to decide who is right. In thousands of cases this professed inability to find out truth becomes an excuse for living without any religion at all.

The saying of our Lord before us is one that demands the serious attention of people in this state of mind. It supplies an argument whose edge and point they will find it hard to evade. It teaches that one secret of getting the key of knowledge is to practice honestly what we know, and that if we conscientiously use the light that we now have, we shall soon find more light coming down into our minds. In short, there is a sense in which it is true, that by *doing* we shall come to *knowing*.

There is a mine of truth in this principle. Well would it be for men if they would act upon it. Instead of saying, as some do – "I must first know everything clearly, and then I will act," – we should say – "I will diligently use such knowledge as I possess and believe that in the using, fresh knowledge will be given to me." How many mysteries this simple plan would solve! How many hard things would soon become plain if men would honestly live up to their light and "follow on to know the Lord" (Hosea 6:3).

It should never be forgotten that God deals with us as moral beings and not as beasts or stones. He loves to encourage us to self-exertion and diligent use of such means as we have in our hands. The plain things in religion are undeniably very many. Let a man honestly attend to them, and he shall be taught the deep things of God.

Whatever some may say about their inability to find out truth, you will rarely find one of them who does not know better than he practices. Then if he is sincere, let him begin here at once. Let him humbly use what little knowledge he has got, and God will soon give him more. "If thine eye is sincere, thy whole body shall be full of light" (Matthew 6:22).

We learn, secondly, in this passage, that *a self-exalting spirit in ministers of religion is entirely opposed to the mind of Christ.* Our Lord says, "He that speaketh of himself seeketh his own glory; but he that seeketh His glory that sent him, the same is true, and no unrighteousness is in him."

The wisdom and truth of this sentence will be evident at once to any reflecting mind. The minister truly called of God will be deeply sensible of his Master's majesty and his own infirmity and will see in himself nothing but unworthiness. He, on the other hand, who knows that he is not "inwardly moved by the Holy Spirit," will try to cover over his defects by magnifying himself and his office. The very desire to exalt ourselves is a bad symptom. It is a sure sign of something wrong within.

Does any one ask illustrations of the truth before us? He will find them, on the one side, in the Scribes and Pharisees of our Lord's times. If one thing more than another distinguished these unhappy men, it was their desire to get praise for themselves. He will find them, on the other side, in the character of the Apostle Paul. The keynote that runs through all his Epistles is personal humility and zeal for Christ's glory – "I am less than the least of all saints – I am not meet to be called an Apostle – I am chief of sinners – we preach not ourselves but Christ Jesus the Lord, and ourselves your servants for Jesus' sake" (Ephesians 3:8; 1 Corinthians 15:9; 1 Timothy 1:15; 2 Corinthians 4:5).

Does any one ask for a test by which he may discern the real man of God from the false shepherd in the present day? Let him remember our Lord's weighty words and notice carefully what is the main object that a minister loves to exalt. Not he who is ever crying – "Behold the Church! behold the Sacraments! behold the ministry!" but he who says – "Behold the Lamb!" – is the pastor after God's own heart. Happy indeed is that minister who forgets self in his pulpit and desires to be hid behind the cross. This man shall be blessed in his work, and be a blessing.

We learn, lastly, in this passage, *the danger of forming a hasty judgment.* The Jews at Jerusalem were ready to condemn our Lord as a sinner against the law of Moses, because He had done a miracle of healing on the Sabbath day. They forgot in their blind enmity that the fourth commandment was not meant to prevent works of necessity or works of mercy. A work on the Sabbath our Lord had done, no doubt, but not a work forbidden by the law. And hence they drew down on themselves the rebuke, "Judge not according to the appearance, but judge righteous judgment."[25]

The practical value of the lesson before us is very great. We shall do well to remember it as we travel through life and to correct our estimate of people and things by the light which it supplies.

We are often too ready to be deceived by an appearance of good. We are in danger of rating some men as very good Christians, because of a little outward profession of religion and a decent Sunday formality – because, in short, they talk the language of Canaan and wear the garb of pilgrims. We forget that all is not good that appears good, even as all is not gold that glitters, and that daily practice, choice, tastes, habits, conduct, private character are the true evidence of what a man

---

25   There is perhaps a reference here to Isaiah's prophecy about Messiah, "He shall not judge after the sight of His eyes" (Isaiah 11:3).

is. In a word, we forget our Lord's saying – "Judge not according to the appearance."

We are too ready, on the other hand, to be deceived by the appearance of evil. We are in danger of setting down some men as not true Christians, because of a few faults or inconsistencies, and "making them offenders because of a word" (Isaiah 29:21). We must remember that the best of men are but men at their very best, and that the most eminent saints may be overtaken by temptation and yet be saints at heart after all. We must not hastily suppose that all is evil, where there is an occasional appearance of evil. The holiest man may fall sadly for a time, and yet the grace within him may finally get a victory. Is a man's general character godly? Then let us suspend our judgment a little when he falls, and hope on. Let us "judge righteous judgment."

In any case let us take care that we pass fair judgment on ourselves. Whatever we think of others, let us beware of making mistakes about our own character. There, at any rate, let us be just, honest, and fair. Let us not flatter ourselves that all is right, because all is apparently right before men. "The Lord," we must remember, "looks on the heart" (1 Samuel 16:7). Then let us judge ourselves with righteous judgment and condemn ourselves while we live, lest we be judged of the Lord and condemned forever at the last day (1 Corinthians 11:31).

John 7:25-36

Then one of those of Jerusalem said, Is not this he whom they seek to kill? But, behold, he speaks boldly, and they say nothing unto him. Have the rulers truly understood that this is indeed the Christ? But we know where this man is from; but when the Christ comes, no one shall know where he is from. Then Jesus cried out in the temple as he taught, saying, Ye know me, and ye know from where I come, but I have not come of myself, but he that sent me is true, whom ye know not. But I know him, for I am from him, and he has sent me. Then they sought to take him, but no one laid hands on him because his hour was not yet come. And many of the people

believed in him and said, When the Christ comes, will he
do more signs than these which this man has done? The
Pharisees heard the people that murmured such things con-
cerning him, and the princes of the priests and the Pharisees
sent officers to take him. Then Jesus said unto them, Yet a
little while I shall be with you, and then I shall go unto him
that sent me. Ye shall seek me and shall not find me, and
where I shall be, ye shall not be able to come. Then the Jews
said among themselves, Where will he go that we shall not
find him? Will he go unto the dispersed among the Greeks
and teach the Greeks? What manner of saying is this that
he said, Ye shall seek me and shall not find me, and where I
shall be ye shall not be able to come?

We see in these verses, *the obstinate blindness of the unbelieving Jews.*
We find them defending their denial of our Lord's Messiahship by saying, "But we know this man whence He is: but when Christ cometh,
no man knoweth whence he is." And yet in both these assertions they
were wrong!

They were wrong in saying that they "knew whence our Lord came."
They meant no doubt to say that He was born at Nazareth, and belonged
to Nazareth, and was therefore a Galilean. Yet the fact was that our
Lord was born at Bethlehem, that He belonged legally to the tribe of
Judah, and that His mother and Joseph were of the house and lineage
of David. It is incredible to suppose that the Jews could not have found
this out, if they had honestly searched and inquired. It is notorious that
pedigrees, genealogies, and family histories were most carefully kept
by the Jewish nation. Their ignorance was without excuse.

They were wrong again in saying, "that no man was to know whence
Christ came." There was a well-known prophecy with which their
whole nation was familiar that Christ was to come out of the town of
Bethlehem (Micah 5:2; Matthew 2:5; John 7:42). It is absurd to suppose that they had forgotten this prophecy. But apparently they found
it inconvenient to remember it on this occasion. Men's memories are
often sadly dependent on their wills.

The Apostle Peter, in a certain place, speaks of some as "willingly ignorant" (2 Peter 3:5). He had good reason to use the expression. It is a sore spiritual disease and one most painfully common among men. There are thousands in the present day just as blind in their way as the Jews. They shut their eyes against the plainest facts and doctrines of Christianity. They pretend to say that they do not understand and cannot therefore believe the things that we press on their attention as needful to salvation. But, alas! in nineteen cases out of twenty, it is a willful ignorance. They do not believe what they do not like to believe. They will neither read, nor listen, nor search, nor think, nor inquire, honestly after truth. Can any one wonder if such people are ignorant? Faithful and true is that old proverb – "There are none so blind as those who will not see."

We see, for another thing, in these verses, *the overruling hand of God over all His enemies*. We find that the unbelieving Jews "Sought to take our Lord – but no man laid hands on Him, because his hour was not yet come." They had the will to hurt him, but by an invisible restraint from above, they had not the power.

There is a mine of deep truth in the words before us, which deserves close attention. They show us plainly that all our Lord's sufferings were undergone voluntarily and of His own free will. He did not go to the cross because He could not help it. He did not die because He could not prevent His death. Neither Jew nor Gentile, Pharisee nor Sadducee, Annas nor Caiaphas, Herod nor Pontius Pilate could have injured our Lord, except power had been given them from above. All that they did was done under control and by permission. The crucifixion was part of the eternal counsels of the Trinity. The sufferings and death of our Lord could not begin until the very hour which God had appointed. This is a great mystery. But it is a truth.

The servants of Christ in every age should treasure up the doctrine before us and remember it in time of need. It is "full of sweet, pleasant, and unspeakable comfort to godly persons." Let such never forget that they live in a world where God overrules all times and events and where nothing can happen but by God's permission. The very hairs of their heads are all numbered. Sorrow and sickness, and poverty, and persecution, can never touch them, unless God sees fit. They may boldly say to every cross – "Thou couldst have no power against me, except it were given thee from above." Then let them work on confidently. They are immortal, until their work is done. Let them suffer patiently, if needs be that they suffer. Their "times are in God's hand" (Psalm 31:15). That hand guides and governs all things here below and makes no mistakes.

We see lastly, in these verses, *the miserable end to which unbelievers may one day come.* We find our Lord saying to His enemies – "Ye shall seek me, and shall not find me; and where I am thither ye cannot come."

We can hardly doubt that these words were meant to have a prophetical sense. Whether our Lord had in view individual cases of unbelief among His hearers or whether He looked forward to the national remorse which many would feel too late in the final siege of Jerusalem are points which we cannot perhaps decide. But that many Jews did remember Christ's sayings long after He had ascended into heaven and did in a way seek Him and wish for Him when it was too late, we may be very sure.

It is far too much forgotten that there is such a thing as finding out truth too late. There may be convictions of sin, discoveries of our own folly, desires after peace, anxieties about heaven, fears of hell, but all too late. The teaching of Scripture on this point is clear and express. It is written in Proverbs – "Then shall they call upon me, but I will not answer; they shall seek me early, but they shall not find me" (Proverbs 1:28). It is written of the foolish virgins in the parable that when they found the door shut, they knocked in vain, saying, "Lord, Lord, open to us" (Matthew 25:11). Dreadful as it may seem, it is possible, by continually resisting light and warnings, to sin away our own souls. It sounds frightening, but it is true.

Let us take heed to ourselves lest we sin after the example of the unbelieving Jews and never seek the Lord Jesus as a Savior until it is too late. The door of mercy is still open. The throne of grace is still waiting for us. Let us give diligence to make sure our interest in Christ, while it is called today. Better never have been born than hear the Son of God say at last, "Where I am, there you cannot come."

John 7:37-39

In the last day, that great day of the feast, Jesus stood and
cried out, saying, If any man thirsts, let him come unto me
and drink. He that believes in me, as the scripture has said,
out of his belly shall flow rivers of living water. (But this he
spoke concerning the Spirit, which those that believe on him
should receive, for the Holy Spirit was not yet given because
Jesus was not yet glorified.)

It has been said that there are some passages in Scripture which deserve
to be printed in letters of gold. Of such passages the verses before us
form one. They contain one of those wide, full, free invitations to mankind, which make the Gospel of Christ so eminently the "good news of
God." Let us see of what it consists.

We have, first, in these verses, *a case supposed.* The Lord Jesus says,
"If any man thirst."[26] These words no doubt were meant to have a spiritual meaning. The thirst before us is of a purely spiritual kind. It means
anxiety of soul – conviction of sin – desire of pardon – longing after
peace of conscience. When a man feels his sins and wants forgiveness –
is deeply sensible of his soul's need, and earnestly desires help and relief
– then he is in that state of mind which our Lord had in view, when he
said, "If any man thirst."[27] The Jews who heard Peter preach on the day
of Pentecost and were "pricked in their hearts," – the Philippian jailer
who cried to Paul and Silas, "What must I do to be saved?" are both
examples of what the expression means. In both cases there was "thirst."

Such thirst as this, unhappily, is known by few. All ought to feel it,
and all would feel it if they were wise. Sinful, mortal, dying creatures as
we all are, with souls that will one day be judged and spend eternity in
heaven or hell, there lives not the man or woman on earth who ought
not to "thirst" after salvation. And yet the many thirst after everything

---

26 Some have thought, because the feast of tabernacles was specially intended to remind the
Jews of their sojourn in the wilderness, that our Lord had in view the miraculous supply
of water from the rock, which followed Israel everywhere, and that He wished the Jews to
see in Him the fulfillment of that type, the true Rock (1 Corinthians 10:4).

27 We should note the breadth of the invitation. It is for "any man." No matter who and what
he may have been – no matter how bad and wicked his former life – the hand is held out,
and the offer made to Him: "If any man thirst, let him come." Let no man say that the
Gospel is narrow in its offers.

except salvation. Money, pleasure, honor, rank, self-indulgence – these are the things which they desire. There is no clearer proof of the fall of man, and the utter corruption of human nature, than the careless indifference of most people about their souls. No wonder the Bible calls the natural man "blind," and "asleep," and "dead," when so few can be found who are awake, alive, and athirst about salvation.

Happy are those who know something by experience of spiritual "thirst." The beginning of all true Christianity is to discover that we are guilty, empty, needy sinners. Until we know that we are lost, we are not in the way to be saved. The very first step toward heaven is to be thoroughly convinced that we deserve hell. That sense of sin which sometimes alarms a man and makes him think his own case desperate is a good sign. It is in fact a symptom of spiritual life – "Blessed indeed are they which do hunger and thirst after righteousness, for they shall be filled" (Matthew 5:6).

We have, secondly, in these verses, *a remedy proposed.* The Lord Jesus says, "If any man thirst, let him come unto me and drink." He declares that He is the true fountain of life, the supplier of all spiritual necessities, the reliever of all spiritual needs. He invites all who feel the burden of sin heavy to apply to Him and proclaims Himself their helper.

Those words "let him come unto me" are few and very simple. But they settle a mighty question which all the wisdom of Greek and Roman philosophers could never settle; they show how man can have peace with God. They show that peace is to be had in Christ by trusting in Him as our mediator and substitute, in one word, by believing. To "come" to Christ is to believe on Him, and to "believe" on Him is to come. The remedy may seem a very simple one, too simple to be true. But there is no other remedy than this; and all the wisdom of the world can never find a flaw in it or devise a better one.

To use this grand prescription of Christ is the secret of all saving Christianity. The saints of God in every age have been men and women who drank of this fountain by faith, and were relieved. They felt their guilt and emptiness and thirsted for deliverance. They heard of a full supply of pardon, mercy, and grace in Christ crucified for all penitent believers. They believed the good news and acted upon it. They cast aside all confidence in their own goodness and worthiness and came to Christ by faith as sinners. So coming they found relief. So coming daily they lived. So coming they died. Really to feel the sinfulness of sin and to thirst and really to come to Christ and believe are the two steps which lead to heaven. But they are mighty steps. Thousands are too proud and careless to take them. Few, alas! think and still fewer believe.

We have, lastly, in these verses, *a promise held out.* The Lord Jesus says, "He that believeth on me, as the scripture hath said, out of his belly shall flow rivers of living water." These words of course were meant to have a figurative sense. They have a double application. They teach, for one thing, that all who come to Christ by faith shall find in Him abundant satisfaction. They teach, for another thing, that believers shall not only have enough for the needs of their own souls, but shall also become fountains of blessings to others.

The fulfillment of the first part of the promise could be testified by thousands of living Christians in the present day. They would say, if their evidence could be collected, that when they came to Christ by faith, they found in Him more than they expected. They have tasted peace, and hope, and comfort, since they first believed, which, with all their doubts and fears, they would not exchange for anything in this world. They have found grace according to their need, and strength according to their days. In themselves and their own hearts, they have often been disappointed; but they have never been disappointed in Christ.

The fulfillment of the other half of the promise will never be fully known until the judgment day. That day alone shall reveal the amount of good that every believer is made the instrument of doing to others from the very day of his conversion. Some do good while they live, by their tongues; like the Apostles and first preachers of the Gospel. Some do good when they are dying; like Stephen and the penitent thief and our own martyred Reformers at the stake. Some do good long after they are dead by their writings; like Baxter and Bunyan and M'Cheyne. But in one way or another, probably, almost all believers will be found to have been fountains of blessings. By word or by deed, by precept or by example, directly or indirectly, they are always leaving their marks on others. They know it not now; but they will find at last that it is true. Christ's saying shall be fulfilled.

Do we ourselves know anything of "coming to Christ?" This is the question that should arise in our hearts as we leave this passage. The worst of all states of soul is to be without feeling or concern about eternity – to be without "thirst." The greatest of all mistakes is to try to find relief in any other way than the one before us – the way of simply "coming to Christ." It is one thing to come to Christ's Church, Christ's ministers, and Christ's ordinances. It is quite another thing to come to Christ Himself. Happy is he who not only knows these things, but acts upon them!

John 7:40-53

Then many of the people, when they heard this word, said, Truly this is the Prophet. Others said, This is the Christ. But some said, Shall the Christ come out of Galilee? Has not the scripture said, That the Christ comes of the seed of David and out of the town of Bethlehem where David was? So there was a division among the people because of him. And some of them would have taken him, but no one laid hands on him. Then the officers to the chief priests and Pharisees came, and they said unto them, Why have ye not brought him? The officers answered, Never has anyone spoken like this man. Then the Pharisees answered them, Are ye also deceived? Have any of the princes or of the Pharisees believed on him? But this people who do not know the law are cursed. Nicodemus said unto them (he that came to Jesus by night, being one of them), Does our law judge any man before it hears him and knows what he does? They answered and said unto him, Art thou also of Galilee? Search and see, for a prophet has never arisen out of Galilee. And each one went unto his own house.

These verses show us, for one thing, *how useless is knowledge in religion, if it is not accompanied by grace in the heart.* We are told that some of our Lord's hearers knew clearly where Christ was to be born. They referred to Scripture, like men familiar with its contents. "Has not the Scripture said that Christ comes of the seed of David and out of the town of Bethlehem, where David was?" And yet the eyes of their understanding were not enlightened. Their own Messiah stood before them, and they neither received, nor believed, nor obeyed Him.

A certain degree of religious knowledge, beyond doubt, is of vast importance. Ignorance is certainly not the mother of true devotion and helps nobody toward heaven. An "unknown God" can never be the object of a reasonable worship. Happy indeed would it be for Christians if they all knew the Scriptures as well as the Jews seem to have done, when our Lord was on earth!

But while we value religious knowledge, we must take care that we do not overvalue it. We must not think it enough to know the facts and doctrines of our faith, unless our hearts and lives are thoroughly influenced by what we know. The demons know the creed intellectually and "believe and tremble," but remain demons still (James 2:19). It is quite possible to be familiar with the letter of Scripture and to be able to quote texts appropriately and reason about the theory of Christianity and yet to remain dead in trespasses and sins. Like many of the generation to which our Lord preached, we may know the Bible well and yet remain faithless and unconverted.

Heart knowledge, we must always remember, is the one thing needful. It is something which schools and universities cannot confer. It is the gift of God. To find out the plague of our own hearts and hate sin – to become familiar with the throne of grace and the fountain of Christ's blood – to sit daily at the feet of Jesus and humbly learn of Him – this is the highest degree of knowledge to which mortal man can attain. Let anyone thank God who knows anything of these things. He may be ignorant of Greek, Latin, Hebrew, and mathematics, but he shall be saved.

These verses show us, for another thing, *how eminent must have been our Lord's gifts, as a public Teacher of religion*. We are told that even the officers of the chief priests, who were sent to take Him, were struck and amazed. They were, of course, not likely to be prejudiced in His favor. Yet even they reported – "Never man spoke like this Man."

Of the *manner* of our Lord's public speaking, we can of necessity form little idea. Action, and voice, and delivery are things that must be seen and heard to be appreciated. That our Lord's manner was peculiarly solemn, arresting, and impressive, we need not doubt. It was probably something very unlike what the Jewish officers were accustomed to hear. There is much in what is said in another place – "He taught them as One having authority, and not as the Scribes" (Matthew 7:29).

Of the *matter* of our Lord's public speaking, we may form some conception from the discourses which are recorded in the four Gospels. The leading features of these discourses are plain and unmistakable. The world has never seen anything like them, since the gift of speech was given to man. They often contain deep truths, which we have no line to fathom. But they often contain simple things, which even a child can understand. They are bold and outspoken in denouncing national and ecclesiastical sins, and yet they are wise and discreet in never giving needless offence. They are faithful and direct in their warnings, and yet loving and tender, in their invitations. For a combination of power and simplicity, of courage and prudence, of faithfulness and tenderness, we may well say, "Never man spoke like this Man!"

It would be well for the Church of Christ if ministers and teachers of religion would strive more to speak after their Lord's pattern. Let them remember that elegant bombastic language and a sensational, theatrical style of address are utterly unlike their Master. Let them realize that an eloquent simplicity is the highest attainment of public speaking. Of this their Master left them a glorious example. Surely they need never be ashamed of walking in His steps.

These verses show us, lastly, *how slowly and gradually the work of grace goes on in some hearts.* We are told that Nicodemus stood up in the council of our Lord's enemies and mildly pleaded that He deserved fair dealing. "Does our law judge any man," he asked, "before it hear him, and know what he doeth?"

This very Nicodemus, we must remember, is the man who, eighteen months before, had come to our Lord by night as an ignorant inquirer. He evidently knew little then and dared not come to Christ in open day. But now, after eighteen months, he has got on so far that he dares to say something on our Lord's side. It was but little that he said, no doubt, but it was better than nothing at all. And a day was yet to come, when he would go further still. He was to help Joseph of Arimathaea in doing honor to our Lord's dead body, when even His chosen Apostles had forsaken Him and fled.

The case of Nicodemus is full of useful instruction. It teaches us that there are diversities in the operation of the Holy Spirit. All are undoubtedly led to the same Savior, but all are not led precisely in the same way. It teaches us that the work of the Spirit does not always go forward with the same speed in the hearts of men. In some cases it may go forward very slowly indeed and yet may be real and true.

We shall do well to remember these things, in forming our opinion of other Christians. We are often ready to condemn some as graceless, because their experience does not exactly tally with our own, or to set them down as not in the narrow way at all, because they cannot run as fast as ourselves. We must beware of hasty judgments. It is not always the fastest runner that wins the race. It is not always those who begin suddenly in religion and profess themselves rejoicing Christians, who continue steadfast to the end. Slow work is sometimes the surest and most enduring. Nicodemus stood firm, when Judas Iscariot fell away and went to his own place. No doubt it would be a pleasant thing if everybody who was converted came out boldly, took up the cross, and confessed Christ in the day of his conversion. But it is not always given to God's children to do so.

Have we any grace in our hearts at all? This, after all, is the grand question that concerns us. It may be small – but have we any? It may grow slowly, as in the case of Nicodemus – but does it grow at all? Better a little grace than none! Better move slowly than stand still in sin and the world!

John Chapter 8

John 8:1-11

Jesus went unto the mount of Olives. And early in the morning he came again into the temple, and all the people came unto him; and he sat down and taught them. Then the scribes and Pharisees brought unto him a woman taken in adultery, and when they had set her in the midst, they said unto him, Master, this woman was taken in adultery in the very act. Now Moses in the law commanded us that such should be stoned, but what sayest thou? This they said, tempting him, that they might be able to accuse him. But Jesus stooped down and with his finger wrote on the ground. So when they continued asking him, he lifted himself up and said unto them, He that is without sin among you, let him be the first to cast a stone at her. And again he stooped down and wrote on the ground. And those who heard it, being convicted by their own conscience, went out one by one, beginning at the eldest even unto the last; and Jesus was left alone and the woman that had been in the midst. Jesus, lifting himself up and seeing no one but the woman, said unto her, Woman, where are thine accusers? Has no one condemned thee? And she said, No one, Lord. Then Jesus said unto her, Neither do I condemn thee; go and sin no more.

THE NARRATIVE WHICH BEGINS the eighth chapter of John's Gospel is of a rather peculiar character. In some respects it stands alone. There is nothing quite like it in the whole range of the four Gospels. In every age some scrupulous minds have stumbled at the passage, and have doubted whether it was ever written by John at all. But the justice of such scruples is a point that cannot easily be proved.

To suppose, as some have thought, that the narrative before us palliates the sin of adultery and exhibits our Lord as making light of the seventh commandment is surely a great mistake. There is nothing in the passage to justify such an assertion. There is not a sentence in it to warrant our saying anything of the kind. Let us calmly weigh the matter and examine the contents of the passage.

Our Lord's enemies brought before Him a woman guilty of adultery and asked him to say what punishment she deserved. We are distinctly told that they asked the question "to trap Him." They hoped to entrap Him into saying something for which they might accuse Him. They fancied perhaps that He who preached pardon and salvation to "publicans and harlots" might be induced to say something which would either contradict the law of Moses or His own words.

Our Lord knew the hearts of the malicious questioners before Him and dealt with them with perfect wisdom, as He had done in the case of the "tribute-money" (Matthew 22:17). He refused to be a "judge" and lawgiver among them and specially in a case which their own law had already decided. He gave them at first no answer at all.

But "when they continued asking," our Lord silenced them with a withering and heart-searching reply. "He that is without sin among you," he said, "let him first cast a stone at her." He did not say that the woman had not sinned, or that her sin was a trifling and excusable one. But He reminded her accusers that they at any rate were not the people to bring a charge against her. Their own motives and lives were far from pure. They themselves did not come into the case with clean hands. What they really desired was not to vindicate the purity of God's law and punish a sinner, but to wreak their malice on Himself.

Last of all, when those who had brought the unhappy woman to our Lord had gone out from His presence, "convicted by their own conscience," He dismissed the guilty sinner with the solemn words, "Neither do I condemn thee: go and sin no more." That she did not deserve punishment He did not say. But He had not come to be a judge. Moreover, in the absence of all witnesses or accusers, there was no case before Him. Let her then depart as one whose guilt was "not proven," even though she was really guilty and let her "sin no more."

To say in the face of these simple facts that our Lord made light of the sin of adultery is not fair. There is nothing in the passage before us to prove it. Of all whose words are recorded in the Bible there is none who has spoken so strongly about the breach of the seventh commandment as our divine Master. It is He who has taught that it may be broken by a look or a thought, as well as by an open act (Matthew 5:28). It is He who has spoken more strongly than any about the sanctity of the marriage relation (Matthew 19:5). In all that is recorded here, we see nothing inconsistent with the rest of His teaching. He simply refused to usurp the office of the judge and to pronounce condemnation on a guilty woman for the gratification of His deadly enemies.

In leaving this passage, we must not forget that it contains two lessons of great importance. Whatever difficulties the verses before us may present, these two lessons at any rate are clear, plain, and unmistakable.

We learn, for one thing, *the power of conscience*. We read of the woman's accusers that when they heard our Lord's appeal, "being convicted by their own conscience, they went out one by one, beginning at the eldest, even into the last." Wicked and hardened as they were, they felt something within which made them cowards. Fallen as human nature is, God has taken care to leave within every man a witness that will be heard.

Conscience is a most important part of our inward man and plays a most prominent part in our spiritual history. It cannot save us. It never yet led any one to Christ. It is blind and liable to be misled. It is lame and powerless and cannot guide us to heaven. Yet conscience is not to be despised. It is the minister's best friend, when he stands up to rebuke sin from the pulpit. It is the mother's best friend, when she tries to restrain her children from evil and quicken them to good. It is the teacher's best friend, when he presses home on boys and girls their moral duties. Happy is he who never stifles his conscience but strives to keep it tender! Still happier is he who prays to have it enlightened by the Holy Spirit and sprinkled with Christ's blood.

We learn, for another thing, *the nature of true repentance*. When our Lord had said to the sinful woman, "Neither do I condemn you," He dismissed her with the solemn words, "go and sin no more." He did not merely say, "go home and repent." He pointed out the chief thing which her case required – the necessity of immediate breaking off from her sin.

Let us never forget this lesson. It is the very essence of genuine repentance, as the Church catechism well teaches, to "forsake sin." That repentance which consists in nothing more than feeling, talking, professing, wishing, meaning, hoping, and resolving is worthless in God's sight. Action is the very life of "repentance unto salvation not to be repented of." Until a man ceases to do evil and turns from his sins, he does not really repent. Would we know whether we are truly converted to God and know anything of godly sorrow for sin and repentance such as causes "joy in heaven"? Let us search and see whether we forsake sin. Let us not rest until we can say as in God's sight, "I hate all sin, and desire to sin no more."

John 8:12-20

Then Jesus spoke again unto them, saying, I AM the light of the world; he that follows me shall not walk in darkness but shall have the light of life. Then the Pharisees said unto him, Thou dost bear witness of thyself; thy witness is not true. Jesus answered and said unto them, Though I bear witness of myself, my witness is true, for I know from where I came and where I go; but ye do not know where I came from and where I go. Ye judge after the flesh, but I judge no one. And yet if I judge, my judgment is true, for I am not alone, but I and the Father that sent me. It is also written in your law that the testimony of two men is true. I AM one that bears witness of myself, and the Father that sent me bears witness of me. Then they said unto him, Where is thy Father? Jesus answered, Ye neither know me, nor my Father; if ye had known me, ye should have known my Father also. Jesus spoke these words in the treasury as he taught in the temple, and no one laid hands on him, for his hour was not yet come.

The conversation between our Lord and the Jews, which begins with these verses, is full of difficulties. The connection between one part and another and the precise meaning of some of the expressions which fell from our Lord's lips are "things hard to be understood." In passages like this it is true wisdom to acknowledge the great imperfection of our spiritual vision and to be thankful if we can glean a few handfuls of truth.

Let us notice, for one thing, in these verses, *what the Lord Jesus says of Himself.* He proclaims, "I am the light of the world."[28]

These words imply that the world needs light and is naturally in a dark condition. It is so in a moral and spiritual point of view – and it has been so for nearly 6,000 years. In ancient Egypt, Greece, and Rome, in modern England, France, and Germany, the same report is true. The vast majority of men neither see nor understand the value of their souls, the true nature of God, nor the reality of a world to come! Notwithstanding all the discoveries of art and science, "darkness still covers the earth, and gross darkness the people" (Isaiah 60:2).

For this state of things, the Lord Jesus Christ declares Himself to be the only remedy. He has risen like the sun to diffuse light, and life, and peace, and salvation in the midst of a dark world. He invites all who want spiritual help and guidance to turn to Him and take Him for their leader. What the sun is to the whole solar system – the center of light, and heat, and life, and fertility – that He has come into the world to be to sinners.

Let this saying sink down into our hearts. It is weighty and full of meaning. False lights on every side invite man's attention in the present day. Reason, philosophy, earnestness, liberalism, conscience, and the voice of the Church are all, in their various ways, crying loudly that they have got "the light" to show us. Their advocates know not what they say. Wretched are those who believe their high professions! He only is the true light who came into the world to save sinners, who

---

28 In this glorious expression, our Lord, we cannot doubt, declares Himself to be the promised Messiah or Savior, of whom the prophets had spoken. The Jews would remember the words – "I will give thee for a light of the Gentiles ("Isaiah 42:6; 49:6). So also Simeon had said, he would be a "light to lighten the Gentiles" (Luke 2:32).

died as our substitute on the cross and sits at God's right hand to be our Friend. "In His light we shall see light" (Psalm 36:9).

Let us notice, secondly, in these verses, *what the Lord Jesus says of those who follow Him.* He promises, "He that followeth Me shall not walk in darkness, but shall have the light of life."

To follow Christ is to commit ourselves wholly and entirely to Him as our only leader and Savior and to submit ourselves to Him in every matter, both of doctrine and practice. "Following" is only another word for "believing." It is the same act of soul, only seen from a different point of view. As Israel followed the pillar of cloud and fire in all their journeyings – moving whenever it moved, stopping whenever it tarried, asking no questions, marching on in faith – so must a man deal with Christ. He must "follow the Lamb wherever he goes" (Revelation 14:4).

He that so follows Christ shall "not walk in darkness." He shall not be left in ignorance like the many around him. He shall not grope in doubt and uncertainty but shall see the way to heaven and know where he is going. He "shall have the light of life." He shall feel within him the light of God's countenance shining on him. He shall find in his conscience and understanding a living light, which nothing can altogether quench. The lights with which many please themselves shall go out in the valley of the shadow of death and prove worse than useless. But the light that Christ gives to every one that follows Him shall never fail.

Let us notice, lastly, in these verses, *what the Lord Jesus says of His enemies.* He tells the Pharisees that with all their pretended wisdom, they were ignorant of God. "Ye neither know Me nor my Father: if ye had known Me, ye should have known my Father also."

Ignorance like this is only too common. There are thousands who are conversant with many branches of human learning and can even argue and reason about religion, and yet know nothing really about God. That there is such a Being as God they fully admit. But His character and attributes revealed in Scripture, His holiness, His purity, His justice, His perfect knowledge, His unchangeableness are things with which they are little acquainted. In fact, the subject of God's nature and character makes them uncomfortable, and they do not like to dwell upon it.

The grand secret of knowing God is to draw near to Him through

Jesus Christ. Approached from this side, there is nothing that need make us afraid. Viewed from this standpoint, God is the sinner's friend. God, out of Christ, may well fill us with alarm. How shall we dare to look at so high and holy a Being? God in Christ is full of mercy, grace, and peace. His law's demands are satisfied. His holiness need not make us afraid. Christ in one word is the way and door by which we must ever draw near to the Father. If we know Christ, we shall know the Father. It is His own word – "No man cometh unto the Father but by Me" (John 14:6). Ignorance of Christ is the root of ignorance of God. Wrong at the starting point, the whole sum of a man's religion is full of error.

And now, where are we ourselves? Do we know? Many are living and dying in a kind of fog. Where are we going? Can we give a satisfactory answer? Hundreds go out of existence in utter uncertainty. Let us leave nothing uncertain that concerns our everlasting salvation. Christ, the light of the world, is for us as well as for others, if we humbly follow Him, cast our souls on Him, and become His disciples. Let us not, like thousands, waste our lives in doubting, and arguing, and reasoning, but simply follow. The child that says, "I will not learn anything until I know something" will never learn at all. The man that says, "I must first understand everything before I become a Christian," will die in his sins. Let us begin by "following," and then we shall find light.

John 8:21-30

Then Jesus said again unto them, I am going away, and ye shall seek me, but ye shall die in your sins; where I go, ye shall not be able to come. Then the Jews said, Will he kill himself? because he says, Where I go, ye shall not be able to come. And he said unto them, Ye are from below, I am from above; ye are of this world, I am not of this world. Therefore I said unto you that ye shall die in your sins, for if ye do not believe that I AM, ye shall die in your sins. And said they unto him, Who art thou? Then Jesus said unto them, He that I said unto you also from the beginning. I have many things to say and to judge regarding you, but he that sent me

*is true; and those things which I have heard of him, I speak
in the world. But they did not understand that he spoke to
them of the Father. Then Jesus said unto them, When ye
have lifted up the Son of man, then ye shall know that I AM
and that I do nothing of myself, but as my Father has taught
me, I speak these things. And he that sent me is with me: the
Father has not left me alone, for I always do those things that
please him. As he spoke these words, many believed in him.*

This passage contains deep things, so deep that we have no line to
fathom them. As we read it we should call to mind the Psalmist's words
– "Thy thoughts are very deep" (Psalm 92:5). But it also contains, in the
opening verses, some things which are clear, plain, and unmistakable.
To these let us give our attention and root them firmly in our hearts.

We learn, for one thing, *that it is possible to seek Christ in vain.* Our
Lord says to the unbelieving Jews, "Ye shall seek Me, and shall die in
your sins." He meant, by these words, that the Jews would one day seek
Him in vain.

The lesson before us is a very painful one. That such a Savior as the
Lord Jesus, so full of love, so willing to save, should ever be sought
"in vain" is a sorrowful thought. Yet so it is! A man may have many
religious feelings about Christ without any saving religion. Sickness,
sudden affliction, the fear of death, the failure of usual sources of comfort – all these causes may draw out of a man a good deal of "religious-
ness." Under the immediate pressure of these, he may say his prayers
fervently, exhibit a strong spiritual feeling, and profess for a season to
"seek Christ" and be a different man. And yet all this time his heart
may never be touched at all! Take away the peculiar circumstances that
affected him, and he may possibly return at once to his old ways. He
sought Christ "in vain," because he sought Him from false motives,
and not with his whole heart.

Unhappily this is not all. There is such a thing as a settled habit of
resisting light and knowledge, until we seek Christ "in vain." Scripture
and experience alike prove that men may reject God until God rejects
them and will not hear their prayer. They may go on stifling their
convictions, quenching the light of conscience, fighting against their

own better knowledge, until God is provoked to give them over and let them alone. It is not for nothing that these words are written – "Then shall they call upon Me, but I will not answer; they shall seek Me early, but they shall not find Me: for that they hated knowledge, and did not choose the fear of the Lord" (Proverbs 1:28, 29). Such cases may not be common; but they are possible, and they are sometimes seen. Some ministers can testify that they have visited people on their deathbeds who seem to seek Christ and yet to seek in vain.

There is no safety but in seeking Christ while He may be found and calling on Him while He is near – seeking Him with a true heart and calling on Him with an honest spirit. Such seeking, we may be very sure, is never in vain. It will never be recorded of such seekers that they "died in their sins." He that really comes to Christ shall never be "cast out." The Lord has solemnly declared that "I do not desire the death of him that dies" – and that "He delights in mercy" (Ezekiel 18:32; Micah 7:18).

We learn for another thing, *how wide is the difference between Christ and the ungodly.* Our Lord says to the unbelieving Jews – "Ye are from beneath, I am from above: ye are of this world, I am not of this world."

These words, no doubt, have a special application to our Lord Jesus Christ Himself. In the highest and most literal sense, there never was but One who could truly say, "I am from above – I am not of this world." That One is He who came forth from the Father and was before the world – even the Son of God.

But there is a lower sense in which these words are applicable to all Christ's living members. Compared to the thoughtless multitude around them, they are "from above" and "not of this world," like their Master. The thoughts of the ungodly are about things beneath; the true Christian's affections are set on things above. The ungodly man is full of this world; its cares, and pleasures, and profits absorb his whole attention. The true Christian, though in the world, is not of it; his citizenship is in heaven, and his best things are yet to come.

The true Christian will do well never to forget this line of demarcation. If he loves his soul and desires to serve God, he must be content to find himself separated from many around him by a gulf that cannot be passed. He may not like to seem peculiar and unlike others; but it is the certain consequence of grace reigning within him. He may find it brings on him hatred, ridicule, and hard speeches; but it is the cup which his Master drank and of which his Master forewarned all His disciples. "If ye were of the world, the world would love His own, but because ye are not of the world, but I have chosen you out of the world, therefore the world hates you" (John 15:19). Then let the Christian never be ashamed to stand alone and show his colors. He must carry the cross if he would wear the crown. If he has within him a new principle "from above," it must be seen.

We learn, lastly, *how dreadful is the end to which unbelief can bring man.* Our Lord says to his enemies, "If ye believe not that I am He, ye shall die in your sins."

These solemn words are invested with peculiar solemnity when we consider from whose lips they came. Who is this that speaks of men dying "in their sins," unpardoned, unforgiven, unfit to meet God – of men going into another world with all their sins upon them? He that says this is no other than the Savior of mankind, who laid down His life for His sheep – the loving, gracious, merciful, compassionate Friend of sinners. It is Christ Himself! Let this simple fact not be overlooked.

They are greatly mistaken who suppose that it is harsh and unkind to speak of hell and future punishment. How can such people get over such language as that which is before us? How can they account for many a like expression which our Lord used, and specially for such passages as those in which He speaks of the "worm that dieth not, and the fire that is not quenched" (Mark 9:46)? They cannot answer these questions. Misled by a false charity and a morbid amiability, they are condemning the plain teaching of the Scripture and are wise above that which is written.

Let us settle it in our minds, as one of the great foundation truths of our faith that there is a hell. Just as we believe firmly that there is an eternal heaven for the godly, so let us believe firmly that there is an eternal hell for the wicked. Let us never suppose that there is any lack of charity in speaking of hell. Let us rather maintain that it is the highest love to warn men plainly of danger and to beseech them to "flee from the wrath to come." It was Satan, the deceiver, murderer, and liar, who said to Eve in the beginning, "Ye shall not surely die" (Genesis 3:4). To shrink from telling men that except they believe they will "die in their sins" may please the devil, but surely it cannot please God.

Finally, let us never forget that *unbelief is the special sin that ruins men's souls.* Had the Jews believed on our Lord, all manner of sin and blasphemy might have been forgiven them. But unbelief bars the door in mercy's face and cuts off hope. Let us watch and pray hard against it. Immorality slays its thousands, but unbelief its tens of thousands. One of the strongest sayings ever used by our Lord was this – "He that believeth not shall be damned" (Mark 16:16).

John 8:31-36

Then Jesus said to those Jews who had believed him, If ye abide in my word, ye shall be my disciples indeed; and ye shall know the truth, and the truth shall set you free. They answered him, We are Abraham's seed, and we have never served anyone; how sayest thou, Ye shall be set free? Jesus answered them, Verily, verily, I say unto you, Whosoever commits sin is the slave of sin. And the slave does not abide in the house for ever, but the Son abides for ever. If the Son therefore shall set you free, ye shall be free indeed.

These verses show us, for one thing, *the importance of steady perseverance in Christ's service.* There were many, it seems, at this particular period, who professed to believe on our Lord and expressed a desire to become His disciples. There is nothing to show that they had true faith. They appear to have acted under the influence of temporary excitement without considering what they were doing. And to them our Lord addresses this instructive warning – "If ye continue in My word, then are ye My disciples indeed."

This sentence contains a mine of wisdom. To make a beginning in religious life is comparatively easy. Not a few mixed motives assist us. The love of novelty, the praise of well-meaning but imprudent professors, the secret self-satisfaction of feeling "how good I am," the universal excitement attending a new position – all these things combine to aid the young beginner. Aided by them he begins to run the race that leads to heaven, lays aside many bad habits, takes up many good ones, has many comfortable frames and feelings, and gets on splendidly for a time. But when the newness of his position is past and gone, when the freshness of his feelings is rubbed off and lost, when the world and the devil begin to pull hard at him, when the weakness of his own heart begins to appear, then it is that he finds out the real difficulties of vital Christianity. Then it is that he discovers the deep wisdom of our Lord's saying now before us. It is not beginning, but "continuing" a religious profession, that is the test of true grace.

We should remember these things in forming our estimate of other people's religion. No doubt we ought to be thankful when we see any one ceasing to do evil and learning to do well. We must not "despise the day of small things" (Zechariah 4:10). But we must not forget that to begin is one thing, and to go on is quite another. Patient continuance in well-doing is the only sure evidence of grace. Not he that runs fast and furiously at first, but he that keeps up his speed is he that "runs so as to obtain." By all means let us be hopeful when we see anything like conversion. But let us not make too sure that it is real conversion, until time has set its seal upon it. Time and wear test metals and prove whether they are solid or plated. Time and wear, in like manner, are the surest tests of a man's religion. Where there is spiritual life there will be continuance and steady perseverance. It is the man who goes on as well as begins that is "the disciple indeed."

These verses show us, for another thing, *the nature of true slavery.* The Jews were fond of boasting, though without any just cause, that they were politically free and were not in bondage to any foreign power. Our Lord reminds them that there was another bondage to which they were giving no heed, although enslaved by it. "Whosoever commits sin is the slave of sin."

How true that is! How many on every side are total slaves, although they do not acknowledge it! They are led captive by their besetting corruptions and infirmities and seem to have no power to get free. Ambition, the love of money, the passion for drink, the craving for pleasure and excitement, gambling, gluttony, illicit relationships – all these are so many tyrants among men. Each and all have crowds of unhappy prisoners bound hand and foot in their chains. The wretched prisoners will not admit their bondage. They will even boast sometimes that they are eminently *free*. But many of them know better. There are times when the iron enters into their souls, and they feel bitterly that they are slaves.

There is no slavery like this. Sin is indeed the hardest of all taskmasters. Misery and disappointment in the way, despair and hell in the end – these are the only wages that sin pays to its servants. To deliver men from this bondage is the grand object of the Gospel. To awaken people to a sense of their degradation, to show them their chains, to make them arise and struggle to be free – this is the great end for which Christ sent forth His ministers. Happy is he who has opened his eyes and found out his danger. To know that we are being led captive is the very first step toward deliverance.

These verses, show us, lastly, *the nature of true liberty.* Our Lord declares this to the Jews in one comprehensive sentence. He says, "If the Son shall make you free, ye shall be free indeed."

Liberty, most Englishmen know, is rightly esteemed one of the highest temporal blessings. Freedom from foreign dominion, a free constitution, free trade, a free press, civil and religious liberty – what a world of meaning lies beneath these phrases! How many would sacrifice life and fortune to maintain the things which they represent! Yet, after all our boasting, there are many so-called freemen who are nothing better than slaves. There are many who are totally ignorant of the highest, purest form of liberty. The noblest liberty is that which is the property of the true Christian. Those only are perfectly free people whom the Son of God "makes free." All else will sooner or later be found slaves.

Wherein does the liberty of true Christians consist? Of what is their freedom made up? They are freed from the guilt and consequences of sin by the blood of Christ. Justified, pardoned, forgiven, they can look forward boldly to the day of judgment and cry "Who shall lay anything to our charge? Who is he that condemneth?" They are freed from the power of sin by the grace of Christ's Spirit. Sin has no longer dominion over them. Renewed, converted, sanctified, they mortify and tread down sin and are no longer led captive by it. Liberty, like this, is the portion of all true Christians in the day that they flee to Christ by faith and commit their souls to Him. That day they become free men. Liberty, like this, is their portion forevermore. Death cannot stop it. The grave cannot even hold their bodies for more than a little season. Those whom Christ makes free are free to all eternity.

Let us never rest until we have some personal experience of this freedom ourselves. Without it all other freedom is a worthless privilege. Free speech, free laws, political freedom, commercial freedom, national freedom – all these cannot smooth down a dying pillow, or disarm death of his sting, or fill our consciences with peace. Nothing can do that but the freedom which Christ alone bestows. He gives it freely to all who seek it humbly. Then let us never rest until it is our own.

John 8:37-47

I know that ye are Abraham's seed, but ye seek to kill me because my word has no place in you. I speak that which I have seen with my Father, and ye do that which ye have seen with your father. They answered and said unto him, Abraham is our father. Jesus said unto them, If ye were Abraham's sons, ye would do the works of Abraham. But now ye seek to kill me, a man that has told you the truth, which I have heard of God; Abraham did not do this. Ye do the deeds of your father. Then they said to him, We are not born of fornication; we have one Father, even God. Jesus said unto them, If God were your Father, ye would surely love me, for I proceeded forth and came from God; neither did I come of myself, but he sent me. Why do ye not understand my speech? even because ye cannot hear my word. Ye are of your father the devil, and the desires of your father ye desire to do. He was a murderer from the beginning and abode not in the truth because there is no truth in him. When he speaks a lie, he speaks of his own, for he is a liar and the father of it. And because I tell you the truth, ye do not believe me. Which of

you reproves me of sin? And if I say the truth, why do ye not
believe me? He that is of God hears God's words; ye therefore
hear them not because ye are not of God.

There are things taught in this passage of Scripture which are peculiarly truth for the times. Well would it be for the Churches if all Christians would ponder carefully the matter which it contains.

We are taught for one thing *the ignorant self-righteousness of the natural man*. We find the Jews pluming themselves on their natural descent from Abraham, as if that must of necessity cover all deficiencies – "Abraham is our father." We find them going even further than this and claiming to be God's special favorites and God's own family – "We have one Father, even God." They forgot that fleshly relationship to Abraham was useless, unless they shared Abraham's grace. They forgot that God's choice of their father to be head of a favored nation was never meant to carry salvation to the children, unless they walked in their father's footsteps. All this in their blind self-conceit they refused to see. "We are Jews. We are God's children. We are the true Church. We are in the covenant. We must be all right." This was their whole argument!

Strange as it may seem, there are multitudes of so-called Christians who are exactly like these Jews. Their whole religion consists of a few notions neither wiser nor better than those propounded by the enemies of our Lord. They will tell you "that they are regular Church people; they have been baptized; they go to the Lord's table" – but they can tell you no more. Of all the essential doctrines of the Gospel they are totally ignorant. Of faith, and grace, and repentance, and holiness, and spiritual mindedness, they know nothing at all. Unquestionably they are Churchmen, and so they hope to go to heaven! There are myriads in this condition. It sounds sad, but unhappily it is only too true.

Let us settle firmly in our minds that connection with a good Church and good ancestors is no proof whatever that we ourselves are in a way to be saved. We need something more than this. We must be joined to Christ himself by a living faith. We must know something experimentally of the work of the Spirit in our hearts. "Church principles" and "sound Churchmanship" are fine words and excellent party cries.

But they will not deliver our souls from the wrath to come or give us boldness in the day of judgment.

We are taught for another thing *the true marks of spiritual sonship.* Our Lord makes this point most plain by two mighty sayings. Did the Jews say, "We have Abraham to our father"? He replies, "If ye were Abraham's children ye would do the work of Abraham." Did the Jews say, "We have one Father, even God"? He replies, "If God were your Father ye would love Me."

Let these two sayings of Christ sink down into our hearts. They supply an answer to two of the most mischievous, yet most common, errors of the present day. What more common, on one side, than vague talk about the universal Fatherhood of God? "All men," we are told, "are God's children, whatever be their creed or religion; all are finally to have a place in the Father's house, "where there are many mansions." What more common, on another side, than high-sounding statements about the effect of baptism and the privileges of Church membership?

"By baptism," we are confidently told, "all baptized people are made children of God; all members of the Church, without distinction, have a right to be addressed as sons and daughters of the Lord Almighty."

Statements like these can never be reconciled with the plain language of our Lord in the passage before us. If words mean anything, no man is really a child of God, who does not love Jesus Christ. The charitable judgment of a baptismal service or the hopeful estimate of a catechism may call him by the name of a son and reckon him among God's children. But the reality of sonship to God and all its blessings, no one possesses who does not love the Lord Jesus Christ in sincerity (Ephesians 6:24). In matters like these we need not be shaken by mere assertions. We may well afford to despise the charge of undervaluing the sacraments. We have only to ask one question – "What is written? What says the Lord?" And with this saying before us, we can only come to one conclusion – "Where there is no love to Christ, there is no sonship to God."

We are taught, lastly, in these verses, *the reality and character of the devil.* Our Lord speaks of him as one whose personality and existence are beyond dispute. In solemn words of stern rebuke He says to His unbelieving enemies, "Ye are of your father the devil" – led by him, doing his will, and showing unhappily that you are like him. And then He paints his picture in dark colors, describing him as a "murderer" from the beginning, as a "liar" and the father of lies.

There is a devil! We have a mighty invisible enemy always near us – one who never slumbers and never sleeps – one who is about our path and about our bed, and spies out all our ways, and will never leave us until we die. He is a murderer! His great aim and object is to ruin us forever and kill our souls. To destroy, to rob us of eternal life, to bring us down to the second death in hell are the things for which he is unceasingly working. He is ever going about, seeking whom he may devour. He is a liar! He is continually trying to deceive us by false representations, just as he deceived Eve at the beginning. He is always telling us that good is evil and evil good – truth is falsehood and falsehood truth – the broad way good and the narrow way bad. Millions are led captive by his deceit and follow him, both rich and poor, both high and low, both learned and unlearned. Lies are his chosen weapons. By lies he slays many.

These are dreadful things; but they are true. Let us live as if we believed them. Let us not be like many who mock, and sneer, and scoff, and deny the existence of the very being who is invisibly leading them to hell. Let us believe there is a devil, and watch, and pray, and fight hard against his temptations. Strong as he is, there is One stronger than him, who said to Peter, "I have prayed for thee, that thy faith fail not," and who still intercedes at God's right hand. Let us commit our souls to Him (Luke 22:32). With such a being as the devil going to and fro in the world, we never need wonder to see evil abounding. But with Christ on our side, we need not be afraid. Greater is He that is for us than he that is against us. It is written, "Resist the devil, and he shall flee from you." "The God of peace shall bruise Satan under your feet shortly" (James 4:7; Romans 16:20).

John 8:48-59

Then the Jews answered, and said unto him, Do we not say well that thou art a Samaritan and hast a demon? Jesus answered, I do not have a demon; but I honour my Father, and ye do dishonour me. And I seek not my own glory; there is one that seeks it and judges. Verily, verily, I say unto you, If anyone keeps my word, he shall not see death forever. Then the Jews said unto him, Now we know that thou hast a demon. Abraham died and the prophets; and thou sayest, If a man keeps my word, he shall not taste death forever? Art thou greater than our father Abraham who died? and the prophets died; whom makest thou thyself? Jesus answered, If I glorify myself, my glory is nothing; it is my Father that glorifies me, of whom ye say that he is your God; yet ye have not known him, but I know him; and if I should say, I do not know him, I shall be a liar like unto you; but I know him and keep his word. Your father Abraham rejoiced to see my day, and he saw it and was glad. Then the Jews said unto him, Thou art not yet fifty years old, and hast thou seen Abraham? Jesus said unto them, Verily, verily, I say unto you, Before Abraham was, I AM. Then they took up stones to cast at him, but Jesus concealed himself and went out of the temple, and going through the midst of them, went away.

We should observe, first, in this passage, *what blasphemous and slanderous language was addressed to our Lord by His enemies.* We read that the Jews "said unto Him, Say we not well that thou art a Samaritan and hast a devil?" Silenced in argument, these wicked men resorted to personal abuse. To lose temper and call names is a common sign of a defeated cause.

Nicknames, insulting epithets, and violent language are favorite weapons with the devil. When other means of carrying on his warfare fail, he stirs up his servants to smite with the tongue. Grievous indeed are the sufferings which the saints of God have had to endure from the tongue in every age. Their characters have been slandered. Evil reports have been circulated about them. Lying stories have been diligently invented and greedily swallowed about their conduct. No wonder that David said, "Deliver my soul, O Lord, from lying lips, and from a deceitful tongue" (Psalm 120:2).

The true Christian in the present day must never be surprised to find that he has constant trials to endure from this quarter. Sinful human nature never changes. So long as he serves the world and walks in the broad way, little perhaps will be said against him. Once let him take up the cross and follow Christ, and there is no lie too monstrous and no story too absurd for some to tell against him and for others to believe. But let him take comfort in the thought that he is only drinking the cup which his blessed Master drank before him. The lies of his enemies do him no injury in heaven, whatever they may on earth. Let him bear them patiently, and not fret or lose his temper. When Christ was reviled, "He reviled not again" (1 Peter 2:23). Let the Christian do likewise.

We should observe, secondly, *what glorious encouragement our Lord holds out to His believing people.* We read that He said, "I tell you the solemn truth, if anyone obeys my teaching, he will never see death."

Of course these words do not mean that true Christians shall never die. On the contrary, we all know that they must go down to the grave, and cross the river just like others. But the words do mean that they shall not be hurt by the second death – that final ruin of the whole man in hell of which the first death is only a faint type or figure (Revelation 21:8). And they do mean that the sting of the first death shall be removed from the true Christian. His flesh may fail, and his bones may be racked with strong pain; but the bitter sense of unpardoned sins shall not crush him down. This is the worst part of death – and in this he shall have the "victory through our Lord Jesus Christ" (1 Corinthians 15:57).

This blessed promise, we must not forget to notice, is the peculiar property of the man who "keeps Christ's sayings." That expression, it is clear, can never be applicable to the mere outward professing Christian, who neither knows nor cares anything about the Gospel. It belongs to him who receives into his heart and obeys in his life the message which the Lord Jesus brought from heaven. It belongs, in short, to those who are Christians, not in name and form only, but in deed and in truth. It is written – "He that overcomes shall not be hurt by the second death" (Revelation 2:11).

We should observe, thirdly, in this passage, *what clear knowledge of Christ Abraham possessed.* We read that our Lord said to the Jews, "Your father Abraham rejoiced to see My day: and he saw it and was glad."

When our Lord used these remarkable words, Abraham had been dead and buried at least 1850 years! And yet he is said to have seen our Lord's day! How astonishing that sounds! Yet it was quite true. Not only did Abraham "see" our Lord and talk to Him when He "appeared unto him in the plains of Mamre," the night before Sodom was destroyed (Genesis 18:1), but by faith he looked forward to the day of our Lord's incarnation yet to come, and as he looked he "was glad." That he saw many things, through a glass darkly, we need not doubt. That he could have explained fully the whole manner and circumstances of our Lord's sacrifice on Calvary, we are not obliged to suppose. But we need not shrink from believing that he saw in the far distance a Redeemer, whose advent would finally make all the earth rejoice. And as he saw it, he "was glad."

The plain truth is that we are too apt to forget that there never was but one way of salvation, one Savior, and one hope for sinners, and that Abraham and all the Old Testaments saints looked to the same Christ that we look to ourselves. We shall do well to call to mind the Seventh Article of the Church of England – "The Old Testament is not contrary to the New – for both in the Old and New Testament everlasting life is offered through Christ, who is the only Mediator between God and man, being both God and man. Wherefore they are not to be heard, who assume that the old Fathers did look only for transitory promises." This is truth that we must never forget in reading the Old Testament. This is sound speech that cannot be condemned.

We should observe, lastly, in this prophecy, *how distinctly our Lord declares His own pre-existence.* We read that He said to the Jews, "Before Abraham was, I am."[29]

---

29   Let us carefully note what a strong proof we have here of the pre-existence and divinity of our Lord Jesus Christ. He applies to Himself the very name by which God made Himself known when He undertook to redeem Israel. It was "I AM" who brought them out of the land of Egypt. It was "I AM" who died for us upon the cross. The amazing strength of the foundation of a sinner's hope appears here.

Without a controversy, these remarkable words are a great deep. They contain things which we have no eyes to see through or mind to fathom. But if language means anything, they teach us that our Lord Jesus Christ existed long before He came into the world. Before the days of Abraham, He was. Before man was created, He was. In short, they teach us that the Lord Jesus was no mere man like Moses or David. He was One whose goings forth were from everlasting, the same yesterday, today, and forever, very and eternal God.

Deep as these words are, they are full of practical comfort. They show us the length, and breadth, and depth, and height of that great foundation on which sinners are invited to rest their souls. He to whom the Gospel bids us come with our sins, and believe for pardon and peace, is no mere man. He is nothing less than very God, and therefore "able to save to the uttermost" all who come to Him. Then let us begin coming to Him with confidence. Let us continue leaning on Him without fear. The Lord Jesus Christ is the true God and our eternal life is secure.

John Chapter 9

John 9:1-12

And as Jesus passed by, he saw a man who was blind from his birth. And his disciples asked him, saying, Rabbi, who sinned, this man or his parents, that he was born blind? Jesus answered, Neither has this man sinned nor his parents, but that the works of God should be made manifest in him. It is expedient that I do the works of him that sent me while it is day; the night comes, when no one can work. As long as I am in the world, I am the light of the world. When he had thus spoken, he spat on the ground and made clay of the spittle, and he anointed the eyes of the blind man with the clay and said unto him, Go, wash in the pool of Siloam (which is by interpretation, Sent). Then he went and washed and came back seeing. The neighbours, therefore, and those who before had seen him that he was blind said, Is not this he that sat and begged? Some said, This is he; others said, He is like him; but he said, I am he. Then they said unto him, How were thine eyes opened? He answered and said, A man that is called Jesus made clay and anointed my eyes and said unto me, Go to the pool of Siloam, and wash; and I went and washed, and I received sight. Then said they unto him, Where is he? He said, I know not.

THE CHAPTER WE NOW begin records one of the few great works of Christ which John has reported. It tells us how our Lord gave sight to a man who had been "blind from his birth."[30] Here, as elsewhere in

---

30   In the miracle which occupies the whole of this chapter, the following special circumstances deserve notice: (1) It is only related by John. (2) Like each of the few miracles in John, it is described with great minuteness and particularity. (3) It is one of the four miracles wrought in

this Gospel, we find the circumstances of the miracle narrated with peculiar fullness, minuteness, and particularity. Here too, as elsewhere, we find the narrative rich in spiritual lessons.

We should observe, first, in this passage, *how much sorrow sin has brought into the world.* A sorrowful case is brought before us. We are told of a man "who was blind from his birth." A more serious affliction can hardly be conceived. Of all the bodily crosses that can be laid on man without taking away life, none perhaps is greater than the loss of sight. It cuts us off from some of the greatest enjoyments of life. It shuts us up within a narrow world of our own. It makes us painfully helpless and dependent on others. In fact, until men lose their eyesight, they never fully realize its value.

Now blindness, like every other bodily infirmity, is one of the fruits of sin. If Adam had never fallen, we cannot doubt that people would never have been blind, or deaf, or mute. The many ills that flesh is heir to, the countless pains, and diseases, and physical defects to which we are all liable, came in when the curse came upon the earth. "By one man sin entered into the world, and death by sin" (Romans 5:12).

Let us learn to hate sin with a godly hatred, as the root of more than half of our cares and sorrows. Let us fight against it, mortify it, crucify it, and abhor it both in ourselves and others. There cannot be a clearer proof that man is a fallen creature than the fact that he can love sin and take pleasure in it.

We should observe, secondly, in this passage, *what a solemn lesson Christ gives us about the use of opportunities.* He says to the disciples who asked Him about the blind man, "I must work while it is called today: the night cometh, when no man can work."

That saying was eminently true when applied to our Lord Himself. He knew well that his own earthly ministry would only last three years

---

Judaea or near Jerusalem mentioned in John. He records eight great miracles altogether: four in Galilee – turning the water into wine, healing the nobleman's son, feeding the multitude, and walking on the water; and four in Judaea – purifying the temple, healing the impotent man, restoring sight to the blind, and raising Lazarus. (4) It is one of those miracles which the Jews were especially taught to expect in Messiah's time: "In that day shall the eyes of the blind see out of obscurity (Isaiah 29:18). (5) It is one of those signs of Messiah having come, to which Jesus particularly directed John the Baptist's attention: "The blind receive their sight" (Matthew 11:5). (6) It was a miracle worked in so public a place, and on a man so well known, that it was impossible for the Jerusalem Jews to deny it.

altogether, and knowing this He diligently redeemed the time. He let slip no opportunity of doing works of mercy and attending to His Father's business. Morning, noon, and night He was always carrying on the work which the Father gave Him to do. It was His food and drink to do His Father's will and to finish His work. His whole life breathed one sentiment – "I must work – the night cometh, when no man can work."

The saying is one which should be remembered by all professing Christians. The life that we now live in the flesh is our day. Let us take care that we use it well for the glory of God and the good of our souls. Let us work out our salvation with fear and trembling, while it is called today. There is no work nor labor in the grave toward which we are all fast hastening. Let us pray, and read, and keep our Sabbaths holy, and hear God's Word, and do good in our generation like men who never forget that "the night is at hand." Our time is very short. Our daylight will soon be gone. Opportunities once lost can never be retrieved. A second lease of life is granted to no man. Then let us resist procrastination as we would resist the devil. Whatever our hand finds to do, let us do it with our might. "The night cometh, when no man can work."

We should observe, thirdly, in this passage, *what different means Christ used in working miracles on different occasions.* In healing the blind man He might, if He had thought fit, have merely touched Him with his finger or given command with His tongue. But He did not rest content with doing so. We are told that "He spat on the ground, and made clay of the spittle, and He anointed the eyes of the blind man with the clay." In all these means of course there was no inherent healing virtue. But for wise reasons the Lord was pleased to use them.

We need not doubt that in this, as in every other action of our Lord, there is an instructive lesson. It teaches us, we may well believe, that the Lord of heaven and earth will not be tied down to the use of any one means or instrumentality. In conferring blessings on man, He will work in His own way and will allow no one to prescribe to Him. Above all, it should teach those who have received anything at Christ's hands to be careful how they measure other men's experience by their own. Have we been healed by Christ and made to see and live? Let us thank God for it, and be humbled. But let us beware of saying that no other man has been healed, except he has been brought to spiritual life in precisely the same manner. The great question is – "Are the eyes of our understanding opened? Do we see? Have we spiritual life?" – Enough for us if the cure is effected and health restored. If it is, we must leave it to the great Physician to choose the instrument, the means, and the manner – the clay, the touch, or the command.

We should observe, lastly, in this passage, *the almighty power that Christ holds in His hands.* We see Him doing that which in itself was impossible. Without medicines He cures an incurable case. He actually gives eyesight to one who was born blind.

Such a miracle as this is meant to teach an old truth, which we can never know too well. It shows us that Jesus the Savior of sinners "has all power in heaven – and earth." Such mighty works could never have been done by one that was merely man. In the cure of this blind man we see nothing less than the finger of God.

Such a miracle, above all, is meant to make us hopeful about our own souls and the souls of others. Why should we despair of salvation while we have such a Savior? Where is the spiritual disease that He cannot take away? He can open the eyes of the most sinful and ignorant and make them see things they never saw before. He can send light into the darkest heart and cause blindness and prejudice to pass away.

Surely, if we are not saved, the fault will be all our own. There lives at God's right hand One who can heal us if we apply to Him. Let us take heed lest those solemn words are found true of us – "Light is come into the world but men loved darkness rather than light, because their deeds were evil" (John 3:19). "Ye will not come to Me that ye might have life" (5:40).

John 9:13-25

They brought to the Pharisees him that beforehand had been blind. And it was the sabbath day when Jesus had made the clay and had opened his eyes. Then again the Pharisees also asked him how he had received his sight. He said unto them, He put clay upon my eyes, and I washed and do see.

Therefore some of the Pharisees said, This man is not of God because he does not keep the sabbath day. Others said, How can a man that is a sinner do such signs? And there was a division among them. They said unto the blind man again, What sayest thou of him, that has opened thine eyes? He said, He is a prophet. But the Jews did not believe concerning him that he had been blind and received his sight until they called the parents of him that had received his sight. And they asked them, saying, Is this your son, who ye say was born blind? how then does he now see? His parents answered them and said, We know that this is our son and that he was born blind; but by what means he now sees, we know not; or who has opened his eyes, we know not; he is of age, ask him; he shall speak for himself. These words spoke his parents because they feared the Jews, for the Jews had agreed already that if anyone did confess that he was the Christ, he should be put out of the synagogue. Therefore his parents said, He is of age, ask him. Then they called again the man that had been blind and said unto him, Give glory to God; we know that this man is a sinner. He answered and said, Whether he is a sinner or not, I do not know; one thing I know, that having been blind, now I see.

These verses show us *how little the Jews of our Lord's time understood the right use of the Sabbath day.* We read that some of the Pharisees found fault because a blind man was miraculously healed on the Sabbath. They said, "This man is not of God, because He keepeth not the Sabbath day." A good work had manifestly been done to a helpless fellow creature. A heavy bodily infirmity had been removed. A mighty act of mercy had been performed. But the blind-hearted enemies of Christ could see no beauty in the act. They called it a breach of the Fourth Commandment!

These would-be wise men completely mistook the intention of the Sabbath. They did not see that it was "made for man" and meant for the good of man's body, mind, and soul. It was a day to be set apart from others, no doubt, and to be carefully sanctified and kept holy. But its sanctification was never intended to prevent works of necessity and acts of mercy. To heal a sick man was no breach of the Sabbath day. In finding fault with our Lord for so doing, the Jews only exposed their ignorance of their own law. They had forgotten that it is as great a sin to add to a commandment, as to take it away.

Here, as in other places, we must take care that we do not put a wrong meaning on our Lord's conduct. We must not for a moment suppose that the Sabbath is no longer binding on Christians, and that they have nothing to do with the Fourth Commandment. This is a great mistake and the root of great evil. Not one of the ten commandments has ever been repealed or put aside. Our Lord never meant the Sabbath to become a day of pleasure, or a day of business, or a day of traveling and idle dissipation. He meant it to be "kept holy" as long as the world stands. It is one thing to employ the Sabbath in works of mercy, in ministering to the sick, and doing good to the distressed. It is quite another thing to spend the day in visiting, feasting, and self-indulgence. Whatever men may please to say, the way in which we use the Sabbath is a sure test of the state of our religion. By the Sabbath may be found out whether we love communion with God. By the Sabbath may be found out whether we are in tune for heaven. By the Sabbath, in short, the secrets of many hearts are revealed. There are only too many of whom we may say with sorrow, "These men are not of God, because they keep not the Sabbath day."

These verses show us, secondly, *the desperate lengths to which prejudice will sometimes carry wicked men.* We read that the "Jews agreed that if any man did confess that Jesus was Christ, he should be put out of the synagogue." They were determined not to believe. They were resolved that no evidence should change their minds and no proofs influence their will. They were like men who shut their eyes and tie a bandage over them, and refuse to have it untied. Just as in after times they stopped their ears when Stephen preached and refused to listen when Paul made his defense, so they behaved at this period of our Lord's ministry.

Of all states of mind into which unconverted men can fall, this is by far the most dangerous to the soul. So long as a person is open, fair, and honest-minded, there is hope for him, however ignorant he may be. He may be much in the dark at present. But is he willing to follow the light, if set before him? He may be walking in the broad road with all his might. But is he ready to listen to any one who will show him a more excellent way? In a word, is he teachable, childlike, and unfettered by prejudice? If these questions can be answered satisfactorily, we never need despair about the man's soul.

The state of mind we should always desire to possess is that of the noble-minded Bereans. When they first heard the Apostle Paul preach, they listened with attention. They received the Word "with all readiness of mind." They "searched the Scriptures" and compared what they heard with God's Word. "And therefore," we are told, "many of them believed." Happy are those who go and do likewise! (Acts 17:11, 12).

These verses show us, lastly, that *nothing convinces a man so thoroughly as his own senses and feelings.* We read that the unbelieving Jews tried in vain to persuade the blind man whom Jesus healed that nothing had been done for him. They only got from him one plain answer – "One thing I know, that whereas I was blind, now I see." How the miracle had been worked, he did not pretend to explain. Whether the person who had healed him was a sinner, he did not profess to know. But that something had been done for him he stoutly maintained. He was not to be reasoned out of his senses. Whatever the Jews might think, there were two distinct facts of which he was conscious – "I was blind – now I see."

There is no kind of evidence so satisfactory as this to the heart of a real Christian. His knowledge may be small. His faith may be feeble. His doctrinal views may be at present confused and indistinct. But if Christ has really wrought a work of grace in his heart by His Spirit, he feels within him something that you cannot overthrow. "I was dark, and now I have light. I was afraid of God, and now I love Him. I was fond of sin, and now I hate it. I was blind, and now I see." Let us never rest until we know and feel within us some real work of the Holy Spirit. Let us not be content with the name and form of Christianity. Let us desire to have true experimental acquaintance with it. Feelings, no doubt, are deceitful and are not everything in religion. But if we have no inward feelings about spiritual matters, it is a very bad sign. The hungry man eats and feels strengthened; the thirsty man drinks and feels refreshed.

Surely the man who has within him the grace of God ought to be able to say, "I feel its power."

John 9:26-41

Then said they to him again, What did he do to thee? How did he open thine eyes? He answered them, I have told you already, and ye have heard; what more would ye hear? Do ye also desire to be his disciples? Then they reviled him and said, Be thou his disciple, but we are disciples of Moses. We know that God spoke unto Moses; as for this fellow, we do not know where he is from. The man answered and said unto them, Indeed this is a marvellous thing that ye do not know where he is from, and yet he has opened my eyes. Now we know that God does not hear sinners, but if anyone should fear God and do his will, him he will hear. Since the world began it has not been heard of that anyone opened the eyes of one that was born blind. If this man were not of God, he could do nothing. They answered and said unto him, Thou wast altogether born in sins, and dost thou teach us? And they cast him out. Jesus heard that they had cast him out; and finding him, he said unto him, Dost thou believe in the Son of God? He answered and said, Who is he, Lord, that I might believe in him? And Jesus said unto him, Thou hast seen him, and it is he that talks with thee. And he said, Lord, I believe. And he worshipped him. And Jesus said, For judgment I have come into this world, that those who do not see might see and that those who see might be blinded. And some of the Pharisees who were with him heard these words and said unto him, Are we blind also? Jesus said unto them, If ye were blind, ye should have no sin; but now because ye say, We see, therefore your sin abides.

We see in these verses *how much wiser the poor sometimes are than the rich*. The man whom our Lord healed of his blindness was evidently a person of very humble condition. It is written that he was one who "sat and begged" (see v. 8). Yet he saw things which the proud rulers of the Jews could not see and would not receive. He saw in our Lord's miracle an unanswerable proof of our Lord's divine commission. "If this Man were not of God," he cries, "He could do nothing." In fact, from the day of his cure his position was completely altered. He had eyes, and the Pharisees were blind.

The same thing may be seen in other places of Scripture. The servants of Pharaoh saw "the finger of God" in the plagues of Egypt, when their master's heart was hardened. The servants of Naaman saw the wisdom of Elisha's advice, when their master was turning away in a rage. The high, the great, and the noble are often the last to learn spiritual lessons. Their possessions and their position often blind the eyes of their understanding and keep them back from the kingdom of God. It is written that "not many wise men after the flesh, not many mighty, not many noble, are called" (1 Corinthians 1:26).

The Christian poor man never need be ashamed of his poverty. It is a sin to be proud, and worldly minded, and unbelieving; but it is no sin to be poor. The very riches which many long to possess are often veils over the eyes of men's souls and prevent their seeing Christ. The teaching of the Holy Spirit is more frequently to be seen among men of low degree than among men of rank and education. The words of our Lord are continually proved most true, "How hardly shall they that have riches enter into the kingdom of God" (Mark 10:23). "Thou hast hid these things from the wise and understanding and hast revealed them unto children" (Matthew 11:25).

We see, secondly, in these verses, *how cruelly and unjustly uncon-verted men will sometimes treat those who disagree with them.* When the Pharisees could not frighten the blind man who had been cured, they expelled him from the Jewish Church. Because he manfully refused to deny the evidence of his own senses, they excommunicated him and put him to an open shame. They cast him out "as a heathen man and a publican."

The temporal injury that such treatment did to a poor Jew was very great indeed. It cut him off from the outward privileges of the Jewish Church. It made him an object of scorn and suspicion among all true

Israelites. But it could do no harm to his soul. That which wicked men bind on earth is not bound in heaven. "The curse causeless shall not come" (Proverbs 26:2).

The children of God in every age have only too frequently met with like treatment. Excommunication, persecution, and imprisonment have generally been favorite weapons with ecclesiastical tyrants. Unable, like the Pharisees, to answer arguments, they have resorted to violence and injustice. Let the child of God console himself with the thought that there is a true Church out of which no man can cast him and a Church membership which no earthly power can take away. He only is blessed whom Christ calls blessed; and he only is accursed whom Christ shall pronounce accursed at the last day.

We see, thirdly, in these verses, *how great is the kindness and condescension of Christ.* No sooner was this poor blind man cast out of the Jewish Church than Jesus finds him and speaks words of comfort. He knew full well how heavy an affliction excommunication was to an Israelite and at once cheered him with kind words. He now revealed Himself more fully to this man than He did to any one except the Samaritan woman. In reply to the question, "Who is the Son of God?" He says plainly, "Thou hast both seen Him, and it is He that talketh with thee."

We have here one among many beautiful illustrations of the mind of Christ. He sees all that His people go through for His sake and feels for all, from the highest to the lowest. He keeps account of all their losses, crosses, and persecutions. "Are they not all written in His book?" (Psalm. 56:8). He knows how to come to their hearts with consolation in their time of need and to speak peace to them when all men seem to hate them. The time when men forsake us is often the very time when Christ draws near, saying, "Fear thou not, for I am with thee: be not dismayed, for I am thy God: I will strengthen thee: yea, I will help thee; I will uphold thee with the right hand of my righteousness" (Isaiah 41:10).

We see, lastly, in these verses, *how dangerous it is to possess knowledge, if we do not make a good use of it.* The rulers of the Jews were fully persuaded that they knew all religious truth. They were indignant at the very idea of being ignorant and devoid of spiritual eyesight. "Are we blind also?" they cried. And then came the mighty sentence, "If ye were blind, ye should have no sin: but now ye say, We see; therefore your sin abides."

Knowledge undoubtedly is a very great blessing. The man who cannot read and is utterly ignorant of Scripture is in a pitiable condition. He is at the mercy of any false teacher who comes across him and may be taught to take up any absurd creed or to follow any vicious practice. Almost any education is better than no education at all.

But when knowledge only sticks in a man's head and has no influence over his heart and life, it becomes a most perilous possession. And when, in addition to this, its possessor is self-conceited and self-satisfied and imagines he knows everything, the result is one of the worst states of soul into which man can fall. There is far more hope about him who says, "I am a poor blind sinner and want God to teach me" than about him who is ever saying, "I know it, I know it, I am not ignorant" and yet cleaves to his sins. The sin of that man "abides."

Let us use diligently whatever religious knowledge we possess and ask continually that God would give us more. Let us never forget that the devil himself is a creature of vast head knowledge and yet none the better for it, because it is not rightly used. Let our constant prayer be that which David so often sent up in the hundred and nineteenth Psalm. "Lord, teach me thy statutes: give me understanding: unite my heart to fear Thy name."

John Chapter 10

John 10:1-9

Verily, verily, I say unto you, He that enters not by the door into the sheepfold, but climbs up some other way, the same is a thief and a robber. But he that enters in by the door is the shepherd of the sheep. To him the porter opens, and the sheep hear his voice, and he calls his own sheep by name and leads them out. And when he puts forth his own sheep, he goes before them; and the sheep follow him, for they know his voice. And they will not follow a stranger, but will flee from him, for they do not know the voice of strangers. Jesus spoke this parable unto them, but they did not understand what it was that he spoke unto them. Then said Jesus unto them again, Verily, verily, I say unto you, I AM the door of the sheep. All that ever came before me are thieves and robbers, but the sheep did not hear them. I AM the door; whosoever enters in by me shall be saved and shall go in and out and find pasture.

THE CHAPTER WE HAVE now begun is closely connected with the preceding one. The parable before us was spoken with direct reference to the blind teachers of the Jewish Church. The Scribes and Pharisees were the people our Lord had in view, when He described the false shepherd. The very men who had just said, "We see," were denounced with holy boldness, as "thieves and robbers."

We have, for one thing, in these verses, *a vivid picture of a false teacher of religion.* Our Lord says that he is one who "enters not by the door into the sheepfold, but climbs up some other way."

The "door," in this sentence, must evidently mean something far more than outward calling and commission. The Jewish teachers, at any rate, were not deficient in this point – they could probably trace up their orders in direct succession to Aaron himself. Ordination is no proof whatever that a man is fit to show others the way to heaven. He may have been regularly set apart by those who have authority to call ministers, and yet all his life may never come near the door and at last may die nothing better than "a thief and a robber."

The true sense of the "door" must be sought in our Lord's own interpretation. It is Christ Himself who is "the door." The true shepherd of souls is he who enters the ministry with a single eye to Christ, desiring to glorify Christ, doing all in the strength of Christ, preaching Christ's doctrine, walking in Christ's steps, and laboring to bring men and women to Christ. The false shepherd of souls is he who enters the ministerial office with little or no thought about Christ, from worldly and self-exalting motives, but from no desire to exalt Jesus and the great salvation that is in Him. Christ, in one word, is the grand touchstone of the minister of religion. The man who makes much of Christ is a pastor after God's own heart, whom God delights to honor. The minister who makes little of Christ is one whom God regards as an impostor – as one who has climbed up to his holy office not by the door but by "some other way."

The sentence before us is a sorrowful and humbling one. That it condemns the Jewish teachers of our Lord's time all men can see. There was no "door" in their ministry. They taught nothing rightly about Messiah. They rejected Christ Himself when He appeared – but all men do not see that the sentence condemns thousands of so-called Christian teachers, quite as much as the leaders and teachers of the Jews. Thousands of ordained men in the present day know nothing whatever about Christ, except His name. They have not entered "the door" themselves, and they are unable to show it to others. Well would it be for Christendom if this were more widely known and more seriously considered! Unconverted ministers are the dry-rot of the Church. "When the blind lead the blind" both must fall into the ditch. If we would know the value of a man's ministry, we must never fail to ask, Where is the Lamb? Where is the Door? Does he bring forward Christ and give Him his rightful place?

We have, for another thing, in these verses, *a peculiar picture of true Christians.* Our Lord describes them as sheep who "hear the voice of a true Shepherd and know His voice;" and as "sheep who will not follow a stranger, but will flee from him, for they know not the voice of strangers."

The thing taught in these words is a very curious one and may seem "foolishness" to the world. There is a spiritual instinct in most true believers, which generally enables them to distinguish between true and false teaching. When they hear unsound religious instruction, there is something within them that says, "This is wrong." When they hear the real truth as it is in Jesus, there is something in their hearts which responds, "This is right." The careless man of the world may see no difference whatever between minister and minister, sermon and sermon. The poorest sheep of Christ, as a general rule, will "distinguish things that differ," though he may sometimes be unable to explain why.

Let us beware of despising this spiritual instinct. Whatever a sneering world may please to say, it is one of the peculiar marks of the indwelling of the Holy Spirit. As such, it is specially mentioned by John, when he says, "Ye have an unction from the Holy One, and ye know all things" (1 John 2:20). Let us rather pray for it daily, in order that we may be kept from the influence of false shepherds. To lose all power of distinguishing between bitter and sweet is one of the worst symptoms of bodily disease. To be unable to see any difference between law and gospel, truth and error, Protestantism and Popery, the doctrine of Christ and the doctrine of man is a sure proof that we are yet dead in heart and need conversion.

We have, lastly, in these verses, *a most instructive picture of Christ Himself.* He utters one of those golden sayings which ought to be dear to all true Christians. They apply to people as well as to ministers. "I am the door: by me if any man enter in, he shall be saved, and shall go in and out, and find pasture." We are all by nature separate and far off from God. Sin, like a great barrier wall, rises between us and our Maker. The sense of guilt makes us afraid of Him. The sense of His holiness keeps us at a distance from Him.

Born with a heart at enmity with God, we become more and more alienated from Him, by practice, the longer we live. The very first questions in religion that must be answered are these – "How can I draw near to God? How can I be justified? How can a sinner like me be reconciled to my Maker?"

The Lord Jesus Christ has provided an answer to these mighty questions. By His sacrifice for us on the cross, He has opened a way through the great barrier and provided pardon and peace for sinners. He has "suffered for sin, the just for the unjust, to bring us to God." He has opened a way into the holiest through His blood, by which we may draw near to God with boldness and approach God without fear. And now He is able to save to the uttermost all who come unto God by Him. In the highest sense He is "the door." No one "can come to the Father" but by Him.

Let us take heed that we use this door and do not merely stand outside looking at it. It is a door free and open to the chief of sinners – "If any man enter in by it, he shall be saved." It is a door within which we shall find a full and constant supply for every need of our souls. We shall find that we can "go in and out" and enjoy liberty and peace. The day comes when this door will be shut forever, and men shall strive to enter in but not be able. Then let us make sure work of our own salvation. Let us not stand tarrying outside and halting between two opinions. Let us enter in and be saved.

John 10:10-18

The thief comes not but for to steal and to kill and to destroy the sheep; I am come that they might have life and that they might have it in abundance. I AM the good shepherd; the good shepherd gives his life for the sheep. But the hireling, who is not a shepherd, whose own the sheep are not, sees the wolf coming and leaves the sheep and flees; and the wolf catches them and scatters the sheep. The hireling flees because he is a hireling, and the sheep do not belong to him. I AM the good shepherd, and know my sheep and am known of mine. As the Father knows me, even so I know the Father, and I lay down my soul for the sheep. And I have other sheep which are not of this fold; it is expedient that I bring them also, and they shall hear my voice, and there shall be one fold and one shepherd. Therefore does my Father love me, because I lay down my soul that I might take it again. No man takes it from me, but I lay it down of myself. I have power to lay it down, and I have power to take it again. This commandment I have received of my Father.

These verses show us, for one thing, *the great object for which Christ came into the world.* He says, I have come that men "might have life, and that they might have it more abundantly."

The truth contained in these words is of vast importance. They supply an antidote to many crude and unsound notions which are abroad in the world. Christ did not come to be only a teacher of new morality, or an example of holiness and self-denial, or a founder of new ceremonies, as some have vainly asserted. He left heaven and dwelt for thirty-three years on earth for far higher ends than these. He came to procure eternal life for man by the price of His own vicarious death. He came to be a mighty fountain of spiritual life for all mankind, to which sinners coming by faith might drink; and drinking, might live for evermore. By Moses came laws, rules, ordinances, ceremonies. By Christ came grace, truth, and eternal life.

Important as this doctrine is, it requires to be fenced with one word of caution. We must not overstrain the meaning of our Lord Jesus Christ's words. We must not suppose that eternal life was a thing entirely unknown until Christ came, or that the Old Testament saints were in utter darkness about the world to come. The way of life by faith in a Savior was a way well known to Abraham and Moses and David. A Redeemer and a Sacrifice was the hope of all God's children from Abel down to John the Baptist; but their vision of these things was necessarily imperfect. They saw them afar off, and not distinctly. They saw them in outline only, and not completely. It was the coming of Christ which made all things plain and caused the shadows to pass away. Life and immortality were brought into full light by the Gospel.

In short, to use our Lord's own words, even those who had life had it "more abundantly," when Christ came into the world.

These verses show us, for another thing, *one of the principal offices which Jesus Christ fills for true Christians.* Twice over our Lord uses an expression which, to an Eastern hearer, would be singularly full of meaning. Twice over he says emphatically, "I am the Good Shepherd." It is a saying rich in consolation and instruction.

Like a good shepherd, Christ knows all His believing people. Their names, their families, their dwelling-places, their circumstances, their private history, their experience, their trials – with all these things Jesus is perfectly acquainted. There is not a thing about the least and lowest of them with which He is not familiar. The children of this world may not know Christians and may count their lives folly; but the Good Shepherd knows them thoroughly and, wonderful to say, though He knows them, does not despise them.

Like a Good Shepherd, Christ cares tenderly for all His believing people. He provides for all their needs in the wilderness of this world and leads them by the right way to a city of habitation. He bears patiently with their many weaknesses and infirmities and does not cast them off because they are wayward, erring, sick, footsore, or lame. He guards and protects them against all their enemies, as Jacob did the flock of Laban; and of those that the Father has given Him, He will be found at last to have lost none.

Like a Good Shepherd, Christ lays down His life for the sheep. He did it once for all, when He was crucified for them. When He saw that nothing could deliver them from hell and the devil but His blood, He willingly made His soul an offering for their sins. The merit of that death He is now presenting before the Father's throne. The sheep are saved for evermore, because the Good Shepherd died for them. This is indeed a love that passes knowledge! "Greater love hath no man than this, that a man lay down his life for his friends" (John 15:13).

Let us only take heed that this office of Christ is not set before us in vain. It will profit us nothing at the last day that Jesus was a Shepherd, if during our lifetime, we never heard His voice and followed Him. If we love life, let us join His flock without delay. Except we do this, we shall be found at the left hand in the day of judgment and lost for evermore.

These verses show us, lastly, that *when Christ died, He died of His own voluntary free will.* He uses a remarkable expression to teach this – "I lay down my life that I might take it again. No man taketh it from Me, but I lay it down of myself. I have power to lay it down, and I have power to take it again."

The point before us is of no small importance. We must never suppose for a moment that our Lord had no power to prevent His sufferings, and that He was delivered up to His enemies and crucified because He could not help it. Nothing could be further from the truth than such an idea. The treachery of Judas, the armed band of priests' servants, the enmity of Scribes and Pharisees, the injustice of Pontius Pilate, the crude hands of Roman soldiers, the scourge, the nails, and the spear – all these could not have harmed a hair of our Lord's head, unless He had allowed them. Well might He say those remarkable words, "Thinkest thou that I cannot now pray to my Father, and He shall presently give Me more than twelve legions of angels? But how, then, shall the Scripture be fulfilled?" (Matthew 26:53).

His death was not the death of a martyr, who sinks at last over-whelmed by enemies, but the death of a triumphant conqueror, who knows that even in dying he wins for himself and his people a kingdom and a crown of glory.

Let us lean back our souls on these mighty truths and be thankful. A willing Savior, a loving Savior, a Savior who came specially into the world to bring life to man is just the Savior that we need. If we hear His voice, repent and believe, He is our own.

John 10:19-30

There was a division therefore again among the Jews for these words. And many of them said, He has a demon and is beside himself; why do ye hear him? Others said, These are not the words of him that has a demon. Can a demon open the eyes of the blind? And they celebrated the dedication

*in Jerusalem, and it was winter. And Jesus walked in the
temple in Solomon's porch. Then the Jews came round about
him and said unto him, Until when wilt thou hold our soul
in suspense? If thou art the Christ, tell us plainly. Jesus
answered them, I have told you, and ye do not believe; the
works that I do in my Father's name, they bear witness of
me. But ye believe not because ye are not of my sheep, as I
said unto you. My sheep hear my voice, and I know them,
and they follow me; and I give unto them eternal life; and
they shall never perish, neither shall anyone pluck them out
of my hand. My Father, who gave them to me, is greater
than all; and no one is able to pluck them out of my Father's
hand. I and my Father are one.*

We should notice, first, in this passage, *what strifes and controversies
our Lord occasioned when He was on earth.* We read that "there was
a division among the Jews for His sayings" – and that "many of them
said He hath a devil, and is mad," while others took an opposite view.
It may seem strange, at first sight, that He who came to preach peace
between God and man should be the cause of contention. But herein
were His own words literally fulfilled – "I came not to send peace, but
a sword" (Matthew 10:34). The fault was not in Christ or His doctrine,
but in the carnal mind of His Jewish hearers.

Let us never be surprised if we see the same thing in our own day.
Human nature never changes. So long as the heart of man is without
grace, so long we must expect to see it dislike the Gospel of Christ. Just
as oil and water, acids and alkalis, cannot combine, so in the same way
unconverted people cannot really like the people of God. "The carnal
mind is enmity against God" (Romans 8:7). "The natural man does not
perceive the things of the Spirit of God" (1 Corinthians 2:14).

The servant of Christ must think it no strange thing if he goes
through the same experience as his Master. He will often find his ways
and opinions in religion the cause of strife in his own family. He will
have to endure ridicule, harsh words, and petty persecution from the
children of this world. He may even discover that he is thought a fool
or a madman on account of his Christianity. Let none of these things

move him. The thought that he is a partaker of the afflictions of Christ ought to steel him against every trial. "If they have called the Master of the house Beelzebub, how much more shall they call them of his household" (Matthew 10:25).

One thing, at any rate, should never be forgotten. We must not allow ourselves to think the worse of religion because of the strifes and dissensions to which it gives rise. Whatever men may please to say, it is human nature and not religion, which is to blame. We do not blame the glorious sun because its rays draw forth noxious vapors from the marsh. We must not find fault with the glorious Gospel, if it stirs up men's corruptions and causes the "thoughts of many hearts to be revealed" (Luke 2:35).

We should notice, secondly, *the name which Christ gives to true Christians.* He uses a figurative expression which, like all His language, is full of deep meaning. He calls them, "My sheep."

The word "sheep," no doubt, points to something in the character and ways of true Christians. It would be easy to show that weakness, helplessness, harmlessness, usefulness are all points of resemblance between the sheep and the believer. But the leading idea in our Lord's mind was the entire dependence of the sheep upon its Shepherd. Just as sheep hear the voice of their own shepherd and follow him, so do believers follow Christ. By faith they listen to His call. By faith they submit themselves to His guidance. By faith they lean on Him and commit their souls implicitly to His direction. The ways of a shepherd and his sheep are a most useful illustration of the relation between Christ and the true Christian.

The expression, "My sheep," points to the close connection that exists between Christ and believers. They are His by gift from the Father, His by purchase, His by calling and choice, and His by their own consent and heart submission. In the highest sense they are Christ's property; and just as a man feels a special interest in that which he has bought at a great price and made his own, so does the Lord Jesus feel a peculiar interest in His people.

Expressions like these should be carefully treasured up in the memories of true Christians. They will be found cheering and heart-strengthening in days of trial. The world may see no beauty in the ways of a godly man and may often pour contempt on him. But he who knows that he is one of Christ's sheep has no cause to be ashamed. He has within him a "well of water springing up into everlasting life" (John 4:14).

We should notice, lastly, in this passage, *the vast privileges which the Lord Jesus Christ bestows on true Christians.* He uses words about them of singular richness and strength. "I know them. I give unto them eternal life. They shall never perish – neither shall any man pluck them out of my hand." This sentence is like the cluster of grapes which came from Eshcol. A stronger form of speech perhaps can hardly be found in the whole range of the Bible.

Christ "knows" his people with a special knowledge of approbation, interest, and affection. By the world around them they are comparatively unknown, uncared for, or despised. But they are never forgotten or overlooked by Christ.

Christ "gives" his people "eternal life." He bestows on them freely a right and title to heaven, pardoning their many sins and clothing them with a perfect righteousness. Money, and health, and worldly prosperity He often wisely withholds from them. But He never fails to give them grace, peace, and glory.

Christ declares that His people "shall never perish." Weak as they are they shall all be saved. Not one of them shall be lost and cast away – not one of them shall miss heaven. If they err, they shall be brought back; if they fall, they shall be raised. The enemies of their souls may be strong and mighty, but their Savior is mightier; and none shall pluck them out of their Savior's hands.

A promise like this deserves the closest attention. If words mean anything, it contains that great doctrine, the perseverance, or continuance in grace, of true believers. That doctrine is literally hated by worldly people. No doubt, like every other truth of Scripture, it is liable to be abused. But the words of Christ are too plain to be evaded. He has said it, and He will make it good – "My sheep shall never perish."

Whatever men may please to say against this doctrine, it is one which God's children ought to hold fast and defend with all their might. To all who feel within them the workings of the Holy Spirit, it is a doctrine full of encouragement and consolation.

Would we get the benefit of this glorious promise? Let us take care that we belong to Christ's flock. Let us hear His voice and follow Him. The man who, under a real sense of sin, flees to Christ and trusts in Him, is one of those who shall never be plucked out of Christ's hand.

John 10:31-42

Then the Jews took up stones again to stone him. Jesus answered them, Many good works have I showed you from my Father; for which of those works do ye stone me? The Jews answered him, saying, For a good work we do not stone thee, but for blasphemy; and because thou, being a man, makest thyself God. Jesus answered them, Is it not written in your law, I said, Ye are gods? If he called them gods unto whom the word of God came (and the scripture cannot be broken), do ye say of him whom the Father has sanctified and sent into the world, Thou blasphemest, because I said, I am the Son of God? If I do not do the works of my Father, do not believe me. But if I do, though ye do not believe me, believe the works that ye may know and believe that the Father is in me and I in him. Therefore they sought again to take him, but he escaped out of their hand and went away again beyond Jordan into the place where John at first baptized, and there he abode. And many came unto him and said, John certainly did no sign, but all the things that John spoke of this man were true. And many believed in him there.

We should observe, in these verses, *the extreme wickedness of human nature.* The unbelieving Jews at Jerusalem were neither moved by our Lord's miracles nor by His preaching. They were determined not to receive Him as their Messiah. Once more it is written that "they took up stones to stone Him."

Our Lord had done the Jews no injury. He was no robber, murderer, or rebel against the law of the land. He was one whose whole life was love, and who "went about doing good" (Acts 10:38). There was no fault or inconsistency in His character. There was no crime that could be laid to His charge. So perfect and spotless a man had never walked on the face of this earth. But yet the Jews hated Him and thirsted for His blood. How true are the words of Scripture – "They hated Him without a cause" (John 15:25). How just the remark of an old divine – "Unconverted men would kill God Himself if they could only get at Him."

The true Christian has surely no right to wonder if he meets with the same kind of treatment as our blessed Lord. In fact, the more like he is to his Master and the more holy and spiritual his life, the more probable is it that he will have to endure hatred and persecution. Let him not suppose that any degree of consistency will deliver him from this cross. It is not his faults, but his graces, which call forth the enmity of men. The world hates to see anything of God's image. The children of the world are vexed and pierced in conscience when they see others better than themselves. Why did Cain hate his brother Abel and slay him? "Because," says John, "his own works were evil, and his brother's righteous" (1 John 3:12). Why did the Jews hate Christ? Because He exposed their sins and false doctrines; and they knew in their own hearts that he was right and they were wrong. "The world," said our Lord, "hateth Me, because I testify of it, that the works thereof are evil" (John 7:7). Let Christians make up their minds to drink the same cup, and let them drink it patiently and without surprise. There is One in heaven who said, "If the world hate you, ye know that it hated Me before it hated you" (John 15:18). Let them remember this and take courage. The time is short. We are traveling on towards a day when all shall be set right, and every man shall receive according to his works. "There is an end: and our expectation shall not be cut off" (Proverbs 23:18).

We should observe, secondly, in these verses, *the high honor that Jesus Christ puts on the Holy Scriptures.* We find Him using a text out of the Psalms as an argument against His enemies, in which the whole point lies in the single word "gods." And then having quoted the text, He lays down the great principle, "the Scripture cannot be broken." It is as though He said, "Wherever the Scripture speaks plainly on any subject, there can be no more question about it. The cause is settled and decided. Every jot and tittle of Scripture is true, and must be received as conclusive."

The principle here laid down by our Lord is one of vast importance. Let us grasp it firmly, and never let it go. Let us maintain boldly the complete inspiration of every word of the original Hebrew and Greek Scriptures. Let us believe that not only every book of the Bible, but every chapter – and not only every chapter, but every verse, and not only every verse, but every word was originally given by inspiration of God. Inspiration, we must never shrink from asserting, extends not only to the thoughts and ideas of Scripture, but to the least words.

The principle before us, no doubt, is rudely assaulted in the present day. Let no Christian's heart fail because of these assaults. Let us stand our ground manfully, and defend the principle of plenary inspiration as we would the apple of our eye. There are difficulties in Scripture, we need not shrink from conceding, things hard to explain, hard to reconcile, and hard to understand. But in almost all these difficulties, the fault, we may justly suspect, is not so much in Scripture as in our own weak minds. In all cases we may well be content to wait for more light and to believe that all shall be made clear at last. One thing we may rest assured is very certain – if the difficulties of plenary inspiration are to be numbered by thousands, the difficulties of any other view of inspiration are to be numbered by tens of thousands. The wisest course is to walk in the old path – the path of faith and humility; and say, "I cannot give up a single word of my Bible. All Scripture is given by inspiration of God. The Scripture cannot be broken."

We should observe, lastly, in these verses, *the importance which our Lord Jesus Christ attaches to His miracles.* He appeals to them as the best evidence of His own Divine mission. He bids the Jews look at them and deny them if they can. "If I do not the works of my Father, believe me not. But if I do, though ye believe not Me, believe the works."

The mighty miracles which our Lord performed during the three years of His earthly ministry are probably not considered as much as they ought to be in the present day. These miracles were not few in number. Forty times and more we read in the Gospels of His doing things entirely out of the ordinary course of nature – healing sick people in a moment, raising the dead with a word, casting out devils, calming winds and waves in an instant, walking on the water as on solid ground. These miracles were not all done in private among friends. Many of them were wrought in the most public manner, under the eyes of unfriendly witnesses. We are so familiar with these things that we are apt to forget the mighty lesson they teach. They teach that He who worked these miracles must be nothing less than very God. They stamp His doctrines and precepts with the mark of Divine authority. He only who created all things at the beginning could suspend the laws of creation at His will. He who could suspend the laws of creation must be One who ought to be thoroughly believed and implicitly obeyed. To reject One who confirmed His mission by such mighty works is the height of madness and folly.

Hundreds of unbelieving men, no doubt, in every age, have tried to pour contempt on Christ's miracles and to deny that they were ever worked at all. But they labor in vain. Proofs upon proofs exist that our Lord's ministry was accompanied by miracles; and that this was acknowledged by those who lived in our Lord's time. Objectors of this sort would do well to take up the one single miracle of our Lord's resurrection from the dead, and disprove it if they can. If they cannot disprove that, they ought, as honest men, to confess that miracles are possible. And then, if their hearts are truly humble, they ought to admit that He whose mission was confirmed by such evidence must have been the Son of God.

Let us thank God, as we turn from this passage, that Christianity has such abundant evidence that it is a religion from God. Whether we appeal to the internal evidence of the Bible or to the lives of the first Christians, or to prophecy, or to miracles; or to history, we get one and the same answer. All say with one voice, "Jesus is the Son of God, and believers have life through His name."

John Chapter 11

John 11:1-6

Now a certain man was sick, named Lazarus, of Bethany, the town of Mary and her sister Martha. (It was that Mary who anointed the Lord with ointment and wiped his feet with her hair whose brother Lazarus was sick.) Therefore his sisters sent unto him, saying, Lord, behold, he whom thou lovest is sick. When Jesus heard that, he said, This sickness is not unto death, but for the glory of God, that the Son of God might be glorified thereby. Now Jesus loved Martha and her sister and Lazarus. When he had heard therefore that he was sick, he abode two days still in the same place where he was.

THE CHAPTER WE HAVE now begun is one of the most remarkable in the New Testament. For grandeur and simplicity, for pathos and solemnity, nothing was ever written like it. It describes a miracle which is not recorded in the other Gospels – the raising of Lazarus from the dead. Nowhere shall we find such convincing proofs of our Lord's Divine power. As God, He makes the grave itself yield up its tenants. Nowhere shall we find such striking illustrations of our Lord's ability to sympathize with His people. As man, He can be touched with the feelings of our infirmities. Such a miracle well became the end of such a ministry. It was fit and right that the victory of Bethany should closely precede the crucifixion at Calvary.

These verses teach us that *true Christians may be sick and ill as well as others.* We read that Lazarus of Bethany was one "whom Jesus loved," and a brother of two well-known holy women. Yet Lazarus was sick, even unto death! The Lord Jesus, who had power over all diseases, could no doubt have prevented this illness, if He had thought fit. But He did not do so. He allowed Lazarus to be sick, and in pain, and weary, and to languish and suffer like any other man.

The lesson is one which ought to be deeply engraved in our memories. Living in a world full of disease and death, we are sure to need it some day. Sickness, in the very nature of things, can never be anything but trying to flesh and blood. Our bodies and souls are strangely linked together, and that which vexes and weakens the body can hardly fail to vex the mind and soul. But sickness, we must always remember, is no sign that God is displeased with us; no, more, it is generally sent for the good of our souls. It tends to draw our affections away from this world, and to direct them to things above. It sends us to our Bibles and teaches us to pray better. It helps to prove our faith and patience and shows us the real value of our hope in Christ. It reminds us that we are not to live always and tunes and trains our hearts for our great change. Then let us be patient and cheerful when we are laid aside by illness. Let us believe that the Lord Jesus loves us when we are sick no less than when we are well.

These verses teach us, secondly, that *Jesus Christ is the Christian's best Friend in the time of need.* We read that when Lazarus was sick, his sisters at once sent to Jesus and laid the matter before Him. Beautiful, touching, and simple was the message they sent. They did not ask Him to come at once or to work a miracle and command the disease to depart. They only said, "Lord, he whom You love is sick" and left the matter there, in the full belief that He would do what was best. Here was the true faith and humility of saints! Here was gracious submission of will!

The servants of Christ, in every age and climate, will do well to follow this excellent example. No doubt when those whom we love are sick, we are to use diligently every reasonable means for their recovery. We must spare no pains to obtain the best medical advice. We must assist nature in every possible manner to fight a good fight against its enemy. But in all our doing, we must never forget that the best and ablest and wisest Helper is in heaven at God's right hand. Like afflicted Job our first action must be to fall on our knees and worship. Like Hezekiah, we must spread our matters before the Lord. Like the holy sisters at Bethany, we must send up a prayer to Christ. Let us not forget, in the hurry and excitement of our feelings, that none can help like Him, and that He is merciful, loving, and gracious.

These verses teach us, thirdly, that *Christ loves all who are true Christians.* We read that "Jesus loved Martha, and her sister, and Lazarus." The characters of these three good people seem to have been somewhat different. Of Martha, we are told in a certain place, that she was "careful and troubled about many things," while Mary "sat at Jesus' feet, and heard His word." Of Lazarus we are told nothing distinctive at all. Yet all these were loved by the Lord Jesus. They all belonged to His family, and He loved them all.

We must carefully bear this in mind in forming our estimate of Christians. We must never forget that there are varieties in character, and that the grace of God does not cast all believers into one and the same mold. Admitting fully that the foundations of Christian character are always the same, and that all God's children repent, believe, are holy, prayerful, and Scripture-loving, we must make allowances for wide varieties in their temperaments and habits of mind. We must not undervalue others because they are not exactly like ourselves. The flowers in a garden may differ widely, and yet the gardener feels interest in all. The children of a family may be curiously unlike one another, and yet the parents care for all. It is just so with the Church of Christ. There are degrees of grace, and varieties of grace; but the least, the weakest, the feeblest disciples are all loved by the Lord Jesus. Then let no believer's heart fail because of his infirmities; and, above all, let no believer dare to despise and undervalue a brother.

These verses teach us, lastly, that *Christ knows best at what time to do anything for His people.* We read that "when He had heard that Lazarus was sick, He abode two days still in the same place where He was." In fact, He purposely delayed His journey and did not come to Bethany until Lazarus had been four days in the grave. No doubt He knew well what was going on; but He never moved until the time came which He saw was best. For the sake of the Church and the world, for the good of friends and enemies, He kept away.

The children of God must constantly school their minds to learn the great lesson now before us. Nothing so helps us to bear patiently the trials of life as an abiding conviction of the perfect wisdom by which everything around us is managed. Let us try to believe not only that all that happens to us is well done, but that it is done in the best manner, by the right instrument, and at the right time. We are all naturally impatient in the day of trial. We are apt to say, like Moses, when beloved ones are sick, "Heal her now, Lord, we beseech thee" (Numbers 12:13). We forget that Christ is too wise a Physician to make any mistakes. It is the duty of faith to say, "My times are in Thy hand. Do with me as Thou wilt, how Thou wilt, what Thou wilt, and when Thou wilt. Not my will, but Thine be done." The highest degree of faith is to be able to wait, sit still, and not complain.

Let us turn from the passage with a settled determination to trust Christ entirely with all the concerns of this world, both public and private. Let us believe that He by whom all things were made at first is He who is managing all with perfect wisdom. The affairs of kingdoms, families, and private individuals are all alike overruled by Him. He chooses all the portions of His people. When we are sick, it is because He knows it to be for our good; when He delays coming to help us, it is for some wise reason. The hand that was nailed to the cross is too wise and loving to smite without a needs-be or to keep us waiting for relief without a cause.

John 11:7-16

Then after that he said to his disciples, Let us go into Judea again. His disciples said unto him, Rabbi, the Jews of late sought to stone thee, and goest thou there again? Jesus answered, Are there not twelve hours in the day? If anyone walks in the day, he does not stumble because he sees the light of this world. But he who walks in the night stumbles because there is no light in him. Having said that he said unto them, Our friend Lazarus sleeps, but I go that I may awake him out of sleep. Then his disciples said, Lord, if he sleeps, he shall be saved. But Jesus had spoken of his death, and they thought that he had spoken of taking of rest in sleep. Then Jesus said unto them plainly, Lazarus has died. And I am glad for your sakes that I was not there, in order that ye may believe; nevertheless let us go unto him. Then Thomas said, who is called Didymus, unto his fellowdisciples, Let us go also, that we may die with him.

We should notice, in this passage, *how mysterious are the ways in which Christ sometimes leads His people.* We are told that when He talked of going back to Judea, His disciples were perplexed. It was the very place where the Jews had lately tried to stone their Master – to return there was to plunge into the midst of danger. These timid Galileans could not see the necessity or prudence of such a step. "Are You going there again?" they cried.

Things such as these are often going on around us. The servants of Christ are often placed in circumstances just as puzzling and perplexing as those of the disciples. They are led in ways of which they cannot see the purpose and object; they are called to fill positions from which they naturally shrink, and which they would never have chosen for themselves. Thousands in every age are continually learning this by their own experience. The path they are obliged to walk in is not the path of their own choice. At present they cannot see its usefulness or wisdom.

At times like these a Christian must call into exercise his faith and patience. He must believe that his Master knows best by what road His servant ought to travel, and that He is leading him by the right way to a city of habitation. He may rest assured that the circumstances in which he is placed are precisely those which are most likely to promote his graces and to check his besetting sins. He need not doubt that what he cannot see now, he will understand hereafter. He will find one day that there was wisdom in every step of his journey, though flesh and blood could not see it at the time. If the twelve disciples had not been taken back into Judea, they would not have seen the glorious miracle of Bethany. If Christians were allowed to choose their own course through life, they would never learn hundreds of lessons about Christ and His grace, which they are now taught in God's ways. Let us remember these things. The time may come when we shall be called to take some journey in life which we greatly dislike. When that time comes, let us set out cheerfully and believe that all is right.

We should notice, secondly, in this passage, *how tenderly Christ speaks of the death of believers.* He announces the fact of Lazarus being dead in language of singular beauty and gentleness – "Our friend Lazarus sleeps." Every true Christian has a Friend in heaven, of almighty power and boundless love. He is thought of, cared for, provided for, defended by God's eternal Son. He has an unfailing Protector, who never slumbers or sleeps and watches continually over his interests. The world may despise him, but he has no cause to be ashamed. Father and mother even may cast him out, but Christ having once taken him up will never let him go. He is the "friend of Christ" even after he is dead! The friendships of this world are often fair weather friendships and fail us like summer-dried fountains, when our need is the greatest; but the friendship of the Son of God is stronger than death and goes beyond the grave. The Friend of sinners is a Friend that sticks closer than a brother.

The death of true Christians is "sleep" and not annihilation. It is a solemn and miraculous change, no doubt, but not a change to be regarded with alarm. They have nothing to fear for their souls in the change, for their sins are washed away in Christ's blood. The sharpest sting of death is the sense of unpardoned sin. Christians have nothing to fear for their bodies in the change; they will rise again by and by, refreshed and renewed, after the image of the Lord. The grave itself is a conquered enemy. It must render back its tenants safe and sound, the very moment that Christ calls for them at the last day.

Let us remember these things when those whom we love fall asleep in Christ, or when we ourselves receive our notice to depart this world. Let us call to mind, in such an hour, that our great Friend takes thought for our bodies as well as for our souls, and that He will not allow one hair of our heads to perish. Let us never forget that the grave is the place where the Lord Himself lay, and that as He rose again triumphant from that cold bed, so also shall all His people. To a mere worldly man, death must needs be a terrible thing; but he that has Christian faith may boldly say, as he lays down life, "I will both lay me down in peace, and sleep: for Thou, Lord, only makest me dwell in safety."

We should notice, lastly, in this passage, *how much of natural temperament clings to a believer even after conversion.* We read that when Thomas saw that Lazarus was dead, and that Jesus was determined in spite of all danger to return into Judea, he said, "Let us also go, that we may die with Him." There can only be one meaning in that expression – it was the language of a despairing and desponding mind, which could see nothing but dark clouds in the picture. The very man who afterwards could not believe that his Master had risen again, and thought the news too good to be true, is just the one of the twelve who thinks that if they go back to Judea they must all die!

Things such as these are deeply instructive and are doubtless recorded for our learning. They show us that the grace of God in conversion does not so remold a man as to leave no trace of his natural bent of character. The sanguine do not altogether cease to be sanguine, nor the desponding to be desponding, when they pass from death to life and become true Christians. They show us that we must make large allowances for natural temperament in forming our estimate of individual Christians. We must not expect all God's children to be exactly one and the same. Each tree in a forest has its own peculiarities of shape and growth, and yet all at a distance look one mass of leaf and verdure. Each member of Christ's body has his own distinctive bias, and yet all in the main are led by one Spirit and love one Lord. The two sisters Martha and Mary, the apostles Peter and John and Thomas, were certainly very unlike one another in many respects. But they had all one point in common – they loved Christ and were His friends.

Let us take heed that we really belong to Christ. This is the one thing needful. If this is made sure, we shall be led by the right way and end well at last. We may not have the cheerfulness of one brother, or the fiery zeal of another, or the gentleness of another. But if grace reigns within us, and we know what repentance and faith are by experience, we shall stand on the right hand in the great day. Happy is the man of whom, with all his defects, Christ says to saints and angels, "This is our friend."

John 11:17-29

Then when Jesus came, he found that he had lain in the grave four days already. Now Bethany was near unto Jerusalem, about fifteen furlongs off; and many of the Jews had come to Martha and Mary to comfort them concerning their brother. Then Martha, as soon as she heard that Jesus was coming, went and met him; but Mary sat still in the house. Then Martha said unto Jesus, Lord, if thou hadst been here, my brother would not have died. But I know that even now whatsoever thou wilt ask of God, God will give it unto thee. Jesus said unto her, Thy brother shall rise again. Martha said unto him, I know that he shall rise again in the resurrection in the last day. Jesus said unto her, I AM the resurrection and the life; he that believes in me, though he is dead, yet shall he live; and whosoever lives and believes in me shall never die. Believest thou this? She said unto him, Yes, Lord, I believe that thou art the Christ, the Son of God, who should come into the world. And having said this, she went away and called Mary her sister secretly, saying, The Master is come, and calls for thee. As soon as she heard that, she arose quickly and came unto him.

There is a grand simplicity about this passage, which is almost spoiled by any human exposition. To comment on it seems like gilding gold or painting lilies. Yet it throws much light on a subject which we can never understand too well; that is, the true character of Christ's people. The portraits of Christians in the Bible are faithful likenesses. They show us saints just as they are.

We learn, firstly, *what a strange mixture of grace and weakness is to be found even in the hearts of true believers.*

We see this strikingly illustrated in the language used by Martha and Mary. Both these holy women had faith enough to say, "Lord, if Thou had been here, my brother had not died." Yet neither of them seems to have remembered that the death of Lazarus did not depend on Christ's absence, and that our Lord, had He thought fit, could have prevented his death with a word without coming to Bethany. Martha

192

had knowledge enough to say, "I know, that even now, whatsoever Thou wilt ask of God, God wilt give it Thee – I know that my brother shall rise again at the last day – I believe that Thou art the Christ, the Son of God." But even she could get no further. Her dim eyes and trembling hands could not grasp the grand truth that He who stood before her had the keys of life and death, and that in her Master dwelt "all the fullness of the Godhead bodily" (Colossians 2:9). She saw indeed, but through a glass darkly. She knew, but only in part. She believed, but her faith was mingled with much unbelief. Yet both Martha and Mary were genuine children of God and true Christians.

These things are graciously written for our learning. It is good to remember what true Christians really are. Many and great are the mistakes into which people fall by forming a false estimate of the Christian's character. Many are the bitter things which people write against themselves by expecting to find in their hearts what cannot be found on this side of heaven. Let us settle it in our minds that saints on earth are not perfect angels, but only converted sinners. They are sinners renewed, changed, sanctified, no doubt; but they are yet sinners and will be until they die. Like Martha and Mary, their faith is often entangled with much unbelief, and their grace compassed round with much infirmity. Happy is that child of God who understands these things and has learned to judge rightly both of himself and others. Rarely indeed shall we find the saint who does not often need that prayer, "Lord, I believe – help Thou mine unbelief."

We learn, secondly, *what need many believers have of clear views of Christ's person, office, and power.* This is a point which is forcibly brought out in the well-known sentence which our Lord addressed to Martha. In reply to her vague and faltering expression of belief in the resurrection at the last day, He proclaims the glorious truth, "I am the resurrection and the life" – "I, even I, thy Master, am He that has the keys of life and death in His hands." And then He presses on her once more that old lesson, which she had doubtless often heard but never fully realized – "He that believeth in Me, though he were dead, yet shall he live; and whosoever liveth and believeth in Me shall never die."

There is matter here which deserves the close consideration of all true Christians. Many of them complain of lack of sensible comfort in their religion. They do not feel the inward peace which they desire. Let them know that vague and indefinite views of Christ are too often the cause of all their perplexities. They must try to see more clearly the great object on which their faith rests. They must grasp more firmly His love and power toward those who believe and the riches He has laid up for them even now in this world. We are, many of us, sadly like Martha. A little general knowledge of Christ as the only Savior is often all that we possess. But of the fullness that dwells in Him, of His resurrection, His priesthood, His intercession, His unfailing compassion, we have tasted little or nothing at all. They are things of which our Lord might well say to many, as he did to Martha, "Believest thou this?"

Let us take shame to ourselves that we have named the name of Christ so long, and yet know so little about Him. What right have we to wonder that we feel so little sensible comfort in our Christianity? Our slight and imperfect knowledge of Christ is the true reason of our discomfort. Let the time past suffice us to have been lazy students in Christ's school; let the time to come find us more diligent in trying to "know Him and the power of His resurrection" (Philippians 3:10). If true Christians would only strive, as Paul says, to "comprehend what is the breadth, and length, and depth, and height, and to know the love of Christ, which passeth knowledge," they would be amazed at the discoveries they would make. They would soon find, like Hagar, that there are wells of water near them of which they had no knowledge. They would soon discover that there is more heaven to be enjoyed on earth than they had ever thought possible. The root of a happy religion is clear, distinct, well-defined knowledge of Jesus Christ. More knowledge would have saved Martha many sighs and tears. Knowledge alone no doubt, if unsanctified, only "puffs up" (1 Corinthians 8:1). Yet without clear knowledge of Christ in all His offices, we cannot expect to be established in the faith and steady in the time of need.

John 11:30-37

(Now Jesus was not yet come into the town, but was in that place where Martha met him.) Then the Jews who were with her in the house and comforted her, when they saw Mary, that she rose up hastily and went out, followed her, saying, She goes unto the grave to weep there. Then when Mary was come where Jesus was and saw him, she fell down at his feet, saying unto him, Lord, if thou hadst been here, my brother would not have died. When Jesus therefore saw her weeping and the Jews also weeping who came with her, he became enraged in the Spirit and stirred himself up and said, Where have ye laid him? They said unto him, Lord, come and see. Jesus wept. Then the Jews said, Behold how he loved him! And some of them said, Could not this man, who opened the eyes of the blind, have also caused that this man should not have died?

Not many passages in the New Testament are more wonderful than the simple narrative contained in these eight verses. It brings out, in a most beautiful light, the sympathizing character of our Lord Jesus Christ. It shows us Him who is "able to save to the uttermost all who come to God by Him," as able to feel as He is to save. It shows us Him who is One with the Father and the Maker of all things entering into human sorrows and shedding human tears.

We learn, for one thing, in these verses, *how great a blessing God sometimes bestows on actions of kindness and sympathy.*

It seems that the house of Martha and Mary at Bethany was filled with mourners when Jesus arrived. Many of these mourners, no doubt, knew nothing of the inner life of these holy women. Their faith, their hope, their love to Christ, their discipleship were things of which they were wholly ignorant. But they felt for them in their heavy bereavement and kindly came to offer what comfort they could. By so doing they reaped a rich and unexpected reward. They beheld the greatest miracle that Jesus ever wrought. They were eye-witnesses when Lazarus came forth from the tomb. To many of them, we may well believe, that day was a spiritual birth. The raising of Lazarus led to a resurrection in their souls. How small sometimes are the hinges on which eternal life appears to depend! If these people had not sympathized they might never have been saved.

We need not doubt that these things were written for our learning. To show sympathy and kindness to the sorrowful is good for our own souls, whether we know it or not. To visit the fatherless and widows in their affliction, to weep with those who weep, to try to bear one another's burdens and lighten one another's cares – all this will make no atonement for sin and will not take us to heaven. Yet it is healthy employment for our hearts and employment which none ought to despise. Few perhaps are aware that one secret of being miserable is to live only for ourselves, and one secret of being happy is to try to make others happy and to do a little good in the world. It is not for nothing that these words were written by Solomon, "It is better to go to the house of mourning than to the house of feasting." "The heart of the wise is in the house of mourning, but the heart of fools is in the house of mirth" (Ecclesiastes 7:2, 4). The saying of our Lord is too much overlooked – "Whosoever shall give to drink to one of these little ones a cup of cold water only in the name of a disciple, verily I say unto you he shall in no wise lose his reward" (Matthew 10:42). The friends of Martha and Mary found that promise wonderfully verified. In an age of inordinate selfishness and self-indulgence, it would be well if they had more imitators.

We learn, for another thing, *what a depth of tender sympathy there is in Christ's heart towards His people.* We read that when our Lord saw Mary weeping and the Jews also weeping with her, "He groaned in the spirit and was troubled." We read even more than this. He gave outward expression to His feelings – He "wept." He knew perfectly well that the sorrow of the family of Bethany would soon be turned into joy, and that Lazarus in a few minutes would be restored to his sisters. But though he knew all this, he "wept."[31]

This weeping of Christ is deeply instructive. It shows us that it is not sinful to sorrow. Weeping and mourning are sadly trying to flesh

---

31 The Greek word rendered "wept" is not the same as that used for "weeping" in the thirty-third verse, but totally different. There the weeping is a weeping accompanied by demonstrative lamentation. Here the word would be more literally and accurately rendered "shed tears." In fact it is the only place in the New Testament where this word for "weep" is used.

and blood and make us feel the weakness of our mortal nature. But they are not in themselves wrong. Even the Son of God wept. It shows us that deep feeling is not a thing of which we need be ashamed. To be cold and stoical and unmoved in the sight of sorrow is no sign of grace. There is nothing unworthy of a child of God in tears. Even the Son of God could weep. It shows us, above all, that the Savior in whom believers trust is a most tender and feeling Savior. He is one who can be touched with sympathy for our infirmities. When we turn to Him in the hour of trouble and pour out our hearts before Him, He knows what we go through and can pity. And He is One who never changes. Though He now sits at God's right hand in heaven, His heart is still the same that it was upon earth. We have an Advocate with the Father who, when He was upon earth, could weep.

Let us remember these things in daily life and never be ashamed of walking in our Master's footsteps. Let us strive to be men and women of a tender heart and a sympathizing spirit. Let us never be ashamed to weep with those who weep and rejoice with those who rejoice. Well would it be for the Church and the world if there were more Christians of this stamp and character! The Church would be far more beautiful, and the world be far more happy.

John 11:38-46

Jesus therefore, becoming enraged again in himself, came to the grave. It was a cave, and a stone lay upon it. Jesus said, Take ye away the stone. Martha, the sister of him that had died, said unto him, Lord, by this time he stinks, for he has been dead four days. Jesus said unto her, Did I not say unto thee that if thou wouldest believe thou shalt see the glory of God? Then they took away the stone from the place where the dead was laid. And Jesus, lifting up his eyes, said, Father, I thank thee that thou hast heard me. And I knew that thou hearest me always, but because of the people who stand by I said it, that they may believe that thou hast sent me. And having said these things, he cried with a loud voice, Lazarus,

come forth. Then he that had been dead came forth, bound
hand and foot with graveclothes, and his face was bound
about with a napkin. Jesus said unto them, Loose him, and
let him go. Then many of the Jews who had come to Mary
and had seen what Jesus did believed on him. But some of
them went unto the Pharisees and told them what Jesus had
done.

These verses record one of the greatest miracles the Lord Jesus Christ
ever worked and supply an unanswerable proof of His divinity. He whose
voice could bring back from the grave one that had been four days dead
must indeed have been very God! The miracle itself is described in such
simple language that no human comment can throw light upon it. But
the *sayings* of our Lord on this occasion are peculiarly interesting and
demand special notice.

We should mark, first, *our Lord's words about the stone which lay
upon the grave of Lazarus.* We read that He said to those around Him,
when he came to the place of burial, "Take ye away the stone."

Now why did our Lord say this? It was doubtless as easy for Him
to command the stone to roll away untouched as to call a dead body
from the tomb. But such was not His mode of proceeding. Here, as in
other cases, He chose to give man something to do. Here, as elsewhere,
He taught the great lesson that His almighty power was not meant to
destroy man's responsibility. Even when He was ready and willing to
raise the dead, He would not have man stand by altogether idle.

Let us treasure up this in our memories. It involves a point of great
importance. In doing spiritual good to others – in training up our children for heaven – in following after holiness in our own daily walk – in
all these things it is undoubtedly true that we are weak and helpless.
"Without Christ we can do nothing." But still we must remember that
Christ expects us to do what we can. "Take ye away the stone" is the daily
command which He gives us. Let us beware that we do not stand still
in idleness under the pretense of humility. Let us daily try to do what
we can, and in the trying Christ will meet us and grant His blessing.

We should mark, secondly, *the words which our Lord addressed to
Martha, when she objected to the stone being removed from the grave.*

The faith of this holy woman completely broke down, when the cave where her beloved brother lay was about to be thrown open. She could not believe that it was of any use. "Lord," she cries, "by this time he stinketh." And then comes in the solemn reproof of our Lord – "Said I not unto thee that if thou wouldst believe thou shouldst see the glory of God?"

That sentence is rich in meaning. It is far from unlikely that it contains a reference to the message which had been sent to Martha and Mary, when their brother first fell sick. It may be meant to remind Martha that her Master had sent her word, "This sickness is not unto death, but for the glory of God." But it is perhaps more likely that our Lord desired to recall to Martha's mind the old lesson He had taught her all through His ministry the duty of always believing. It is as though He said, "Martha, Martha, you are forgetting the great doctrine of faith, which I have ever taught thee. Believe, and all will be well. Fear not: only believe."

The lesson is one which we can never know too well. How apt our faith is to break down in time of trial! How easy it is to talk of faith in the days of health and prosperity, and how hard to practice it in the days of darkness, when neither sun, moon, nor stars appear! Let us lay to heart what our Lord says in this place. Let us pray for such stores of inward faith that when our turn comes to suffer, we may suffer patiently and believe all is well. The Christian who has ceased to say, "I must see, and then I will believe," and has learned to say, "I believe, and by and by I shall see," has reached a high degree in the school of Christ.

We should mark, thirdly, *the words which our Lord addressed to God the Father, when the stone was taken from the grave.* We read that He said, "Father, I thank Thee that Thou hast heard Me. And I knew that Thou hearest Me always: but because of the people which stand by I said it, that they may believe that Thou hast sent Me."

This wonderful language is totally unlike anything said by Prophets or Apostles, when they worked miracles. In fact, it is not prayer, but praise. It evidently implies a constant mysterious communion going on between Jesus and His Father in heaven, which it is past the power of man either to explain or conceive. We need not doubt that here, as elsewhere in John, our Lord meant to teach the Jews the entire and complete unity there was between Him and His Father, in all that He did, as well as in all that He taught. Once more He would remind them that he did not come among them as a mere Prophet, but as the Messiah who was sent by the Father, and who was one with the Father. Once more He would have them know that as the words which He spoke were the very words which the Father gave Him to speak, so the works which He wrought were the very works which the Father gave Him to do. In short, He was the promised Messiah, whom the Father always hears, because He and the Father are One.

Deep and high as this truth is, it is for the peace of our souls to believe it thoroughly and to grasp it tightly. Let it be a settled principle of our religion that the Savior in whom we trust is nothing less than eternal God, One whom the Father hears always, One who in very deed is God's Fellow. A clear view of the dignity of our Mediator's Person is one secret of inward comfort. Happy is he who can say, "I know whom I have believed, and that He is able to keep that which I have committed to Him" (2 Timothy 1:12).

We should mark, lastly, *the words which our Lord addressed to Lazarus when he raised him from the grave.* We read that "He cried with a loud voice, Lazarus, come forth!" At the sound of that voice, the king of terrors at once yielded up his lawful captive, and the insatiable grave gave up its prey. At once "He that was dead came forth, bound hand and foot with grave-clothes."

The greatness of this miracle cannot possibly be exaggerated. The mind of man can scarcely take in the vastness of the work that was done. Here, in open day, and before many hostile witnesses, a man, four days dead, was restored to life in a moment. Here was public proof that our Lord had absolute power over the material world! A corpse, already corrupt, was made alive! – Here was public proof that our Lord had absolute power over the world of spirits! A soul that had left its earthly tenement was called back from Paradise and joined once more to its owner's body. Well may the Church of Christ maintain that He who could work such works was "God over all blessed forever" (Romans 9:5).

Let us turn from the whole passage with thoughts of comfort and consolation. Comfortable is the thought that the loving Savior of sinners, on whose mercy our souls entirely depend, is one who has all power in heaven, and earth, and is mighty to save. Comfortable is the thought that there is no sinner too far gone in sin for Christ to raise and convert. He that stood by the grave of Lazarus can say to the vilest of men, "Come forth loose him, and let him go." Comfortable, not least, is the thought that when we ourselves lie down in the grave, we may lie down in the full assurance that we shall rise again. The voice that called Lazarus forth will one day pierce our tombs and bid soul and body come together. "The trumpets shall sound, and the dead shall be raised incorruptible, and we shall be changed" (1 Corinthians 15:52).

John 11:47-57

Then the high priests and the Pharisees gathered a council and said, What shall we do? for this man does many signs. If we let him thus alone, everyone will believe on him, and the Romans shall come and take away both our place and the nation. And one of them, named Caiaphas, being the high priest that same year, said unto them, Ye know nothing at all nor consider that it is expedient for us that one man should die for the people, and not that the whole nation be lost. And this he spoke not of himself; but being high priest that year, he prophesied that Jesus should die for the nation; and not for that nation only, but that he should also gather together in one the sons of God that were scattered abroad. So that from that day forth they took counsel together to kill him. Jesus therefore no longer walked openly among the Jews, but went from there unto a country near to the wilderness into a city called Ephraim and there continued with his disciples. And the passover of the Jews was now at hand, and many went out of the country up to Jerusalem before the passover to purify themselves; and they sought for Jesus and spoke among themselves as they stood in the temple, What think ye, that he will not come to the feast? Now both the high priests and the Pharisees had given a commandment, that if anyone knew where he was he should show it, that they might take him.

These concluding verses of the eleventh chapter of John contain a melancholy picture of human nature. As we turn away from Jesus Christ and the grave at Bethany and look at Jerusalem and the rulers of the Jews, we may well say, "Lord, what is man?"

We should observe, for one thing, in these verses, *the desperate wickedness of man's natural heart.* A mighty miracle was wrought within an easy walk of Jerusalem. A man four days dead was raised to life in the sight of many witnesses. The fact was unmistakable and could not be denied; and yet the chief priests and Pharisees would not believe that He who did this miracle ought to be received as the Messiah. In the face of overwhelming evidence, they shut their eyes and refused to be convinced. "This man," they admitted, "does many miracles." But so far from yielding to this testimony, they only plunged into further wickedness and "took counsel to put Him to death." Great, indeed, is the power of unbelief!

Let us beware of supposing that miracles alone have any power to convert men's souls and to make them Christians. The idea is a complete delusion. To fancy, as some do, that if they saw something wonderful done before their eyes in confirmation of the Gospel, they would at once cast off all indecision and serve Christ, is a mere idle dream. It is the grace of the Spirit in our hearts, and not miracles, that our souls require. The Jews of our Lord's day are a standing proof to mankind that men may see signs and wonders and yet remain hard as stone. It is a deep and true saying, "If men believe not Moses and the Prophets, neither would they be persuaded though one rose from the dead" (Luke 16:31).

We must never wonder if we see abounding unbelief in our own times and around our own homes. It may seem at first unexplainable to us how men cannot see the truth which seems so clear to ourselves and do not receive the Gospel which appears so worthy of acceptance. But the plain truth is that man's unbelief is a far more deeply seated disease than it is generally reckoned. It is proof against the logic of facts, against reasoning, against argument, against moral persuasion. Nothing can melt it down but the grace of God. If we ourselves believe, we can never be too thankful. But we must never count it a strange thing if we see many of our fellows just as hardened and unbelieving as the Jews.

We should observe, for another thing, *the blind ignorance with which God's enemies often act and reason.* These rulers of the Jews said to one another, "If we let this Christ alone we shall be ruined. If we do not stop His course and make an end of His miracles, the Romans will interfere and make an end of our nation." Never, the event afterward proved, was there a more short-sighted and erring judgment than this. They rushed madly on the path they had chosen, and the very thing they feared came to pass. They did not leave our Lord alone, but crucified and slew Him. And what happened then? After a few years, the very calamity they had dreaded took place – the Roman armies did come, destroyed Jerusalem, burned the temple, and carried away the whole nation into captivity.

The well-read Christian need hardly be reminded of many such like things in the history of Christ's Church. The Roman emperors persecuted the Christians in the first three centuries and thought it a positive duty to not let them alone. But the more they persecuted them, the more they increased. The blood of the martyrs became the seed of the Church. The English Papists, in the days of Queen Mary, persecuted the Protestants and thought that truth was in danger if they were let alone. But the more they burned our forefathers, the more they confirmed men's minds in steadfast attachment to the doctrines of the Reformation. In short, the words of the second Psalm are continually verified in this world – "The kings of the earth set themselves, and the rulers take counsel together against the Lord." But "He that sitteth in the heavens shall laugh; the Lord shall have them in derision." God can make the designs of His enemies work together for the good of His people and cause the wrath of man to praise Him. In days of trouble, and rebuke, and blasphemy, believers may rest patiently in the Lord. The very things that at one time seem likely to hurt them shall prove in the end to be for their gain.

We should observe, lastly, *what importance unsaved men sometimes attach to outward ceremonies, while their hearts are full of sin.* We are told that many Jews "went up out of the country to Jerusalem, before the Passover, to purify themselves." The most of them, it may be feared, neither knew nor cared anything about inward purity of heart. They made much ado about the washings, and fastings, and ascetic observances, which formed the essence of popular Jewish religion in our Lord's time; and yet they were willing in a very few days to shed innocent blood. Strange as it may appear, these very sticklers for outward ceremonies were found ready to do the will of the Pharisees and to put their own Messiah to a violent death.

Extremes like this meeting together in the same person are, unhappily, far from uncommon. Experience shows that a bad conscience will often try to satisfy itself by a show of zeal for the cause of religion, while the "weightier matters" of the faith are entirely neglected. The very same man who is ready to compass sea and land to attain ceremonial purity is often the very man who, if he had fit opportunity, would not shrink from helping to crucify Christ. Startling as these assertions may seem, they are abundantly borne out by plain facts. The cities where Lent is kept at this day with the most extravagant strictness are the very cities where the carnival after Lent is a season of glaring excess and immorality. The people in some parts of Christendom, who make much ado one week about fasting and priestly absolution, are the very people who another week will think nothing of murder. These things are simple realities. The hideous inconsistency of the Jewish formalists in our Lord's time has never been without a long succession of followers.

Let us settle it firmly in our minds that a religion which expends itself in zeal for outward formalities is utterly worthless in God's sight. The purity that God desires to see is not the purity of bodily washing and fasting, of holy water and self-imposed asceticism, but purity of heart. External worship and ceremonialism may "satisfy the flesh," but they do not tend to promote real godliness. The standard of Christ's kingdom must be sought in the sermon on the Mount – "Blessed are the pure in heart, for they shall see God" (Matthew 5:8; Colossians 2:23).

John Chapter 12

John 12:1-11

Jesus, therefore, six days before the passover, came to Bethany, where Lazarus was who had been dead, whom he raised from the dead. There they made him a supper; and Martha served, but Lazarus was one of those that sat at the table with him. Then Mary took a pound of ointment of spikenard, very costly, and anointed the feet of Jesus and wiped his feet with her hair; and the house was filled with the odour of the ointment. Then said one of his disciples, Judas Iscariot, Simon's son, who should betray him, Why was this ointment not sold for three hundred denarius and given to the poor? This he said, not that he cared for the poor, but because he was a thief and had the bag and would take from what was put therein. Therefore Jesus said, Let her alone; against the day of my burying she has kept this; for the poor ye always have with you, but ye shall not always have me. A great multitude of the Jews therefore knew that he was there; and they came not only for Jesus' sake, but that they might see Lazarus also, whom he had raised from the dead. So the princes of the priests took counsel that they might also put Lazarus to death because by reason of him many of the Jews went away and believed on Jesus.

THE CHAPTER WE HAVE now begun finishes a most important division of John's Gospel. Our Lord's *public* addresses to the unbelieving Jews of Jerusalem are here brought to an end. After this chapter, John records nothing but what was said in private to the disciples.

We see, for one thing, in this passage, *what abounding proofs exist of the truth of our Lord's greatest miracles.*

We read of a supper at Bethany, where Lazarus "sat at the table" among the guests – Lazarus, who had been publicly raised from the dead after lying four days in the grave. No one could pretend to say that his resurrection was a mere optical delusion, and that the eyes of the bystanders must have been deceived by a spirit or vision. Here was the very same Lazarus, after several weeks, sitting among his fellow-men with a real material body and eating and drinking real material food. It is hard to understand what stronger evidence of a fact could be supplied. He that is not convinced by such evidence as this may as well say that he is determined to believe nothing at all.

It is a comfortable thought, that the very same proofs which exist about the resurrection of Lazarus are the proofs which surround that still mightier fact, the resurrection of Christ from the dead. Was Lazarus seen for several weeks by the people of Bethany, going in and coming out among them? So was the Lord Jesus seen by His disciples. Did Lazarus take material food before the eyes of his friends? So did the Lord Jesus eat and drink before His ascension. No one, in his sober senses, who saw Jesus take "broiled fish and a honeycomb" and eat it before several witnesses, would doubt that He had a real body (Luke 24:42).

We shall do well to remember this. In an age of abounding unbelief and scepticism, we shall find that the resurrection of Christ will bear any weight that we can lay upon it. Just as He placed beyond reasonable doubt the rising again of a beloved disciple within two miles of Jerusalem, so in a very few weeks He placed beyond doubt His own victory over the grave. If we believe that Lazarus rose again, we need not doubt that Jesus rose again also. If we believe that Jesus rose again, we need not doubt the truth of His Messiahship, the reality of His acceptance as our Mediator, and the certainty of our own resurrection. Christ has risen indeed, and wicked men may well tremble. Christ has risen from the dead, and believers may well rejoice.

We see, for another thing, in this passage, *what unkindness and discouragement Christ's friends sometimes meet with from man.*

We read that, at the supper in Bethany, Mary, the sister of Lazarus, anointed the feet of Jesus with precious ointment and wiped them with the hair of her head. Nor was this ointment poured on with a meager hand. She did it so liberally and profusely that "the house was filled with the odor of the ointment." She did it under the influence of a heart full of love and gratitude. She thought nothing too great and good to bestow on such a Savior. Sitting at His feet in days gone by and hearing His words, she had found peace for her conscience and pardon for her sins. At this very moment she saw Lazarus, alive and well, sitting by her Master's side – her own brother Lazarus, whom He had brought back to her from the grave. Greatly loved, she thought she could not show too much love in return. Having freely received, she freely gave.

But there were some present who found fault with Mary's conduct and blamed her as guilty of wasteful extravagance. One especially, an apostle, a man of whom better things might have been expected, declared openly that the ointment would have been better employed if it had been sold, and the price "given to the poor." The heart which could conceive such thoughts must have had low views of the dignity of Christ's person and still lower views of our obligations to Him. A cold heart and a stingy hand will generally go together.

There are only too many professing Christians of a like spirit in the present day. Myriads of baptized people cannot understand zeal of any sort for the honor of Christ. Tell them of any vast outlay of money to push trade or to advance the cause of science, and they approve of it as right and wise. Tell them of any expense incurred for the preaching of the Gospel at home or abroad, for spreading God's Word, for extending the knowledge of Christ on earth, and they tell you plainly that they think it waste. They never give a farthing to such objects as these, and count those people fools who do. Worst of all, they often cover over their own backwardness to help purely Christian objects by a pretended concern for the poor at home. Yet they find it convenient to forget the well known fact that those who do most for the cause of Christ are precisely those who do most for the poor.

We must never allow ourselves to be moved from "patient continuance in well-doing" by the unkind remarks of such people. It is vain to expect a man to do much for Christ, when he has no sense of debt to

Christ. We must pity the blindness of our unkind critics and work on. He who pleaded the cause of loving Mary and said, "Let her alone," is sitting at the right hand of God and keeps a book of remembrance. A day is soon coming when a wondering world will see that every cup of cold water given for Christ's sake, as well as every box of precious ointment, was recorded in heaven and has its rewards. In that great day those who thought that anyone could give too much to Christ will find they had better never have been born.

We see, lastly, in this passage, *what desperate hardness and unbelief there is in the heart of man.*

Unbelief appears in the chief priests, who "consulted that they might put Lazarus to death." They could not deny the fact of his having been raised again. Living, and moving, and eating, and drinking within two miles of Jerusalem after lying four days in the grave, Lazarus was a witness to the truth of Christ's Messiahship, whom they could not possibly answer or put to silence. Yet these proud men would not give way. They would rather commit a murder than throw down the arms of rebellion and confess themselves in the wrong. No wonder that the Lord Jesus in a certain place "marveled" at unbelief. Well might He say, in a well-known parable, "If they believe not Moses and the Prophets, neither will they be persuaded though one rose from the dead" (Mark 6:6; Luke 16:31).

Hardness appears in Judas Iscariot who, after being a chosen Apostle and a preacher of the kingdom of heaven, turns out at last a thief and a traitor. So long as the world stands, this unhappy man will be a lasting proof of the depth of human corruption. That anyone could follow Christ as a disciple for three years, see all His miracles, hear all His teaching, receive at His hand repeated kindnesses, be counted an Apostle, and yet prove rotten at heart in the end, all this at first sight appears incredible and impossible! Yet the case of Judas shows plainly that the thing can be. Few things, perhaps, are so little realized as the extent of what desperate hardness and unbelief there is in the heart of man.

Let us thank God if we know anything of faith and can say, with all our sense of weakness and infirmity, "I believe." Let us pray that our faith may be real, true, genuine, and sincere, and not a mere temporary impression like the morning cloud and the early dew. Not least, let us watch and pray against the love of the world. It ruined one who basked in the full sunshine of privileges and heard Christ Himself teaching every day. Then "let him that thinks he stands take heed lest he fall" (1 Corinthians 10:12).

John 12:12-19

On the next day the multitude that were come to the feast, when they heard that Jesus was coming to Jerusalem, took branches of palm trees and went forth to meet him and cried, Hosanna; Blessed is he that comes in the name of the Lord, the King of Israel. And Jesus, when he had found a young ass, sat upon it, as it is written, Fear not, daughter of Sion; behold, thy King comes, sitting on an ass's colt. His disciples did not understand these things at first, but when Jesus was glorified, then they remembered that these things were written of him and that they had done these things unto him. The multitude, therefore, that was with him when he called Lazarus out of his grave and raised him from the dead, bore witness. For this cause the multitude also met him, for they had heard that he had done this sign. The Pharisees therefore said among themselves, Perceive ye how ye prevail nothing? behold, the world is gone after him.

A careful reader of the Gospels can hardly fail to observe that our Lord Jesus Christ's conduct, at this stage of His earthly ministry, is very peculiar. It is unlike anything else recorded of Him in the New Testament. Hitherto we have seen Him withdrawing as much as possible from public notice, retiring into the wilderness, and checking those who would have brought Him forward and made Him a king. As a rule He did not court popular attention. He did not "cry or strive, or cause His voice to be heard in the streets" (Matthew 12:19). Here, on the contrary, we see Him making a public entry into Jerusalem, attended by an immense crowd of people, and causing even the Pharisees to say, "Behold, the world has gone after Him."

The explanation of this apparent inconsistency is not hard to find out. The time had come at last when Christ was to die for the sins of the world. The time had come when the true passover Lamb was to be slain, when the true blood of atonement was to be shed, when Messiah was to be "cut off" according to prophecy (Daniel 9:26), when the way into the holiest was to be opened by the true High Priest to all mankind. Knowing all this, our Lord purposely drew attention to Himself. Knowing this, He placed Himself prominently under the notice of the whole Jewish nation. It was only fit and right that this thing should not be "done in a corner" (Acts 26:26). If ever there was a transaction in our Lord's earthly ministry which was public, it was the Sacrifice which He offered up on the cross of Calvary. He died at the time of year when all the tribes were assembled at Jerusalem for the passover feast. Nor was this all. He died in a week when, by His remarkable public entry into Jerusalem, He had caused the eyes of all Israel to be specially fixed upon Himself.

We learn, for one thing, in these verses, *how entirely voluntary the sufferings of Christ were.* It is impossible not to see in the history before us that our Lord had a mysterious influence over the minds and wills of all around Him, whenever He thought fit to use it. Nothing else can account for the effect which His approach to Jerusalem had on the multitudes which accompanied Him. They seem to have been carried forward by a secret constraining power, which they were obliged to obey, in spite of the disapproval of the leaders of the nation. In short, just as our Lord was able to make winds, and waves, and diseases, and devils obey Him, so was He able, when it pleased Him, to turn, the minds of men according to His will.

For the case before us does not stand alone. The men of Nazareth could not hold Him when He chose to "pass through the midst of them and go His way" (Luke 4:30). The angry Jews of Jerusalem could not detain him when they would have laid violent hands on Him in the Temple; but, "going through the midst of them, He passed by" (John 8:59). Above all, the very soldiers who apprehended Him in the garden, at first "went backward and fell to the ground" (John 18:6). In each of these instances there is but one explanation. A Divine influence was put forth. There was about our Lord during His whole earthly ministry a mysterious "hiding of His power" (Habakkuk 3:4). But He had almighty power when He was pleased to use it.

Why, then, did He not resist His enemies at last? Why did He not scatter the band of soldiers who came to seize Him like chaff before the wind? There is but one answer. He was a *willing Sufferer* in order to procure redemption for a lost and ruined soul. He had undertaken to give His own life as a ransom that we might live forever, and He laid it down on the cross with all the desire of His heart. He did not bleed and suffer and die because He was vanquished by superior force and could not help Himself, but because He loved us and rejoiced to give Himself for us as our Substitute. He did not die because He could not avoid death, but because He was willing with all His heart to make His soul an offering for sin.

Forever let us rest our hearts on this most comfortable thought. We have a most willing and loving Savior. It was His delight to do His Father's will and to make a way for lost and guilty man to draw near to God in peace. He loved the work He had taken in hand and the poor sinful world which He came to save. Never, then, let us give way to the unworthy thought that our Savior does not love to see sinners coming to Him and does not rejoice to save them. He who was a most willing Sacrifice on the cross is also a most willing Savior at the right hand of God. He is just as willing to receive sinners who come to Him now for peace, as He was to die for sinners, when He held back His power and willingly suffered on Calvary.

We learn, for another thing, in these verses, *how minutely the prophecies concerning Christ's first coming were fulfilled.* The riding into Jerusalem on a donkey, which is here recorded, might seem at first sight a simple action and in no way remarkable.[32] But when we turn to

---

32 To ride upon an ass, we must always remember, was not so low and ignominious a mode of travelling as it may seem to us. . . . Asses are specially named as part of the wealth of Abraham, Jacob, and Job (Genesis 12:16; 30:43; Job 13:12). Solomon had an officer specially over the asses (1 Chronicles 27:30). Abraham, Balaam, Achsah, Abigail, and the Shunamite rich woman, all rode on asses. To ride on white asses was a mark of great men in the days of the Judges (Judges 5:10). . . . By riding on an ass, our Lord had fulfilled the prophecy of Zechariah, in which, 500 years before, the prophet had foretold that the King of Zion

the Old Testament, we find that this very thing had been predicted by the Prophet Zechariah five hundred years before (Zechariah 9:9). We find that the coming of a Redeemer someday was not the only thing which the Holy Spirit had revealed to the Fathers, but that even the least particulars of His earthly career were predicted and written down with precise accuracy.

Such fulfillments of prophecy as this deserve the special attention of all who love the Bible and read it with reverence. They show us that every word of Holy Scripture was given by inspiration of God. They teach us to beware of the mischievous practice of spiritualizing and explaining away the language of Scripture. We must settle it in our minds that the plain, literal meaning of the Bible is generally the true and correct meaning. Here is a prediction of Zechariah literally and exactly fulfilled. Our Lord was not merely a very humble person as some spiritualizing interpreters would have explained Zechariah's words to mean, but He literally rode into Jerusalem on a donkey.

Above all, such fulfillments teach us what we may expect in looking forward to the second advent of Jesus Christ. They show us that we must look for a literal accomplishment of the prophecies concerning that second coming and not for a figurative and a spiritual one. Forever let us hold fast this great principle. Happy is that Bible reader who believes the words of the Bible to mean exactly what they seem to mean. Such a man has the true key of knowledge in looking forward to things to come. To know that predictions about the second advent of Christ will be fulfilled literally, just as predictions about the first advent of Christ were fulfilled literally, is the first step towards a right understanding of unfulfilled prophecy.

John 12:20-26

And there were certain Greeks among them that came up to worship at the feast; the same came therefore to Philip, who

---

would one day appear "riding upon an ass." At the time when he prophesied this, there were no kings in Jerusalem. The kingdom had ceased at the captivity. We cannot doubt that this prophecy was well known among the Scribes and Pharisees, and taken together with the fact that Daniel's 70 weeks were expiring, our Lord's entry into Jerusalem In this fashion must have raised many thoughts in their hearts.

*was of Bethsaida of Galilee, and asked him, saying, Lord, we
desire to see Jesus. Philip came and told Andrew, and then
Andrew and Philip told Jesus. And Jesus answered them,
saying, The hour comes in which the Son of man shall be
clarified. Verily, verily, I say unto you, Except the grain of
wheat falls into the ground and dies, it abides alone; but if
it dies, it brings forth much fruit. He that loves his life shall
lose it, and he that hates his life in this world shall keep it
unto life eternal. If anyone serves me, let them follow me;
and where I am, there shall my servant be also; the one that
serves me, will my Father honour.*

There is more going on in some people's minds than we are aware of.
The case of the Greeks before us is a remarkable proof of this. Who
would have thought when Christ was on earth that foreigners from a
distant land would have come forward in Jerusalem and said, "Sir, we
would like to see Jesus"? Who these Greeks were, what they meant, why
they desired to see Jesus, what their inward motives were – all these
are questions we cannot answer. Like Zacchaeus, they may have been
influenced by curiosity. Like the wise men from the East, they may
have surmised that Jesus was the promised King of the Jews, whom
all the eastern world was expecting. Enough for us to know that they
showed more interest in Christ than Caiaphas and all his companions.
Enough to know that they drew from our Lord's lips sayings which
are still read in one hundred and fifty languages, from one end of the
world to the other.

We learn, for one thing, from our Lord's words in this passage, that
death is the way to spiritual life and glory. "Except a corn of wheat fall into
the ground, it abideth alone; but if it die, it bringeth forth much fruit."

This sentence was primarily meant to teach the wondering Greeks
the true nature of Messiah's kingdom. If they thought to see a King like
the kings of this world, they were greatly mistaken. Our Lord would
have them know that He came to carry a cross and not to wear a crown.
He came not to live a life of honor, ease, and magnificence, but to die a
shameful and dishonored death. The kingdom He came to set up was
to begin with a crucifixion and not with a coronation. Its glory was to

take its rise not from victories won by the sword and from accumulated treasures of gold and silver, but from the death of its King.

But this sentence was also meant to teach a wider and broader lesson still. It revealed, under a striking figure, the mighty foundation truth that Christ's death was to be the source of spiritual life to the world. From His cross and sufferings was to spring up a mighty harvest of benefit to all mankind. His death, like a grain of seed, was to be the root of blessings and mercies to countless millions of immortal souls. In short, the great principle of the Gospel was once more exhibited – that Christ's vicarious death (not His life, or miracles, or teaching, but His death) was to bring forth fruit to the praise of God and to provide redemption for a lost world.

This deep and mighty sentence was followed by a practical application, which closely concerns ourselves. "He that hateth his life shall keep it." He that would be saved must be ready to give up life itself, if necessary, in order to obtain salvation. He must bury his love of the world, with its riches, honors, pleasures, and rewards, with a full belief that in so doing he will reap a better harvest, both here and hereafter. He who loves the life that now is so much, that he cannot deny himself anything for the sake of his soul, will find at length that he has lost everything. He, on the contrary, who is ready to cast away everything most dear to him in this life, if it stands in the way of his soul, and to crucify the flesh with its affections and lusts, will find at length that he is no loser. In a word, his losses will prove nothing in comparison to his gains.

Truths such as these should sink deeply into our hearts and stir up self-inquiry. It is as true of Christians as it is of Christ – there can be no life without death, there can be no sweet without bitter, there can be no crown without a cross. Without Christ's death there would have been no life for the world. Unless we are willing to die to sin and crucify all that is most dear to flesh and blood, we cannot expect any benefit from Christ's death. Let us remember these things and take up our cross daily like men. Let us, for the joy set before us, endure the cross and despise the shame, and in the end we shall sit down with our Master at God's right hand. The way of self-crucifixion and sanctification may seem foolishness and wasteful to the world, just as burying good seed seems wasteful to the child and the fool. But there never lived the man who did not find that by sowing to the Spirit, he reaped life everlasting.

We learn, for another thing, from our Lord's words, that *if we profess to serve Christ, we must follow Him.* "If any man serve Me," is the saying, "let him follow Me."

That expression, "following," is one of wide signification and brings before our minds many familiar ideas. As the soldier follows his general, as the servant follows his master, as the scholar follows his teacher; as the sheep follows its shepherd, just so ought the professing Christian to follow Christ. Faith and obedience are the leading marks of real followers and will always be seen in true believing Christians. Their knowledge may be very small and their infirmities very great; their grace very weak and their hope very dim. But they believe what Christ says and strive to do what Christ commands. And of such Christ declares, "They serve Me, they are Mine."

Christianity like this receives little from man. It is too thorough, too decided, too strong, too real. To serve Christ in name and form is easy work and satisfies most people, but to follow Him in faith and life demands more trouble than the generality of men will take about their souls. Laughter, ridicule, opposition, persecution are often the only reward which Christ's followers get from the world. Their religion is one "whose praise is not of men, but of God" (Romans 2:29).

Yet to him who follows, let us never forget, the Lord Jesus holds out abundant encouragement – "Where I am," He declares, "there also shall my servant be; if any man serve Me, him will my Father honor." Let us lay to heart these comfortable promises and go forward in the narrow way without fear. The world may cast out our name as evil and turn us out of its society; but when we dwell with Christ in glory, we shall have a home from which we can never be ejected. The world may pour contempt on our religion and laugh us and our Christianity to scorn; but when the Father honors us at the last day, before the assembly of angels and men, we shall find that His praise makes amends for all.

John 12:27-33

Now is my soul troubled; and what shall I say? Father, save
me from this hour, but for this have I come in this hour.
Father, clarify thy name. Then there came a voice from the
heaven, saying, I have clarified it and will clarify it again.
The people, therefore, that were present and heard it, said
that it thundered; others said, An angel spoke to him. Jesus
answered and said, This voice came not because of me, but
for your sakes. Now is the judgment of this world; now shall
the prince of this world be cast out. And I, if I be lifted up
from the earth, will draw all men unto me. This he said, sig-
nifying what death he should die.

"There are some things hard to be understood" in Scripture (2 Peter 3:16). There are depths here which we have no line to fathom thoroughly. This need not surprise us or shake our faith. The Bible would not be a book "given by inspiration of God," if it did not contain many things which pass man's finite understanding. With its difficulties, the Bible contains thousands of passages which the most unlearned may easily comprehend. Even here, if we look steadily at these verses, we may gather from them lessons of considerable importance.

We have, first, in these verses, *a great doctrine indirectly proved.* That doctrine is the imputation of man's sin to Christ. We see the Savior of the world, the eternal Son of God, troubled and disturbed in mind – "Now is my soul troubled." We see Him who could heal diseases with a touch, cast out devils with a word, and command the waves and winds to obey Him in great agony and conflict of spirit. Now how can this be explained?

To say, as some do, that the only cause of our Lord's trouble was the prospect of His own painful death on the cross is a very unsatisfactory explanation. At this rate it might justly be said that many a martyr has shown more calmness and courage than the Son of God. Such a conclusion is, to say the least, most revolting. Yet this is the conclusion to which men are driven if they adopt the modern notion that Christ's death was only a great example of self-sacrifice.

Nothing can ever explain our Lord's trouble of soul, both here and in Gethsemane, except the old doctrine that He felt the burden of man's sin pressing Him down. It was the mighty weight of a world's guilt imputed to Him and meeting on his head, which made Him groan and agonize and cry, "Now is my soul troubled." Forever let us cling to that doctrine, not only as untying the knot of the passage before us, but as the only ground of solid comfort for the heart of a Christian. That our sins have been really laid on our Divine Substitute and borne by Him and that His righteousness is really imputed to us and accounted ours – this is the real warrant for Christian peace. And if any man asks how we know that our sins were laid on Christ, we bid him read such passages as that which is before us and explain them on any other principle if he can. Christ has borne our sins, carried our sins, groaned under the burden of our sins, been "troubled" in soul by the weight of our sins, and really taken away our sins. This, we may rest assured, is sound doctrine: this is Scriptural theology.

We have, secondly, in these verses, *a great mystery unfolded.* That mystery is the possibility of much inward conflict of soul without sin.

We cannot fail to see in the passage before us a mighty mental struggle in our blessed Savior. Of its depth and intensity we can probably form very little conception. But the agonizing cry, "My soul is troubled," – the solemn question, "What shall I say?" – the prayer of suffering flesh and blood, "Father, save Me from this hour," – the meek confession, "For this cause came I unto this hour," – the petition of a perfectly submissive will, "Father, glorify Thy name," – what does all this mean? Surely there can be only one answer. These sentences tell of a struggle within our Savior's breast, a struggle arising from the natural feelings of one who was perfect man and as man could suffer all that man is capable of suffering. Yet He in whom this struggle took place was the Holy Son of God. "In Him is no sin" (1 John 3:5).

There is a fountain of comfort here for all true servants of Christ, which ought never to be overlooked. Let them learn from their Lord's example that inward conflict of soul is not necessarily in itself a sinful thing. Too many, we believe, from not understanding this point, go heavily all their days on their way to heaven. They fancy they have no grace, because they find a fight in their own hearts. They refuse to take comfort in the Gospel, because they feel a battle between the flesh and the Spirit. Let them mark the experience of their Lord and Master and lay aside their desponding fears. Let them study the experience of His saints in every age, from Paul downwards, and understand that as Christ had inward conflicts, so must Christians expect to have them also. To give way to doubts and unbelief, no doubt is wrong, and robs us of our peace. There is a faithless despondency, unquestionably, which is blameworthy and must be resisted, repented of, and brought to the fountain for all sin, that it may be pardoned. But the mere presence of fight and strife and conflict in our hearts is in itself no sin. The believer may be known by his inward warfare as well as by his inward peace.

We have, thirdly, in these verses, *a great miracle exhibited.* That miracle is the heavenly Voice described in this passage – a voice which was heard so plainly that people said it thundered – proclaiming, "I have glorified my name, and will glorify it again."

This wondrous Voice was heard three times during our Lord's earthly ministry. Once it was heard at His baptism, when the heavens were opened and the Holy Spirit descended on Him. Once it was heard at His transfiguration, when Moses and Elijah appeared for a season with Him, before Peter, James, and John. Once it was heard here at Jerusalem, in the midst of a mixed crowd of disciples and unbelieving Jews. On each occasion we know that it was the Voice of God the Father. But why this Voice was only heard on these occasions we are left to conjecture. The thing was a deep mystery, and we cannot now speak particularly of it.

Let it suffice us to believe that this was meant to show the intimate relations and unbroken union of God the Father and God the Son, throughout the period of the Son's earthly ministry. At no period during His incarnation was there a time when the eternal Father was not close to Him, though unseen by man.

Let us also believe that this was meant to signify to bystanders the entire approval of the Son by the Father, as the Messiah, the Redeemer, and the Savior of man. That approval the Father was pleased to signify by voice three times, as well as to declare by signs and mighty deeds, performed by the Son in His name. These things we may well believe.

We have, lastly, in these verses, *a great prophecy delivered.* The Lord Jesus declared, "I, if I be lifted up from the earth, will draw all men unto me." Concerning the true meaning of these words, there can be but one opinion in any honest mind. They do not mean, as is often supposed, that if the doctrine of Christ crucified is lifted up and exalted by ministers and teachers, it will have a drawing effect on hearers. This is undeniably a truth, but it is not the truth of the text. They simply mean that the death of Christ on the cross would have a drawing effect on all mankind. His death as our Substitute and the Sacrifice for our sins would draw multitudes out of every nation to believe on Him and receive Him as their Savior. By being crucified for us and not by ascending a temporal throne, He would set up a kingdom in the world and gather subjects to Himself.

How thoroughly this prophecy has been fulfilled for eighteen centuries, the history of the Church is an abundant proof. Whenever Christ crucified has been preached, and the story of the cross fully told, souls have been converted and drawn to Christ, in every part of the world, just as iron filings are drawn to a magnet. No truth so exactly suits the needs of all children of Adam, of every color, climate, and language, as the truth about Christ crucified.

And the prophecy is not yet exhausted. It shall yet receive a more complete accomplishment. A day shall come when every knee shall bow before the Lamb that was slain, and every tongue confess that He is Lord to the glory of God the Father. He who was "lifted up" on the cross shall yet sit on the throne of glory, and before Him shall be gathered all nations. Friends and foes, each in their own order, shall be "drawn" from their graves and appear before the judgment seat of Christ. Let us take heed in that day that we are found on His right hand!

John 12:34-43

The people answered him, We have heard out of the law that the Christ abides for ever; and how sayest thou, It is expedient that the Son of man be lifted up? Who is this Son of man? Then Jesus said unto them, Yet a little while is the

*Light with you. Walk while ye have the light, lest darkness
come upon you; for he that walks in darkness does not know
where he goes. While ye have the Light, believe in the Light
that ye may be the sons of light. Jesus spoke these things and
departed and hid himself from them. But although he had
done so many signs before them, yet they did not believe in
him, that the word of Isaiah the prophet might be fulfilled,
which he spoke, Lord, who shall believe our report? and to
whom has the arm of the Lord been revealed? Therefore they
could not believe, because Isaiah said again, He has blinded
their eyes and hardened their heart, that they should not
see with their eyes nor understand with their heart and be
converted, and I should heal them. Isaiah said these things
when he saw his glory and spoke of him. Nevertheless, even
among the princes many believed in him, but because of the
Pharisees they did not confess him, lest they should be put
out of the synagogue; for they loved the glory of men more
than the glory of God.*

We may learn, from these verses, *the duty of using present opportunities.*
The Lord Jesus says to us all, "Yet a little while is the light with you.
Walk while ye have the light, lest darkness come upon you. While ye
have light believe in the light." Let us not think that these things were
only spoken for the sake of the Jews. They were written for us also, upon
whom the ends of the world are come.

The lesson of the words is generally applicable to the whole professing Church of Christ. Its time for doing good in the world is short
and limited. The throne of grace will not always be standing – it will
be removed one day, and the throne of judgment will be set up in its
place. The door of salvation by faith in Christ will not always be open
– it will be shut one day forever, and the number of God's elect will be
completed. The fountain for all sin and uncleanness will not always be
accessible; the way to it will one day be barred, and there will remain
nothing but the lake that burns with fire and brimstone.

These are solemn thoughts; but they are true. They cry aloud to
sleeping Churchmen and drowsy congregations and ought to arouse

great searchings of heart. "Can nothing more be done to spread the Gospel at home and abroad? Has every means been tried for extending the knowledge of Christ crucified? Can we lay our hands on our hearts, and say that the Churches have left nothing undone in the matter of missions? Can we look forward to the Second Advent with no feelings of humiliation, and say that the talents of wealth, and influence, and opportunities have not been buried in the ground?" Such questions may well humble us, when we look, on one side, at the state of professing Christendom, and on the other, at the state of the heathen world. We must confess with shame that the Church is not walking worthy of its light.

But the lesson of the words is specially applicable to ourselves as individuals. Our own time for getting good is short and limited; let us take heed that we make good use of it. Let us "walk while we have the light." Have we Bibles? Let us not neglect to read them. Have we heard the Gospel of Jesus Christ? Let us not linger halting between two opinions, but believe to the saving of our souls. Have we Sabbaths? Let us not waste them in idleness, carelessness, and indifference, but throw our whole hearts into their sacred employments and turn them to good account. Light is about us and around us and near us on every side. Let us each resolve to walk in the light while we have it, lest we find ourselves at length cast out into outer darkness forever. It is a true saying of an old divine, that the recollection of lost and misspent opportunities will be the very essence of hell.

We may learn, secondly, from these verses, *the desperate hardness of the human heart.* It is written of our Lord's hearers at Jerusalem that "though he had done so many miracles before them, yet they believed not on Him."

We err greatly if we suppose that seeing wonderful miraculous things will ever convert souls. Thousands live and die in this delusion. They fancy if they saw some miraculous sight or witnessed some supernatural exercise of Divine grace, they would lay aside their doubts and at once become decided Christians. It is a total mistake. Nothing short of a new heart and a new nature implanted in us by the Holy Spirit will ever make us real disciples of Christ. Without this, a miracle might raise within us a little temporary excitement; but, the novelty once gone, we would find ourselves just as cold and unbelieving as the Jews.

The prevalence of unbelief and indifference in the present day ought not to surprise us. It is just one of the evidences of that mighty foundational doctrine, the total corruption and fall of man. How feebly we grasp and realize that doctrine is proved by our surprise at human incredulity. We only half believe the heart's deceitfulness. Let us read our Bibles more attentively and search their contents more carefully. Even when Christ wrought miracles and preached sermons, there were numbers of His hearers who remained utterly unmoved. What right have we to wonder if the hearers of modern sermons in countless instances remain unbelieving? "The disciple is not greater than his Master." If even the hearers of Christ did not believe, how much more should we expect to find unbelief among the hearers of His ministers! Let the truth be spoken and confessed. Man's obstinate unbelief is one among many indirect proofs that the Bible is true. The clearest prophecy in Isaiah begins with the solemn question, "Who hath believed?" (Isaiah 53:1).

We may learn, thirdly, from these verses, *the amazing power which the love of the world has over men.* We read that "among the chief rulers many believed on Christ; but because of the Pharisees they did not confess Him, lest they should be put out of the synagogue. For they loved the praise of men more than the praise of God."

These unhappy men were evidently convinced that Jesus was the true Messiah. Reason, and intellect, and mind, and conscience, obliged them secretly to admit that no one could do the miracles which He did, unless God was with Him, and that the preacher of Nazareth really was the Christ of God. But they had not courage to confess it. They dared not face the storm of ridicule, if not persecution, which confession would have entailed. And so, like cowards, they held their peace and kept their convictions to themselves.

Their case, it may be feared, is a sadly common one. There are thousands of people who know far more in religion than they act up to. They know they ought to come forward as decided Christians. They know that they are not living up to their light. But the fear of man keeps them back. They are afraid of being laughed at, jeered at, and despised by the world. They dread losing the good opinion of society and the favorable judgment of men and women like themselves. And so they go on from year to year, secretly ill at ease and dissatisfied with themselves – knowing too much of religion to be happy in the world and clinging too much to the world to enjoy any religion.

Faith is the only cure for soul ailments like this. A believing view of an unseen God, an unseen Christ, an unseen heaven, and an unseen judgment-day – this is the grand secret of overcoming the fear of man. The expulsive power of a new principle is required to heal the disease. "This is the victory that overcomes the world, even our faith" (1 John 5:4). Let us pray for faith, if we would conquer that deadly enemy of souls, the fear of man, and the love of man's praise. And if we have any faith, let us pray for more. Let our daily cry be, "Lord, increase our faith." We may easily have too much money or too much worldly prosperity; but we can never have too much faith.

John 12:44-50

But Jesus cried and said, He that believes in me, believes not in me, but in him that sent me, and he that sees me sees him that sent me. I am come as a light into the world that whosoever believes in me should not abide in darkness. And if anyone hears my words and believes not, I judge him not, for I came not to judge the world but to save the world. He that rejects me and does not receive my words has one that judges him: the word that I have spoken, the same shall judge him in the last day. For I have not spoken of myself; but the Father who sent me, he gave me a commandment, what I should say and what I should speak. And I know that his commandment is eternal life; whatsoever I speak therefore, even as the Father said unto me, so I speak.

These verses throw light on two subjects which we can never understand too well. Our daily peace and our practice of daily watchfulness over ourselves are closely connected with a clear knowledge of these two subjects.

One thing shown in these verses is *the dignity of our Lord Jesus Christ.* We find Him saying, "He that sees Me, sees Him that sent Me. I have come a Light into the world, that whosoever believes in Me should not abide in darkness." Christ's oneness with the Father and Christ's office are clearly exhibited in these words.

Concerning the unity of the Father and the Son, we must be content to believe reverently what we cannot grasp mentally or explain distinctly. Let it suffice us to know that our Savior was not like the prophets and patriarchs, a man sent by God the Father, a friend of God, and a witness for God. He was something far higher and greater than this. He was in His Divine nature essentially one with the Father – and in seeing Him, men saw the Father who sent Him. This is a great mystery; but a truth of vast importance to our souls. He that casts His sins on Jesus Christ by faith is building on a rock. Believing on Christ, he believes not merely on Him, but on Him that sent Him.

Concerning the office of Christ, there can be little doubt that in this place He compares Himself to the sun. Like the sun, He has risen on this sin-darkened world with healing on His wings and shines for the common benefit of all mankind. Like the sun, He is the great source and center of all spiritual life. Like the sun, He illuminates the whole earth, and no one need miss the way to heaven, if he will only use the light offered for his acceptance.

Forever let us make much of Christ in all our religion. We can never trust Him too much, follow Him too closely, or commune with Him too unreservedly. He has all power in heaven and earth. He is able to save to the uttermost all who come to God by Him. None can pluck us out of the hand of Him who is one with the Father. He can make all our way to heaven bright and plain and cheerful, like the morning sun cheering the traveler. Looking unto Him, we shall find light in our understandings, see light on the path of life we have to travel, feel light in our hearts, and find the days of darkness, which will come sometimes, stripped of half their gloom. Only let us abide in Him and look to Him with a single eye. There is a mine of meaning in His words, "If thine eye be single, thy whole body shall be full of light" (Matthew 6:22).

Another thing shown in these verses is *the certainty of a judgment to come*. We find our Lord saying, "He that rejects Me, and does not receive my words, has One that judges him – the word that I have spoken, the same shall judge him in the last day."

There is a last day! The world shall not always go on as it does now. Buying and selling, sowing and reaping, planting and building, marrying and giving in marriage – all this shall come to an end at last. There is a time appointed by the Father when the whole machinery of creation shall stop, and the present dispensation shall be changed for another. It had a beginning, and it shall also have an end. Banks shall at length close their doors forever. Stock exchanges shall be shut. Governments shall be dissolved. The very sun, which since Noah's flood has done his daily work so faithfully, shall rise and set no more. Well would it be if we thought more of this day! Paydays, birthdays, wedding days are often regarded as days of absorbing interest; but they are nothing compared to the last day.

There is a judgment coming! Men have their reckoning days, and God will at last have His. The trumpet shall sound. The dead shall be raised incorruptible. The living shall be changed. All, of every name and nation, and people and tongue, shall stand before the judgment seat of Christ. The books shall be opened, and the evidence brought forth. Our true character will come out before the world. There will be no concealment, no evasion, no false coloring. Every one shall give account of himself to God, and all shall be judged according to their works. The wicked shall go away into everlasting fire, and the righteous into life eternal.

These are dreadful truths! But they are truths and ought to be told. No wonder that the Roman governor Felix trembled when Paul the prisoner discoursed about "righteousness, temperance, and judgment to come" (Acts 24:25). Yet the believer in the Lord Jesus Christ has no cause to be afraid.[33] For him, at any rate, there is no condemnation,

---

33 These verses are also meant to correct the Jewish impression that Messiah was to come only to judge, to execute vengeance, to smite down His enemies, and to punish His adversaries. This impression arose from misapplied views of the Second Advent and the judgment

and the last assize (judgment; assessment) need have no terrors. The bias of his life shall witness for him, while the shortcomings of his life shall not condemn him. It is the man who rejects Christ and will not hear His call to repentance – he is the man who in the judgment day will have reason to be cast down and afraid.

Let the thought of judgment to come have a practical effect on our religion. Let us daily judge ourselves with righteous judgment that we may not be judged and condemned of the Lord. Let us so speak and so act as men who will be judged by the law of liberty. Let us make conscience of all our hourly conduct and never forget that for every idle word we must give account at the last day. In a word, let us live like those who believe in the truth of judgment, heaven, and hell. So living, we shall be Christians indeed and in truth and have boldness in the day of Christ's appearing.

Let the judgment day be the Christian's answer and apology when men ridicule him as too strict, too precise, and too particular in his religion. Irreligion may do tolerably well for a season, so long as a man is in health and prosperous and looks at nothing but this world. But he who believes that he must give account to the Judge of quick and dead at His appearing and kingdom will never be content with an ungodly life. He will say, "There is a judgment. I can never serve God too much. Christ died for me. I can never do too much for Him."

---

yet to come. Our Lord, for the last time, declares that He came for no such purpose. . . . Verse 47 means that our Lord came at His First Advent not to be judge, but a Savior not to inflict punishment, but to provide mercy. He came to provide salvation for all the world, so that any one in the world may be saved. But no one gets any benefit from this salvation excepting those that believe. The true key to the meaning of this sentence is the contrast between Christ's first coming and His second one. The first was to set up a throne of grace: the second will be to set up a throne of judgment. The expression in John 3:17 is precisely parallel – "God sent not His Son into the world to condemn the world, but that the world through Him might be saved."

John Chapter 13

John 13:1-5

Now before the feast of the passover, when Jesus knew that his hour was come that he should depart out of this world unto the Father, having loved his own who were in the world, he loved them unto the end. And supper being ended, the devil having now put into the heart of Judas Iscariot, Simon's son, to betray him, Jesus knowing that the Father had given all things into his hands and that he had come from God and was going to God, arose from the supper and laid aside his garments and took a towel and girded himself. After that, he poured water into a basin and began to wash the disciples' feet and to wipe them with the towel with which he was girded.

THE PASSAGE WE HAVE now read begins one of the most interesting portions of John's Gospel. For five consecutive chapters we find the Evangelist recording matters which are not mentioned by Matthew, Mark, and Luke. We can never be thankful enough that the Holy Spirit has caused them to be written for our learning! In every age the contents of these chapters have been justly regarded as one of the most precious parts of the Bible. They have been the food and drink, the strength and comfort of all true-hearted Christians. Let us ever approach them with peculiar reverence. The place whereon we stand is holy ground.

We learn, for one thing, from these verses, *what patient and continuing love there is in Christ's heart towards His people.* It is written that "having loved His own which were in the world, He loved them unto the end." Knowing perfectly well that they were about to forsake

Him shamefully in a very few hours, in full view of their approaching display of weakness and infirmity, our blessed Master did not cease to have loving thoughts of His disciples. He was not weary of them – He loved them to the last.

The love of Christ to sinners is the very essence and marrow of the Gospel. That He should love us at all and care for our souls – that He should love us before we love Him or even know anything about Him – that He should love us so much as to come into the world to save us, take our nature on Him, bear our sins, and die for us on the cross – all this is wonderful indeed! It is a kind of love to which there is nothing like it among men. The narrow selfishness of human nature cannot fully comprehend it. It is one of those things which even the angels of God "desire to look into." It is a truth which Christian preachers and teachers should proclaim incessantly and never be weary of proclaiming.

But the love of Christ to saints is no less wonderful, in its way, than His love to sinners, though far less considered. That He should bear with all their countless infirmities from grace to glory – that He should never be tired of their endless inconsistencies and petty provocations – that He should go on forgiving and forgetting incessantly and never be provoked to cast them off and give them up – all this is marvelous indeed! No mother watching over the waywardness of her feeble babe in the days of its infancy has her patience so thoroughly tried as the patience of Christ is tried by Christians. Yet His patience is infinite. His compassions are a well that is never exhausted. His love is "a love that passeth knowledge."

Let no man be afraid of beginning with Christ, if he desires to be saved. The chief of sinners may come to Him with boldness and trust Him for pardon with confidence. This loving Savior is One who delights to "receive sinners" (Luke 15:2). Let no man be afraid of going on with Christ after he has once come to Him and believed. Let him not fancy that Christ will cast him off because of failures, and dismiss him into his former hopelessness on account of infirmities. Such thoughts are entirely unwarranted by anything in the Scriptures. Jesus will never reject any servant because of feeble service and weak performance. Those whom He receives He always keeps. Those whom He loves at first He loves at last. His promise shall never be broken, and it is for saints as well as sinners – "He that comes to Me I will in no wise cast out" (John 6:37).

We learn, for another thing, from these verses, *what deep corruption may sometimes be found in the heart of a great professor of religion*. It is written that "the devil put into the heart of Judas Iscariot, Simon's son, to betray Christ."

This Judas, we must always remember, was one of the twelve Apostles. He had been chosen by Christ Himself at the same time with Peter, James, John, and their companions. For three years he had walked in Christ's society, had seen His miracles, had heard His preaching, had experienced many proofs of His loving-kindness. He had even preached himself and wrought miracles in Christ's name; and when our Lord sent out His disciples two and two, Judas Iscariot no doubt must have been one of some couple that was sent. Yet here we see this very man possessed by the devil and rushing headlong to destruction.

On all the coasts of England there is not such a beacon to warn sailors of danger as Judas Iscariot is to warn Christians. He shows us what length a man may go in religious profession, and yet turn out a rotten hypocrite at last, and prove never to have been converted. He shows us the uselessness of the highest privileges, unless we have a heart to value them and turn them to good account. Privileges alone without grace save nobody and will only make hell deeper. He shows us the uselessness of mere head knowledge. To know things with our brains and be able to talk and preach and speak to others is no proof that our own feet are in the way of peace. These are terrible lessons – but they are true.

Let us never be surprised if we see hypocrisy and false profession among Christians in modern days. There is nothing new in it, nothing peculiar, nothing that did not happen even among Christ's own immediate followers and under Christ's own eyes. Counterfeit money is a strong proof that there is good money somewhere. Hypocrisy is a strong indirect evidence that there is such a thing as true religion.

Above all, let us pray daily that our own Christianity may at any rate be genuine, sincere, real and true. Our faith may be feeble, our hope dim, our knowledge small, our failures frequent, our faults many. But at all events let us be real and true. Let us be able to say with poor, weak, erring Peter, "Thou, Lord, who knowest all things, knowest that I love Thee" (John 21:17).

John 13:6-15

Then he came to Simon Peter, and Peter said unto him, Lord, dost thou wash my feet? Jesus answered and said unto him, What I do thou dost not understand now, but thou shalt understand afterwards. Peter said unto him, Thou shalt never wash my feet. Jesus answered him, If I wash thee not, thou shalt have no part with me. Simon Peter said unto him, Lord, not my feet only, but also my hands and my head. Jesus said to him, He that is washed needs only to wash his feet because he is completely clean, and ye are clean, but not all. For he knew who should betray him; therefore, said he, Ye are not all clean. So after he had washed their feet and had taken his garments and had sat down again, he said unto them, Know ye what I have done to you? Ye call me Master and Lord; and ye say well, for so I am. If I then, the Lord and the Master, have washed your feet, ye also ought to wash one another's feet. For I have given you an example that ye should do as I have done to you.

The verses we have now read conclude the story of our Lord's washing the feet of His disciples, the night before He was crucified. It is a story full of touching interest, which for some wise reason no Evangelist records except John. The wonderful condescension of Christ in doing such a menial action can hardly fail to strike any reader. The mere fact that the Master should wash the feet of the servants might well fill us with surprise. But the circumstances and sayings which arose out of the action are just as interesting as the action itself. Let us see what they were.

We should notice, firstly, *the hasty ignorance of the Apostle Peter.* One moment we find him refusing to allow his Master to do such a servile work as He is about to do – "Dost thou wash my feet?" "Thou shalt never wash my feet." Another moment we find him rushing with characteristic impetuosity into the other extreme – "Lord, wash not my feet only, but my hands and my head." But throughout the transaction we find him unable to take in the real meaning of what his eyes behold. He sees, but he does not understand.

Let us learn from Peter's conduct that a man may have plenty of faith and love and yet be sadly destitute of clear knowledge. We must not set down men as graceless and godless because they are dull, and stupid, and blundering in their religion. The heart may often be quite right when the head is quite wrong. We must make allowances for the corruption of the understanding, as well as of the will. We must not be surprised to find that the brains as well as the affections of Adam's children have been hurt by the fall. It is a humbling lesson and one seldom fully learned except by long experience. But the longer we live the more true shall we find it that a believer, like Peter, may make many mistakes and lack understanding and yet, like Peter, have a heart right before God and get to heaven at last.

Even at our best estate we shall find that many of Christ's dealings with us are hard to understand in this life. The "why" and "wherefore" of many a providence will often puzzle and perplex us quite as much as the washing puzzled Peter. The wisdom, and fitness, and necessity of many a thing will often be hidden from our eyes. But at times like these we must remember the Master's words and fall back upon them – "What I do thou dost not understand now, but thou shalt understand afterwards." There came days, long after Christ had left the world, when Peter saw the full meaning of all that happened on the memorable night before the crucifixion. Even so there will be a day when every dark page in our life's history will be explained, and when, as we stand with Christ in glory, we shall know all.

We should notice, secondly, in this passage, *the plain practical lesson which lies upon its surface.* That lesson is read out to us by our Lord. He says, "I have given you an example, that ye should do as I have done to you."

Humility is evidently one part of the lesson. If the only-begotten Son of God, the King of kings, did not think it beneath Him to do the humblest work of a servant, there is nothing which His disciples should think themselves too great or too good to do. No sin is so offensive to

God and so injurious to the soul as pride. No grace is so commended, both by precept and example, as humility. "Be clothed with humility" (1 Peter 5:5). "He that humbles himself shall be exalted" (Luke 18:14). "Let this mind be in you, which was also in Christ Jesus; who, being in the form of God, thought it not robbery to be equal with God: but made Himself of no reputation, and took upon Him the form of a servant, and was made in the likeness of men: and being found in fashion as a man, He humbled Himself" (Philippians 2:5-8). Well would it be for the Church if this very simple truth was more remembered, and real humility was not so sadly rare. Perhaps there is no sight so displeasing in God's eyes as a self-conceited, self-satisfied, self-contented, stuck-up professor of religion. Alas, it is a sight only too common! Yet the words which John here records have never been repealed. They will be a swift witness against many at the last day, except they repent.

Love is manifestly the other part of the great practical lesson. Our Lord would have us love others so much that we should delight to do anything which can promote their happiness. We ought to rejoice in doing kindnesses, even in little things. We ought to count it a pleasure to lessen sorrow and multiply joy, even when it costs us some self-sacrifice and self-denial. We ought to love every child of Adam so well that if in the least trifle we can do anything to make him more happy and comfortable, we should be glad to do it. This was the mind of the Master, and this the ruling principle of His conduct upon earth. There are but few who walk in His steps, it may be feared; but these few are men and women after His own heart.

The lesson before us may seem a very simple one, but its importance can never be overrated. Humility and love are precisely the graces which the men of the world can understand, if they do not comprehend doctrines. They are graces about which there is no mystery, and they are within reach of all Christians. The poorest and most ignorant Christian can every day find occasion for practicing love and humility. Then if we would do good to the world and make our calling and election sure, let no man forget our Lord's example in this passage. Like Him, let us be humble and loving towards all.

We should notice, lastly, in this passage, *the deep spiritual lessons which lie beneath its surface.* They are three in number and lie at the very root of religion, though we can only touch them briefly.

For one thing, we learn that all need to be washed by Christ. "If I wash thee not, thou hast no part in Me." No man or woman can be saved unless his sins are washed away in Christ's precious blood. Nothing else can make us clean or acceptable before God. We must be "washed, sanctified, and justified, in the name of the Lord Jesus, and by the Spirit of our God" (1 Corinthians 6:11). Christ must wash us, if we are ever to sit down with saints in glory. Then let us take heed that we apply to Him by faith, wash and become clean. They only are washed who believe.

For another thing, we learn that even those who are cleansed and forgiven need a daily application to the blood of Christ for daily pardon. We cannot pass through this evil world without defilement. There is not a day in our lives but we fail and come short in many things and need fresh supplies of mercy. Even "he that is washed needs to wash his feet" and to wash them in the same fountain where he found peace of conscience when he first believed. Then let us daily use that fountain without fear. With the blood of Christ we must begin, and with the blood of Christ we must go on.

Finally, we learn that even those who kept company with Christ and were baptized with water as His disciples were "not all" washed from their sin. These words are very solemn – "Ye are clean: but not all." Then let us take heed to ourselves and beware of false profession. If even Christ's own disciples are not all cleansed and justified, we have reason to be on our guard. Baptism and Churchmanship are no proof that we are right in the sight of God.

John 13:16-20

Verily, verily, I say unto you, The slave is not greater than his lord; neither is the apostle greater than he that sent him. If ye know these things, ye shall be blessed if ye do them. I speak not of you all; I know whom I have chosen; but that the scripture may be fulfilled, He that eats bread with me has lifted up his heel against me, now I tell you before it is done, so that, when it is come to pass, ye may believe that I AM. Verily, verily, I say unto you, He that receives whomsoever I send receives me, and he that receives me receives him that sent me.

If we would understand the full meaning of these verses, we must mark carefully where they stand in the chapter. They follow right after the remarkable passage in which we read of Christ washing His disciples' feet. They stand in close connection with His solemn command that the disciples should do as they had seen Him do. Then come the five verses which we have now to consider.

We are taught, for one thing, in these verses, that *Christians must never be ashamed of doing anything that Christ has done.* We read, "Verily, I say unto you, The slave is not greater than his Lord; neither is the apostle greater than he that sent him."

There seems little doubt that our Lord's all-seeing eye saw a rising unwillingness in the minds of the Apostles to do such menial things as they had just seen Him do. Puffed up with their old Jewish expectation of thrones and kingdoms in this world, secretly self-satisfied with their own position as our Lord's friends, these poor Galileans were startled at the idea of washing people's feet! They could not bring themselves to believe that Messiah's service entailed work like this. They could not yet take in the grand truth that true Christian greatness consisted in doing good to others. And hence they needed our Lord's word of warning. If He had humbled Himself to do humbling work, His disciples must not hesitate to do the same.

The lesson is one of which we all need to be reminded. We are all too apt to dislike any work which seems to entail trouble, self-denial, and going down to our inferiors. We are only too ready to relegate such work to others and to excuse ourselves by saying, "It is not in our way." When feelings of this kind arise within us, we shall find it good to remember our Lord's words in this passage, no less than our Lord's example. We ought never to think it beneath us to show kindness to the lowest of men. We ought never to hold our hand because the objects of our kindness are ungrateful or unworthy. Such was not the mind of

Him who washed the feet of Judas Iscariot as well as Peter. He who in these matters cannot stoop to follow Christ's example gives little evidence of possessing true love or true humility.

We are taught, for another thing, in these verses, *the uselessness of religious knowledge if not accompanied by practice.* We read, "If ye know these things, happy are ye if ye do them." It sounds as if our Lord would warn His disciples that they would never be really happy in His service if they were content with a barren head knowledge of duty and did not live according to their knowledge.

The lesson is one which deserves the continual remembrance of all professing Christians. Nothing is more common than to hear people saying of doctrine or duty – "We know it, we know it;" while they sit still in unbelief or disobedience. They actually seem to flatter themselves that there is something creditable and redeeming in knowledge, even when it bears no fruit in heart, character, or life. Yet the truth is precisely the other way. To know what we ought to be, believe, and do, and yet to be unaffected by our knowledge, only adds to our guilt in the sight of God. To know that Christians should be humble and loving, while we continue proud and selfish, will only sink us deeper in the pit, unless we awake and repent. Practice, in short, is the very life of religion. "To him that knows to do good, and does it not, to him it is sin" (James 4:17).

Of course we must never *despise* knowledge. It is in one sense the beginning of Christianity in the soul. So long as we know nothing of sin, or God, or Christ, or grace, or repentance, or faith, or conscience, we are of course nothing better than heathens. But we must not overrate knowledge. It is altogether valueless unless it produces results in our conduct, and influences our lives, and moves our wills. In fact, knowledge without practice does not raise us above the level of the devil. He could say to Jesus, "I know Thee who Thou art, the Holy One of God." The devils, says James, "believe and tremble" (James 2:19). Satan knows truth, but has no will to obey it and is miserable. He that would be happy in Christ's service must not only know, but do.

We are taught, for another thing, in these verses, *the perfect knowledge which Christ has of all His people.* He can distinguish between false profession and true grace. The Church may be deceived and rank men as Apostles who are nothing better than brethren of Judas Iscariot. But Jesus is never deceived, for He can read hearts. And here He declares with peculiar emphasis, "I know whom I have chosen."

This perfect knowledge of our Lord Jesus Christ is a very solemn thought and one which cuts two ways. It ought to fill the hypocrite with alarm and drive him to repentance. Let him remember that the eyes of the all-seeing Judge already see him through and through and detect the absence of a wedding garment. If he would not be put to shame before assembled worlds, let him cast aside his false profession and confess his sin before it is too late. Believers, on the other hand, may think of an all-knowing Savior with comfort. They may remember, when misunderstood and slandered by an evil world, that their Master knows all. He knows that they are true and sincere, however weak and failing. A time is coming when He will confess them before His Father and bring forth their characters clear and bright as the summer sun at noon-day.

We are taught, finally, in these verses, *the true dignity of Christ's disciples.* The world may despise and ridicule the Apostles because they care more for works of love and humility than the pursuits of the world. But the Master bids them remember their commission and not be ashamed. They are God's ambassadors and have no cause to be cast down. "Verily, verily," He declares, "He that receiveth whomsoever I send receiveth Me; and he that receiveth Me receiveth Him that sent Me."

The doctrine here laid down is full of encouragement. It ought to cheer and hearten all who lay themselves out to do good, and specially to do good to the fallen and the poor. Work of this kind gets little praise from men, and they who give themselves up to it are often regarded as miserable enthusiasts and meet with much opposition. Let them however work on and take comfort in the words of Christ which we are now considering. To spend and be spent in trying to do good makes a man far more honorable in the eyes of Jesus than to command armies or amass a fortune. The few who work for God in Christ's way have no cause to be ashamed. Let them not be cast down if the children of the world laugh and sneer and despise them. A day comes when they will hear the words, "Come ye blessed children of my Father, inherit the kingdom prepared for you" (Matthew 25:34).

John 13:21-30

*When Jesus had thus said, he was troubled in spirit and tes-
tified and said, Verily, verily, I say unto you, that one of you
shall betray me. Then the disciples looked one on another,
doubting of whom he spoke. And one of his disciples, whom
Jesus loved, was seated at the table beside Jesus. Simon Peter
therefore beckoned to this one that he should ask him who
it was of whom he spoke. He then, reclining on Jesus' breast,
said unto him, Lord, who is it? Jesus answered, He it is to
whom I shall give a sop when I have dipped it. And when he
had dipped the sop, he gave it to Judas Iscariot, the son of
Simon. And after the sop Satan entered into him. Then Jesus
said unto him, That which thou shalt do, do it more quickly.
Now no one at the table understood for what purpose he
spoke this unto him. For some of them thought, because
Judas had the bag, that Jesus had said unto him, Buy those
things that we need for the feast, or that he should give
something to the poor. He then having received the sop went
immediately out, and it was now night.*

The subject of the verses before us is a very painful one. They describe the last scene between our Lord Jesus Christ and the false Apostle Judas Iscariot. They contain the last words which passed between them before they parted forever in this world. They never seem to have met again on earth, excepting in the garden when our Lord was taken prisoner. Within a short time both the holy Master and the treacherous servant were dead. They will never meet again in the body until the trumpet sounds, and the dead are raised, and the judgment is set, and the books are opened. What a dreadful meeting will that be!

Let us mark, firstly, in this passage, *what trouble our Lord Jesus went through for the sake of our souls.* We are told that shortly after washing the disciples' feet, He "was troubled in spirit, and said, One of you shall betray Me."

The whole length and breadth and depth of our Master's troubles during His earthly ministry are far beyond the conception of most people. His death and suffering on the cross were only the heading up and completion of His sorrows. But all throughout His life – partly from the general unbelief of the Jews – partly from the special hatred of the Pharisees and Sadducees – partly from the weakness and infirmity of His few followers – He must have been in a peculiar degree "a Man of sorrows and acquainted with grief" (Isaiah 53:3).

But the trouble before us was a singular and exceptional one. It was the bitter sorrow of seeing a chosen Apostle deliberately becoming an apostate, a backslider, and an ungrateful traitor. That it was a foreseen sorrow from the beginning we need not doubt; but sorrow is not less acute because long foreseen. That it was a peculiarly cutting sorrow is very evident. Nothing is found so hard for flesh and blood to bear as ingratitude. Even a poet of our own has said that it is "sharper than a serpent's tooth to have a thankless child." Absalom's rebellion seems to have been David's heaviest trouble, and Judas Iscariot's treachery may have been one of the heaviest trials of the Son of David.

Passages like these should make us see the amazing love of Christ to sinners. How many cups of sorrow He drained to the dregs in working out our salvation beside the mighty cup of bearing our sins. They show us how little reason we have for complaining when friends fail us, and men disappoint us. If we share our Master's lot, we have no cause to be surprised. Above all, they show us the perfect suitableness of Christ to be our Savior. He can sympathize with us. He has suffered Himself and can feel for those who are ill used and forsaken.

Let us mark, secondly, in these verses, *the power and malignity of our great enemy the devil.* We are told in the beginning of the chapter that he "put it into the heart" of Judas to betray our Lord. We are told here that he "entered into" him. First he suggests – then he commands. First he knocks at the door and asks permission to come in – then, once admitted, he takes complete possession and rules the whole inward man like a tyrant.

Let us take heed that we are not "ignorant of Satan's devices." He is still going to and fro in the earth, seeking whom he may devour. He is about our path, and about our bed, and spies out all our ways. Our only safety lies in resisting him at the first and not listening to his first advances. For this we are all responsible. Strong as he is, he has no power to do us harm, if we cry to the stronger One in heaven and use the means which He has appointed. It is a standing principle of Christianity and will ever be found true. "Resist the devil, and he will flee from you" (James 4:7).

Once let a man begin tampering with the devil, and he never knows how far he may fall. Trifling with the first thoughts of sin – making light of evil ideas when first offered to our hearts – allowing Satan to talk to us, and flatter us, and put bad notions into our hearts – all this may seem a small matter to many. It is precisely at this point that the road to ruin often begins. He that allows Satan to sow wicked thoughts will soon find within his heart a crop of wicked habits. Happy is he who really believes that there is a devil, and believing, watches and prays daily that he may be kept from his temptations.

Let us mark, lastly, in these verses, *the extreme hardness which comes over the heart of a backsliding professor of religion.* This is a thing which is most painfully brought out in the case of Judas Iscariot. One might have thought that the sight of our Lord's trouble and the solemn warning, "One of you shall betray Me," would have stirred the conscience of this unhappy man. But it did not do so. One might have thought that the solemn words, "what thou doest, do quickly," would have arrested him, and made him ashamed of his intended sin. But nothing seems to have moved him. Like one whose conscience was dead, buried, and gone, he rises and goes out to do his wicked work and parts with his Lord forever.

The extent to which we may harden ourselves by resisting light and knowledge is one of the most fearful facts in our nature. We may become past feeling, like those whose limbs are mortified before they die. We may lose entirely all sense of fear, or shame, or remorse, and have a heart as hard as the nether millstone, blind to every warning, and deaf to every appeal. It is a painful disease, but one which unhappily is not uncommon among professing Christians. None seem so liable to it as those who, having great light and privilege, deliberately turn their backs on Christ and return to the world. Nothing seems likely to touch such people but the voice of the archangel and the trumpet of God. Let us watch jealously over our hearts and beware of giving way to the beginnings of sin. Happy is he who fears always and walks humbly with his God (Proverbs 28:14). The strongest Christian is the one who feels his weakness most and cries most frequently, "Hold me up, and I shall be saved" (Psalm 119:117).

John 13:31-38

Therefore, when he was gone out, Jesus said, Now is the Son of man clarified, and God is clarified in him. If God is clarified in him, God shall also clarify him in himself and shall straightway clarify him. Little children, yet a little while I am with you. Ye shall seek me; and as I said unto the Jews, Where I go, ye cannot come, so now I say to you. A new commandment I give unto you, That ye love one another; as I have loved you, that ye also love one another. By this shall everyone know that ye are my disciples, if ye have love one to another. Simon Peter said unto him, Lord, where goest thou? Jesus answered him, Where I go, thou canst not follow me now; but thou shalt follow me afterwards. Peter said unto him, Lord, why cannot I follow thee now? I will lay down my soul for thy sake. Jesus answered him, Wilt thou lay down thy soul for my sake? Verily, verily, I say unto thee, The cock shall not crow until thou hast denied me three times.

In this passage we find the Lord Jesus at last alone with His eleven faithful disciples. The traitor, Judas Iscariot, had left the room and gone out to do his wicked deed of darkness. Freed from his painful company, our Lord opens His heart to His little flock more fully than He had ever done before. Speaking to them for the last time before His passion, He begins a discourse which for touching interest surpasses any portion of Scripture.

These verses show us *what glory the crucifixion brought both to God the Father and to God the Son.* It seems impossible to avoid the conclusion that this was what our Lord had in His mind when He said, "Now is the Son of man glorified, and God is glorified in Him." It is as though He said, "The time of my crucifixion is at hand. My work on earth is finished. An event is about to take place tomorrow, which, however painful to you who love Me, is in reality most glorifying both to Me and My Father."

This was a dark and mysterious saying, and we may well believe that the eleven did not understand it. And no wonder! In all the agony of the death on the cross, in all the ignominy and humiliation which they saw afar off, or heard of next day, in hanging in great pain for six hours between two thieves – in all this there was no appearance of glory! – On the contrary, it was an event calculated to fill the minds of the Apostles with shame, disappointment, and dismay. And yet our Lord's saying was true.

The crucifixion brought glory to the Father. It glorified His wisdom, faithfulness, holiness, and love. It showed Him wise in providing a plan whereby He could be just and yet the Justifier of the ungodly. It showed Him faithful in keeping His promise that the seed of the woman should bruise the serpent's head. It showed Him holy in requiring His law's demands to be satisfied by our great Substitute. It showed Him loving in providing such a Mediator, such a Redeemer, and such a Friend for sinful man as His co-eternal Son.

The crucifixion brought glory to the Son. It glorified His compassion, His patience, and His power. It showed Him most compassionate in dying for us, suffering in our stead, allowing Himself to be counted sin and a curse for us and buying our redemption with the price of His own blood. It showed Him most patient in not dying the common death of most men, but in willingly submitting to such horrors and unknown agonies as no mind can conceive, when with a word he could have summoned His Father's angels and been set free. It showed Him most powerful in bearing the weight of all a world's transgressions and vanquishing Satan and despoiling him of his prey.

Forever let us cling to these thoughts about the crucifixion. Let us remember that painting and sculpture can never tell a tenth part of what took place on the cross. Crucifixes and pictures at best can only show us a human being agonizing in a painful death. But of the length and breadth and depth and height of the work transacted on the cross – of God's law honored, man's sins borne, sin punished in a Substitute, free salvation bought for man – of all this they can tell nothing. Yet all this lies hid under the crucifixion. No wonder Paul cries, "God forbid that I should glory, save in the cross of our Lord Jesus Christ" (Galatians 6:14).

These verses show us, secondly, *what great importance our Lord Jesus attaches to the grace of brotherly love.* Almost as soon as the false Apostle had left the faithful eleven, comes the injunction, "Love one another." Immediately after the sad announcement that He would leave them soon, the commandment is given, "Love one another." It is called a "new" commandment, not because it had never been given before, but because it was to be more honored to occupy a higher position, to be backed by a higher example than it ever had been before. Above all, it was to be the test of Christianity before the world. "By this shall all men know that ye are my disciples, if ye have love one to another."

Let us take heed that this well-known Christian grace is not merely a notion in our heads, but a practice in our lives. Of all the commands of our Master there is none which is so much talked about and so little obeyed as this. Yet, if we mean anything when we profess to have charity and love toward all men, it ought to be seen in our tempers and our words, our bearing and our doing, our behavior at home and abroad, our conduct in every relation of life. Specially it ought to show itself forth in all our dealing with other Christians. We should regard them as brethren and sisters, and delight to do anything to promote their happiness. We should abhor the idea of envy, malice, and jealousy towards a member of Christ and regard it as a downright sin. This is what our Lord meant when He told us to love one another.

Christ's cause in the earth would prosper far more than it does if this simple law was more honored. There is nothing that the world understands and values more than true charity. The very men who cannot comprehend doctrine and know nothing of theology can appreciate charity. It arrests their attention and makes them think. For the world's sake, if for no other cause, let us follow after charity more and more.

These verses show us, lastly, *how much self-ignorance there may be in the heart of a true believer.* We see Simon Peter declaring that he was ready to lay down his life for his Master. We see his Master telling him that in that very night he would "deny Him three times." And we all know how the matter ended. The Master was right, and Peter was wrong.

Let it be a settled principle in our religion, that there is an amount of weakness in all our hearts of which we have no adequate conception, and that we never know how far we might fall if we were tempted. We fancy sometimes, like Peter, that there are some things we could not possibly do. We look pitifully upon others who fall and please ourselves in the thought that at any rate we would not have done so. We know nothing at all. The seeds of every sin are latent in our hearts even when renewed, and they only need occasion, or carelessness and the withdrawal of God's grace for a season, to put forth an abundant crop. Like Peter, we may think we can do wonders for Christ, and like Peter, we may learn by bitter experience that we have no power and might at all.

The servant of Christ will do wisely to remember these things. "Let him that thinks he stands, take heed lest he fall" (1 Corinthians 10:12). A humble sense of our own innate weakness, a constant dependence on the Strong for strength, a daily prayer to be held up, because we cannot hold up ourselves – these are the true secrets of safety. The great Apostle of the Gentiles said, "When I am weak, then I am strong" (2 Corinthians 12:10).

John Chapter 14

John 14:1-3

Let not your heart be troubled; ye believe in God, believe also in me. In my Father's house are many dwelling places; if it were not so, I would have told you. I go to prepare a place for you. And if I go and prepare a place for you, I will come again and take you unto myself; that where I am, there ye may be also.

THE THREE VERSES WE have now read are rich in precious truth. For eighteen centuries they have been peculiarly dear to Christ's believing servants in every part of the world. Many are the sick rooms which they have lightened! Many are the dying hearts which they have cheered! Let us see what they contain.

We have, first, in this passage *a precious remedy against an old disease.* That disease is trouble of heart. That remedy is faith.

Heart trouble is the commonest thing in the world. No rank, or class, or condition is exempt from it. No bars, or bolts, or locks can keep it out. Partly from inward causes and partly from outward causes – partly from the body and partly from the mind – partly from what we love and partly from what we fear, the journey of life is full of trouble. Even the best of Christians have many bitter cups to drink between grace and glory. Even the holiest saints find the world a valley of tears.

Faith in the Lord Jesus is the only sure medicine for troubled hearts. To believe more thoroughly, trust more entirely, rest more unreservedly, lay hold more firmly, lean back more completely – this is the prescription which our Master urges on the attention of all His disciples. No doubt the members of that little band which sat round the table at the last supper had believed already. They had proved the reality of their faith by giving up everything for Christ's sake. Yet what does their Lord say to them here? Once more He presses on them the old lesson, the lesson with which they first began – "Believe! Believe more! Believe on Me!" (Isaiah 26:3).

Never let us forget that there are degrees in faith, and that there is a wide difference between weak and strong believers. The weakest faith is enough to give a man a saving interest in Christ and ought not to be despised, but it will not give a man such inward comfort as a strong faith. Vagueness and dimness of perception are the defect of weak believers. They do not see clearly what they believe and why they believe. In such cases more faith is the one thing needed. Like Peter on the water, they need to look more steadily at Jesus and less at the waves and wind. Is it not written, "Thou wilt keep him in perfect peace whose mind is stayed on Thee"? (Isaiah. 26:3).

We have, secondly, in this passage *a very comfortable account of heaven, or the future abode of saints.* It is but little that we understand about heaven while we are here in the body, and that little is generally taught us in the Bible by negatives much more than positives. But here, at any rate, there are some plain things.

Heaven is "a Father's house" – the house of that God of whom Jesus says, "I go to my Father, and your Father." It is, in a word, home – the home of Christ and Christians.[34] This is a sweet and touching expression. Home, as we all know, is the place where we are generally loved for our own sakes and not for our gifts or possessions; the place where we are loved to the end, never forgotten, and always welcome. This is one idea of heaven. Believers are in a strange land and at school in this life. In the life to come they will be at home.

Heaven is a place of "mansions" – of lasting, permanent, and eternal dwellings. Here in the body we are in temporary lodgings, tents, and tabernacles and must submit to many changes. In heaven we shall be settled at last and go out no more. "Here we have no continuing city"

---

34 God needs no literal house, with walls and roof as we do. But where He dwells is called His house (Deuteronomy 26:15; Psalm 33:14; 2 Chronicles 38:27; 2 Corinthians 5:1). There is something very touching and comforting in the thought that the heaven we go to is "our Father's house." It is home.

(Hebrews 13:14). Our house not made with hands shall never be taken down.

Heaven is a place of "many mansions." There will be room for all believers and room for all sorts, for little saints as well as great ones, for the weakest believer as well as for the strongest. The feeblest child of God need not fear there will be no place for him. None will be shut out but impenitent sinners and obstinate unbelievers.

Heaven is a place where Christ Himself shall be present.[35] He will not be content to dwell without His people – "Where I am, there ye shall be also." We need not think that we shall be alone and neglected. Our Savior – our elder Brother – our Redeemer, who loved us and gave Himself for us, shall be in the midst of us forever. What we shall see, and whom we shall see in heaven, we cannot fully conceive yet, while we are in the body. But one thing is certain – we shall see Christ.

Let these things sink down into our minds. To the worldly and careless, they may seem nothing at all. To all who feel in themselves the working of the Spirit of God they are full of unspeakable comfort. If we hope to be in heaven, it is pleasant to know what heaven is like.

We have, lastly, in this passage *a solid ground for expecting good things to come.* The evil heart of unbelief within us is apt to rob us of our comfort about heaven. "We wish we could think it was all true." "We fear we shall never be admitted into heaven." Let us hear what Jesus says to encourage us.

One cheering word is this – "I go to prepare a place for you." Heaven is a prepared place for a prepared people – a place which we shall find Christ Himself has made ready for true Christians. He has prepared it by procuring a right for every sinner who believes to enter in. None can stop us and say we have no business there. He has prepared it by going before us as our Head and Representative and taking possession of it for all the members of His mystical body. As our Forerunner He has marched in, leading captivity captive, and has planted His banner in the land of glory. He has prepared it by carrying our names with Him as our High Priest into the holy of holies and making angels ready to

---

35 Let us note that one of the simplest, plainest ideas of heaven is here. It is being "ever with the Lord." Whatever else we see or do not see in heaven, we shall see Christ. Whatever kind of a place, it is a place where Christ is (Philippians 1:23; 1 Thessalonians 4:17).

receive us. Those who enter heaven will find they are neither unknown nor unexpected.

Another cheering word is this – "I will come again and receive you unto myself." Christ will not wait for believers to come up to Him, but will come down to them, to raise them from their graves and escort them to their heavenly home. As Joseph came to meet Jacob, so will Jesus come to call His people together and guide them to their inheritance. The second advent ought never to be forgotten. Great is the blessedness of looking back to Christ coming the first time to suffer for us, but no less great is the comfort of looking forward to Christ coming the second time to raise and reward His saints.

Let us leave the whole passage with solemnized feelings and serious self-examination. How much they miss who live in a dying world and yet know nothing of God as their Father and Christ as their Savior! How much they possess who live the life of faith in the Son of God and believe in Jesus! With all their weaknesses and crosses, they have that which the world can neither give nor take away. They have a true Friend while they live and a true home when they die.

John 14:4-11

So that ye know where I go, and ye know the way. Thomas said unto him, Lord, we know not where thou goest; how, therefore, can we know the way? Jesus said unto him, I AM the way, the truth, and the life; no one comes unto the Father, but by me. If ye had known me, ye should have known my Father also; and from now on ye know him and have seen him. Philip said unto him, Lord, show us the Father, and it will suffice us. Jesus said unto him, Have I been such a long time with you, and yet thou hast not known me, Philip? He that has seen me has seen the Father; and how sayest thou then, Show us the Father? Believest thou not that I am in the Father and the Father in me? The words that I speak unto you I speak not of myself; but the Father that dwells in me, he does the works. Believe me that I am in the

Father and the Father in me, or else believe me for the very works' sake.

We should mark in these verses *how much better Jesus speaks of believers than they speak of themselves.* He says to His disciples, "Ye know where I go, and ye know the way." And yet Thomas at once breaks in with the remark, "We know not where thou goest; how, therefore, can we know the way?" The apparent contradiction demands explanation. It is more seeming than real.

Certainly, in one point of view, the knowledge of the disciples was very small. They knew little before the crucifixion and resurrection compared to what they might have known and little compared to what they afterwards knew after the day of Pentecost. About our Lord's purpose in coming into the world, about His sacrificial death and substitution for us on the cross, their ignorance was glaring and great. It might well be said that they "knew in part" only, and were children in understanding.

And yet, in another point of view, the knowledge of the disciples was very great. They knew far more than the great majority of the Jewish nation and received truths which the Scribes and Pharisees entirely rejected. Compared to the world around them, they were in the highest sense enlightened. They knew and believed that their Master was the promised Messiah, the Son of the living God; and to know Him was the first step towards heaven. All things go by comparison. Before we lightly esteem the disciples because of their ignorance, let us take care that we do not underrate their knowledge. They knew more precious truth than they were aware of themselves. Their hearts were better than their heads.

The plain truth is that all believers are apt to undervalue the work of the Spirit in their own souls and to fancy they know nothing because they do not know everything. Many true Christians are thought more of in heaven while they live than they think of themselves and will find it out to their surprise at the last day. There is One above who takes far more account of heart knowledge than head knowledge. Many go mourning all the way to heaven because they know so little, and fancy they will miss the way altogether, and yet have hearts with which God is well pleased.

We should mark, secondly, in these verses, *what glorious names the Lord Jesus gives Himself.* He says, "I am the way, the truth, and the life." The fullness of these precious words can probably never be taken in by man. He that attempts to unfold them does little more than scratch the surface of a rich soil.

Christ is "the way" – the way to heaven and peace with God. He is not only the guide, and teacher, and lawgiver, like Moses; He is Himself the door, the ladder, and the road through whom we must draw near to God. He has opened the way to the tree of life, which was closed when Adam and Eve fell, by the satisfaction He made for us on the cross. Through His blood we may draw near with boldness and have access with confidence into God's presence.

Christ is "the truth" – the whole substance of true religion which the mind of man requires. Without Him the wisest heathen groped in gross darkness and knew nothing about God. Before He came even the Jews saw "through a glass darkly" and discerned nothing distinctly under the types, figures, and ceremonies of the Mosaic law. Christ is the whole truth and meets and satisfies every desire of the human mind.

Christ is "the life" – the sinner's title to eternal life and pardon, the believer's root of spiritual life and holiness, the surety of the Christian's resurrection life. He that believes on Christ has everlasting life. He that abides in Him, as the branch abides in the vine, shall bring forth much fruit. He that believes on Him, though he were dead, yet shall he live. The root of all life, for soul and for body, is Christ.

Forever let us grasp and hold fast these truths. To use Christ daily as the way, to believe Christ daily as the truth, to live on Christ daily as the life, this is to be a well-informed, a thoroughly furnished and an established Christian.

We should mark, thirdly, in these verses, *how expressly the Lord Jesus shuts out all ways of salvation but Himself.* "No man," He declares, "No man cometh unto the Father but by Me."[36]

---

36   We should mark carefully what an unanswerable argument this sentence supplies against the modern notion that it does not matter what a man believes – that all religions will lead men to heaven if they are sincere – that creeds and doctrines are of no importance – that heaven is a place for all mankind – whether heathen, Mohammedan, or Christian – and that the Fatherhood of God is enough to save all at last, of all sects, kinds, and characters! Our Lord's words should never be forgotten. "There is no way to the Father but by Me."

It avails nothing that a man is clever, learned, highly gifted, amiable, charitable, kindhearted, and zealous about some sort of religion. All this will not save his soul if he does not draw near to God by Christ's atonement and make use of God's own Son as his Mediator and Savior. God is so holy that all men are guilty and debtors in His sight. Sin is so sinful that no mortal man can make satisfaction for it. There must be a mediator, a ransom-payer, a redeemer between ourselves and God, or else we can never be saved. There is only one door, one bridge, one ladder between earth and heaven – the crucified Son of God. Whoever will enter in by that door may be saved; but to him who refuses to use that door, the Bible holds out no hope at all. Without shedding of blood there is no remission.

Let us beware, if we love life, of supposing that mere earnestness will take a man to heaven, though he knows nothing of Christ. The idea is a deadly and ruinous error. Sincerity will never wipe away our sins. It is not true that every man will be saved by his own religion, no matter what he believes, so long as he is diligent and sincere. We must not pretend to be wiser than God. Christ has said, and Christ will stand to it, "No man cometh unto the Father but by Me."

We should mark, lastly, in these verses, *how close and mysterious is the union of God the Father and God the Son.* Four times over, this mighty truth is put before us in words that cannot be mistaken. "If ye had known Me, ye would have known my Father." "He that hath seen Me hath seen the Father." "I am in the Father, and the Father in Me." "The Father that dwelleth in Me, He doeth the works."

Sayings like these are full of deep mystery. We have no eyes to see their meaning fully – no line to fathom it – no language to express it – no mind to take it in. We must be content to believe when we cannot explain and to admire and revere when we cannot interpret. Let it suffice us to know and hold that the Father is God and the Son is God, and yet that they are one in essence though two distinct Persons – ineffably one and yet ineffably distinct. These are high things, and we cannot attain to a full comprehension of them.

Let us however take comfort in the simple truth that Christ is very

---

God is a Father to none but to those who believe in Christ. In short, there are not many ways to heaven. There is only one way.

God of very God; equal with the Father in all things and One with Him. He who loved us, and shed His blood for us on the cross, and bids us trust Him for pardon is no mere man like ourselves. He is "God over all, blessed forever," and able to save to the uttermost the chief of sinners. Though our sins be as scarlet, He can make them white as snow. He that casts his soul on Christ has an Almighty Friend – a Friend who is One with the Father and very God.

John 14:12-17

Verily, verily, I say unto you, He that believes in me, the works that I do he shall do also; and greater works than these shall he do because I go unto my Father. And whatsoever ye shall ask the Father in my name, that will I do, that the Father may be glorified in the Son. If ye ask any thing in my name, I will do it. If ye love me, keep my commandments; and I will ask the Father, and he shall give you another Comforter, that he may abide with you for ever, even the Spirit of truth, whom the world cannot receive because it does not see him, or know him; but ye know him, for he dwells with you and shall be in you.

These verses are an example of our Lord's tender consideration for the weakness of His disciples. He saw them troubled and faint-hearted at the prospect of being left alone in the world. He cheers them by three promises peculiarly suited to their circumstances. "A word spoken in season, how good is it!"

We have first in this passage, a striking promise about *the works that Christians may do*. Our Lord says, "He that believes in Me, the works that I do he shall do also; and greater works than these shall he do; because I go unto my Father."

The full meaning of this promise is not to be sought in the miracles which the Apostles wrought after Christ left the world. Such a notion seems hardly borne out by facts. We read of no Apostle walking on the water or raising a person four days dead like Lazarus. What our Lord has in view seems to be the far greater number of conversions, the far wider spread of the Gospel, which would take place under the ministry of the Apostles than under his own teaching. This was the case, we know from the Acts of the Apostles. We read of no sermon preached by Christ under which three thousand were converted in one day, as they were on the day of Pentecost. In short, "greater works" mean more conversions. There is no greater work possible than the conversion of a soul.

Let us admire the condescension of our Master in allowing to the ministry of His weak servants more success than to His own. Let us learn that His visible presence is not absolutely necessary to the progress of His kingdom. He can help forward His cause on earth quite as much by sitting at the right hand of the Father and sending forth the Holy Spirit as by walking to and fro in the world. Let us believe that there is nothing too hard or too great for believers to do, so long as their Lord intercedes for them in heaven. Let us work on in faith and expect great things, though we feel weak and lonely like the disciples. Our Lord is working with us and for us, though we cannot see Him. It was not so much the sword of Joshua that defeated Amalek, as the intercession of Moses on the hill (Exodus 17:11).

We have, secondly, in this passage, a striking promise *about things that Christians may get by prayer.* Our Lord says, "Whatsoever ye shall ask in my name, that will I do . . . If ye shall ask anything in my name, I will do it."

These words are a direct encouragement to the simple yet great duty of praying. Everyone who kneels daily before God and from his heart "says his prayers" has a right to take comfort in these words. Weak and imperfect as his supplications may be, so long as they are put in Christ's hands and offered in Christ's name, they shall not be in vain. We have a Friend at Court, an Advocate with the Father; and if we honor Him by sending all our petitions through Him, He pledges His word that they shall succeed. Of course it is taken for granted that the things we ask are for our souls' good and not mere temporal benefits. "Anything" and "whatsoever" do not include wealth, and money, and worldly prosperity. These things are not always good for us, and our Lord loves us too well to let us have them. But whatever is really good for our souls, we need not doubt we shall have, if we ask in Christ's name.

How is it that many true Christians have so little? How is it that they go halting and mourning on the way to heaven, and enjoy so little peace, and show so little strength in Christ's service? The answer is simple and plain. "They have not, because they ask not." They have little because they ask little. They are no better than they are because they do not ask their Lord to make them better. Our languid desires are the reason of our languid performances. We are not straitened in our Lord but in ourselves. Happy are they who never forget the words, "Open thy mouth wide, and I will fill it" (Psalm 81:10). He that does much for Christ and leaves his mark in the world will always prove to be one who prays much.

We have, lastly, in this passage, a striking promise *about the Holy Spirit.* Our Lord says, "I will ask the Father, and He shall give you another Comforter, even the Spirit of truth."

This is the first time that the Holy Spirit is mentioned as Christ's special gift to His people. Of course we are not to suppose that He did not dwell in the hearts of all the Old Testament saints. But He was given with peculiar influence and power to believers when the New Testament dispensation came in, and this is the special promise of the passage before us. We shall find it useful, therefore, to observe closely the things that are here said about Him.

The Holy Spirit is spoken of as "a Person." To apply the language before us to a mere influence or inward feeling is an unreasonable strain of words.

The Holy Spirit is called "the Spirit of truth." It is His special office to apply truth to the hearts of Christians, to guide them into all truth, and to sanctify them by the truth.

The Holy Spirit is said to be one whom "the world cannot receive and does not know." His operations are in the strongest sense foolishness to the natural man. The inward feelings of conviction, repentance, faith, hope, fear, and love, which He always produces, are precisely that part of religion which the world cannot understand.

The Holy Spirit is said to "dwell in" believers and to be known by them. They know the feelings that He creates and the fruits that He produces, though they may not be able to explain them or see at first whence they come. But they all are what they are – new men, new creatures, light and salt in the earth, compared to the worldly, by the indwelling of the Holy Spirit.

The Holy Spirit is given to the Church of the elect "to abide with them" until Christ comes the second time. He is meant to supply all the needs of believers and to fill up all that is lacking while Christ's visible presence is removed. He is sent to abide with and help them until Christ returns.

These are truths of vast importance. Let us take care that we grasp them firmly and never let them go. Next to the whole truth about Christ, it concerns our safety and peace to see the whole truth about the Holy Spirit. Any doctrine about the Church, the ministry, or the Sacraments, which obscures the Spirit's inward work or turns it into mere form, is to be avoided as deadly error. Let us never rest until we feel and know that He dwells in us. "If any man have not the Spirit of Christ, he is none of His" (Romans 8:9).

John 14:18-20

I will not leave you orphans; I will come to you. Yet a little while, and the world shall see me no more, but ye shall see me; because I live, ye shall live also. At that day ye shall know that I am in my Father, and ye in me, and I in you.

The short passage before us is singularly rich in "precious promises." Twice our Lord Jesus Christ says, "I will." Twice He says to believers, "Ye shall."

We learn from this passage, that *Christ's second coming is meant to be the special comfort of believers.* He says to His disciples, "I will not leave you orphans – I will come to you."

Now what is the "coming" here spoken of? It is only fair to say that this is a disputed point among Christians. Many refer it to our Lord's coming to His disciples after His resurrection. Many refer it to His invisible coming into the hearts of His people by the grace of the Holy Spirit. Many refer it to His coming by the outpouring of the Holy Spirit on the day of Pentecost. It may well be doubted, however, whether any one of these three views conveys the full meaning of our Lord's words, "I will come."

The true sense of the expression appears to be the second personal coming of Christ at the end of the world. It is a wide, broad, sweeping promise, intended for all believers, in every age, and not for the Apostles alone – "I will not stay always in heaven – I will one day come back to you." It is like the message which the angels brought to the disciples after the ascension – "This same Jesus shall come in like manner as ye have seen Him go" (Acts 1:11). It is like the last promise which winds up the Book of Revelation – "Surely I come quickly" (Revelation 22:20). Just in the same way the parting consolation held out to believers the night before the crucifixion is a personal return – "I will come."

Let us settle it in our minds that all believers are comparatively "orphans" and children in their minority until the second advent. Our best things are yet to come. Faith has yet to be exchanged for sight and hope for certainty. Our peace and joy are at present very imperfect. They are as nothing to what we shall have when Christ returns. For the return let us look and long and pray. Let us place it in the forefront of all our doctrinal system, next to the atoning death and the interceding life of our Lord. The highest style of Christians are the men who look for and love the Lord's appearing (2 Timothy 4:8).

We learn for another thing, that *Christ's life secures the life of His believing people.* He says, "Because I live ye shall live also."

There is a mysterious and indissoluble union between Christ and every true Christian. The man that is once joined to Him by faith is as closely united as a member of the body is united to the head. So long as Christ, his Head, lives, so long he will live. He cannot die unless Christ can be plucked from heaven, and Christ's life destroyed. But this, since Christ is very God, is totally impossible! "Christ, having been raised from the dead, dies no more: death has no more dominion over Him" (Romans 6:9). That which is divine, in the very nature of things, cannot die.

Christ's life secures the continuance of *spiritual life* to His people. They shall not fall away. They shall persevere unto the end. The divine nature of which they are partakers shall not perish. The incorruptible seed within them shall not be destroyed by the devil and the world. Weak as they are in themselves, they are closely knit to an immortal Head, and not one member of His mystical body shall ever perish.

Christ's life secures the *resurrection life* of His people. Just as He rose again from the grave, because death could not hold Him one moment beyond the appointed time, so shall all His believing members rise again in the day when He calls them from the tomb. The victory that Jesus won when He rolled the stone away and came forth from the tomb was a victory not only for Himself but for His people. If the Head rose, much more shall the members.

Truths like these ought to be often pondered by true Christians. The careless world knows little of a believer's privileges. It sees little but the outside of him. It does not understand the secret of his present strength, and of his strong hope of good things to come. And what is that secret? Invisible union with an invisible Savior in heaven! Each child of God is invisibly linked to the throne of the Rock of Ages. When that throne can be shaken, and not until then, we may despair. But Christ lives, and we shall live also.

We learn, finally, from this passage, that *full and perfect knowledge of divine things will never be attained by believers until the second advent.* Our Lord says, "At that day," the day of my coming, "ye shall know that I am in my Father, and ye in Me, and I in you."

The best of saints knows but little so long as he is in the body. The fall of our father Adam has corrupted our understandings, as well as our consciences, hearts, and wills. Even after conversion we see through a glass darkly, and on no point do we see so dimly as on the nature of our own union with Christ and of the union of Christ and the Father. These are matters in which we must be content to believe humbly and, like little children, to receive on trust the things which we cannot explain.

But it is a blessed and cheering thought that when Christ comes again, the remains of ignorance shall be rolled away. Raised from the dead, freed from the darkness of this world, no longer tempted by the devil and tried by the flesh, believers shall see as they have been seen and know as they have been known. We shall have light enough one day. What we know not now, we shall know hereafter.

Let us rest our souls on this comfortable thought, when we see the mournful divisions which rend the Church of Christ. Let us remember that a large portion of them arise from ignorance. We know in part and therefore misunderstand one another. A day comes when Lutherans shall no longer wrangle with Zwinglians, nor Calvinist with Arminian, nor Churchman with Dissenter. That day is the day of Christ's second coming. Then and then only will the promise receive its complete fulfillment – "At that day ye shall know."

John 14:21-26

He that has my commandments and keeps them, he it is that loves me; and he that loves me shall be loved of my Father, and I will love him and will manifest myself to him. Judas, not Iscariot, said unto him, Lord, how is it that thou wilt manifest thyself unto us and not unto the world? Jesus answered and said unto him, He who loves me will keep my words, and my Father will love him, and we will come unto him and dwell with him. He that does not love me does not keep my words, and the word which ye have heard is not mine, but of the Father who sent me. I have spoken these things unto you, being yet present with you. But the Comforter, which is the Holy Spirit, whom the Father will send in my name, he shall teach you all things and bring to your remembrance all the things that I have said unto you.

We learn from these verses that *keeping Christ's commandments is the best test of love to Christ*. This is a lesson of vast importance and one that needs continually pressing on the attention of Christians. It is not talking about religion, and talking fluently and well too, but steadily doing Christ's will and walking in Christ's ways that is the proof of our being true believers. Good feelings and desires are useless if they are not accompanied by action. They may even become mischievous to the soul, induce hardness of conscience, and do certain harm. Passive impressions which do not lead to action gradually deaden and paralyze the heart. Living and doing are the only real evidence of grace. Where the Holy Spirit is, there will always be a holy life. A jealous watchfulness over tempers, words, and deeds, a constant endeavor to live by the rule of the Sermon on the Mount, this is the best proof that we love Christ.

Of course such maxims as these must not be wrested and misunderstood. We are not to suppose for a moment that "keeping Christ's commandments" can save us. Our best works are full of imperfection. When we have done all we can, we are feeble and unprofitable servants. "By grace are ye saved through faith – not of works" (Ephesians 2:8). But while we hold one class of truths, we must not forget another. Faith in the blood of Christ must always be attended by loving obedience to the will of Christ. What the Master has joined together, the disciple must not put asunder. Do we profess to love Christ? Then let us show it by our lives. The Apostle who said, "Thou knowest that I love Thee!" received the charge, "Feed my lambs." That meant, "Do something. Be useful – follow my example" (John 21:17).

We learn, secondly, from these verses, that *there are special comforts laid up for those who love Christ, and prove it by keeping His words.* This, at any rate, seems the general sense of our Lord's language – "My Father will love him, and we will come unto him, and make our abode with him."

The full meaning of this promise, no doubt, is a deep thing. We have no line to fathom it. It is a thing which no man can understand except he that receives and experiences it. But we need not shrink from believing that eminent holiness brings eminent comfort with it, and that no man has such sensible enjoyment of his religion as the man who, like Enoch and Abraham, walks closely with God. There is more of heaven on earth to be obtained than most Christians are aware of. "The secret of the Lord is with them that fear Him, and He will show them His covenant" (Psalm 25:14). "If any man hear my voice and open the door, I will come in to him, and sup with him, and he with Me" (Revelation 3:20). Promises like these, we may be sure, mean something and were not written in vain.

How is it, people often ask, that so many professing believers have so little happiness in their religion? How is it that so many know little of "joy and peace in believing" and go mourning and heavy-hearted towards heaven? The answer to these questions is a sorrowful one, but it must be given. Few believers attend as strictly as they should to Christ's practical sayings and words. There is far too much loose and careless obedience to Christ's commandments. There is far too much forgetfulness that while good works cannot justify us, they are not to be despised. Let these things sink down into our hearts. If we want to be eminently happy, we must strive to be eminently holy.

We learn, lastly, from these verses, that *one part of the Holy Spirit's work is to teach, and to bring things to remembrance.* It is written, "The Comforter shall teach you all things, and bring all things to your remembrance."

To confine this promise to the eleven Apostles, as some do, seems a narrow and unsatisfactory mode of interpreting Scripture. It appears to reach far beyond the day of Pentecost and the gift of writing inspired books of God's Holy Word. It is safer, wiser, and more consistent with the whole tone of our Lord's last discourse to regard the promise as the common property of all believers in every age of the world. Our Lord knows the ignorance and forgetfulness of our nature in spiritual things. He graciously declares that when He leaves the world, His people shall have a teacher and remembrancer.

Are we sensible of spiritual ignorance? Do we feel that at best we know in part and see in part? Do we desire to understand more clearly the doctrines of the Gospel? Let us pray daily for the help of the "teaching" Spirit. It is His office to illuminate the soul, to open the eyes of the understanding, and to guide us into all truth. He can make dark places light and rough places smooth.

Do we find our memory of spiritual things defective? Do we complain that though we read and hear, we seem to lose as fast as we gain? Let us pray daily for the help of the Holy Spirit. He can bring things to our remembrance. He can make us remember "old things and new." He can keep in our minds the whole system of truth and duty and make us ready for every good word and work.

John 14:27-31

Peace I leave with you, my peace I give unto you; not as the world gives, give I unto you. Let not your heart be troubled, neither let it be afraid. Ye have heard how I said unto you, I go away and come again unto you. If ye loved me, ye would rejoice because I said, I go unto the Father; for my Father is greater than I. And now I have told you before it comes to pass, that when it is come to pass, ye might believe. Hereafter I will not talk much with you, for the prince of this world comes and has nothing in me. But that the world may know that I love the Father; and as the Father gave me command-ment, even so I do. Arise, let us go from here.

We ought not to leave the closing portion of this wonderful chapter without noticing one striking feature in it. That feature is the singular frequency with which our Lord uses the expression, "My Father," and "the Father." In the last five verses we find it four times. In the whole chapter it occurs no less than twenty-two times. In this respect the chapter stands alone in the Bible.

The reason of this frequent use of the expression is a deep subject. Perhaps the less we speculate and dogmatize about it the better. Our Lord was one who never spoke a word without a meaning, and we need not doubt there was a meaning here. Yet may we not reverently suppose that He desired to leave on the minds of His disciples a strong impression of his entire unity with the Father? Seldom does our Lord lay claim to such high dignity and such power of giving and supplying comfort to His Church as in this discourse. Was there not, then, a fit-ness in His continually reminding His disciples that in all His giving He was one with the Father and did nothing without the Father? This, at any rate, seems a fair conjecture. Let it be taken for what it is worth.

We should observe, for one thing, in this passage, *Christ's last legacy to His people.* We find Him saying, "Peace I leave with you, my peace I give unto you; not as the world gives, give I unto you."

Peace is Christ's distinctive gift – not money, not worldly ease, not temporal prosperity. These are at best very questionable possessions. They often do more harm than good to the soul. They act as clogs and weights to our spiritual life. Inward peace of conscience, arising from a sense of pardoned sin and reconciliation with God, is a far greater blessing. This peace is the property of all believers, whether high or low, rich or poor.

The peace which Christ gives He calls "my peace." It is specially His own to give, because He bought it by His own blood, purchased it by His own substitution, and is appointed by the Father to dispense it to a perishing world. Just as Joseph was sealed and commissioned to give grain to the starving Egyptians, so is Christ specially commissioned, in the counsels of the Eternal Trinity, to give peace to mankind.

The peace that Christ gives is not given as the world gives. What He gives, the world cannot give at all, and what He gives is given neither unwillingly, nor sparingly, nor for a little time. Christ is far more willing to give than the world is to receive. What He gives He gives to all eternity and never takes away. He is ready to give abundantly above all that we can ask or think. "Open your mouth wide," He says, "and I will fill it" (Psalm 81:10).

Who can wonder that a legacy like this should be backed by the renewed emphatic charge, "Let not your heart be troubled, neither let it be afraid?" There is nothing lacking on Christ's part for our comfort, if we will only come to Him, believe, and receive. The chief of sinners has no cause to be afraid. If we will only look to the one true Savior, there is medicine for every trouble of heart. Half our doubts and fears arise from dim perceptions of the real nature of Christ's Gospel.

We should observe, for another thing, in this passage, *Christ's perfect holiness.* We find Him saying, "The prince of this world cometh, and hath nothing in Me."

The meaning of these remarkable words admits of only one interpretation. Our Lord would have his disciples know that Satan, "the prince of this world," was about to make his last and most violent attack on Him. He was mustering all his strength for one more tremendous onset. He was coming up with his utmost malice to try the second Adam in the garden of Gethsemane and on the cross of Calvary. But our blessed Master declares, "He hath nothing in Me." "There is nothing he can lay hold on. There is no weak and defective point in Me. I have kept my Father's commandment and finished the work He gave me to do. Satan, therefore, cannot overthrow Me. He can lay nothing to my charge. He cannot condemn Me. I shall come forth from the trial more than conqueror."

Let us mark the difference between Christ and all others who have been born of woman. He is the only one in whom Satan has no power over. He came to Adam and Eve and found weakness. He came to Noah, Abraham, Moses, David, and all the saints and found imperfection. He came to Christ and found "nothing" at all. He was a Lamb "without blemish and without spot," a suitable Sacrifice for a world of sinners, a suitable Head for a redeemed race.

Let us thank God that we have such a perfect, sinless Savior that His righteousness is a perfect righteousness, and His life a blameless life. In ourselves and our doings we shall find everything imperfect; and if we had no other hope than our own goodness, we might well despair. But in Christ we have a perfect, sinless, Representative and Substitute. Well may we say, with the triumphant Apostle, "Who shall lay anything to our charge?" (Romans 8:33). Christ has died for us and suffered in our stead. In Him Satan can find nothing. We are hidden in Him. The Father sees us in Him, unworthy as we are, and for His sake is well pleased.

John Chapter 15

John 15:1-6

I AM the true vine, and my Father is the husbandman.
Every branch in me that does not bear fruit he shall take
away; and every one that bears fruit, he shall purge that they
may bring forth more fruit. Now ye are clean through the
word which I have spoken unto you. Abide in me, and I in
you. As the branch cannot bear fruit of itself, except it abides
in the vine, no more can ye, except ye abide in me. I AM the
vine, ye are the branches: he that abides in me, and I in him,
the same brings forth much fruit; for without me ye can do
nothing. He who does not abide in me shall be cast forth as
an unsound branch and shall wither, and they are gathered
and cast into the fire and are burned.

THESE VERSES, WE MUST carefully remember, contain a parable. In interpreting it we must not forget the great rule which applies to all Christ's parables. The general lesson of each parable is the main thing to be noticed. The minor details must not be tortured and pressed to an excess in order to extract a meaning from them. The mistakes into which Christians have fallen by neglecting this rule are neither few nor small.

We are meant to learn first, from these verses, that *the union between Christ and believers is very close.* He is "the Vine," and they are "the branches."

The union between the branch of a vine and the main stem is the closest that can be conceived. It is the whole secret of the branch's life, strength, vigor, beauty, and fertility. Separate from the parent stem, it has no life of its own. The sap and juice that flow from the stem are the origin and maintaining power of all its leaves, buds, blossoms, and fruit. Cut off from the stem, it must soon wither and die.

The union between Christ and believers is just as close and just as real. In themselves believers have no life, or strength, or spiritual power. All that they have of vital religion comes from Christ. They are what they are, and feel what they feel, and do what they do, because they draw out of Jesus a continual supply of grace, help, and ability. Joined to the Lord by faith and united in mysterious union with Him by the Spirit, they stand, and walk, and continue, and run the Christian race. But every jot of good about them is drawn from their spiritual Head, Jesus Christ.

The thought before us is both comfortable and instructive. Believers have no cause to despair of their own salvation and to think they will never reach heaven. Let them consider that they are not left to themselves and their own strength. Their root is Christ, and all that there is in the root is for the benefit of the branches. Because He lives, they shall live also. Worldly people have no cause to wonder at the continuance and perseverance of believers. Weak as they are in themselves, their Root is in heaven and never dies. "When I am weak," said Paul, "then am I strong" (2 Corinthians 12:10).

We are meant to learn, secondly, from these verses, that *there are false Christians as well as true ones.* There are "branches in the vine" which appear to be joined to the parent stem and yet bear no fruit. There are men and women who appear to be members of Christ and yet will prove finally to have had no vital union with Him.

There are myriads of professing Christians in every Church whose union with Christ is only outward and formal. Some of them are joined to Christ by baptism and Church membership. Some of them go even further than this and are regular communicants and loud talkers about religion. But they all lack the one thing needful. Notwithstanding services, and sermons, and sacrament, they have no grace in their hearts, no faith, no inward work of the Holy Spirit. They are not one with Christ, and Christ in them. Their union with Him is only nominal and not real. They have "a name to live," but in the sight of God, they are dead.

Christians of this stamp are aptly represented by branches in a vine which bear no fruit. Useless and unsightly, such branches are only fit to be cut off and burned. They draw nothing out of the parent stem and make no return for the place they occupy. Just so will it be at the last day with false professors and nominal Christians. Their end, except they repent, will be destruction. They will be separated from the company of true believers and cast out as withered, useless branches into everlasting fire. They will find at last, whatever they thought in this world, that there is a worm that never dies, and a fire that is not quenched.

We are meant to learn, thirdly, from these verses, that *the fruits of the Spirit are the only satisfactory evidence of a man being a true Christian.* The disciple that "abides in Christ," like a branch abiding in the vine, will always bear fruit.

He that would know what the word "fruit" means need not wait long for an answer. Repentance toward God, faith toward our Lord Jesus Christ, holiness of life and conduct, these are what the New Testament calls "fruit." These are the distinguishing marks of the man who is a living branch of the true Vine. Where these things are lacking, it is vain to talk of possessing *dormant* grace and spiritual life. Where there is no fruit there is no life. He that lacks these things is "dead while he liveth."

True grace, we must not forget, is never idle. It never slumbers and never sleeps. It is a vain notion to suppose that we are living members of Christ, if the example of Christ is the only satisfactory evidence of saving union between Christ and our souls. Where there is no fruit of the Spirit to be seen, there is no vital religion in the heart. The Spirit of Life in Christ Jesus will always make Himself known in the daily conduct of those in whom He dwells. The Master Himself declares, "Every tree is known by his own fruit" (Luke 6:44).

We are meant, lastly, to learn from these verses, that *God will often increase the holiness of true Christians by His providential dealings with them.* "Every branch," it is written, "that bears fruit, He purges it, that it may bear more fruit."

The meaning of this language is clear and plain. Just as the gardener prunes and cuts back the branches of a fruitful vine in order to make them more fruitful, so does God purify and sanctify believers by the circumstances of life in which He places them.

Trial, to speak plainly, is the instrument by which our Father in heaven makes Christians more holy. By trial He calls out their passive graces and proves whether they can suffer His will as well as do it. By trial He weans them from the world, draws them to Christ, drives them to the Bible and prayer, shows them their own hearts, and makes them humble. This is the process by which He "prunes" them and makes them more fruitful. The lives of the saints in every age are the best and truest comment on the text. Never, hardly, do we find an eminent saint, either in the Old Testament or the New, who was not purified by suffering and, like His Master, a "man of sorrows."

Let us learn to be patient in the days of darkness, if we know anything of vital union with Christ. Let us remember the doctrine of the passage before us and not murmur and complain because of trials. Our trials are not meant to do us harm, but good. God chastens us "for our profit, that we may be partakers of His holiness" (Hebrews 12:10). Fruit is the thing that our Master desires to see in us, and He will not spare the pruning knife if He sees we need it. In the last day we shall see that all was well done.

John 15:7-11

If ye abide in me and my words abide in you, ye shall ask what ye will, and it shall be done unto you. In this is my Father clarified, in that ye bear much fruit; and in this manner ye shall be my disciples. As the Father has loved me, so I have loved you; abide in my love. If ye keep my commandments, ye shall abide in my love, even as I have kept my Father's commandments and abide in his love. These things I have spoken unto you that my joy may abide in you and that your joy might be fulfilled.

There is a wide difference between believers in Christ. In some things they are all alike. All feel their sins; all trust in Christ; all repent and strive to be holy. All have grace, and faith, and new hearts. But they differ widely in the degree of their attainments. Some are far happier and holier Christians than others and have far more influence on the world.

Now what are the inducements which the Lord Jesus holds out to His people to make them aim at eminent holiness? This is a question which ought to be deeply interesting to every pious mind. Who would not like to be a singularly useful and happy servant of Christ? The passage before us throws light on the subject in three ways.

In the first place, our Lord declares, "If ye abide in Me, and my words abide in you, ye shall ask what ye will, and it shall be done unto you." This is *a distinct promise of power and success in prayer.* And what does it turn upon? We must "abide in Christ," and Christ's "words must abide in us."

To abide in Christ means to keep up a habit of constant close communion with Him – to be always leaning on Him, resting on Him, pouring out our hearts to Him, and using Him as our Fountain of life and strength as our chief Companion and best Friend. To have His words abiding in us is to keep His sayings and precepts continually before our memories and minds and to make them the guide of our actions and the rule of our daily conduct and behavior.

Christians of this stamp, we are told, shall not pray in vain. Whatever they ask they shall obtain, so long as they ask things according to God's mind. No work shall be found too hard and no difficulty insurmountable. Asking they shall receive, and seeking they shall find. Such men were Martin Luther, the German Reformer, and our own martyr, Bishop Latimer. Such a man was John Knox of whom Queen Mary said that she feared his prayers more than an army of twenty thousand men. It is written in a certain place, "The effectual fervent prayer of a righteous man availeth much" (James 5:16).

Now, why is there so little power of prayer like this in our own time? Simply because there is so little close communion with Christ and so little strict conformity to His will. Men do not "abide in Christ" and therefore pray in vain. Christ's words do not abide in them as their standard of practice, and therefore their prayers seem not to be heard. They ask and receive not, because they ask amiss. Let this lesson sink down into our hearts. He that would have answers to his prayers must carefully remember Christ's directions. We must keep up intimate friendship with the great Advocate in heaven, if our petitions are to prosper.

In the second place, our Lord declares, "Herein is my Father glorified, that ye bear much fruit; so shall ye be my disciples." The meaning of this promise seems to be that *fruitfulness in Christian practice will not only bring glory to God, but will supply the best evidence to our own hearts that we are real disciples of Christ.*

Assurance of our own interest in Christ, and our consequent eternal safety, is one of the highest privileges in religion. To be always doubting and fearing is miserable work. Nothing is worse than suspense in any matter of importance and above all in the matter of our souls. He that would know one of the best receipts for obtaining assurance should diligently study Christ's words now before us. Let him strive to bear much fruit in his life, his habits, his temper, his words, and his works. So doing he shall feel the "witness of the Spirit" in his heart and give abundant proof that he is a living branch of the true Vine. He shall find inward evidence in his own soul that he is a child of God and shall supply the world with outward evidence that cannot be disputed. He shall leave no room for doubt that he is a disciple.

Would we know why so many professing Christians have little comfort in their religion and go fearing and doubting along the road to heaven? The question receives a solution in the saying of our Lord we are now considering. Men are content with a little Christianity and a little fruit of the Spirit and do not labor to be holy in all of life. They must not wonder if they enjoy little peace, feel little hope, and leave behind them little evidence. The fault lies with themselves. God has linked together holiness and happiness; and what God has joined together we must not think to put asunder.

In the third place, our Lord declares, "If ye keep my commandments, ye shall abide in my love." The meaning of this promise is near akin to that of the preceding one. *The man who makes conscience of diligently observing Christ's precepts, is the man who shall continually enjoy a sense of Christ's love in his soul.*

Of course we must not misunderstand our Lord's words when He speaks of "keeping His commandments." There is a sense in which no one can keep them. Our best works are imperfect and defective, and when we have done our best, we may well cry, "God be merciful to me a sinner." Yet we must not run into the other extreme and give way to the lazy idea that we can do nothing at all. By the grace of God, we may make Christ's laws our rule of life and show daily that we desire to please Him. So doing, our gracious Master will give us a constant sense of His favor and make us feel His face smiling on us, like the sun shining on a fine day. "The secret of the Lord is with them that fear Him, and He will show them His covenant" (Psalm 25:14).

Lessons like these may be *legal* to some and bring down much blame on those who advocate them. Such is the narrow mindedness of human nature that few can look on more than one side of truth! Let the servant of Christ call no man his master. Let him hold on his way and never be ashamed of diligence, fruitfulness, and jealous watchfulness in his obedience to Christ's commands. These things are perfectly consistent with salvation by grace and justification by faith, whatever any one may say to the contrary.

Let us hear the conclusion of the whole matter. The Christian who is careful over his words and tempers and works will generally be the most happy Christian. "Joy and peace in believing" will never accompany an inconsistent life. It is not for nothing that our Lord concludes the passage – "These things have I spoken unto you, that your joy might be full."

John 15:12-16

This is my commandment, That ye love one another as I have loved you. Greater love has no man than this, that a man lay down his soul for his friends. Ye are my friends if ye do whatsoever I command you. From now on I do not call you slaves, for the slave does not know what his lord does; but I have called you friends, for all things that I have heard of my Father I have made known unto you. Ye have not chosen me, but I have chosen you and ordained you, that ye should go and bring forth fruit, and that your fruit should remain; that whatever ye shall ask of the Father in my name, he may give it unto you.

Three weighty points demand our attention in this passage. On each of these the language of our Lord Jesus Christ is full of striking instruction.

We should observe first *how our Lord speaks of the grace of brotherly love.*

He returns to it a second time, though He has already spoken of it in the former part of His discourse. He would have us know that we can never think too highly of love, attach too much weight to it, labor too much to practice it. Truths, which our Master thinks it needful to enforce on us by repetition, must needs be of first class importance.

He commands us to love one another. "This is my commandment." It is a positive duty laid on our consciences to practice this grace. We have no more right to neglect it than any of the ten precepts given on Mount Sinai.

He supplies the highest standard of love – "Love one another as I have loved you." No lower measure must content us. The weakest, the lowest, the most ignorant, the most defective disciple is not to be despised. All are to be loved with an active, self-denying, self-sacrificing love. He that cannot do this, or will not try to do it, is disobeying the command of his Master.

A precept like this should stir up in us great searchings of heart. It condemns the selfish, ill-natured, jealous, ill-tempered spirit of many professing Christians with a sweeping condemnation. Sound views of doctrine and knowledge of controversy will avail us nothing at last, if we have known nothing of love. Without charity we may pass muster very well as Churchmen. But without charity we are no better, says Paul, than "sounding brass and tinkling cymbal" (1 Corinthians 13:1). Where there is no Christlike love, there is no grace, no work of the Spirit, and no reality in our religion. Blessed are those who do not forget Christ's commandment! They are those who shall have right to the tree of life and enter the celestial city. The unloving professor is unfit for heaven.

We should observe, secondly, *how our Lord speaks of the relation between Himself and true believers.* He says, "From now on I do not call you slaves . . . but I have called you friends."

This is indeed a glorious privilege. To know Christ, serve Christ, follow Christ, obey Christ, work in Christ's vineyard, fight Christ's battles, all this is no small matter. But for sinful men and women like ourselves to be called "friends of Christ" is something that our weak minds can hardly grasp and take in. The King of kings and Lord of lords not only pities and saves all those who believe in Him but actually calls them His "friends." We need not wonder, in the face of such language as this, that Paul should say, the "love of Christ passeth knowledge" (Ephesians 3:19).

Let the expression before us encourage Christians to deal familiarly with Christ in prayer. Why should we be afraid to pour out all our hearts, and disclose all our secrets, in speaking to one who calls us His "friends"? Let it cheer us in all the troubles and sorrows of life and increase our confidence in our Lord. "He that hath friends," says Solomon, "will show himself friendly" (Proverbs 18:24). Certainly our great Master in heaven will never forsake His "friends." Poor and unworthy as we are, He will not cast us off but will stand by us and keep us to the end. David never forgot Jonathan, and the Son of David will never forget His people. None so rich, so strong, so well off, so thoroughly provided for, as the man of whom Christ says, "This is my friend!"

We should observe, lastly, *how our Lord speaks of the doctrine of election.* He says, "Ye have not chosen Me, but I have chosen you, that you should go and bring forth fruit." The choosing here mentioned is evidently twofold. It includes not only the election to the Apostolic office, which was peculiar to the eleven, but the election to eternal life, which is the privilege of all believers. To this last "choosing," as it specially concerns ourselves, we may profitably direct our attention.

Election to eternal life is a truth of Scripture which we must receive humbly and believe implicitly. Why the Lord Jesus calls some and does not call others, quickens whom He will, and leaves others alone in their sins, these are deep things which we cannot explain. Let it suffice us to know that it is a fact. God must begin the work of grace in a man's heart, or else a man will never be saved. Christ must first choose us and call us by His Spirit, or else we shall never choose Christ. Beyond doubt, if not saved, we shall have none to blame but ourselves. But if saved, we shall certainly trace up the beginning of our salvation to the choosing grace of Christ. Our song to all eternity will be that which fell from the lips of Jonah – "Salvation is of the Lord" (Jonah 2:9).

Election is always to sanctification. Those whom Christ chooses out of mankind, He chooses not only that they may be saved, but that they may bear fruit, and fruit that can be seen. All other election beside this is a mere vain delusion and a miserable invention of man. It was the faith and hope and love of the Thessalonians, which made Paul say, "I know your election of God" (1 Thessalonians 1:4). Where there is no visible fruit of sanctification, we may be sure there is no election.

Armed with such principles as these, we have no cause to be afraid of the doctrine of election. Like any other truth of the Gospel, it is liable to be abused and perverted. But to a pious mind, as the seventeenth Article of the Church of England truly says, it is a doctrine "full of sweet, pleasant, and unspeakable comfort."

John 15:17-21

This I command you, that ye love one another. If the world hates you, ye know that it hated me before it hated you. If ye were of the world, the world would love its own; but because ye are not of the world, but I have chosen you out of the world, therefore the world hates you. Remember the word that I said unto you, The slave is not greater than his lord. If they have persecuted me, they will also persecute you; if they have kept my word, they will keep yours also. But they will do all these things unto you for my name's sake, because they do not know him that sent me.

The passage before us opens with a renewed exhortation to brotherly love. For the third time in this discourse our Lord thinks it needful to press this precious grace on the attention of His disciples. Rare, indeed, must genuine charity be, when such repeated mention of it is made! In the present instance the connection in which it stands should be carefully observed. Christian love is placed in contrast to the hatred of the world.

We are shown first, in this passage, *what true Christians must expect to meet in this world – hatred and persecution.* If the disciples looked for kindness and gratitude from man, they would be painfully disappointed. They must lay their account to be ill-treated like their Master. "The world hates you. Be not moved or surprised. If they have persecuted Me, they will also persecute you; if they have kept my saying, they will keep yours also."

Facts, painful facts in every age, supply abundant proof that our Lord's warning was not without cause. Persecution was the lot of the Apostles and their companions wherever they went. Not more than one or two of them died quietly in his bed. Persecution has been the lot of true believers throughout the eighteen Christian centuries of history. The doings of Roman Emperors and Roman Popes, the Spanish inquisition, the martyrdoms of Queen Mary's reign, all tell the same story. Persecution is the lot of all really godly people at this very day. Ridicule, mockery, slander, misrepresentations still show the feeling of unconverted people against the true Christian. As it was in Paul's day, so it is now. In public and in private, at school and at college, at home and abroad, "all that will live godly in Christ Jesus shall suffer persecution" (2 Timothy 3:12). Mere churchmanship and outward profession are a cheap religion, of course, and cost a man nothing. But real vital Christianity will always bring with it a cross.

To know and understand these things is of the utmost importance to our comfort. Nothing is so mischievous as the habit of indulging false expectations. Let us realize that human nature never changes, that "the carnal mind is enmity against God" and against God's image in His people. Let us settle it in our minds that no holiness of life or consistency of conduct will ever prevent wicked people hating the servants of Christ, just as they hated their blameless Master. Let us remember these things, and then we shall not be disappointed.

We are shown secondly, in this passage, *two reasons for patience under the persecution of this world.* Each is weighty and supplies matter for much thought.

For one thing, persecution is the cup of which Christ Himself drank. Faultless as He was in everything, in temper, word, and deed

– unwearied as He was in works of kindness, always going about doing good – never was any one so hated as Jesus was to the last day of His earthly ministry. Scribes and High Priests, Pharisees and Sadducees, Jews and Gentiles united in pouring contempt on Him and opposing Him and never rested until He was put to death.

Surely this simple fact alone should sustain our spirits and prevent our being cast down by the hatred of man. Let us consider that we are only walking in our Master's footsteps and sharing our Master's portion. Do we deserve to be better treated? Are we better than He? Let us fight against these murmuring thoughts. Let us drink quietly the cup which our Father gives us. Above all, let us often call to mind the saying, "Remember the word that I spake unto you, The servant is not greater than his Master."

For another thing, persecution helps to prove that we are children of God and have treasure in heaven. It supplies evidence that we are really born again, that we have grace in our hearts and are heirs of glory – "If ye were of the world, the world would love his own: but because ye are not of the world, but I have chosen you out of the world, therefore the world hates you." Persecution, in short, is like the goldsmith's stamp on real silver and gold – it is one of the marks of a converted man.

Let us nerve our minds with this cheering thought, when we feel ready to faint and give way under the world's hatred. No doubt it is hard to bear, and even harder when our conscience tells us we are innocent. But after all let us never forget that it is a token for good. It is a symptom of a work begun within us by the Holy Spirit, which can never be overthrown. We may fall back on that wonderful promise, "Blessed are ye when men shall revile you, and persecute you, and shall say all manner of evil against you falsely, for my sake. Rejoice, and be exceeding glad: for great is your reward in heaven" (Matthew 5:11, 12). When the world has said and done its worst, it cannot rob believers of that promise.

Let us leave the whole subject with a feeling of deep pity for those who persecute others on account of their religion. Often, very often, as our Lord says, they do it because they know no better. "They know not Him that sent Me."[37] Like our Divine Master and His servant Stephen,

---

37 The judicial blindness and hardness of the Jewish nation in the time of our Lord and His apostles is a thing that ought to be carefully observed by all Bible readers (Acts 3:17; 13:27;

let us pray for those who despitefully use us and persecute us. Their persecution rarely does us harm and often drives us nearer to Christ, the Bible, and the throne of grace. Our intercession, if heard on high, may bring down blessings on their souls.

John 15:22-27

If I had not come and spoken unto them, they would not have sin; but now they have no excuse for their sin. He that hates me hates my Father also. If I had not done among them works which no other man has done, they would not have sin; but now they have seen them and hate both me and my Father. But this comes to pass that the word might be fulfilled that is written in their law, They hated me without a cause. But when the Comforter is come, whom I will send unto you from the Father, even the Spirit of truth, which proceeds from the Father, he shall testify of me; and ye also shall bear witness because ye have been with me from the beginning.

In these verses our Lord Jesus Christ handles three subjects of great importance. They are difficult subjects, no doubt, subjects on which we may easily fall into error. But the words before us throw much light upon them.

We should observe, for one thing, how our Lord speaks of *the misuse of religious privileges*. It intensifies man's guilt and will increase his condemnation. He tells His disciples that if He had not "spoken" and "done" among the Jews things which none ever spoke or did before, "they had not had sin." By this, we must remember, He means, "they had not been so sinful and so guilty as they are now." But now they were utterly without excuse. They had seen Christ's works and heard Christ's teaching and yet remained unbelieving. What more could be done for

---

28:25-27; 1 Corinthians 2:8; 2 Corinthians 3:14). It was a peculiar judicial blindness, we must remember, to which the whole nation was given over, like Pharaoh, as a final punishment for many centuries of idolatry, wickedness, and unbelief. Nothing but this seems thoroughly to account for the extraordinary unbelief of many of our Lord's hearers.

them? Nothing – absolutely nothing! They willfully sinned against the clearest possible light and were of all men most guilty.

Let us settle it down as a first principle in our religion, that religious privileges are in a certain sense very dangerous things. If they do not help us toward heaven, they will only sink us deeper into hell. They add to our responsibility. "To whomsoever much is given, of him shall much be required" (Luke 12:48). He that dwells in a land of open Bibles and preached Gospel, and yet dreams that he will stand in the judgment day on the same level with an untaught Chinese, is fearfully deceived. He will find to his own cost, except he repents, that his judgment will be according to his light. The mere fact that he had knowledge and did not improve it will of itself prove one of his greatest sins. "He that knew His Master's will and did it not, shall be beaten with many stripes" (Luke 12:47).

Well would it be for all professing Christians in England, if this point was more thoroughly considered! Nothing is more common than to hear men taking comfort in the thought that they "know what" is right, while at the same time they are evidently unconverted and unfit to die. They rest in that unhappy phrase, "We know it, we know it," as if knowledge could wash away all their sins – forgetting that the devil has more knowledge than any of us and yet is no better for it. Let the burning words of our Lord in the passage now before us sink down into our hearts and never be forgotten – "If I had not come and spoken unto them, they had not had sin: but now they have no cloak for their sin." To see light and not use it, to possess knowledge and yet not turn it to account, to be able to say "I know," and yet not to say "I believe" will place us at the lowest place on Christ's left hand, in the great day of judgment.

We should observe, for another thing, in these verses, *how our Lord speaks of the Holy Spirit.* He is "the Comforter" who is to come; He is One sent and "proceeding;" He is One whose office it is to "testify." These are not words that can be used of a mere influence or inward feeling. So to interpret them is to contradict common sense and to strain the meaning of plain language.

Again, our Lord speaks of the Holy Spirit as One whom He "will send from the Father" and One "who proceeds from the Father." These are deep sayings, no doubt, so deep that we have no line to fathom them. The mere fact that for centuries the Eastern and Western Churches of Christendom have been divided about their meaning should teach us to handle them with modesty and reverence. One thing, at all events, is very clear and plain. There is a close and intimate connection between the Spirit, the Father, and the Son. Why the Holy Spirit should be said to be sent by the Son and to proceed from the Father in this verse, we cannot tell. But we may quietly repose our minds in the thought expressed in an ancient creed that "In this Trinity none is afore or after other: none is greater or less than another." "Such as the Father is such is the Son, and such is the Holy Spirit." Above all, we may rest in the comfortable truth that in the salvation of our souls all three Persons in the Trinity equally co-operate. It was God in Trinity who said, "Let us create," and it is God in Trinity who says, "Let us save."

Forever let us take heed to our doctrine about the Holy Spirit. Let us make sure that we hold sound and Scriptural views of His nature, His Person, and His operations. A religion which entirely leaves Him out and gives Him no place is far too common. Let us beware that such a religion is not ours. "Where is the Lamb, the Lord Jesus Christ?" should be the first testing question about our Christianity. "Where is the Holy Spirit?" should be the second question. Let us take good heed that the work of the Spirit is not so buried under extravagant views of the Church, the ministry, and the Sacraments that the real Holy Spirit of Scripture is completely put out of sight. "If any man have not the Spirit of Christ, he is none of His" (Romans 8:9). No religion deserves to be called Scriptural and apostolic in which the work of the Spirit does not stand forth prominently and occupy a principal place.

We should observe lastly, in these verses, *how our Lord speaks of the special office of the Apostles.* They were to be His witnesses in the world. "Ye also shall bear witness."

The expression is singularly instructive and full of meaning. It taught the eleven what they must expect their portion to be, so long as they lived. They would have to bear testimony to facts which many would not believe and to truths which the natural heart would dislike.

They would often have to stand alone, a few against many, a little flock against a great multitude. None of these things must move them. They must count it no strange thing to be persecuted, hated, opposed, and discredited. They must not mind it. To witness of Christ was their grand duty, whether men believed them or not. So witnessing, their record would be on high in God's book of remembrance; and so witnessing, sooner or later, the Judge of all would give them a crown of glory that fades not away.

Let us never forget, as we leave this passage, that the position of the Apostles is that which, in a certain sense, every true Christian must fill, as long as the world stands. We must all be witnesses for Christ. We must not be ashamed to stand up for Christ's cause, to speak out for Christ, and to persist in maintaining the truth of Christ's Gospel. Wherever we live, in town or in country, in public or in private, abroad or at home, we must boldly confess our Master on every opportunity. So doing, we shall walk in the steps of the Apostles, though at a long interval. So doing, we shall please our Master and may hope at last that we shall receive the Apostles' reward.

John Chapter 16

John 16:1-7

These things I have spoken unto you that ye should not be offended. They shall put you out of the synagogues, and the hour will even come when whosoever kills you will think that he does God service. And they will do these things unto you because they do not know the Father, nor me. But I have told you these things that when that hour shall come, ye may remember that I told you of them. And I did not say these things unto you at the beginning because I was with you. But now I go unto him that sent me, and none of you asks me, Where goest thou? But because I have said these things unto you, sorrow has filled your heart. Nevertheless I tell you the truth: It is expedient for you that I go away; for if I do not go away, the Comforter will not come unto you; but if I depart, I will send him unto you.

THE OPENING VERSES OF this chapter contain three important utterances of Christ, which deserve our special attention.

For one thing, we find *our Lord delivering a remarkable prophecy.* He tells His disciples that they will be cast out of the Jewish Church and persecuted even to the death – "They shall put you out of the synagogues: yea, the time cometh, that whosoever killeth you will think that he doeth God service."

How strange that seems at first sight! Excommunication, suffering, and death, are the portion that the Prince of Peace predicts to His disciples. So far from receiving them and their message with gratitude, the world would hate them, despitefully use them, and put them to death.

And, worst of all, their persecutors would actually persuade themselves that it was right to persecute and would inflict the cruelest injuries in the sacred name of religion.

How true the prediction has turned out! Like every other prophecy of Scripture, it has been fulfilled to the very letter. The Acts of the Apostles show us how the unbelieving Jews persecuted the early Christians. The pages of history tell us what horrible crimes have been committed by the Popish Inquisition. The annals of our own country inform us how our holy Reformers were burned at the stake for their religion by men who professed to do all they did from zeal for pure Christianity. Unlikely and incredible as it might seem at the time, the great Prophet of the Church has been found in this, as in everything else, to have predicted nothing but literal truth.

Let it never surprise us to hear of true Christians being persecuted in one way or another, even in our own day. Human nature never changes. Grace is never really popular. The quantity of persecution which God's children have to suffer in every rank of life, even now, if they confess their Master, is far greater than the thoughtless world supposes. They only know it who go through it at school, at college, in the counting house, in the barracks room, on board the ship. Those words shall always be found true – "All that will live godly in Christ Jesus, shall suffer persecution" (2 Timothy 3:12).

Let us never forget that religious earnestness alone is no proof that a man is a sound Christian. Not all zeal is right – it may be a zeal without knowledge. No one is so mischievous as a blundering, ignorant zealot. Not all earnestness is trustworthy – without the leading of God's Spirit, it may lead a man so far astray that, like Saul, he will persecute Christ himself. Some bigots imagine they are doing God service, when they are actually fighting against His truth and trampling on His people. Let us pray that we may have light as well as zeal.

For another thing, we find *our Lord explaining His special reason for delivering the prophecy just referred to,* as well as all His discourse. "These things," He says, "I have spoken unto you, that ye should not be offended."

Well did our Lord know that nothing is so dangerous to our comfort as to indulge false expectations. He therefore prepared His disciples for what they must expect to meet with in His service. Forewarned, forearmed! They must not look for a smooth course and a peaceful journey. They must make up their minds to battles, conflicts, wounds, opposition, persecution, and perhaps even death. Like a wise general, He did not conceal from His soldiers the nature of the campaign they were beginning. He told them all that was before them, in faithfulness and love, that when the time of trial came, they might remember His words and not be disappointed and offended. He wisely forewarned them that the cross was the way to the crown.

To count the cost is one of the first duties that ought to be pressed on Christians in every age. It is no kindness to young beginners to paint the service of Christ in false colors and to keep back from them the old truth, "Through much tribulation we must enter the kingdom of God." By prophesying smooth things and crying, "Peace," we may easily fill the ranks of Christ's army with professing soldiers. But they are just the soldiers who, like the stony-ground hearers, in time of tribulation will fall away and turn back in the day of battle.

No Christian is in a healthy state of mind who is not prepared for trouble and persecution. He that expects to cross the troubled waters of this world and to reach heaven with wind and tide always in his favor knows nothing yet as he ought to know. We never can tell what is before us in life. But of one thing we may be very sure – we must carry the cross if we would wear the crown. Let us grasp this principle firmly and never forget it. Then, when the hour of trial comes, we shall "not be offended."

In the last place, we find *our Lord giving a special reason why it was expedient for Him to go away from His disciples.* "If I do not go away," He says, "the Comforter will not come unto you."

We can well suppose that our gracious Lord saw the minds of His disciples crushed at the idea of His leaving them. Little as they realized His full meaning on this, as well as on other occasions, they evidently had a vague notion that they were about to be left like orphans in a cold and unkind world by their Almighty Friend. Their hearts quailed and shrunk back at the thought. Most graciously does our Lord cheer them by words of deep and mysterious meaning. He tells them that His departure, however painful it might seem, was not an evil, but a good. They would actually find it was not a loss, but a gain. His bodily absence would be more useful than His presence.

It is vain to deny that this is a somewhat mysterious saying. It seems at first sight hard to understand how in any sense it could be good that Christ should go away from His disciples. Yet a little reflection may show us that, like our Lord's sayings, this remarkable utterance was wise, and right, and true. The following points, at any rate, deserve attentive consideration.

If Christ had not died, risen again, and ascended up into heaven, it is plain that the Holy Spirit could not have come down with special power on the day of Pentecost and bestowed His manifold gifts on the Church. Mysterious as it may be, there was a connection in the eternal counsels of God between the ascension of Christ and the outpouring of the Spirit.

If Christ had remained bodily with the disciples, He could not have been in more places than one at the same time. The presence of the Spirit, whom He sent down, would fill every place where believers were assembled in His name in every part of the world.

If Christ had remained upon earth and not gone up into heaven, He could not have become a High Priest for His people in the same full and perfect manner that He became after His ascension. He went away to sit down at the right hand of God and to appear for us, in our human nature glorified, as our Advocate with the Father.

Finally, if Christ had always remained bodily with His disciples, there would have been far less room for the exercise of their faith and hope and trust than there was when He went away. Their graces would not have been called into such active exercise, and they would have had less opportunity of glorifying God and exhibiting His power in the world.

After all, there remains the broad fact that after the Lord Jesus went away, and the Comforter came down on the day of Pentecost, the religion of the disciples became a new thing altogether. The growth of their knowledge, and faith, and hope, and zeal, and courage was so remarkable that they were twice the men they were before. They did far more for Christ when He was absent than they had ever done when He was present. What stronger proof can we require that it was expedient for them that their Master should go away!

Let us leave the whole subject with a deep conviction that it is not the bodily presence of Christ in the midst of us, so much as the presence of the Holy Spirit in our hearts, that is essential to a high standard of Christianity. What we should all desire and long for is not Christ's body literally touched with our hands and received into our mouths, but Christ dwelling spiritually in our hearts by the grace of the Holy Spirit.

John 16:8-15

And when he is come, he will reprove the world of sin and of righteousness and of judgment: of sin, because they do not believe in me; of righteousness, because I go to my Father, and ye see me no more; of judgment, because the prince of this world is judged. I have yet many things to say unto you, but ye cannot bear them now. Howbeit when he, the Spirit of truth, is come, he will guide you into all truth, for he shall not speak of himself; but whatsoever he shall hear, that shall he speak, and he will cause you to know the things which are to come. He shall clarify me, for he shall take of that which is mine and shall cause you to know it. All that the Father has is mine; therefore I said that he shall take of that which is mine and shall cause you to know it.

When our Lord in this passage speaks of the Holy Spirit "coming," we must take care that we do not misunderstand His meaning. On the one hand, we must remember that the Holy Spirit was for all of the Lord's people, even in the Old Testament days, from the very beginning. No man was ever saved from the power of sin and made a saint, except by the renewing of the Holy Spirit. Abraham, and Isaac, and Samuel, and David, and the Prophets were made what they were by the operation of the Holy Spirit.

On the other hand, we must never forget that after Christ's ascension, the Holy Spirit was poured down on men with far greater energy as individuals and with far wider influence on the nations of the world at large than He has ever poured out before. It is this increased energy and influence that our Lord has in view in the verses before us. He meant that after His own ascension, the Holy Spirit would "come" down into the world with such *a* vastly increased power, that it would seem as if He had "come" for the first time and had never been in the world before.

The difficulty of rightly explaining the wondrous sayings of our Lord in this place is undeniably very great. It may well be doubted whether the full meaning of His words has ever been entirely grasped by man, and whether there is not something at the bottom which has not been completely unfolded. The common, superficial explanation that our Lord only meant that the work of the Spirit in saving individual believers is to convince them of their own sins, of Christ's righteousness, and of the certainty of judgment at last will hardly satisfy thinking minds. It is a shortcut and superficial way of getting over Scripture difficulties. It contains excellent and sound doctrine, no doubt, but it does not meet the full meaning of our Lord's words. It is truth, but not the truth of the text. It is not individuals here and there whom He says the Spirit is to convince, but the world. Let us see whether we cannot find a fuller and more satisfactory interpretation.

For one thing, our Lord probably meant to *show us what the Holy Spirit would do to the world of unbelieving Jews.* He would convince them "of sin, and righteousness, and judgment."

He would convince the Jews "of sin." He would compel them to feel and acknowledge in their own minds that in rejecting Jesus of Nazareth they had committed a great sin and were guilty of gross unbelief.

He would convince the Jews of "righteousness." He would press home on their consciences that Jesus of Nazareth was not an impostor and a deceiver, as they had said, but a holy, just, and blameless Person, whom God had owned by receiving up into heaven.

He would convince the Jews of "judgment." He would oblige them to see that Jesus of Nazareth had conquered, overcome, and judged the devil and all his host and was exalted to be a Prince and a Savior at the right hand of God.

That the Holy Spirit did actually so convince the Jewish nation after the day of Pentecost is clearly shown by the Acts of the Apostles. It was He who gave the humble fishermen of Galilee such grace and might in testifying of Christ that their adversaries were put to silence. It was His reproving and convincing power which enabled them to "fill Jerusalem with their doctrine." Not a few of the nation, we know, were savingly convinced like Paul, and "a great company of priests" became obedient to the faith. Myriads more, we have every reason to believe, were mentally convinced, if they had not courage to come out and take up the cross. The whole tone of the Jewish people towards the end of the Acts of the Apostles is unlike what it is at the beginning. A vast reproving and convincing influence, even where not saving, seems to have gone over their minds. Surely this was partly what our Lord had in view in these verses when He said, "The Holy Spirit shall reprove and convince."

For another thing, our Lord probably meant to *foretell what the Holy Spirit would do for the whole of mankind, both Gentiles as well as Jews.*

He would reprove in every part of the earth the current ideas of men about sin, righteousness, judgment and convince people of some far higher ideas on these points than they had before acknowledged. He would make men see more clearly the nature of sin, the need of righteousness, the certainty of judgment. In a word, He would insensibly be an Advocate and convincing Pleader for God throughout the whole world and raise up a standard of morality, purity, and knowledge of which formerly men had no conception.

That the Holy Spirit actually did so in every part of the earth after the day of Pentecost is a simple matter of fact. The unlearned and lowly Jews, whom He sent forth and strengthened to preach the Gospel after our Lord's ascension, "turned the world upside down" and in two or three centuries altered the habits, tastes, and practices of the whole civilized world. The power of the devil received a decided check. Even infidels dare not deny that the doctrines of Christianity had an enormous effect on men's ways, lives, and opinions when they were first preached, and that there were no special graces or eloquence in the preachers that can account for it. In truth, the world was "reproved and convinced" in spite of itself; and even those who did not become believers became better men. Surely this also was partly what our Lord had in view when He said to His disciples, "When the Holy Spirit comes, He shall convince the world of sin, and righteousness, and judgment."

Let us leave the whole passage, deep and difficult as it is, with a thankful remembrance of one comfortable promise which it contains. "The Spirit of truth," says our Lord to His weak and half-informed followers, "shall guide you into all truth." That promise was for our sakes, no doubt, as well as for theirs. Whatever we need to know for our present peace and sanctification, the Holy Spirit is ready to teach us. All truth in science, nature, and philosophy of course is not included in this promise. But into all spiritual truth that is really profitable, and that our minds can comprehend and bear, the Holy Spirit is ready and willing to guide us. Then let us never forget, in reading the Bible, to pray for the teaching of the Holy Spirit. We must not wonder if we find the Bible a dark and difficult book, if we do not regularly seek light from Him by whom it was first inspired. In this, as in many other things, "we have not because we ask not."

John 16:16-24

A little while, and ye shall not see me; and again, a little while, and ye shall see me, because I go to the Father. Then some of his disciples said among themselves, What is this that he says unto us, A little while, and ye shall not see me; and again, a little while, and ye shall see me; and, Because I go to the Father? They said therefore, What is this that he says, A little while? we cannot understand what he says. Now Jesus knew that they were desirous to ask him and said unto them, Do ye enquire among yourselves of what I said, A little while, and ye shall not see me; and again, a little while, and ye shall see me? Verily, verily, I say unto you, That ye shall weep and lament, and the world shall rejoice; but even though ye shall be sorrowful, your sorrow shall be turned into joy. The woman, when she is in travail, has pain, because her hour is come; but as soon as she is delivered of the child, she remembers the

anguish no more, for joy that a man is born into the world.
And ye now therefore have sorrow; but I will see you again,
and your heart shall rejoice, and no one shall take your joy
from you. And in that day ye shall ask me nothing. Verily,
verily, I say unto you, Whatever ye shall ask the Father in my
name, he will give you. Until now ye have asked nothing in my
name; ask, and ye shall receive, that your joy may be fulfilled.

Not all Christ's sayings were understood by His disciples. We are told this distinctly in the passage we have now read. "What is this that he says unto us? We cannot tell what he says." None ever spoke so plainly as Jesus. None were so thoroughly accustomed to His style of teaching as the Apostles. Yet even the Apostles did not always take in their Master's meaning. Surely we have no right to be surprised if we cannot interpret Christ's words. There are many depths in them which we have no line to fathom. But let us thank God that there are many sayings of our Lord recorded which no honest mind can fail to understand. Let us use diligently the light that we have and not doubt that "to him that hath, more shall be given."

We learn, for one thing, in these verses, that *Christ's absence from the earth will be a time of sorrow to believers, but of joy to the world.* It is written, "Ye shall weep and lament, but the world shall rejoice." To confine these words to the single point of Christ's approaching death and burial appears a narrow view of their meaning. Like many of our Lord's sayings on the last evening of His earthly ministry, they seem to extend over the whole period of time between His first and second advents.

Christ's personal absence must needs be a sorrow to all true-hearted believers. "The children of the bride chamber cannot but fast when the bridegroom is taken from them." Faith is not sight. Hope is not certainty. Reading and hearing are not the same as beholding. Praying is not the same as speaking face to face. There is something, even in the hearts of the most eminent saints, that will never be fully satisfied as long as they are on earth and Christ is in heaven. So long as they dwell in a body of corruption and see through a glass darkly – so long as they behold creation groaning under the power of sin and all things not put under

Christ – so long their happiness and peace must needs be incomplete. This is what Paul meant when he said, "We ourselves, which have the first fruits of the Spirit, groan within ourselves, waiting for the adoption, to wit, the redemption of our body" (Romans 8:23).

Yet this same personal absence of Christ is no cause of sorrow to the children of this world. It was not sorrow to the unbelieving Jews, we may be sure. When Christ was condemned and crucified, they rejoiced and were glad. They thought that the hated reprover of their sins and false teaching was silenced forever. It is not sorrow to the careless and the wicked of our day, we may be sure. The longer Christ keeps away from this earth and lets them alone, the better will they be pleased. "We do not want this Christ to reign over us" is the feeling of the world. His absence causes them no pain. Their so-called happiness is complete without Him. All this may sound very painful and startling. But where is the thinking reader of the Bible who can deny that it is true? The world does not want Christ back again and thinks that it does very well without Him. What a fearful waking up there will be some day!

We learn, for another thing in this verse, that *Christ's personal return shall be a source of boundless joy to His believing people.* It is written, "I will see you again, and your heart shall rejoice, and your joy no man taketh from you." Once more we must take care that we do not narrow the meaning of these words by tying them down to our Lord's resurrection. They surely reach much further than this. The joy of the disciples when they saw Christ risen from the dead was a joy soon obscured by His ascension and withdrawal into heaven. The true joy, the perfect joy, the joy that can never be taken away will be the joy which Christ's people will feel when Christ returns the second time at the end of this world.

The second personal advent of Christ, to speak plainly, is the one grand object on which our Lord, both here and elsewhere, teaches all believers to fix their eyes. We ought to be always looking for and "loving His appearing" as the perfection of our happiness and the consummation of all our hopes (2 Peter 3:12; 2 Tim. 4:8). That same Jesus who was taken up visibly into heaven shall also come again visibly, even as He went. Let the eyes of our faith be always fixed on this coming. It is not enough that we look *backward* to the cross and rejoice in Christ dying for our sins; and *upwards* to the right hand of God and rejoice in Christ's interceding for every believer. We must do more than this. We must look *forward* to Christ's return from heaven to bless His people and to wind up the work of redemption. Then, and then only, will the prayer of eighteen centuries receive its complete answer – "Thy kingdom come, Thy will be done on earth as it is in heaven." Well may our Lord say that in that day of resurrection and reunion our "hearts shall rejoice." "When we awake up after His likeness we shall be satisfied" (Psalm 17:15).

We learn, lastly, in these verses, that *while Christ is absent believers must ask much in prayer.* It is written, "Hitherto have ye asked nothing in My name: ask and ye shall receive, that your joy may be full."

We may well believe that up to this time the disciples had never realized their Master's full dignity. They had certainly never understood that He was the one Mediator between God and man, in whose name and for whose sake they were to put up their prayers. Here they are distinctly told that henceforward they are to "ask in His name." Nor can we doubt that our Lord would have all His people, in every age, understand that the secret of comfort during His absence is to be instant in prayer. He would have us know that if we cannot see Him with our bodily eyes any longer, we can talk with Him, and through Him have special access to God. "Ask and ye shall receive," He proclaims to all His people in every age; "and your joy shall be full."

Let the lesson sink down deeply into our hearts. Of all the list of Christian duties there is none to which there is such abounding encouragement as prayer. It is a duty which concerns all. High and low, rich and poor, learned and unlearned – all must pray. It is a duty for which all are accountable. All cannot read, or hear, or sing; but all who have the spirit of adoption can pray. Above all, it is a duty in which everything depends on the heart and motive within. Our words may be feeble and ill chosen, and our language broken and ungrammatical and unworthy to be written down. But if the heart be right, it matters not. He that sits in heaven can spell out the meaning of every petition sent up in the name of Jesus and can make the asker know and feel that he receives.

"If we know these things, happy are we if we do them." Let prayer in the name of Jesus be a daily habit with us every morning and evening of our lives. Keeping up that habit, we shall find strength for duty, comfort in trouble, guidance in perplexity, hope in sickness, and support in death. Faithful is He that promised, "Your joy shall be full;" and He will keep His word, if we ask in prayer.

John 16:25-33

I have spoken these things unto you in proverbs, but the hour comes when I shall no longer speak unto you in proverbs, but I shall show you plainly of the Father. In that day ye shall ask in my name, and I do not say unto you that I will ask the Father for you; for the Father himself loves you because ye have loved me and have believed that I came out from God. I came forth from the Father and am come into the world; again, I leave the world and go to the Father. His disciples said unto him, Behold, now thou speakest plainly and speakest no proverb. Now we understand that thou knowest all things and needest not that anyone should ask thee; by this we believe that thou didst come forth from God. Jesus answered them, Do ye now believe? Behold, the hour comes and is now come, that ye shall be scattered, each one to his own, and shall leave me alone; and yet I am not alone, because the Father is with me. These things I have spoken unto you that in me ye might have peace. In the world ye shall have tribulation; but be of good cheer; I have overcome the world.

The passage we have now read is a very remarkable portion of Scripture for two reasons. On the one hand, it forms a suitable conclusion to our Lord's long parting address to His disciples. It was fit and right that such a solemn sermon should have a solemn ending. On the other hand, it contains the most general and unanimous profession of belief that we ever find the Apostles making – "Now are we sure that Thou knowest all things . . . by this we believe that thou didst come forth from God."

That there are things hard to be understood in the passage it would be useless to deny. But there lie on its surface three plain and profitable lessons to which we may usefully confine our attention.

We learn, for one thing, that *clear knowledge of God the Father is one of the foundations of the Christian religion.* Our Lord says to His disciples, "The hour comes when I shall show you plainly of the Father." He does not say, we should mark, "I will show you plainly about myself." It is the Father whom He promises to show.

The wisdom of this remarkable saying is very deep. There are few subjects of which men know so little in reality as the character and attributes of God the Father. It is not for nothing that it is written, "No man knoweth the Father save the Son, and he to whomsoever the Son shall reveal Him" (Matthew 11:27). "The only begotten Son, which is in the bosom of the Father, He has declared Him" (John 1:18). Thousands imagine that they know the Father because they think of Him as great, and almighty, and all-hearing, and wise, and eternal, but they think no further. To think of Him as just and yet the justifier of the sinner who believes in Jesus – as the God who sent His Son to suffer and die – as God in Christ reconciling the world unto Himself – as God specially well-pleased with the atoning sacrifice of His Son whereby His law is honored; to think of God the Father in this way is not given to most men. No wonder that our Master says, "I will show you plainly of the Father."

Let it be part of our daily prayers that we may know more of "the only true God," as well as of Jesus Christ whom He has sent. Let us beware alike of the mistakes which some make, who speak of God as if there was no Christ; and of the mistakes which others make, who speak of Christ as if there was no God. Let us seek to know all three Persons in the blessed Trinity and give to each One the honor due to him. Let us lay hold firmly of the great truth, that the Gospel of our salvation is the result of the eternal counsels of Father, Son, and Holy Spirit; and that we are as thoroughly debtors to the love of the Father, as to the love of the Spirit, or the love of the Son. No one has learned of Christ so deeply as the man who is ever drawing nearer to the Father through the Son – ever feeling more childlike confidence in Him – and ever understanding more thoroughly that in Christ, God is not an angry judge, but a loving Father and Friend.

We learn, for another thing, in this passage, that *our Lord Jesus Christ makes much of a little grace, and speaks kindly of those who have it.* We see Him saying to the disciples – "The Father Himself loveth you, because you have loved Me, and have believed that I came out from God."

How weak was the faith and love of the Apostles! How soon, in a very few hours, they were buried under a cloud of unbelief and cowardice! These very men whom Jesus commends for loving and believing, before the morning sun arose, forsook Him and fled. Yet, weak as their graces were, they were real and true and genuine. They were graces which hundreds of learned priests and scribes and Pharisees never attained and, not attaining, died miserably in their sins.

Let us take great comfort in this blessed truth. The Savior of sinners will not cast off those who believe in Him, because they are babes in faith and knowledge. He will not break the bruised reed or quench the smoking flax. He can see reality under much infirmity, and where He sees it, He is graciously pleased. The followers of such a Savior may well be bold and confident. They have a Friend who despises not the least member of His flock and casts out none who come to Him, however weak and feeble, if they are only true.

We learn, for another thing, in this passage, that *the best Christians know but little of their own hearts.* We see the disciples professing loudly, "Now Thou speakest plainly – now we are sure – now we believe." Brave words these! And yet the very men that spoke them in a very short time were scattered like timid sheep and left their Master alone.

We need not doubt that the profession of the eleven was real and sincere. They honestly meant what they said. But they did not know themselves. They did not know what they were capable of doing under the pressure of the fear of men and of strong temptation. They had not rightly estimated the weakness of the flesh, the power of the devil, the feebleness of their own resolutions, the shallowness of their own faith. All this they had yet to learn by painful experience. Like young recruits, they had yet to learn that it is one thing to know the soldier's drill and wear the uniform and quite another thing to be steadfast in the day of battle.

Let us mark these things and learn wisdom. The true secret of spiritual strength is self-distrust and deep humility. "When I am weak," said a great Christian, "then am I strong" (2 Corinthians 12:10). None of us, perhaps, have the least idea how much we might fall if placed suddenly under the influence of strong temptation. Happy is he who never forgets the words, "Let him that thinketh he standeth take heed lest he fall;" and, remembering our Lord's disciples, prays daily "Hold Thou me up and then I shall be safe."

We learn, lastly, from this passage, that *Christ is the true source of peace.* We read that our Lord winds up all His discourse with these soothing words – "These things have I spoken unto you, that ye might have peace." The end and scope of His parting address, He would have us know, is to draw us nearer to Himself as the only fountain of comfort. He does not tell us that we shall have no trouble in the world. He holds out no promise of freedom from tribulation, while we are in the body. But He bids us rest in the thought that He has fought our battle and won a victory for us. Though tried, and troubled, and vexed with things here below, we shall not be destroyed. "Be of good cheer," is His parting charge – "Be of good cheer; I have overcome the world."

Let us lean back our souls on these comfortable words and take courage. The storms of trial and persecution may sometimes beat heavily on us; but let them only drive us closer to Christ. The sorrows, and losses, and crosses, and disappointments of our life may often make us feel sorely cast down; but let them only make us tighten our hold on Christ. Armed with this very promise let us, under every cross, come boldly to the throne of grace that we may obtain mercy and find grace to help in time of need. Let us often say to our souls, "Why art thou cast down, and why art thou disturbed?" And let us often say to our gracious Master – "Lord, didst not Thou say, Be of good cheer? Lord, do as Thou hast said, and cheer us to the end."

John Chapter 17

John 17:1-8

Jesus spoke these words and lifted up his eyes to heaven and said, Father, the hour is come; clarify thy Son, that thy Son may also clarify thee, as thou hast given him power over all flesh, that he should give eternal life to as many as thou hast given him. And this is life eternal, that they might know thee the only true God and Jesus Christ, whom thou hast sent. I have clarified thee on the earth; I have finished the work which thou didst give me to do. And now, O Father, clarify thou me with thine own self with that clarity which I had with thee before the world was. I have manifested thy name unto the men which thou didst give me out of the world; thine they were, and thou didst give them me; and they have kept thy word. Now they have known that all things whatsoever thou hast given me are of thee. For I have given unto them the words which thou gavest me; and they have received them and have known surely that I came out from thee, and they have believed that thou didst send me.

These verses begin one of the most wonderful chapters in the Bible. It is a chapter in which we see our Lord Jesus Christ addressing a long prayer to God the Father. It is wonderful as a specimen of the communion that was ever kept up between the Father and the Son during the period of the Son's ministry on earth. It is wonderful as a pattern of the intercession which the Son, as an High Priest, is ever carrying on for us in heaven. Not least it is wonderful as an example of the sort of things that believers should mention in prayer. What Christ asks for His people, His people should ask for themselves. It has been well and truly said by an old divine that "the best and fullest sermon ever preached was followed by the best of prayers."

It is needless to say that the chapter before us contains many deep things. It could hardly be otherwise. He that reads the words spoken by one Person of the blessed Trinity to another Person, by the Son to the Father, must surely be prepared to find much that he cannot fully understand, much that he has no line to fathom. There are sentences, words, and expressions in the twenty-six verses of this chapter, which no one probably has ever unfolded completely. We have not minds to do it or to understand the matters it contains, if we could. But there are great truths in the chapter which stand out clearly and plainly on its face, and to these truths we shall do well to direct our best attention.

We should notice, firstly, in these verses, *what a glorious account they contain of our Lord Jesus Christ's office and dignity.* We read that the Father has "given Him power over all flesh, that He should give eternal life." The keys of heaven are in Christ's hands. The salvation of every soul of mankind is at His disposal. We read, furthermore, that "it is life eternal to know the only true God, and Jesus Christ whom He has sent." The mere knowledge of God is not sufficient and saves none. We must know the Son as well as the Father. God known without Christ is a Being whom we can only fear and dare not approach. It is "God in Christ, reconciling the world unto Himself," who alone can give to the soul life and peace. We read, furthermore, that Christ "has finished the work which the Father gave Him to do." He has finished the work of redemption and wrought out a perfect righteousness for His people. Unlike the first Adam, who failed to do God's will and brought sin into the world, the second Adam has done all and left nothing undone that He came to do. Finally, we read that Christ "had glory with the Father before the world was." Unlike Moses and David, He existed from all eternity, long before He came into the world; and He shared glory with the Father, before He was made flesh and born of the Virgin Mary.

Each of these marvelous sayings contains matter which our weak minds have not power fully to comprehend. We must be content to admire and reverence what we cannot thoroughly grasp and explain. But one thing is abundantly clear – sayings like these can only be used of one who is very God. To no patriarch, or prophet, or king, or apostle is any such language ever applied in the Bible. It belongs to none but God.

Forever let us thank God that the hope of a Christian rests on such a solid foundation as a Divine Savior. He to whom we are commanded to flee for pardon and in whom we are bid to rest for peace is God as well as man. To all who really think about their souls and are not careless and worldly, the thought is full of comfort. Such people know and feel that great sinners need a great Savior, and that no mere human redeemer would meet their needs. Then let them rejoice in Christ and lean back confidently on Him. Christ has all power and is able to save to the uttermost, because Christ is divine. Office, power, and pre-existence, all combine to prove that He is divine.

We should notice, secondly, in these verses, *what a gracious account they contain of our Lord Jesus Christ's disciples.* We find our Lord Himself saying of them, "They have kept Thy Word – they have known that all things Thou hast given Me are of Thee – they have received Thy words – they have known surely that I came out from Thee – they have believed that Thou didst send Me."

These are wonderful words when we consider the character of the eleven men to whom they were applied. How weak was their faith! How slender their knowledge! How shallow their spiritual attainments! How faint their hearts in the hour of danger! Yet a very little time after Jesus spoke these words they all forsook Him and fled, and one of them denied Him three times with an oath. No one, in short, can read the four Gospels with attention and fail to see that never had a great master such weak servants as Jesus had in the eleven apostles. Yet these very weak servants were the men of whom the gracious Head of the Church speaks here in high and honorable terms.

The lesson before us is full of comfort and instruction. It is evident that Jesus sees far more in His believing people than they see in themselves or than others see in them. The least degree of faith is very precious in His sight. Though it be no bigger than a grain of mustard seed, it is a plant of heavenly growth and makes a boundless difference between the possessor of it and the man of the world. Wherever the gracious Savior of sinners sees true faith in Himself, however feeble, He looks with compassion on many infirmities and passes by many defects. It was even so with the eleven apostles. They were weak and unstable as water; but they believed and loved their Master when millions refused to own Him. And the language of Him who declared that a cup of cold water given in the name of a disciple should not lose its reward shows clearly that their loyalty was not forgotten.

The true servant of God should mark well the feature in Christ's character which is here brought out, and rest his soul upon it. The best among us must often see in himself a vast amount of defects and infirmities and must feel ashamed of his poor attainments in religion. But do we simply believe in Jesus? Do we cling to Him and roll all our burdens on Him? Can we say with sincerity and truth, as Peter said afterwards, "Lord, Thou knowest all things – Thou knowest that I love Thee"? Then let us take comfort in the words of Christ before us and not give way to despondency. The Lord Jesus did not despise the eleven because of their feebleness but bore with them and saved them to the end, because they believed. And He never changes. What He did for them, He will do for us.

John 17:9-16

I pray for them; I do not pray for the world, but for those whom thou hast given me; for they are thine. And all my things are thine, and thine are mine; and I have been clarified in them. And now I am no longer in the world, but these are in the world, and I come to thee. Holy Father, those whom thou hast given me, keep them in thy name, that they may be one, as we are. While I was with them in the world, I kept them in thy name; those that thou gavest me I have kept, and none of them is lost, but the son of perdition, that the scripture might be fulfilled. And now I come to thee; and these things I speak in the world that they might have my joy fulfilled in themselves. I have given them thy word, and the world has hated them because they are not of the world, even as I am not of the world. I do not pray that thou should take them out of the world, but that thou should keep them from the evil. They are not of the world, even as I am not of the world.

These verses, like every part of this wonderful chapter, contain some deep things which are "hard to be understood." But there are several plain points standing out on the face of the passage which deserve the special attention of all true Christians. Passing by all other points, let us fix our attention on two.

We learn, for one thing, that *the Lord Jesus does things for God's people which He does not do for the wicked and unbelieving.* He helps their souls by special intercession. He says, "I pray for them – I pray not for the world, but for them which Thou hast given Me."

The doctrine before us is one which is especially hated by the world. Nothing gives such offence and stirs up such bitter feeling among the wicked as the idea of God making any distinction between men and loving one person more than another. Yet the world's objections to the doctrine are, as usual, weak and unreasonable. Surely a little reflection might show us that a God who regarded good and bad, holy and unholy, righteous and unrighteous, with equal complacency and favor, would be a very strange kind of God! The special intercession of Christ for His saints is agreeable to reason and to common sense.

Of course, like every other Gospel truth, the doctrine before us needs careful statement and Scriptural guarding. On the one hand, we must not diminish Christ's heart for the world; and on the other, we must not say that it is more or bigger than it actually is. It is true that Christ invites and longs for all to be saved; but it is also true that He specially loves His own whom He sanctifies and glorifies. It is true that He has wrought out a redemption sufficient for all mankind; but it is also true that His redemption is effectual only to those whom are chosen. Just so it is true that He is the Mediator between God and man; but it is also true that He intercedes actively for none but those whom the Father calls His own. Hence it is written, "I pray for them – I pray not for the world."

This special intercession of the Lord Jesus is one grand secret of the believer's safety. He is daily watched, and thought for, and provided for with unfailing care by One whose eye never slumbers and never sleeps. Jesus is "able to save them to the uttermost who come unto God by Him, because He ever liveth to make intercession for them" (Hebrews 7:25). They never perish, because He never ceases to pray for them, and His prayer must prevail. They stand and persevere to the end, not because of their own strength and goodness, but because Jesus intercedes for them. Judas fell never to rise again; while Peter fell, but repented and was restored. The reason of the difference lay under those words of Christ to Peter, "I have prayed for thee, that thy faith fail not" (Luke 22:32).

The true servant of Christ ought to lean back his soul on the truth before us and take comfort in it. It is one of the peculiar privileges and treasures of a believer and ought to be well known. However much it may be wrested and abused by false professors and hypocrites, it is one which those who really feel in themselves the workings of the Spirit should hold firmly and never let go. Well says the judicious Hooker – "No man's condition so safe as ours – the prayer of Christ is more than sufficient both to strengthen us, be we never so weak; and to overthrow all adversary power, be it never so strong and potent."

We learn, for another thing, in these verses, that *Christ does not wish His believing people to be taken out of the world, but to be kept from the evil of it.*

We need not doubt that our Lord's all-seeing eye detected in the hearts of His disciples an impatient desire to get away from this troubled world. Few in number and weak in strength, surrounded on every side by enemies and persecutors, they might well long to be released from the scene of conflict and to go home. Even David had said in a certain place, "Oh, that I had wings like a dove, then would I flee away and be at rest!" (Psalm 55:6). Seeing all this, our Lord has wisely placed on record this part of His prayer for the perpetual benefit of His Church. He has taught us the great lesson that He thinks it better for His people to remain in the world and be kept from its evil than to be taken out of the world and removed from the presence of evil altogether.

Nor is it difficult on reflection to see the wisdom of our Lord's mind about His people in this as in everything else. Pleasant as it might be to flesh and blood to be snatched away from conflict and temptation, we may easily see that it would not be profitable. How could Christ's people do any good in the world if taken away from it immediately after conversion? How could they exhibit the power of grace and make proof of faith, and courage, and patience as good soldiers of a crucified Lord? How could they be duly trained for heaven and taught to value the blood and intercession and patience of their Redeemer unless they purchased their experience by suffering? Questions like these admit of only one kind of answer. To abide here in this valley of tears, tried, tempted, assaulted, and yet kept from falling into sin, is the surest plan to promote the sanctification of Christians and to glorify Christ. To go to heaven at once in the day of conversion would doubtless be an easy course and would save us much trouble. But the easiest course is not always the path of duty. He that would win the crown must carry the cross and show himself light in the midst of darkness and salt in the midst of corruption. "If we suffer, we shall also reign with Him" (2 Timothy 2:12).

If we have any hope that we are Christ's true disciples, let us be satisfied that Christ knows better than we do what is for our good. Let us leave "our times in His hand" and be content to abide here patiently as long as He pleases, however hard our position, so long as He keeps us from evil. That He will so keep us we need not doubt, if we ask Him, because He prays that we may be "kept." Nothing, we may be sure, glorifies grace so much as to live like Daniel in Babylon and the saints in Nero's household – in the world and yet not of the world – tempted on every side and yet conquerors of temptation, not taken out of the reach of evil and yet kept and preserved from its power.

John 17:17-26

Sanctify them in thy truth; thy word is the truth. As thou hast sent me into the world, even so have I also sent them into the world. And for their sakes I sanctify myself, that they also might be sanctified in the truth. Neither do I pray for these alone, but also for those who shall believe in me through their word; that they all may be one; as thou,

Father, art in me, and I in thee, that they also may be one in us, that the world may believe that thou hast sent me. And the clarity which thou gavest me I have given them, that they may be one, even as we are one: I in them, and thou in me, that they may be perfect in one and that the world may know that thou hast sent me and hast loved them as thou hast loved me. Father, I will that they also, whom thou hast given me, be with me where I am, that they may behold my clarity, which thou hast given me, for thou hast loved me from before the foundation of the world. O righteous Father, the world has not known thee; but I have known thee, and these have known that thou hast sent me. And I have manifested unto them thy name and will manifest it still, that the love with which thou hast loved me may be in them, and I in them.

These wonderful verses form a fitting conclusion of the most wonderful prayer that was ever prayed on earth – the last Lord's prayer after the first Lord's Supper. They contain three most important petitions which our Lord offered up in behalf of His disciples. On these three petitions let us fix our attention. Passing by all other things in the passage, let us look steadily at these three points.

We should mark, first, *how Jesus prays that His people may be sanctified.* "Sanctify them," He says, "through thy truth – Thy word is truth."

We need not doubt that, in this place at any rate, the word "sanctify" means "make holy." It is a prayer that the Father would make His people more holy, more spiritual, more pure, more saintly in thought and word and deed, in life and character. Grace had done something for the disciples already – called, converted, renewed, and changed them. The great Head of the Church prays that the work of grace may be carried higher and further, and that His people may be more thoroughly sanctified and made holy in body, soul, and spirit – in fact more like Himself.

Surely we need not say much to show the matchless wisdom of this prayer. More holiness is the very thing to be desired for all servants of Christ. Holy living is the great proof of the reality of Christianity. Men may refuse to see the truth of our arguments, but they cannot evade the evidence of a godly life. Such a life adorns religion and makes it beautiful and sometimes wins those who are not "won by the Word." Holy living trains Christians for heaven. The nearer we live to God while we live, the more ready shall we be to dwell forever in His presence when we die. Our entrance into heaven will be entirely by grace and not of works; but heaven itself would be no heaven to us if we entered it with an unsanctified character. Our hearts must be in tune for heaven if we are to enjoy it. There must be a moral "fitness for the inheritance of the saints in light," as well as a title. Christ's blood alone can give us a title to enter the inheritance. Sanctification must give us a capacity to enjoy it.

Who, in the face of such facts as these, need wonder that increased sanctification should be the first thing that Jesus asks for His people? Who that is really taught of God can fail to know that holiness is happiness and that those who walk with God most closely are always those who walk with Him most comfortably? Let no man deceive us with vain words in this matter. He who despises holiness and neglects good works, under the vain pretense of giving honor to justification by faith, shows plainly that he has not the mind of Christ.

We should mark, secondly, in these verses, *how Jesus prays for the unity and oneness of His people*. "That they all may be one – that they may be one in Us – that they may be one even as We are one" – and "that so the world may believe and know that Thou hast sent Me," – this is a leading petition in our Lord's prayer to His Father.

We can ask no stronger proof of the value of unity among Christians and the sinfulness of division than the great prominence which our Master assigns to the subject in this passage. How painfully true it is that in every age divisions have been the scandal of religion and the weakness of the Church of Christ! How often Christians have wasted their strength in contending against their brethren, instead of contending against sin and the devil! How repeatedly they have given occasion to the world to say, "When you have settled your own internal differences we will believe!" All this, we need not doubt, the Lord Jesus foresaw with prophetic eye. It was the foresight of it which made Him pray so earnestly that believers might be "one."

Let the recollection of this part of Christ's prayer abide in our minds and exercise a constant influence on our behavior as Christians. Let no man think lightly, as some men seem to do, of schism or count it a small thing to multiply sects, parties, and denominations. These very things, we may depend, only help the devil and damage the cause of Christ. "If it be possible, as much as lieth in us, let us live peaceably with all men" (Romans 12:18). Let us bear much, concede much, and put up with much, before we plunge into secessions and separations. They are movements in which there is often much false fire. Let rabid zealots who delight in sect-making and party-forming rail at us and denounce us if they please. We need not mind them. So long as we have Christ and a good conscience, let us patiently hold on our way, follow the things that make for peace, and strive to promote unity. It was not for nothing that our Lord prayed so fervently that His people might be "one."

We should mark, finally, in these verses, *how Jesus prays that His people may at last be with Him and behold His glory.* "I will," He says, "that those whom Thou hast given Me, be with Me where I am – that they may behold my glory."

This is a singularly beautiful and touching conclusion to our Lord's remarkable prayer. We may well believe that it was meant to cheer and comfort those who heard it and to strengthen them for the parting scene which was fast drawing near. But for all who read it even now, this part of his prayer is full of sweet and unspeakable comfort.

We do not see Christ now. We read of Him, hear of Him, believe in Him, and rest our souls in His finished work. But even the best of us, at our best, walk by faith and not by sight, and our poor halting faith often makes us walk very feebly in the way to heaven. There shall be an end of all this state of things one day. We shall at length see Christ as He is and know as we have been known. We shall behold Him face to face and not through a glass darkly. We shall actually be in His presence and company and go out no more. If faith has been pleasant, much more will sight be; and if hope has been sweet, much more will certainty be. No wonder that when Paul has written, "We shall ever be with the Lord," he adds, "Comfort one another with these words" (1 Thessalonians 4:17, 18).

We know little of heaven now. Our thoughts are all confounded, when we try to form an idea of a future state in which pardoned sinners shall be perfectly happy. "It does not yet appear what we shall be" (1 John 3:2). But we may rest ourselves on the blessed thought that after death we shall be "with Christ." Whether before the resurrection in paradise or after the resurrection in final glory, the prospect is still the same. True Christians shall be "with Christ." We need no more information. Where that blessed Person is who was born for us, died for us, and rose again, there can be no lack of anything. David might well say, "In Thy presence is fulness of joy, and at Thy right hand are pleasures forevermore" (Psalm 16:11).

Let us leave this wonderful prayer with a solemn recollection of the three great petitions which it contains. Let holiness and unity by the way, and Christ's company in the end, be subjects never long out of our thoughts or distant from our minds. Happy is that Christian who cares for nothing so much as to be holy and loving like his Master while he lives and a companion of his Master when he dies.

John Chapter 18

John 18:1-11

When Jesus had spoken these things, he went forth with his
disciples over the brook Cedron, where there was a garden,
into which he entered, and his disciples. And Judas also,
who betrayed him, knew the place: for Jesus gathered there
often with his disciples. Judas then, taking a company of sol-
diers and ministers of the high priests and of the Pharisees,
came there with lanterns and torches and weapons. Jesus
therefore, knowing all the things that should come upon
him, went forth, and said unto them, Whom seek ye? They
answered him, Jesus of Nazareth. Jesus said unto them, I
AM. And Judas also, who betrayed him, stood with them.
And when he said unto them, I AM, they went backward
and fell to the ground. Then he asked them again, Whom
seek ye? And they said, Jesus of Nazareth. Jesus answered,
I have told you that I AM; if, therefore, ye seek me, let these
go away, that the word might be fulfilled, which he spoke,
Of those whom thou gavest me I have lost none. Then Simon
Peter, having a sword, drew it and smote the high priest's
slave and cut off his right ear. The slave's name was Malchus.
Then Jesus said unto Peter, Put up thy sword into the sheath;
the cup which my Father has given me, shall I not drink it?

These verses begin John's account of Christ's sufferings and crucifixion.[38]

---

38 The Cedron here mentioned is the same as the Kidron named more than once in the Old
    Testament. The word "brook" means, literally, a "winter torrent" and this, according to
    all travelers, is precisely what the Kidron is. Excepting in winter, or after rains, it is merely
    the dry bed of a watercourse. It lies on the east side of Jerusalem, between the city and the
    Mount of Olives. It is the same Kidron which David passed over weeping, when obliged
    to flee from Jerusalem by the rebellion of Absalom (2 Samuel 15:23). It is the same Kidron
    by the side of which Asa burnt the idol of his mother Maachah (2 Chronicles 15:16), and
    into which Josiah cast the dust of the idolatrous altars which he destroyed (2 Kings 23:12).

We now enter on the closing scene of our Lord's ministry and pass at once from His intercession to His sacrifice. We shall find that, like the other Gospel-writers, the beloved disciple enters fully into the story of the cross. But we shall also find, if we read carefully, that he mentions several interesting points in the story, which Matthew, Mark, and Luke for some wise reasons have passed over.

We should notice, first, in these verses, *the exceeding hardness of heart to which a backsliding professor may attain.* We are told that Judas, one of the twelve Apostles, became guide to those who captured Jesus.[39] We are told that he used his knowledge of the place of our Lord's retirement in order to bring His deadly enemies upon Him;[40] and we are told that when the band of men and officers approached his Master in order to take Him prisoner, Judas "stood with them." Yet this was a man who for three years had been a constant companion of Christ, had seen His miracles, had heard His sermons, had enjoyed the benefit of His private instruction, had professed himself a believer, had even worked and preached in Christ's name! "Lord," we may well say, "what is man?" From the highest degree of privilege down to the lowest depth of sin, there is but a succession of steps. Privileges misused seem to paralyze the conscience. The same fire that melts wax will harden clay.

Let us beware of resting our hopes of salvation on religious knowledge, however great; or religious advantages, however many. We may know all doctrinal truth and be able to teach others and yet prove rotten at heart and go down to the pit with Judas. We may bask in the full sunshine of spiritual privileges and hear the best of Christian teaching and yet bear no fruit to God's glory and be found withered branches of the vine, only fit to be burned. "Let him that thinks he stands, take heed

---

39   It is evident that the agony in Gethsemane took place at this point of the narrative. The order of things is: first, the Lord's Supper, then the long discourse recorded by John alone, then the marvelous prayer, then the going over Cedron into the garden, then the agony, and then the arrival of Judas and the capture of our Lord. It is plain therefore that there is a pause in the narrative of John's Gospel at this point, and that we must allow a little space of time for the agony, after our Lord "went out" of the city and crossed the Cedron. This would make the arrival of Judas and the soldiers far on in the night.

40   The fact that the traitor Judas "knew the place," while our Lord deliberately went there shows . . . that our Lord went to His death willingly and voluntarily; He went to the "garden," knowing well that Judas was acquainted with the place. . . . Almost all commentators notice the curious fact that the fall of Adam and Eve took place in a garden, and Christ's passion also began in a garden, and the sepulcher where Christ was laid was in a garden, and the place where He was crucified was in a garden (John 19:41).

lest he fall" (1 Corinthians 10:12). Above all, let us beware of cherishing within our hearts any secret besetting sin, such as love of money or love of the world. One faulty link in a chain cable may cause a shipwreck. One little leak may sink a ship. One allowed and unmortified sin may ruin a professing Christian. Let him that is tempted to be a careless man in his religious life consider these things and take care. Let him remember Judas Iscariot. His history is meant to be a lesson.

We should notice, secondly, in these verses, *the entire voluntariness of Christ's sufferings.* We are told that the first time that our Lord said to the soldiers, "I am He, they went backward, and fell to the ground."[41] A secret invisible power, no doubt, accompanied the words. In no other way can we account for a band of hardy Roman soldiers falling prostrate before a single unarmed man. The same miraculous influence which tied the priests and Pharisees powerless at the triumphant entry into Jerusalem – which stopped all opposition when the temple was purged of buyers and sellers – that same mysterious influence was present now. A real miracle was wrought, though few had eyes to see it. At the moment when our Lord seemed weak, He showed that He was strong.

Let us carefully remember that our blessed Lord suffered and died of His own free will. He did not die because He could not help it; He did not suffer because He could not escape. All the soldiers of Pilate's army could not have taken Him, if He had not been willing to be taken. They could not have hurt a hair of His head, if He had not given them permission. But here, as in all His earthly ministry, Jesus was a willing sufferer. He loved us and gave Himself for us, cheerfully, willingly, gladly, in order to make atonement for our sins. It was "the joy set before Him" which made Him endure the cross, and despise the shame, and yield Himself up without reluctance into the bands of His enemies. Let this thought abide in our hearts and refresh our souls. We have a Savior who was far more willing to save us than we are willing to be saved. If we

---

41   It looks as if they did not know our Lord by sight or could not believe that the bold speaker before them could be the prisoner they came to apprehend. That many of the party did not know our Lord by sight is clear from the fact mentioned by Matthew and Mark that Judas had given them a sign: "Whomsoever I kiss, that same is He: hold Him fast." This sign, therefore, had not yet been given. Probably there was no time for it. The coming forward and question of our Lord had taken place so suddenly that they took the whole party by surprise.

are not saved, the fault is all our own. Christ is just as willing to receive and pardon as He was willing to be taken prisoner, to bleed, and to die.

We should notice, thirdly, in these verses, *our Lord's tender care for His disciples' safety.* Even at this critical moment, when His own unspeakable sufferings were about to begin, He did not forget the little band of believers who stood around Him. He remembered their weakness. He knew how little fit they were to go into the fiery furnace of the High Priest's Palace and Pilate's judgment hall. He mercifully makes for them a way of escape. "If ye seek Me, let these go their way." It seems most probable that here also a miraculous influence accompanied his words. At any rate, not a hair of the disciples' heads was touched. While the Shepherd was taken, the sheep were allowed to flee away unharmed.

We need not hesitate to see in this incident an instructive type of all our Savior's dealings with His people even at this day. He will not allow them "to be tempted above that which they are able to bear." He will hold the winds and storms in His hands and not allow believers, however sifted and buffeted, to be utterly destroyed. He watches tenderly over every one of His children and, like a wise physician, measures out the right quantity of their trials with unerring skill. "They shall never perish, neither shall any one pluck them out of His hand" (John 10:28). Forever let us lean our souls on this precious truth. In the darkest hour the eye of the Lord Jesus is upon us, and our final safety is sure.

We should notice, lastly, in these verses, *our Lord's perfect submission to his Father's will.* Once, in another place, we find Him saying, "If it be possible, let this cup pass from Me – nevertheless, not as I will, but as Thou wilt." Again, in another place, we find Him saying, "If this cup may not pass away from Me except I drink it, Thy will be done." Here, however, we find even a higher pitch of cheerful acquiescence – "The cup that my Father hath given Me, shall I not drink it?" (Matthew 26:39-42; John 18:11).

Let us see in this blessed frame of mind, a pattern for all who profess and call themselves Christians. Far as we may come short of the Master's standard, let this be the mark at which we continually aim. Determination to have our own way and do only what we like is one great source of unhappiness in the world. The habit of laying all our matters before God in prayer and asking Him to choose our portion is one chief secret of peace. He is the truly wise man who has learned to say at every stage of his journey, "Give me what Thou wilt, place me where Thou wilt, do with me as Thou wilt; but not my will, but Thine be done." This is the man who has the mind of Christ. By self-will Adam and Eve fell and brought sin and misery into the world. Entire submission of will to the will of God is the best preparation for that heaven where God will be all.

John 18:12-27

Then the company of soldiers and the tribune and the ministers of the Jews took Jesus and bound him and led him away to Annas first, for he was father-in-law to Caiaphas, who was the high priest of that year and he sent him bound unto Caiaphas, the high priest. Now Caiaphas was he who had given the counsel to the Jews that it was expedient that one man should die for the people. And Simon Peter followed Jesus, and so did another disciple; that disciple was known unto the high priest and went in with Jesus into the palace of the high priest. But Peter stood at the door without. Then that other disciple, who was known unto the high priest, went out and spoke unto her that kept the door and brought in Peter. Then the damsel that kept the door said unto Peter, Art not thou also one of this man's disciples? He said, I am not. And the slaves and servants stood there, who had made a fire of coals, for it was cold, and they warmed themselves; and Peter stood with them and warmed himself. The high priest then asked Jesus of his disciples and of his doctrine. Jesus answered him, I spoke openly to the world; I always taught in the synagogue and in the temple, where all the Jews gather; and I have said nothing in secret. Why dost thou ask me? Ask those who heard me what I have said unto them; behold, they know what I said. And when he had thus spoken, one of the servants who stood by struck Jesus with the

palm of his hand, saying, Answerest thou the high priest so?
Jesus answered him, If I have spoken evil, bear witness of the
evil, but if well, why dost thou smite me? Thus Annas sent
him bound unto Caiaphas the high priest. And Simon Peter
stood and warmed himself. They said therefore unto him,
Art not thou also one of his disciples? He denied it and said,
I am not. One of the slaves of the high priest, kinsman of the
one whose ear Peter had cut off, said, Did I not see thee in
the garden with him? Peter then denied again, and immedi-
ately the cock crew.

In this part of John's history of Christ's sufferings, three wonderful things stand out upon the surface of the narrative. To these three let us confine our attention.

We should mark, for one thing, *the amazing hardness of unconverted men.* We see this in the conduct of the men by whom our Lord was taken prisoner. Some of them most probably were Roman soldiers, and some of them were Jewish servants of the priests and Pharisees. But in one respect they were all alike. Both parties saw our Lord's divine power exhibited, when they "went backward, and fell to the ground." Both saw a miracle, according to Luke's Gospel, when Jesus touched the ear of Malchus and healed him. Yet both remained unmoved, cold, indifferent and insensible, as if they had seen nothing out of the common way. They went on coolly with their odious business; "They took Jesus, bound Him, and led Him away."

The degree of hardness and insensibility of conscience to which men may attain, when they live twenty or thirty years without the slightest contact with religion, is something dreadful and appalling. God and the things of God seem to sink out of sight and disappear from the mind's eye. The world and the things of the world seem to absorb the whole attention. In such cases we may well believe miracles would produce little or no effect, as in the case before us. The eye would gaze on them like the eye of a beast looking at a romantic landscape without any impression being made on the heart. He who thinks that seeing a miracle would convert him into a thorough Christian has got much to learn.

Let us not wonder if we see cases of hardness and unbelief in our own day and generation. Such cases will continually be found among those classes of mankind, who from their profession or position are completely cut off from means of grace. Twenty or thirty years of total irreligion, without the influence of Sunday, Bible, or Christian teaching, will make a man's heart hard as the nether millstone. His conscience at last will seem dead, buried, and gone. He will appear past feeling. Painful as these cases are, we must not think them peculiar to our own times. They existed under Christ's own eyes, and they will exist until Christ returns. The Church which allows any portion of a population to grow up in practical heathenism must never be surprised to see a rank crop of practical infidelity.

We should mark, for another thing, *the amazing condescension (submission) of our Lord Jesus Christ.* We see the Son of God taken prisoner and led away bound like a malefactor – arraigned before wicked and unjust judges – insulted and treated with contempt. And yet this unresisting prisoner had only to will His deliverance, and He would at once have been free. He had only to command the confusion of His enemies, and they would at once have been confounded. Above all He was One who knew full well that Annas[42] and Caiaphas[43] and all their companions would one day stand before His judgment seat and receive an eternal sentence. He knew all these things, and yet condescended to be treated as a malefactor without resisting.

One thing at any rate is very clear. The love of Christ to sinners is "a love that passeth knowledge." To suffer for those whom we love, and who are in some sense worthy of our affections, is suffering that we can understand. To submit to ill-treatment quietly, when we have no power

---

[42] Being led to Annas is a fact which is mentioned by no Gospel writer except John. The explanation . . . In the time when our Lord Jesus was on earth, the office of the high priest among the Jews was filled up with the utmost disorder and irregularity. Instead of the high priest being high priest for life, he was often elected for a year of two, and then deposed, and his office given to another. There were often living at one time several priests who had served the office of high priest. . . . Remembering this, we may understand our Lord being "led away to Annas first," and then passed on by him to Caiaphas. So intimate were the relations between the two that in Luke 3:2 we are told that "Annas and Caiaphas were high priests." In Acts 4:6, Annas is called "the high priest." Yet it is very certain that Caiaphas was the acting high priest the year that our Lord was crucified.

[43] Let us not forget that this was the very Caiaphas, who after the raising of Lazarus, had said publicly that it was expedient that one man should die for the people. Behold how he is made the unconscious instrument of bringing that saying to pass though in a widely different sense from that which he intended.

to resist, is submission that is both graceful and wise. But to suffer voluntarily, when we a have the power to prevent it and to suffer for a world of unbelieving and ungodly sinners, unasked and unthanked – this is a line of conduct which passes man's understanding. Never let us forget that this is the peculiar beauty of Christ's sufferings, when we read the wondrous story of His cross and passion.

He was led away captive and dragged before the High Priest's bar, not because He could not help Himself but because He had set His whole heart on saving sinners by bearing their sins, by being treated as a sinner, and by being punished in their stead. He was a willing prisoner, that we might be set free. He was willingly arraigned and condemned, that we might be absolved and declared innocent. "He suffered for sins, the just for the unjust, that He might bring us unto God" (1 Peter 3:18). "Though He was rich, yet for your sakes He became poor, that ye through His poverty might be rich" (2 Corinthians 8:9). "For he hath made him to be sin for us, who knew no sin, that we might be made the righteousness of God in Him" (5:21). Surely if there is any doctrine of the Gospel which needs to be clearly known, it is the doctrine of Christ's voluntary substitution. He suffered and died willingly and unresistingly, because He knew that He had come to be our substitute and by substitution to purchase our salvation.

We should mark, lastly, *the amazing degree of weakness that may be found in a real Christian.* We see this exemplified in a most striking manner in the conduct of the Apostle Peter. We see that famous disciple forsaking his Master and acting like a coward – running away when he ought to have stood by His side – ashamed to own Him when he ought to have confessed Him – and finally denying three times that He knew Him. And this takes place immediately after receiving the Lord's' Supper – after hearing the most touching address and prayer that mortal ear ever heard – after the plainest possible warnings – under the pressure of no very serious temptation. "Lord," we may well say, "what is man that Thou art mindful of him?" "Let him that thinks he stands, take heed lest he fall" (1 Corinthians 10:12).

This fall of Peter is doubtless intended to be a lesson to the whole Church of Christ. It is recorded for our learning, that we be kept from like sorrowful overthrow. It is a beacon mercifully set up in Scripture to prevent others making shipwreck. It shows us the danger of pride and self-confidence. If Peter had not been so sure that although all denied Christ, he never would, he would probably never have fallen. It shows us the danger of laziness. If Peter had watched and prayed, when our Lord advised him to do so, he would have found grace to help him in the time of need. It shows us, not least, the painful influence of the fear of man. Few are aware, perhaps, how much more they fear the face of man whom they can see than the eye of God whom they cannot see. These things are written for our admonition. Let us remember Peter and be wise.

After all let us leave the passage with the comfortable reflection that we have a merciful and pitiful High Priest, who can be touched with the feeling of our infirmities and will not break the bruised reed. Peter no doubt fell shamefully and only rose again after heartfelt repentance and bitter tears. But he did rise again. He was not left to reap the consequence of his sin and cast off for evermore. The same pitying hand that saved him from drowning, when his faith failed him on the waters, was once more stretched out to raise him when he fell in the High Priest's hall.[44] Can we doubt that he rose a wiser and better man? If Peter's fall has made Christians see more clearly their own great weakness and Christ's great compassion, then Peter's fall has not been recorded in vain.

John 18:28-40

Then led they Jesus from Caiaphas unto the hall of judgment, and it was early; and they themselves did not go into the judgment hall, lest they should be defiled, but that they might eat the passover. Pilate then went out unto them and said, What accusation bring ye against this man? They answered and said unto him, If he were not a malefactor, we would not have delivered him up unto thee. Then Pilate

---

44 It is noteworthy that some think the houses of Caiaphas and Annas were adjacent, and that "the hall" was common to both of them. I am strongly disposed to think that this is a correct view, and a remembrance of it may help us over several difficulties in the narrative of the four evangelists when compared.

said unto them, Take him, and judge him according to your
law. The Jews therefore said unto him, It is not lawful for
us to put anyone to death; that the saying of Jesus might be
fulfilled, which he spoke, signifying what death he should
die. Then Pilate entered into the judgment hall again and
called Jesus and said unto him, Art thou the King of the
Jews? Jesus answered him, Sayest thou this thing of thyself,
or did others tell it unto thee of me? Pilate answered, Am
I a Jew? Thine own nation and the chief priests have deliv-
ered thee unto me; what hast thou done? Jesus answered,
My kingdom is not of this world; if my kingdom were of this
world, then my servants would fight, that I should not be
delivered to the Jews; now, therefore, my kingdom is not from
here. Pilate therefore said unto him, Art thou a king then?
Jesus answered, Thou sayest that I AM king. To this end I
was born, and for this cause I came into the world, that I
should bear witness unto the truth. Every one that is of the
truth hears my voice. Pilate said unto him, What is truth?
And when he had said this, he went out again unto the Jews,
and said unto them, I find no fault at all in him. But ye have
a custom, that I should release unto you one at the pass-
over; will ye therefore that I release unto you the King of the
Jews? Then they all cried again, saying, Not this man, but
Barabbas. Now Barabbas was a robber.

The verses we have now read contain four striking points, which are
only found in John's narrative of Christ's passion. We need not doubt
that there were good reasons why Matthew, Mark, and Luke were not
inspired to record them. But they are points of such deep interest that
we should feel thankful that they have been brought forward by John.

The first point that we should notice is *the false conscientiousness
of our Lord's wicked enemies*. We are told that the Jews who brought
Christ before Pilate would not go into "the judgment hall, lest they
should be defiled; but that they might eat the passover." That was scru-
pulosity indeed! These hardened men were actually engaged in doing
the wickedest act that mortal man ever did. They wanted to kill their

own Messiah. And yet at this very time they talked of being "defiled" and were very fastidious about the passover!

The conscience of unconverted men is a very curious part of their moral nature. While in some cases it becomes hardened, seared, and dead, until it feels nothing; in others it becomes morbidly scrupulous about the lesser matters of religion. It is no uncommon thing to find people excessively meticulous about the observance of trifling forms and outward ceremonies, while they are the slaves of degrading sins and detestable immoralities. Robbers and murderers in some countries are extremely strict about confession, and absolution, and prayers to saints. Fastings and self-imposed austerities in Lent are often followed by excess of worldliness when Lent is over. There is but a step from Lent to Carnival. The attendants at daily services in the morning are not infrequently the patrons of balls and theaters at night. All these are symptoms of spiritual disease and a heart secretly dissatisfied. Men who know they are wrong in one direction often struggle to make things right by excess of zeal in another direction. That very zeal is their condemnation.

Let us pray that our consciences may always be enlightened by the Holy Spirit, and that we may be kept from a one-sided and deformed Christianity. A religion that makes a man neglect the weightier matters of daily holiness and separation from the world, and concentrate his whole attention on forms, sacraments, ceremonies, and public services is, to say the least, very suspicious. It may be accompanied by immense zeal and show of earnestness, but it is not sound in the sight of God. The Pharisees paid tithe of mint, anise, and cummin and compassed sea and land to make proselytes, while they neglected "judgment, mercy, and faith" (Matthew 23:23). The very Jews who thirsted for Christ's blood were the Jews who feared the defilement of a Roman judgment hall and made much ado about keeping the passover! Let their conduct be a beacon to Christians as long as the world stands. That religion is worth little which does not make us say, "I esteem all Thy commandments concerning all things to be right, and I hate every false way" (Psalm 119:128). That Christianity is worthless which makes us make up for the neglect of heart religion and practical holiness by an extravagant zeal for man-made ceremonies or outward forms.

The second point that we should notice in these verses is *the account that our Lord Jesus Christ gives of His kingdom*. He says, "My kingdom is not of this world." These famous words have been so often perverted and wrested out of their real sense that their true meaning has been almost buried under a heap of false interpretations. Let us make sure that we know what they mean.

Our Lord's main object in saying "My kingdom is not of this world" was to inform Pilate's mind concerning the true nature of His kingdom and to correct any false impression he might have received from the Jews. He tells him that He did not come to set up a kingdom which would interfere with the Roman Government. He did not aim at establishing a temporal power to be supported by armies and maintained by taxes. The only dominion He exercised was over men's hearts, and the only weapons that His subjects employed were spiritual weapons. A kingdom which required neither money nor servants for its support was one of which the Roman Emperors need not be afraid. In the highest sense it was a kingdom "not of this world."[45]

But our Lord did not intend to teach that the kings of this world have nothing to do with religion and ought to ignore God altogether in the government of their subjects. No such idea, we may be sure, was in His mind. He knew perfectly well that it was written, "By Me kings reign" (Proverbs 8:15), and that kings are as much required to use their influence for God as the lowest of their subjects. He knew that the prosperity of kingdoms is wholly dependent on the blessing of God, and that kings are as much bound to encourage righteousness and godliness as to punish unrighteousness and immorality. To suppose that He meant to teach Pilate that in His judgment an infidel might be as good a king as a Christian, and a man like Gallio as good a ruler as David or Solomon, is simply absurd.

---

45   The true meaning of this little sentence is not very clear. May it not mean, "Now, in this dispensation my kingdom is not an earthly one, and is not of this world. A day will come by and by, after my second advent, when my kingdom will be a visible one over the whole earth, and my saints shall rule over the whole earth, and my saints shall rule over the renewed world." – This may seem fanciful to some; but I have a strong impression that it is the true meaning. The adverb "now: is very decided and emphatical.

Let us carefully hold fast the true meaning of our Lord's words in these latter days. Let us never be ashamed to maintain that no Government can expect to prosper which refuses to recognize religion, which deals with its subjects as if they had no souls and cares not whether they serve God, or Baal, or no God at all. Such a Government will find, sooner or later, that its line of policy is suicidal and damaging to its best interests. No doubt the kings of this world cannot make men Christians by laws and statutes. But they can encourage and support Christianity, and they will do so if they are wise. The kingdom where there is the most industry, temperance, truthfulness, and honesty will always be the most prosperous of kingdoms. The king who wants to see these things abound among his subjects should do all that lies in his power to help Christianity and to discourage irreligion.

The third point that we should notice in these verses is *the account that our Lord gives of His own mission.* He says, "To this end was I born, and for this cause came I into the world, that I should bear witness unto the truth."

Of course we are not to suppose our Lord meant that this was the *only* end of His mission. No doubt He spoke with special reference to what He knew was passing through Pilate's mind. He did not come to win a kingdom with the sword and to gather adherents and followers by force. He came armed with no other weapon but "truth." To testify to fallen man the truth about God, about sin, about the need of a Redeemer, about the nature of holiness – to declare and lift up before man's eyes this long lost and buried "truth" – was one great purpose of His ministry. He came to be God's witness to a lost and corrupt world. That the world needed such a testimony, He does not shrink from telling the proud Roman Governor. And this is what Paul had in view, when he tells Timothy, that "before Pontius Pilate Christ witnessed a good confession" (1 Timothy 6:13).

The servants of Christ in every age must remember that our Lord's conduct in this place is meant to be their example. Like Him we are to be witnesses to God's truth, salt in the midst of corruption, light in the midst of darkness, men and women not afraid to stand alone and to testify for God against the ways of sin and the world. To do so may entail on us much trouble and even persecution. But the duty is clear and plain. If we love life, if we would keep a good conscience and be owned by Christ at the last day, we must be "witnesses." It is written, "Whosoever shall be ashamed of Me and of my words in this adulterous and sinful generation, of him also shall the Son of man be ashamed, when He cometh in the glory of His Father with the holy angels" (Mark 8:38).

The last point that we should notice in these verses is *the question that Pontius Pilate addressed to our Lord.* We are told that when our Lord spoke of the truth, the Roman Governor replied, "What is truth?" We are not told with what motive this question was asked, nor does it appear on the face of the narrative that he who asked it waited for an answer. It seems far more likely that the saying was the sarcastic, sneering exclamation of one who did not believe that there was any such thing as "truth." It sounds like the language of one who had heard from his earliest youth so many barren speculations about "truth" among Roman and Greek philosophers that he doubted its very existence. "Truth indeed! What is truth?"

Melancholy as it may appear, there are multitudes in every Christian land whose state of mind is just like that of Pilate. Hundreds, it may be feared among the upper classes, are continually excusing their own irreligion by the specious plea that, like the Roman Governor, they cannot find out "what is truth." They point to the endless controversies of Romanists and Protestants, of High Churchmen and Low Churchmen, of Churchmen and Dissenters and pretend to say that they do not understand who is right and who is wrong. Sheltered under this excuse, they pass through life without any decided religion and in this wretched, comfortless state too often die.

But is it really true that truth cannot be discovered? Nothing of the kind! God never left any honest, diligent inquirer without light and guidance. Pride is one reason why many cannot discover truth. They do not humbly go down on their knees and earnestly ask God to teach them. Laziness is another reason. They do not honestly take pains and search the Scriptures. The followers of unhappy Pilate, as a rule, do not deal fairly and honestly with their consciences. Their favorite question – What is truth? – is nothing better than a pretense and an excuse. The words of Solomon will be found true as long as the world stands – "If thou criest after knowledge, and liftest up thy voice for understanding; if thou seekest her as silver, and searchest for her as for hid treasures; then shall thou understand the fear of the Lord, and find the knowledge of God" (Proverbs 2:4, 5). No man ever followed that advice and missed the way to heaven.

John Chapter 19

John 19:1-16

Then Pilate, therefore, took Jesus and scourged him. And the soldiers platted a crown of thorns and put it on his head, and they put a purple robe on him and said, Hail, King of the Jews! and they smote him with their hands. Pilate therefore went forth again and said unto them, Behold, I bring him forth to you, that ye may know that I find no fault in him. Then Jesus came forth, wearing the crown of thorns and the purple robe. And Pilate said unto them, Behold the man! When the princes of the priests and the servants saw him, they cried out, saying, crucify him, crucify him. [a] Pilate said unto them, Take him, and crucify him, for I find no fault in him. The Jews answered him, We have a law, and by our law he ought to die because he made himself the Son of God. Therefore when Pilate heard that word, he was the more afraid and went again into the judgment hall and said unto Jesus, Where art thou from? But Jesus gave him no answer. Then Pilate said unto him, Speakest thou not unto me? knowest thou not that I have power to crucify thee[b] and have power to release thee? Jesus answered, Thou could have no power at all against me, unless it were given thee from above; therefore he that delivered me unto thee has the greater sin. And from then on Pilate sought to release him, but the Jews cried out, saying, If thou let this man go, thou art not Caesar's friend; whosoever makes himself a king speaks against Caesar. Therefore when Pilate heard that word, he brought Jesus forth and sat down in the judgment seat in a place that is called the Pavement, but in the

*Hebrew, Gabbatha. And it was the preparation of the pass-
over and about the sixth hour; then he said unto the Jews,
Behold your King! But they cried out, Away with him, away
with him, crucify him. Pilate said unto them, Shall I crucify
your King? The high priests answered, We have no king but
Caesar. So that then, he delivered him unto them to be crucified. And they took Jesus and led him away.*

These verses exhibit to our eyes a wonderful picture, a picture which
ought to be deeply interesting to all who profess and call themselves
Christians. Like every great historical picture, it contains special points
on which we should fix our special attention. Above all, it contains three
life-like portraits, which we shall find it useful to examine in order.

The first portrait in the picture is that of our Lord Jesus Christ Himself.
We see the Savior of mankind scourged,[46] crowned with thorns, mocked,
smitten, rejected by His own people, unjustly condemned by a judge
who saw no fault in Him, and finally delivered up to a most painful
death.[47] Yet this was He who was the eternal Son of God, whom the
Father's countless angels delighted to honor. This was He who came
into the world to save sinners and, after living a blameless life for thirty
years, spent the last three years of His time on earth in going about
doing good and preaching the Gospel. Surely the sun never shone on
a more wondrous sight since the day of its creation!

Let us admire that love of Christ which Paul declares, "passeth
knowledge," and let us see an endless depth of meaning in the expression. There is no earthly love with which it can be compared and no
standard by which to measure it. It is a love that stands alone. Never let
us forget when we ponder this tale of suffering that Jesus suffered for our
sins, the Just for the unjust, that He was wounded for our transgressions
and bruised for our iniquities, and that with His stripes we are healed.

---

46 The importance of this particular portion of our Lord's sufferings is strongly shown by
the fact that Isaiah specially says, "by His stripes we are healed;" and that Peter specially
quotes that text in his first epistle (Isaiah 53:5; 1 Peter 2:24). Our Lord Himself particularly
foretold that He would be scourged (Luke 18:33).

47 Let us remember, when we read that word "delivered" that it is expressly written, He was
"delivered for our offences," and that God "spared not His own Son, but delivered Him up
for us all" (Romans 4:25; 8:30). Christ was delivered to death that we might be delivered
from death and set free. Here is substitution.

Let us diligently follow the example of His patience in all the trials and afflictions of life and specially in those which may be brought upon us by religion. When He was reviled, He reviled not again; when He suffered, He threatened not, but committed Himself to Him that judges righteously. Let us arm ourselves with the same mind. Let us consider Him who endured such contradiction of sinners without a murmur and strive to glorify Him by suffering well, no less than by doing well.

The second portrait in the picture before us is that of the unbelieving Jews who favored our Lord's death. We see them for three or four long hours obstinately rejecting Pilate's offer to release our Lord – fiercely demanding His crucifixion – savagely claiming His condemnation to death as a right – persistently refusing to acknowledge Him as their King – declaring that they had no King but Caesar – and finally accumulating on their own heads the greater part of the guilt of His murder. Yet, these were the children of Israel and the seed of Abraham to whom pertained the promises and the Mosaic ceremonial, the temple sacrifices and the temple priesthood. These were men who professed to look for a Prophet like unto Moses and a son of David who was to set up a kingdom as Messiah. Never, surely, was there such an exhibition of the depth of human wickedness since the day when Adam fell.

Let us mark with fear and trembling the enormous danger of long-continued rejection of light and knowledge. There is such a thing as judicial blindness; and it is the last and sorest judgment which God can send upon men. He who, like Pharaoh and Ahab, is often reproved but refuses to receive reproof will finally have a heart harder than the nether millstone and a conscience past feeling and seared as with a hot iron. This was the state of the Jewish nation during the time of our Lord's ministry; and the heading up of their sin was their deliberate rejection of Him, when Pilate desired to let Him go. From such judicial blindness may we all pray to be delivered! There is no worse judgment from God than to be left to ourselves and given over to our own wicked hearts and the devil. There is no surer way to bring that judgment upon us than to persist in refusing warnings and sinning against light. These words of Solomon are very dreadful – "Because I have called, and ye refused; I have stretched out my hand, and no man regarded; but ye have set at nought all my counsel, and would none of my reproof: I also will laugh at your calamity; I will mock when your fear cometh" (Proverbs 1:24-26). Never let it be forgotten that, like the Jews, we may at length be given up to strong delusion, so that we believe lies and think that we are doing God service while we are committing sin (2 Thessalonians 2:11).

The third, and last portrait in the picture before us, is that of Pontius Pilate. We see a Roman Governor – a man of rank and high position – an imperial representative of the most powerful nation on earth – a man who ought to have been the fountain of justice and equity – halting between two opinions in a case as clear as the sun at noonday. We see him knowing what was right and yet afraid to act up to his knowledge – convinced in his own conscience that he ought to acquit the prisoner before him and yet afraid to do it lest he should displease His accusers – sacrificing the claims of justice to the base fear of man – sanctioning from sheer cowardice, an enormous crime – and finally countenancing, from love of man's good opinion, the murder of an innocent person. Never perhaps did human nature make such a contemptible exhibition. Never was there a name so justly handed down to a world's scorn as the name which is embalmed in all our creeds – the name of Pontius Pilate.

Let us learn what miserable creatures great men are when they have no high principles within them and no faith in the reality of a God above them. The lowest laborer who has grace and fears God is a nobler being in the eyes of his Creator than the King, ruler, or statesman, whose first aim it is to please the people. To have one conscience in private and another in public – one rule of duty for our own souls and another for our public actions – to see clearly what is right before God and yet for the sake of popularity to do wrong – this may seem to some both right, and politic, and statesmanlike, and wise. But it is a character which no Christian man can ever regard with respect.

Let us pray that our own country may never be without men in high places who have grace to think right and courage to act up to their knowledge without truckling to the opinion of men. Those who fear God more than man and care for pleasing God more than man are the best rulers of a nation and in the long run of years are always most respected. Men like Pontius Pilate, who are always trimming and compromising, led by popular opinion instead of leading popular opinion, afraid of doing right if it gives offence, ready to do wrong if it makes them personally popular, such men are the worst governors that a country can have. They are often God's heavy judgment on a nation because of a nation's sins.

John 19:17-27

And he, bearing his cross[c], went forth into a place called the place of a skull, which is called in the Hebrew, Golgotha, where they crucified him and two others with him, one on either side and Jesus in the middle. And Pilate also wrote a title and put it above the cross[d]. And the writing was, JESUS OF NAZARETH THE KING OF THE JEWS. And many of the Jews read this title, for the place where Jesus was crucified was near to the city; and it was written in Hebrew and Greek and Latin. Then the high priests of the Jews said to Pilate, Write not, The King of the Jews, but that he said, I AM King of the Jews. Pilate answered, What I have written I have written. Then the soldiers, when they had crucified Jesus, took his garments and made four parts (to each soldier a part); and also his coat: now the coat was without seam, woven from the top throughout. They said therefore among themselves, Let us not rend it, but cast lots for it, whose it shall be; that the scripture might be fulfilled, which says, They parted my garments among them, and for my raiment they did cast lots. These things therefore the soldiers did. Now there stood by the cross[e] of Jesus his mother and his mother's sister, Mary the wife of Cleophas, and Mary Magdalene. When Jesus therefore saw his mother and the disciple standing by, whom he loved, he said unto his mother, Woman, behold thy son! Then he said to the disciple, Behold thy mother! And from that hour that disciple took her unto his own home.

He that can read a passage like this without a deep sense of man's debt to Christ must have a very cold or a very thoughtless heart. Great must be the love of the Lord Jesus to sinners, when He could voluntarily endure such sufferings for their salvation. Great must be the sinfulness of sin, when such an amount of vicarious suffering was needed in order to provide redemption.

We should observe, first, in this passage, *how our Lord had to bear His cross when He went forth from the city to Golgotha.*[48]

We need not doubt that there was a deep meaning in all this circumstance. For one thing, it was part of that depth of humiliation to which our Lord submitted as our substitute. One portion of the punishment imposed on the vilest criminals was that they should carry their own cross when they went to execution; and this portion was laid upon our Lord. In the fullest sense He was reckoned a sinner and counted a curse for our sakes. For another thing, it was a fulfillment of the great type of the sin offering of the Mosaic law. It is written that "The bullock for the sin offering, and the goat for the sin offering, whose blood was brought in to make atonement in the holy place, shall one carry forth without the camp" (Leviticus 16:27). Little did the blinded Jews imagine, when they madly hounded on the Romans to crucify Jesus outside the gates, that they were unconsciously perfecting the mightiest sin offering that was ever seen.[49] It is written, "Jesus, that He might sanctify the people with his own blood, suffered without the gate" (Hebrews 13:12).

The practical lesson which all true Christians should gather from the fact before us is one that should be kept in continual remembrance. Like our Master, we must be content to go forth "without the camp," bearing His reproach. We must come out from the world and be separate and be willing, if need be, to stand alone. Like our Master, we must be willing

---

48 It is hardly necessary to remark that the type of Isaac bearing the wood for the sacrifice on Moriah, in which he himself was to be the victim, was here fulfilled by our Lord.

49 Our Lord went out of the city to be crucified. He was condemned in the open air and "went forth" cannot mean out of Pilate's house, but went outside of Jerusalem, without the gates. Trifling as this incident may seem to a careless reader, it is a striking fulfilment of one of the great types of the Mosaic law. The sin offering on the great day of atonement was to be carried forth "without the camp" (Leviticus 16:27). Our Lord came to be the true sin offering, to give His soul an offering for our sins. Therefore it was divinely over-ruled of God, that in order to fulfill the type perfectly, He should suffer outside the city (Leviticus 6:12-21). Paul specially refers to this when he tells the Hebrew Christians, who were familiar with the law of Moses, that "Jesus suffered without the gate" (Hebrews 13:12). The minutest details of our Lord's passion have a deep meaning.

to take up our cross daily and to be persecuted both for our doctrine and our practice. Well would it be for the Church if there was more of the true cross to be seen among Christians! To wear material crosses as an ornament, to place material crosses on churches and tombs, all this is cheap and easy work and entails no trouble. But to have Christ's cross in our hearts, to carry Christ's cross in our daily walk, to know the fellowship of His sufferings, to be made conformable to His death, to have crucified affections and live crucified lives – all this needs self-denial; and Christians of this stamp are few and far between. Yet, this, we may be sure, is the only cross-bearing and cross-carrying that does good in the world. The times require less of the cross outwardly and more of the cross within.

We should observe, secondly, in this passage, *how our Lord was crucified as a King.* The title placed over our Lord's head made this plain and unmistakable. The reader of Greek, or Latin, or Hebrew could not fail to see that He who hung on the central cross of the three on Golgotha had a royal title over His head. The overruling hand of God so ordered matters that the strong will of Pilate overrode for once the wishes of the malicious Jews. In spite of the chief priests, our Lord was crucified as "the King of the Jews."

It was fit and right that so it should be. Even before our Lord was born, the angel Gabriel declared to the Virgin Mary, "The Lord God shall give unto Him the throne of His father David: and He shall reign over the house of Jacob forever; and of His kingdom there shall be no end" (Luke 1:32, 33). Almost as soon as He was born, there came wise men from the East, saying, "Where is He that is born King of the Jews?" (Matthew 2:2). The week before the crucifixion, the multitude who accompanied our Lord at His triumphal entry into Jerusalem had cried, "Blessed is the King of Israel that cometh in the name of the Lord" (John 12:13). The current belief of all godly Jews was that when Messiah, the Son of David, came, He would come as a King. A kingdom of heaven and a kingdom of God was continually proclaimed by our Lord throughout His ministry. A King indeed He was, as He told Pilate of a kingdom utterly unlike the kingdoms of this world, but for all that a true King of a true kingdom, and a Ruler of true subjects. As such He was born.

As such He lived. As such He was crucified. And as such He will come again and reign over the whole earth, King of kings and Lord of lords.

Let us take care that we ourselves know Christ as our King and that His kingdom is set up within our hearts. They only will find Him their Savior at the last day, who have obeyed Him as King in this world. Let us cheerfully pay Him that tribute of faith, and love, and obedience, which He prizes far above gold. Above all, let us never be afraid to own ourselves His faithful subjects, soldiers, servants and followers, however much He may be despised by the world. A day will soon come when the despised Nazarene who hung on the cross shall take to Himself His great power and reign and put down every enemy under His feet. The kingdoms of this world, as Daniel foretold, shall be swept aside and become the kingdom of our God and of His Christ. And at last every knee shall bow to Him, and every tongue confess that Jesus Christ is Lord.

We should observe, lastly, in these verses, *how tenderly our Lord took thought for Mary, His mother.* We are told that even in the dreadful agonies of body and mind which our Lord endured, He did not forget her of whom He was born. He mercifully remembered her desolate condition and the crushing effect of the sorrowful sight before her. He knew that, while a good Christian, she was only a woman, and that, as a woman, she must deeply feel the death of such a Son. He therefore commended her to the protection of His best-loved and best-loving disciple in brief and touching words – "Woman," He said, "behold thy son! Then saith He to the disciple, Behold thy mother! And from that hour that disciple took her unto his own home."

We surely need no stronger proof than we have here that Mary, the mother of Jesus, was never meant to be honored as divine or to be prayed to, worshiped, and trusted in as the friend and patroness of sinners. Common sense points out that she who needed the care and protection of another was never likely to help men and women to heaven or to be in any sense a mediator between God and man! It is not too much to say, however painful the assertion, that of all the inventions of the Church of Rome, there never was one more utterly devoid of foundation, both in Scripture and reason, than the doctrine of Mary-worship.

Let us turn from points of controversy to a subject of far more practical importance. Let us take comfort in the thought that we have in
Jesus a Savior of matchless tenderness, matchless sympathy, matchless
concern for the condition of His believing people. Let us never forget
His words, "Whosoever shall do the will of God, the same is my brother,
and my sister, and mother" (Mark 3:35). The heart that even on the
cross felt for Mary is a heart that never changes. Jesus never forgets any
who love Him, and even in their worst estate remembers their need.
No wonder that Peter says, "Casting all your care upon Him; for He
careth for you" (1 Peter 5:7).

John 19:28-37

After this, Jesus knowing that all things were now accom-
plished, that the scripture might be fulfilled, said, I thirst.
Now there was set a vessel full of vinegar, and they filled a
sponge with vinegar and put it upon hyssop and put it to
his mouth. When Jesus therefore had received the vinegar,
he said, It is finished, and he bowed his head and gave the
Spirit. The Jews therefore, because it was the preparation,
that the bodies should not remain upon the cross[f] on the
sabbath day (for that sabbath day was a high day) besought
Pilate that their legs might be broken and that they might
be taken away. Then the soldiers came and broke the legs of
the first and of the other who were crucified with him. But
when they came to Jesus and saw that he was dead already,
they did not break his legs, but one of the soldiers with a
spear pierced his side, and forthwith blood and water came
out. And he that saw it gives testimony, and his testimony is
true, and he knows that he says the truth, that ye also might
believe. For these things were done that the scripture should
be fulfilled, A bone of him shall not be broken. And again
another scripture says, They shall look on him whom they
pierced.

This part of John's narrative of Christ's passion contains points of deep interest, which are silently passed over by Matthew, Mark, and Luke. The reason of this silence we are not told. Suffice it for us to remember that, both in what they recorded and in what they did not record, all four Evangelists wrote by inspiration of God.

Let us mark, for one thing, in these verses, *the frequent fulfillments of prophetic Scripture throughout every part of Christ's crucifixion.* Three different predictions are specially mentioned in Exodus, Psalms, and Zechariah, which received their accomplishment at the cross. Others, as every well-informed Bible reader knows, might easily be added.[50] All combine to prove one and the same thing. They prove that the death of our Lord Jesus Christ at Golgotha was a thing foreseen and predetermined by God. Hundreds of years before the crucifixion, every part of the solemn transaction was arranged in the Divine counsels, and the minutest particulars were revealed to the Prophets. From first to last it was a thing foreknown, and every portion of it was in accordance with a settled plan and design. In the highest, fullest sense, when Christ died, He "died according to the Scriptures" (1 Corinthians 15:3).

We need not hesitate to regard such fulfillments of prophecy as strong evidence of the Divine authority of God's Word. The Prophets foretell not only Christ's death but the particulars of His death. It is impossible to explain so many accomplishments of predicted circumstances upon any other theory. To talk of luck, chance, and accidental coincidence as sufficient explanation is preposterous and absurd. The only rational account is the inspiration of God. The Prophets who foretold the particulars of the crucifixion were inspired by Him who foresees the end from the beginning; and the books they wrote under His inspiration ought not to be read as human compositions but Divine. Great indeed

---

50 In verses 36 and 37 John explains distinctly to his readers why two of the facts he has just mentioned, however trifling they might seem to an ignorant person, were in reality of great importance. By one of these facts – the not breaking a bone of our Lord's body – the text was fulfilled which said that not a bone of the Passover lamb should be broken (Exodus 12:46). By the other fact – the piercing of our Lord's side – the prophecy of Zechariah was fulfilled, that the inhabitants of Jerusalem "should look on him whom they pierced" (Zechariah 12:10). . . . It is almost needless to say that the passage, like many others, does not mean that these things were done in order that Scripture might be fulfilled, but that by these things being done the Scripture was fulfilled, and God's perfect foreknowledge about the least details of Christ's death was proved. . . . Let us carefully note here what strong evidence these verses supply in favor of a literal, and not a merely spiritual, fulfillment of Old Testament prophecies.

are the difficulties of all who pretend to deny the inspiration of the Bible. It really requires more unreasoning faith to be an infidel than to be a Christian. The man who regards the repeated fulfillments of minute prophecies about Christ's death, such as the prophecies about His dress, His thirst, His pierced side, and His bones as the result of chance and not of design must indeed be a credulous man.

We should mark, secondly, in these verses, *the peculiarly solemn saying which came from our Lord's lips just before He died.* John relates that "when He had received the vinegar, He said, it is finished; and He bowed His head and gave up the spirit." It is surely not too much to say that of all the seven famous sayings of Christ on the cross, none is more remarkable than this, which John alone has recorded.[51]

The precise meaning of this wondrous expression, "It is finished," is a point which the Holy Spirit has not thought good to reveal to us. There is a depth about it, we must all instinctively feel, which man has probably no line to fathom. Yet there is perhaps no irreverence in conjecturing the thoughts that were in our Lord's mind when the word was spoken. The finishing of all the known and unknown sufferings which He came to endure as our Substitute – the finishing of the ceremonial law, which He came to wind up and fulfill as the true Sacrifice for sin – the finishing of the many prophecies, which He came to accomplish – the finishing of the great work of man's redemption, which was now close at hand – all this, we need not doubt, our Lord had in view when He said, "It is finished." There may have been more behind, for anything we know. But in handling the language of such a Being as our Savior on such an occasion and at so mysterious a crisis of His history, it is well to be cautious. "The place whereon we stand is holy ground."

One comfortable thought, at all events, stands out most clearly on the face of this famous expression. We rest our souls on a "finished

---

51 Three of His seven saying on the cross were before the darkness and four after it or during it. The order of the famous seven sayings was as follows:
   1. "Father, forgive them; for they know not what they do."
   2 "Today shalt thou be with Me in paradise."
   3. "Woman behold thy son. Behold thy mother."
   4. "My God, my God, why hast thou forsaken me."
   5. "I thirst."
   6. "It is finished."
   7. "Father, into thy hands I commend my spirit."

work," if we rest them on the work of Jesus Christ the Lord. We need not fear that either sin, or Satan, or law shall condemn us at the last day. We may lean back on the thought that we have a Savior who has done all, paid all, accomplished all, performed all that is necessary for our salvation. We may take up the challenge of the Apostle, "Who is he that condemneth? It is Christ that died: yea, rather that is risen again; who is even at the right hand of God; who also maketh intercession for us" (Romans 8:34). When we look at our own works, we may well be ashamed of their imperfections. But when we look at the finished work of Christ, we may feel peace. We "are complete in Him," if we believe (Colossians 2:10).

We should mark, lastly, in these verses, *the reality and truth of Christ's death.* We are told that "one of the soldiers with a spear pierced His side, and forthwith came there out blood and water." This incident, small as it may seem at first sight, supplies probable proof that the heart of our blessed Lord was pierced and that life was consequently extinct. He did not merely faint, or swoon away, or become insensible as some have dared to insinuate. His heart actually ceased to beat, and He actually died. Great, indeed, was the importance of this fact. We must all see on a moment's reflection that without a real death there could be no real sacrifice; that without a real death there could be no real resurrection; and that without a real death and real resurrection, the whole of Christianity is a house built on sand and has no foundation at all. Little indeed did that reckless Roman soldier dream that he was a mighty helper of our holy religion, when he thrust his spear into our Lord's side.

That the "blood and water" mentioned in this place had a deep spiritual meaning, we can hardly doubt. John himself seems to refer to them in his first Epistle, as highly significant. "This is He that came by water and blood" (1 John 5:6). The Church in every age has been of one mind in holding that they are emblems of spiritual things. Yet the precise meaning of the blood and water is a subject about which Christians have never agreed and perhaps will never agree until the Lord returns.

The favorite theory that the blood and water mean the two Sacraments, however plausible and popular, may be reasonably regarded as somewhat destitute of solid foundation. Baptism and the Lord's Supper were ordinances already in existence when our Lord died, and they needed no reappointing. It is surely not necessary to drag in these two blessed Sacraments on every occasion and to insist on thrusting them forward as the hidden sense of every disputed text where the number "two" is mentioned. Such pertinacious application of hard places in Scripture to Baptism and the Lord's Supper does no real good and brings no real honor to the Sacraments. It is questionable whether it does not tend to vulgarize them and bring them into contempt.

The true meaning of the blood and water is probably to be sought in the famous prophecy of Zechariah, where he says, "In that day there shall be a fountain opened to the house of David, and to the inhabitants of Jerusalem, for sin and uncleanness" (Zechariah 13:1). When was that fountain so truly and really opened as in the hour when Christ died? What emblem of atonement and purification was so well known to the Jews as blood and water? Why then should we hesitate to believe that the flow of "blood and water" from our Lord's side was a significant declaration to the Jewish nation that the true fountain for sin was at length thrown open, and that henceforth sinners might come boldly to Christ for pardon and wash and be clean? This interpretation, at any rate, deserves serious thought and consideration.[52]

Whatever view we take of the blood and water, let us make sure that we ourselves are "washed and made white in the blood of the Lamb" (Revelation 7:14). It will matter nothing at the last day that we held during life the most exalted view of the sacraments, if we never came to Christ by faith and never had personal dealings with Him. Faith in Christ is the one thing needful. "He that has the Son has life; and he that does not have the Son of God does not have life" (1 John 5:12).

John 19:38-42

After these things, Joseph of Arimathaea, being a disciple
of Jesus but secretly for fear of the Jews, besought Pilate

---

52   Matthew Henry says, "The blood and water signified the two great benefits which all believers partake of through Christ – justification and sanctification. Blood stands for remission, water for regeneration; blood for atonement, water for purification. The two must always go together. Christ hath joined them together, and we must not think to put them asunder. They both flowed from the pierced side of our Redeemer."

*that he might take away the body of Jesus, and Pilate gave
him leave. He came therefore and took the body of Jesus.
Then Nicodemus came also, who at the first came to Jesus
by night, and brought a mixture of myrrh and aloes, about
one hundred pounds. And they took the body of Jesus and
wound it in linen clothes with the spices, as is the manner
of the Jews to bury. Now in the place where he was crucified there was a garden, and in the garden a new sepulchre,
in which no one had yet been laid. Therefore they laid Jesus
there because of the Jews' preparation day, for the sepulchre
was near.*

There is a peculiar interest attached to these five verses of Scripture.
They introduce us to a stranger of whom we never heard before. They
bring in an old friend whose name is known wherever the Bible is read.
They describe the most important funeral that ever took place in this
world. From each of these three points of interest we may learn a very
profitable lesson.

We learn, for one thing, from these verses, that *there are some true
Christians in the world of whom very little is known.* The case of Joseph
of Arimathea teaches this very plainly. Here is a man named among
the friends of Christ, whose very name we never find elsewhere in the
New Testament and whose history, both before and after this crisis, is
completely withheld from the Church. He comes forward to do honor
to Christ, when others had forsaken Him and fled. He cares for Him
and delights to do Him service, even when dead – not because of any
miracle which he saw Him do but out of free and gratuitous love. He
does not hesitate to confess himself one of Christ's friends at a time
when Jews and Romans alike had condemned Him as a malefactor and
put Him to death. Surely the man who could do such things must have
had strong faith! Can we wonder that, wherever the Gospel is preached,
throughout the whole world, this unselfish action of Joseph is told of
as a memorial of him?[53]

---

53 The manner of Jesus' burial was one of the things predicted by Isaiah (53:9) in a verse which
should be translated "His grave was appointed with the wicked; but with the rich man was
His tomb." The details of His burial are carefully recorded by all the four Evangelists. Each
of them names Joseph as the prime agent in the transaction and each mentions something

Let us hope and believe that there are many Christians in every age who, like Joseph, are the Lord's hidden servants, unknown to the Church and the world, but well known to God. Even in Elijah's time there were seven thousand in Israel who had never bowed the knee to Baal, although the desponding prophet knew nothing of it. Perhaps, at this very day, there are saints in the back streets of some of our great towns or in the lanes of some of our country parishes, who make no noise in the world, and yet love Christ and are loved by Him. Ill health, or poverty, or the daily cares of some laborious calling render it impossible for them to come forward in public; and so they live and die comparatively unknown. Yet the last day may show an astonished world that some of these very people, like Joseph, honored Christ as much as any on earth, and that their names were written in heaven. After all, it is special circumstances that bring to the surface special Christians. It is not those who make the greatest show in the Church, who are always found the closest friends of Christ.

We learn, for another thing, from these verses, that *there are some servants of Christ whose latter end is better than their beginning.* The case of Nicodemus teaches that lesson very plainly. The only man who dared to help Joseph in his holy work of burying our Lord was one who at first "came to Jesus by night" and was nothing better than an ignorant inquirer after truth. At a later period in our Lord's ministry, we find this same Nicodemus coming forward with somewhat more boldness and raising in the Council of the Pharisees the question, "Doth our law judge any man, before it hear him, and know what he doeth?" (John 7:51). Finally, we see him in the passage before us, ministering to our Lord's dead body and not ashamed to take an active part in giving to the despised Nazarene an honorable burial. How great the contrast between the man who timidly crept into the Lord's lodging to ask a question and the man who brought a hundred pounds weight of myrrh and aloes to anoint His dead body! Yet it was the same Nicodemus.

---

that the other three Gospel writers do not mention. Matthew alone says that he was "a rich man (27:51). Mark alone says that he was "an honorable counsellor, which also waited for the kingdom of God" (15:43). Luke alone says that he was "a good man and a just," who had "not consented to the counsel and deed of them . . . who himself waited for the kingdom of God" (23:50, 51). John alone says here, that he was "a disciple of Jesus, but secretly, for fear of the Jews."

How great may be a man's growth in grace, and faith, and knowledge, and courage in the short space of three years.

We shall do well to store up these things in our minds and to remember the case of Nicodemus in forming our estimate of other people's religion. We must not condemn others as graceless and godless, because they do not see the whole truth at once and only reach decided Christianity by slow degrees. The Holy Spirit always leads believers to the same foundation truths and into the same highway to heaven. In these there is invariable uniformity. But the Holy Spirit does not always lead believers through the same experience or at the same rate of speed. In this there is much diversity in His operations.

He that says conversion is a needless thing and that an unconverted man may be saved is undoubtedly under a strange delusion. But he that says that no one is converted except he becomes a full-blown and established Christian in a single day is no less under a delusion. Let us not judge others rashly and hastily. Let us believe that a man's beginnings in religion may be very small, and yet his latter end may greatly increase. Has a man real grace? Has he within him the genuine work of the Spirit? This is the grand question. If he has, we may safely hope that his grace will grow, and we should deal with him gently and bear with him charitably, though at present he may be a mere babe in spiritual attainments. The life in a helpless infant is as real and true a thing as the life in a full-grown man – the difference is only one of degree. "Who hath despised the day of small things?" (Zechariah 4:10). The very Christian who begins his religion with a timid night visit and an ignorant inquiry may stand forward alone one day and confess Christ boldly in the full light of the sun.

We learn, lastly, from these verses, that *the burial of the dead is an act which God sanctions and approves.* We need not doubt that this is part of the lesson which the passage before us was meant to convey to our minds. Of course, it supplies unanswerable evidence that our Lord really died and afterwards really rose again; but it also teaches that when the body of a Christian is dead, there is fitness in burying it with decent honor. It is not for nothing that the burials of Abraham, and Isaac, and Jacob, and Joseph, and Moses are carefully recorded in holy writ. It is not for nothing that we are told that John the Baptist was laid in a tomb; and that "devout men carried Stephen to his burial, and made great lamentation over him" (Acts 8:2). It is not for nothing that we are told so particularly about the burial of Christ.

The true Christian need never be ashamed of regarding a funeral with peculiar reverence and solemnity. It is the body, which may be the instrument of committing the greatest sins or of bringing the greatest glory to God. It is the body, which the eternal Son of God honored by dwelling in it for thirty and three years and finally dying in our stead. It is the body, with which He rose again and ascended up into heaven. It is the body, in which He sits at the right hand of God and represents us before the Father as our Advocate and Priest. It is the body, which is now the temple of the Holy Spirit, while the believer lives. It is the body, which will rise again, when the last trumpet sounds and, reunited to the soul, will live in heaven to all eternity. Surely, in the face of such facts as these, we never need suppose that reverence bestowed on the burial of the body is reverence thrown away.

Let us leave the subject with one word of caution. Let us take care that we do not regard a sumptuous funeral as an atonement for a life wasted in carelessness and sin. We may bury a man in the most expensive style and spend thousands of dollars in mourning. We may place over his grave a costly marble stone and inscribe on it a flattering epitaph. But all this will not save our souls or his. The turning point at the last day will not be how we are buried, but whether we were "buried with Christ," and repented and believed (Romans 6:4). Better a thousand times to die the death of the righteous, have a lowly grave and a pauper's funeral, than to die graceless and lie under a marble tomb!

John Chapter 20

John 20:1-10

The first of the sabbaths, Mary Magdalene came early, when it was yet dark, unto the sepulchre and saw the stone taken away from the sepulchre. Then she ran and came to Simon Peter and to the other disciple, whom Jesus loved, and said unto them, They have taken away the Lord out of the sepulchre, and we know not where they have laid him. Peter therefore went forth, and that other disciple, and came to the sepulchre. So they both ran together, and the other disciple outran Peter and came first to the sepulchre. And he, stooping down and looking in, saw the linen clothes lying; yet he did not go in. Then came Simon Peter following him and went into the sepulchre and saw the linen clothes lying and the napkin, that had been placed over his head, not lying with the linen clothes, but wrapped together in a place by itself. Then that other disciple, who came first to the sepulchre, went in also and he saw and believed. For as yet they did not know the scripture, that he must rise again from the dead. Then the disciples went away again unto their own.

The chapter we have now begun takes us from Christ's death to Christ's resurrection. Like Matthew, Mark, and Luke, John dwells on these two great events with peculiar fullness and particularity. And we need not wonder. The whole of saving Christianity hinges on the two facts that Christ died for our sins and rose again for our justification. The chapter before our eyes deserves special attention. Of all the four evangelists, none supplies such deeply interesting evidence of the resurrection as the disciple whom Jesus loved.

We are taught in the passage before us *that those who love Christ most are those who have received most benefit from him.*

The first whom John names among those[54] who came to Christ's sepulcher is Mary Magdalene. The history of this faithful woman, no doubt, is hidden in much obscurity. A vast amount of needless ridicule has been heaped upon her memory, as if she was once a habitual sinner against the seventh commandment. Yet there is literally no evidence whatever that she was anything of the kind! But we are distinctly told that she was one out of whom the Lord had cast "seven devils" (Mark 16:9; Luke 8:2) – one who had been subjected in a peculiar way to Satan's possession – and one whose gratitude to our Lord for deliverance was a gratitude that knew no bounds. In short, of all our Lord's followers on earth, none seem to have loved Him so much as Mary Magdalene. None felt that they owed so much to Christ. None felt so strongly that there was nothing too great to do for Christ. Hence, as Andrews beautifully puts it – "She was last at His cross and first at His grave. She stayed longest there and was soonest here. She could not rest until she was up to seek Him. She sought Him while it was yet dark, even before she had light to seek Him by." In a word, having received much, she loved much; and loving much, she did much, in order to prove the reality of her love.

The case before us throws broad and clear light on a question, which ought to be deeply interesting to every true-hearted servant of Christ. How is it that many who profess and call themselves Christians do so little for the Savior whose name they bear? How is it that many, whose faith and grace it would be uncharitable to deny, work so little, give so little, say so little, take so little pains to promote Christ's cause and bring glory to Christ in the world? These questions admit of only one answer. It is a low sense of debt and obligation to Christ, which is the account of the whole matter. Where sin is not felt at all, nothing is

---

54   The order of Christ's eleven appearances between His resurrection and ascension, I believe to be as follows: (1) to Mary Magdalene alone (Mark 16:9; John 20:14); (2) to certain women returning from the sepulcher (Matthew 28:9, 10); (3) to Simon Peter alone (Luke 24:34); (4) to two disciples going to Emmaus (Luke 24:13); (5) to ten apostles at Jerusalem and some other disciples, Thomas being absent (John 20:19); (6) to eleven apostles at Jerusalem, Thomas being present (John 20:26-29); (7) to seven disciples fishing at the sea of Tiberias (John 21:1); (8) to eleven apostles on a mountain in Galilee, and perhaps some others with them (Matthew 29:16); (9) to above five hundred brethren at once (1 Corinthians 15:7); (10) to James only (1 Corinthians 15:7); (11) to all the apostles and probably some others on Mount Olivet at His ascension.

done; and where sin is little felt, little is done. The man who is deeply conscious of his own guilt and corruption and deeply convinced that without the death and intercession of Christ he would sink deservedly into the lowest hell, this is the man who will spend and be spent for Jesus and think that he can never do enough to show forth His praise. Let us daily pray that we may see the sinfulness of sin and the amazing grace of Christ more clearly and distinctly. Then, and then only, shall we cease to be cool, and lukewarm, and slovenly in our work for Jesus. Then, and then only, shall we understand such burning zeal as that of Mary and comprehend what Paul meant when he said, "The love of Christ constraineth us; because we thus judge that if One died for all, then were all dead: and that He died for all, that they which live should not henceforth live unto themselves, but unto Him which died for them, and rose again" (2 Corinthians 5:14, 15).

We are taught, secondly, in these verses *that there are widely different temperaments in different believers.*

This is a point which is curiously brought out in the conduct of Peter and John, when Mary Magdalene told them that the Lord's body was gone. We are told that they both ran to the sepulcher, but John, the disciple whom Jesus loved, outran Peter and reached the empty grave first. Then comes out the difference between the two men. John, of the two more gentle, quiet, tender, reserved, retiring, deep feeling, stooped down and looked in but went no further. Peter, more hot, and zealous, and impulsive, and fervent, and forward, cannot be content without going down into the sepulcher and actually seeing with his own eyes. Both, we may be sure, were deeply attached to our Lord. The hearts of both at this critical juncture were full of hopes, and fears, and anxieties, and expectations, all tangled together. Yet each behaves in his own characteristic fashion. We need not doubt that these things were intentionally written for our learning.

Let us learn from the case before us to make allowances for wide varieties in the inward character of believers. To do so will save us much trouble in the journey of life and prevent many an uncharitable thought. Let us not judge brethren harshly and set them down in a low place, because they do not see or feel things exactly as we see and feel, and because things do not affect or strike them just as they affect and strike us. The flowers in the Lord's garden are not all of one color and one scent, though they are all planted by one Spirit. The subjects of His kingdom are not all exactly of one tone and temperament, though they all love the same Savior and are written in the same book of life. The Church of Christ has some in its ranks who are like Peter and some who are like John, and a place for all, and a work for all to do. Let us love all who love Christ in sincerity and thank God that they love Him at all. The great thing is to love Jesus.

We are taught, finally, in these verses *that there may be much ignorance even in true believers.*

This is a point which is brought out here with singular force and distinctness. John himself, the writer of this Gospel, records of himself and his companion Peter, "As yet they knew not the Scripture, that He must rise again from the dead." How truly incredible this seems! For three long years these two leading Apostles had heard our Lord speak of His own resurrection as a fact, and yet they had not understood Him. Again and again He had staked the truth of His Messiahship on His rising from the dead, and yet they had never taken in His meaning. We little realize the power over the mind which is exercised by wrong teaching in childhood, and by early prejudices imbibed in our youth. Surely the Christian minister has little right to complain of ignorance among his hearers, when he marks the ignorance of Peter and John under the teaching of Christ Himself.

After all we must remember that true grace, and not head knowledge, is the one thing needful. We are in the hands of a merciful and compassionate Savior, who passes by and pardons much ignorance, when He sees "a heart right in the sight of God." Some things indeed we must know, and without knowing them we cannot be saved. Our own sinfulness and guilt, the office of Christ as a Savior, the necessity of repentance and faith – such things as these are essential to salvation. But he that knows these things may, in other respects, be a very ignorant man. In fact, the extent to which one man may have grace together with much ignorance, and another may have much knowledge and yet no grace, is one of the greatest mysteries in religion and one which the last day alone will unfold. Let us then seek knowledge and be ashamed of ignorance. But above all let us make sure that, like Peter and John, we have grace and right hearts.

John 20:11-18

But Mary stood outside near the sepulchre weeping, and as she wept, she stooped down and looked into the sepulchre and saw two angels in white sitting, the one at the head and the other at the feet, where the body of Jesus had been placed. And they said unto her, Woman, why dost thou weep? She said unto them, Because they have taken away my Lord, and I know not where they have laid him. And when she had said this, she turned around and saw Jesus stand- ing there and did not know that it was Jesus. Jesus said unto her, Woman, why dost thou weep? whom seekest thou? She, supposing him to be the gardener, said unto him, Lord, if thou didst carry him off, tell me where thou hast laid him, and I will take him away. Jesus said unto her, Mary! Turning herself around, she said unto him, Rabboni, which is to say, Master. Jesus said unto her, Touch me not, for I have not yet ascended to my Father; but go to my brethren and say unto them, I ascend unto my Father and your Father, and to my God and your God. Mary Magdalene came giving the news to the disciples, That I have seen the Lord, and he spoke these things unto me.

The interview between the Lord Jesus and Mary Magdalene imme-diately after His resurrection, described in these verses, is a narrative peculiar to John. No other Evangelist has been inspired to record it. Of all the accounts of the appearances of our Lord after He rose from the dead, none perhaps is so affecting and touching as this. He that can read this simple story without a deep interest must have a very cold and unfeeling heart.

We see, first, in these verses *that those who love Christ most diligently and perseveringly are those who receive most privileges from Christ's hand.* It is a touching fact and one to be carefully noted that Mary Magdalene would not leave the sepulcher, when Peter and John went away to their own home. Love to her gracious Master would not let her leave the place where He had been lain. Where He was now she could not tell. What had become of Him she did not know. But love made her linger about the empty tomb where Joseph and Nicodemus had recently laid Him. Love made her honor the last place where His precious body had been seen by mortal eyes. And her love reaped a rich reward. She saw the angels whom Peter and John had never observed. She actually heard them speak and had soothing words addressed to her. She was the first to see our Lord after He rose from the dead, the first to hear His voice, the first to hold conversation with Him. Can anyone doubt that this was written for our learning? Wherever the Gospel is preached throughout the world, this little incident testifies that those who honor Christ will be honored by Christ.

As it was in the morning of the first Resurrection day, so will it be as long as the Church stands. The great principle contained in the passage before us will hold good until the Lord comes again. All believers have not the same degree of faith, or hope, or knowledge, or courage, or wisdom; and it is vain to expect it. But it is a certain fact that those who love Christ most fervently and cleave to Him most closely will always enjoy most communion with Him and feel most of the witness of the Spirit in their hearts. It is precisely those who wait on the Lord in the temper of Mary Magdalene, to whom the Lord will reveal Himself most fully and make them know and feel more than others. To know Christ is good; but to "know that we know Him" is far better.

We see, secondly, in these verses *that the fears and sorrows of believers are often quite needless.* We are told that Mary stood at the sepulcher weeping and wept as if nothing could comfort her. She wept when the angels spoke to her; "Woman," they said, "why are you weeping?" She was weeping still when our Lord spoke to her – "Woman," He also said, "why are you weeping?" And the burden of her complaint was always the same – "They have taken away my Lord, and I know not where they have laid Him." Yet all this time her risen Master was close to her with "body, flesh, and bones, and all things pertaining to the perfection of man's nature." Her tears were needless. Her anxiety was unnecessary. Like Hagar in the wilderness, she had a well of water by her side, but she had not eyes to see it.

What thoughtful Christian can fail to see that we have here a faithful picture of many a believer's experience? How often we are anxious when there is no just cause for anxiety! How often we mourn over the absence of things which in reality are within our grasp and even at our right hand! Two-thirds of the things we fear in life never happen at all, and two-thirds of the tears we shed are thrown away and shed in vain. Let us pray for more faith and patience and allow more time for the full development of God's purposes. Let us believe that things are often working together for our peace and joy, which seem at one time to contain nothing but bitterness and sorrow. Old Jacob said at one time of his life, "all these things are against me" (Genesis 42:36); yet he lived to see Joseph again, rich and prosperous, and to thank God for all that had happened. If Mary had found the seal of the tomb unbroken and her Master's body lying cold within, she might well have wept! The very absence of the body which made her weep was a token for good and a cause of joy for herself and all mankind.

We see, thirdly, in these verses *what low and earthly thoughts of Christ may creep into the mind of a true believer*. It seems impossible to gather any other lesson from the solemn words which our Lord addressed to Mary Magdalene when He said, "Touch Me not; for I am not yet ascended to my Father." No doubt the language is somewhat mysterious and ought to be delicately and reverently handled. Yet it is only reasonable to suppose that the first surprise and the reaction from great sorrow to great joy was more than the mind of Mary could bear. She was only a woman, though a holy and faithful woman. It is highly probable that in the first excess of her joy she threw herself at our Lord's feet and made greater demonstrations of feeling than were seemly or becoming. Very likely she behaved too much like one who thought all must be right if she had her Lord's bodily presence, and all must be wrong in His bodily absence. This was not the highest style of faith. She acted, in short, like one who forgot that her Master was God as well as man. She made too little of His divinity and too much of His

349

humanity. And hence she called forth our Lord's gentle rebuke, "Touch Me not! There is no need of this excessive demonstration of feeling. I am not yet ascending to my Father for forty days – your present duty is not to linger at my feet but to go and tell my brethren that I have risen. Think of the feelings of others as well as of your own."

After all, we must confess that the fault of this holy woman was one into which Christians have always been too ready to fall. In every age there has been a tendency in the minds of many to make too much of Christ's bodily presence and to forget that He is not a mere earthly friend but one who is "God over all, blessed forever" as well as man. The pertinacity with which Romanists and their allies cling to the doctrine of Christ's real corporal presence in the Lord's Supper is only another exhibition of Mary's feeling when she wanted Christ's body or no Christ at all. Let us pray for a right judgment in this matter, as in all other things concerning our Lord's person. Let us be content to have Christ dwelling in our hearts by faith and present when two or three are met in His name and to wait for the real presence of Christ's body until He comes again. What we really need is not His literal flesh, but His Spirit. It is not for nothing that it is written, "The Spirit is he that gives life; the flesh profits nothing" (John 6:63). "If we have known Christ after the flesh, yet henceforth know we Him no more" (2 Corinthians 5:16).

We see, lastly, in these verses *how kindly and graciously our Lord speaks of His disciples.* He bids Mary Magdalene carry a message to them as "His brethren." He bids her tell those who His Father was their Father, and His God their God. It was but three days before that they had all forsaken Him shamefully and fled. Yet this merciful Master speaks as if all was forgiven and forgotten. His first thought is to bring back the wanderers, to bind up the wounds of their consciences, to reanimate their courage, to restore them to their former place. This was indeed a love that passes knowledge. To trust deserters and to show confidence in backsliders was a compassion which man can hardly understand. So true is that word of David – "Like as a Father pitieth his children, so the Lord pitieth them that fear Him. For He knoweth our frame; He remembereth that we are dust" (Psalm 103:13, 14).

Let us leave the passage with the comfortable reflection that Jesus

Christ never changes. He is the same yesterday, today, and forever. As
He dealt with His erring disciples in the morning of His resurrection, so
will He deal with all who believe and love Him, until He comes again.
When we wander out of the way, He will bring us back. When we fall,
He will raise us again. But he will never break His royal word – "Him
that comes to Me, I will in no wise cast out" (John 6:37). The saints in
glory will have one anthem in which every voice and heart will join –
"He hath not dealt with us after our sins, nor rewarded us according
to our iniquities" (Psalm 103:10).

John 20:19-23

Then the same day at evening, being the first of the sabbaths,
when the doors were shut where the disciples were assembled
for fear of the Jews, Jesus came and stood in the midst and
said unto them, Peace be unto you. And having said this, he
showed them his hands and his side. Then the disciples were
glad when they saw the Lord. Then Jesus said to them again,
Peace be unto you; as my Father has sent me, even so send
I you. And when he had said this, he breathed on them and
said unto them, Receive ye the Holy Spirit; unto those whose
sins ye release, they shall be released; and unto those whose
sins ye retain, they shall be retained.

The verses we have now read contain things hard to be understood. Like
all the events which followed our Lord's resurrection, there is much in
the facts before us which is mysterious and requires reverent handling.
Our Lord's actions, in suddenly appearing among the disciples when
the doors were closed and in breathing upon them, might soon draw
us into unprofitable speculation.[55] It is easy, in such cases, to darken

---

55   The action of our Lord, "He breathed on them," is one that stands completely alone in the
      New Testament, and the Greek word is nowhere else used. On no occasion but this do we
      find the Lord "breathing" on any one. Of course it was a symbolical action, and the only
      question is, What did it symbolize? And Why was it used? My own belief is that the true
      explanation is to be found in the account of man's creation in Genesis. There we read, "The
      Lord God formed man of the dust of the ground, and breathed into his nostrils the breath
      of life, and man became a living soul" (Genesis 2:7). Just as there was no life in man until

counsel by words without knowledge. We shall find it safer and wiser to confine our attention to points which are plain and instructive.

We should observe, for one thing, the *remarkable language with which our Lord greeted the apostles, when He first met them after His resurrection.* Twice over he addressed them with the kindly words, "Peace be unto you." We may dismiss as untenable in all probability, the cold and cautious suggestion that this was nothing better than an unmeaning phrase of courtesy. He who "spake as never man spake" said nothing without meaning. He spoke, we may be sure, with special reference to the state of mind of the eleven apostles, with special reference to the events of the last few days, and with special reference to their future ministry. "Peace" and not blame – "peace" and not fault-finding – "peace" and not rebuke – was the first word which this little company heard from their Master's lips after He left the tomb.

It was right and fitting that it should be so, and in full harmony with things that had gone before. "Peace on earth" was the song of the heavenly host, when Christ was born. Peace and rest of soul was the general subject that Christ continually preached for three years. Peace, and not riches, had been the great legacy which He had left with the eleven the night before His crucifixion. Surely it was in full keeping with all the tenor of our Lord's dealings that, when He revisited His little company of disciples after His resurrection, His first word should be "Peace." It was a word that would soothe and calm their minds.

Peace, we may safely conclude, was intended by our Lord to be the keynote to the Christian ministry. That same peace which was so continually on the lips of the Master was to be the grand subject of the teaching of His disciples. Peace between God and man through the precious blood of atonement – peace between man and man through the infusion of grace and charity – to spread such peace as this was to be the work of the Church. Any religion, like that of Mahomet, who made converts with the sword, is not from above but from beneath. Any form of Christianity which burns men at the stake in order to promote its own success carries about with it the stamp of an apostasy. That is the truest and best religion which does most to spread real, true peace.

God breathed into him the breath of life, so I believe our Lord taught the disciples by this action of breathing on them.

We should observe, for another thing, in these verses, *the remarkable evidence which our Lord supplied of His own resurrection.* He graciously appealed to the senses of His trembling disciples. He showed them "His hands and His side." He bade them see with their own eyes that He had a real material body and that He was not a ghost or a spirit. "Handle Me and see" were His words, according to Luke – "a spirit hath not flesh and bone, as ye see Me have." Great indeed was the condescension of our blessed Master in thus coming down to the feeble faith of the eleven Apostles! But great also was the principle which He established for the use of His Church in every age until He returns. That principle is that our Master requires us to believe nothing is contrary to our senses. Things *above* our reason we must expect to find in a religion that comes from God, but not things contrary to reason.

Let us lay firm hold on this great principle and never forget to use it. Specially let us take care that we use it in estimating the effect of the sacraments and the work of the Holy Spirit. To require people to believe that men have the quickening power of the Holy Spirit, when our eyes tell us they are living in habitual carelessness and sin, or that the bread and wine in the Lord's Supper are Christ's real body and blood, when our senses tell us they are still bread and wine – this is to require more belief than Christ ever required of His disciples. It is to require that which is flatly contradictory to reason and common sense. Such requisitions Christ never made. Let us not try to be wiser than our Lord.

We should observe, lastly, in these verses, *the remarkable commission which our Lord conferred upon His eleven Apostles.* We are told that He said, "As the Father hath sent me, even so send I you. And when He had said this, He breathed on them, and saith unto them, Receive ye the Holy Spirit: whose soever sins ye remit, they are remitted unto them; and whose soever sins ye retain, they are retained." It is vain to deny that the true sense of these solemn words has been for centuries a subject of controversy and dispute. It is useless perhaps to expect that the controversy will ever be closed. The utmost that we can hope to do with the passage is to supply a probable exposition.

It seems then highly probable that our Lord in this place solemnly commissioned His Apostles to go into all the world and preach the

353

Gospel as He had preached it. He also conferred on them the power of *declaring* with peculiar authority whose sins were forgiven and whose sins were not forgiven. That this is precisely what the Apostles did is a simple matter of fact, which any one may verify for himself by reading the book of the Acts. When Peter proclaimed to the Jews, "Repent ye, and be converted" (Acts 3:19) – and when Paul declared at Antioch of Iconium – "to you is the word of this salvation sent" – "Through this man is preached the forgiveness of sins, and by Him all that believe are justified" (Acts 13:26-38) – they were doing what this passage commissioned the Apostles to do. They were opening with authority the door of salvation and inviting with authority all sinners to enter in by it and be saved. It seems, on the other hand, most improbable that our Lord intended in this verse to sanction the practice of private absolution after private confession of sins.

Let us leave the whole passage with a deep sense of the importance of the minister's office, when that office is duly exercised according to the mind of Christ. No higher honor can be imagined than that of being Christ's ambassadors and proclaiming in Christ's name the forgiveness of sins to a lost world. But let us ever beware of investing the ministerial office with one jot more of power and authority than Christ conferred upon it. To treat ministers as being in any sense mediators between God and man is to rob Christ of His prerogative, to hide saving truth from sinners, and to exalt ordained men to a position which they are totally unqualified to fill.

John 20:24-31

But Thomas, one of the twelve, called Didymus, was not with them when Jesus came. The other disciples, therefore, said unto him, We have seen the Lord. But he said unto them, Unless I shall see in his hands the print of the nails and put my finger into the print of the nails and thrust my hand into his side, I will not believe. And again eight days later, his disciples were within and Thomas with them; then Jesus came, the doors being shut, and stood in the midst and said,

354

*Peace be unto you. Then he said to Thomas, Reach here thy
finger and behold my hands and reach here thy hand and
thrust it into my side and be not unbelieving, but faithful.
And Thomas answered and said unto him, My Lord and my
God. Jesus said unto him, Thomas, because thou hast seen
me, thou hast believed; blessed are those that have not seen
and yet have believed. And Jesus truly did many other signs
in the presence of his disciples, which are not written in this
book; but these are written that ye might believe that Jesus is
the Christ, the Son of God, and that believing ye might have
life in his name.*

The story of the unbelief of Thomas, related in these verses, is a narrative peculiar to the Gospel of John. For wise and good reasons it is passed over in silence by Matthew, Mark, and Luke and was probably not given to the world until Thomas was dead. It is precisely one of those passages of Scripture which supply strong internal evidence of the honesty of the inspired writers. If impostors and deceivers had compiled the Bible for their own private advantage, they would never have told mankind that one of the first founders of a new religion behaved as Thomas here did.

We should mark, for one thing, in these verses, *how much Christians may lose by not regularly attending the assemblies of God's people.* Thomas was absent the first time that Jesus appeared to the disciples after His resurrection, and consequently Thomas missed a blessing. Of course we have no certain proof that the absence of the Apostle could not admit of explanation. Yet, at such a crisis in the lives of the eleven, it seems highly improbable that he had any good reason for not being with his brethren, and it is far more likely that in some way he was to blame. One thing, at any rate, is clear and plain. By being absent he was kept in suspense and unbelief a whole week, while all around him were rejoicing in the thought of a risen Lord. It is difficult to suppose that this would have been the case, if there had not been a fault somewhere. It is hard to avoid the suspicion that Thomas was absent when he might have been present.

We shall all do well to remember the charge of the Apostle Paul – "Forsake not the assembling of yourselves together, as the manner of some is" (Hebrews 10:25). Never to be absent from God's house on Sundays without good reason – never to miss the Lord's Supper when administered in our own congregation – never to let our place be empty when means of grace are going on, this is one way to be a growing and prosperous Christian. The very sermon that we needlessly miss may contain a precious word in season for our souls. The very assembly for prayer and praise from which we stay away may be the very gathering that would have cheered, and established, and quickened our hearts. We little know how dependent our spiritual health is on little, regular, habitual helps, and how much we suffer if we miss our medicine. The wretched argument that many attend means of grace and are no better for them should be no argument to a Christian. It may satisfy those who are blind to their own state and destitute of grace, but it should never satisfy a real servant of Christ. Such a one should remember the words of Solomon – "Blessed is the man that heareth me, watching daily at my gates, waiting at the posts of my doors" (Proverbs 8:34). Above all he should bind around his heart the Master's promise – "Wheresoever two or three are gathered together in my name, there am I in the midst of them" (Matthew 18:20). Such a man will rarely be left like Thomas, shut out in the cold chill of unbelief, while others are warmed and filled.

We should mark for another thing in this verse, *how kind and merciful Christ is to dull and slow believers.* Nowhere, perhaps, in all the four Gospels, do we find this part of our Lord's character so beautifully illustrated as in the story before our eyes. It is hard to imagine anything more tiresome and provoking than the conduct of Thomas, when even the testimony of ten faithful brethren had no effect on him, and he doggedly declared, "Except I see with my own eyes and touch with my own hands, I will not believe." But it is impossible to imagine anything more patient and compassionate than our Lord's treatment of this weak disciple. He does not reject him, or dismiss him, or excommunicate him. He comes again at the end of a week and apparently for the special benefit of Thomas. He deals with him according to his weakness like a gentle nurse dealing with a froward child – "Reach hither thy finger, and behold my hands; reach hither thy hand, and thrust it into my side." If nothing but the grossest, coarsest, most material evidence could satisfy him, even that evidence was supplied. Surely this was a love that passes knowledge and a patience that passes understanding.

A passage of Scripture like this, we need not doubt, was written for the special comfort of all true believers. The Holy Spirit knew well that the dull, and the slow, and the stupid, and the doubting are by far the commonest type of disciples in this evil world. The Holy Spirit has taken care to supply abundant evidence that Jesus is rich in patience as well as compassion, and that He bears with the infirmities of all His people. Let us take care that we drink into our Lord's spirit and copy His example. Let us never set down men as godless, because their faith is feeble and their love is cold. Let us remember the case of Thomas and be very compassionate and of tender mercy. Our Lord has many weak children in His family, many dull pupils in His school, many raw soldiers in His army, many lame sheep in His flock. Yet He bears with them all and casts none away. Happy is that Christian who has learned to deal likewise with his brethren. There are many in the Church who, like Thomas, are dull and slow, but for all that, like Thomas, are real and true believers.

We should mark, lastly, in these verses, *how Christ was addressed by a disciple as "God," without prohibition or rebuke on His part.* The noble exclamation which burst from the lips of Thomas when convinced that his Lord had risen indeed; the noble exclamation, "My Lord and my God" – admits of only one meaning. It was a distinct testimony to our blessed Lord's divinity. It was a clear, unmistakable declaration that Thomas believed Him, whom he saw and touched that day, to be not only man but God. Above all, it was a testimony which our Lord received and did not prohibit and a declaration which He did not say one word to rebuke. When Cornelius fell down at the feet of Peter and would have worshiped him, the Apostle refused such honor at once – "Stand up; I myself also am a man" (Acts 10:26). When the people of Lystra would have done sacrifice to Paul and Barnabas, "they rent their clothes, and ran in among the people, saying, Sirs, why do ye these things? We also are men of like passions with you" (Acts 14:14). But when Thomas says to Jesus, "My Lord and my God," the words do not elicit a syllable of reproof from our holy and truth-loving Master. Can we doubt that these things were written for our learning?

Let us settle it firmly in our minds that the divinity of Christ is one of the grand foundation truths of Christianity, and let us be willing to go to the stake rather than let it go. Unless our Lord Jesus is very God of very God, there is an end of His mediation, His atonement, His advocacy, His priesthood, His whole work of redemption. These glorious doctrines are useless blasphemies, unless Christ is divine. Forever let us bless God that the divinity of our Lord is taught everywhere in the Scriptures and stands on evidence that can never be overthrown. Above all, let us daily repose our sinful souls on Christ with undoubting confidence, as one who is perfect God as well as perfect man. He is man and therefore can be touched with the feeling of our infirmities. He is God, and therefore is "able to save to the uttermost all who come unto God by Him." That Christian has no cause to fear, who can look to Jesus by faith and say with Thomas, "My Lord and my God." With such a Savior we need not be afraid to begin the life of real religion, and with such a Savior we may boldly go on.

John Chapter 21

John 21:1-14

After these things Jesus manifested himself again to the disciples at the sea of Tiberias, and he manifested himself in this manner: Simon Peter and Thomas, called Didymus, and Nathanael of Cana in Galilee and the sons of Zebedee and two other of his disciples were together. Simon Peter said unto them, I am going fishing. They said unto him, Let us also go with thee. They went forth and entered into a ship immediately, and that night they caught nothing. But when the morning was now come, Jesus stood on the shore, but the disciples did not understand that it was Jesus. Then Jesus said unto them, Children, have ye any food? They answered him, No. And he said unto them, Cast the net on the right hand side of the ship, and ye shall find. They cast therefore, and now they were not able to draw it for the multitude of fishes. Therefore that disciple whom Jesus loved said unto Peter, It is the Lord. Now when Simon Peter heard that it was the Lord, he girt his fisher's coat unto him (for he was naked) and cast himself into the sea. And the other disciples came in the little ship (for they were not far from land, but as it were two hundred cubits), dragging the net with the fishes. As soon then as they were come to land, they saw a fire of coals there, and a fish laid thereon, and bread. Jesus said unto them, Bring of the fish which ye have now caught. Simon Peter went up and drew the net to land full of great fishes, one hundred and fifty-three; and being so many, yet the net was not broken. Jesus said unto them, Come and dine. And none of the disciples dared to ask him, Who art

thou? knowing that it was the Lord. Jesus then came and
took the bread and gave them, and the fish likewise. This
was now the third time that Jesus manifested himself to his
disciples, after he was risen from the dead.

The appearance of our Lord Jesus Christ after His resurrection, described in these verses, is a deeply interesting portion of the Gospel history. The circumstances attending it have always been regarded as highly allegorical and figurative in every age of the Church. It may, however, be justly doubted whether commentators and interpreters have not gone too far in this direction. It is quite possible to spiritualize and filter away the narratives of the Gospels until we completely lose sight of the plain meaning of words. In the present case we shall find it wise to confine ourselves to the great, simple lessons, which the passage undoubtedly contains.

We should observe, for one thing, in these verses, the poverty of the first disciples of Christ. We find them working with their own hands, in order to supply their temporal needs, and working at one of the humblest of callings – the calling of a fisherman. Silver and gold they had none, lands and revenues they had none, and therefore they were not ashamed to return to the business to which they had, most of them, been trained. Striking is the fact, that some of the seven here named were fishing, when our Lord first called them to be Apostles, and again fishing, when He appeared to them almost the last time. We need not doubt that to the minds of Peter, James, and John, the coincidence would come home with peculiar power.

The poverty of the Apostles goes far to prove the divine origin of Christianity. These very men who toiled all night in a boat, dragging about a cold wet net, and taking nothing – these very men who found it necessary to work hard in order that they might eat – these very men were some of the first founders of the mighty Church of Christ, which has now overspread one-third of the globe. These were they who went forth from an obscure corner of the earth, and turned the world upside down. These were the unlearned and ignorant men who boldly confronted the subtle systems of ancient philosophy and silenced its advocates by the preaching of the cross. These were the men who at Ephesus, and

Athens, and Rome emptied the heathen temples of their worshipers and turned away multitudes to a new and better faith. He that can explain these facts, except by admitting that Christianity came down from God, must be a strangely incredulous man. Reason and common sense lead us to only one conclusion in the matter. Nothing can account for the rise and progress of Christianity but the direct interposition of God.

We should observe, for another thing, in these verses, *the different characters of different disciples of Christ*. Once more, on this deeply interesting occasion, we see Peter and John side by side in the same boat, and once more, as at the sepulcher, we see these two good men behaving in different ways. When Jesus stood on the shore in the dim twilight of the morning, John was the first to perceive who it was and to say, "It is the Lord;" but Peter was the first to spring into the water, and to struggle to get close to his Master. In a word, John was the first to see; but Peter was the first to act. John's gentle loving spirit was quickest to discern; but Peter's fiery, impulsive nature was quickest to stir and move. And yet both were believers, both were true-hearted disciples, both loved the Lord in life and were faithful to Him unto death.[56] But their natural temperaments were not the same.

Let us never forget the practical lesson before us. As long as we live, let us diligently use it in forming our estimate of believers. Let us not condemn others as graceless and unconverted solely because they do not see the path of duty from our standpoint or feel things exactly as we feel them. "There are diversities of gifts, but the same Spirit" (1 Corinthians 12:4). The gifts of God's children are not bestowed precisely in the same measure and degree. Some have more of one gift, and some have more of another. Some have gifts which shine more in public, and some which shine more in private. Some are more bright in a passive life, and some are more bright in an active one. Yet each and all the members of God's family, in their own way and in their own season, bring glory to God. Martha was "careful and troubled about much

---

56 Miracle on miracle passed under the eyes of the astonished disciples. Can we doubt that their minds recalled the miraculous draught of fishes on a former occasion, when "their net brake," and our Lord's words, "Fear not; from henceforth thou shalt catch men:" and also his original saying, "Follow Me, and I will make you fishers of men?" And can we doubt that some of them remembered the parable of the kingdom of Heaven being like to "a net cast into the sea," and finally drawn to shore?" (Luke 5:10; Matthew 4:19; 13:47).

serving," when Mary "sat at the feet of Jesus and heard His word." Yet there came a day at Bethany, when Mary was crushed and prostrated by overmuch sorrow, and Martha's faith shone more brightly than her sister's (Luke 10:39, 40; John 11:20-28). Nevertheless both were loved by our Lord. The one thing needful is to have the grace of the Spirit and to love Christ. Let us love all of whom this can be said, though they may not see with our eyes in everything. The Church of Christ needs servants of all kinds and instruments of every sort; penknives as well as swords, axes as well as hammers, chisels as well as saws, Marthas as well as Marys, Peters as well as Johns. Let our ruling maxim be this, "Grace be with all them that love our Lord Jesus Christ in sincerity" (Ephesians 6:24).

We should observe, lastly, in these verses, *the abundant evidence which Scripture supplies of our Lord Jesus Christ's resurrection.* Here, as in other places, we find an unanswerable proof that our Lord rose again with a real material body and a proof seen by seven grown-up men with their own eyes, at one and the same time. We see Him sitting, talking, eating, drinking on the shore of the lake of Galilee and to all appearance for a considerable time. The morning sun of spring shines down on the little party. They are alone by the well-known Galilean lake, far away from the crowd and noise of Jerusalem. In the midst sits the Master with the nail-prints in His hands – the very Master whom they had all followed for three years, and one of them, at least, had seen hanging on the cross. They could not be deceived. Will anyone pretend to say that stronger proof could be given that Jesus rose from the dead? Can any one imagine better evidence of a fact? That Peter was convinced and satisfied we know. He says himself to Cornelius, We did "eat and drink with Him after He rose from the dead" (Acts 10:41). Those who in modern times say they are not convinced may as well say that they are determined not to believe any evidence at all.

Let us all thank God that we have such a cloud of witnesses to prove that our Lord rose again. The resurrection of Christ is the grand proof of Christ's divine mission. He told the Jews they need not believe He was the Messiah, if He did not rise again the third day. The resurrection of Christ is the top-stone of the work of redemption. It proved that He finished the work He came to do and, as our Substitute, had overcome the grave. The resurrection of Christ is a miracle that no infidel can explain away. Men may carp and cavil at Balaam's donkey and Jonah in the whale's belly if they please, but until they can prove that Christ did not rise again, we need not be moved. Above all, the resurrection of Christ is the pledge of our own. As the grave could not detain the Head, so it shall not detain the members. Well may we say with Peter, "Blessed be the God and Father of our Lord Jesus Christ, who hath begotten us again unto a living hope by the resurrection of Jesus Christ from the dead" (1 Peter 1:3).

John 21:15-17

So when they had dined, Jesus said to Simon Peter, Simon, son of Jonas, lovest thou me more than these? He said unto him, Yes, Lord, thou knowest that I love thee. He said unto him, Feed my lambs. He said to him again the second time, Simon, son of Jonas, lovest thou me? He said unto him, Yes, Lord thou knowest that I love thee. He said unto him, Feed my sheep. He said unto him the third time, Simon, son of Jonas, lovest thou me? Peter was grieved because he said unto him the third time, Lovest thou me? And he said, Lord, thou knowest all things; thou knowest that I love thee. Jesus said unto him, Feed my sheep.

These verses describe a remarkable conversation between our Lord Jesus Christ and the Apostle Peter. To the careful Bible reader, who remembers the Apostle's thrice-repeated denial of Christ, the passage cannot fail to be a deeply interesting portion of Scripture. Well would it be for the Church, if all "after-meal" conversations among Christians were as useful and edifying as this.

We should notice first, in these verses, *Christ's question to Peter –* "Simon, son of Jonas, lovest thou Me?" Three times we find the same inquiry made. It seems most probable that this three-fold repetition was meant to remind the Apostle of his own thrice-repeated denial.

Once we find a remarkable addition to the inquiry – "Lovest thou Me more than these?" It is a reasonable supposition that those three words "more than these" were meant to remind Peter of his over-confident assertion – "Though all men deny Thee, yet will not I." It is just as if our Lord would say, "Wilt thou now exalt thyself above others? Hast thou yet learned thine own weakness?"

"Lovest thou Me" may seem at first sight a simple question. In one sense it is so. Even a child can understand love and can say whether he loves another or not. Yet "Lovest thou Me" is, in reality, a very searching question. We may know much, and do much, and profess much, and talk much, and work much, and give much, and go through much, and make much show in our religion, and yet be dead before God from lack of love and at last go down to the pit. Do we love Christ? That is the great question. Without this there is no vitality about our Christianity. We are no better than painted wax figures, lifeless stuffed beasts in a museum, sounding brass and tinkling cymbals. There is no life where there is no love.

Let us take heed that there is some feeling in our religion. Knowledge, orthodoxy, correct views, regular use of forms, a respectable moral life – all these do not make up a true Christian. There must be some personal feeling towards Christ. Feeling alone, no doubt, is a poor useless thing and may be here today and gone tomorrow. But the entire absence of feeling is a very bad symptom and speaks ill for the state of a man's soul. The men and women to whom Paul wrote his Epistles had feelings and were not ashamed of them. There was One in heaven whom they loved, and that One was Jesus the Son of God. Let us strive to be like them and to have some real feeling in our Christianity, if we hope to share their reward.

We should notice, secondly, in these verses, *Peter's answer to Christ's question*. Three times we find the Apostle saying, "Thou knowest that I love Thee." Once we are told that he said, "Thou knowest all things." Once we have the touching remark made that he was "grieved to be asked the third time." We need not doubt that our Lord, like a skillful physician, stirred up this grief intentionally. He intended to pierce the Apostle's conscience and to teach him a solemn lesson. If it was grievous to the disciple to be questioned, how much more grievous must it have been to the Master to be denied!

The answer that the humbled Apostle gave is the one account that the true servant of Christ in every age can give of his religion. Such a one may be weak, and fearful, and ignorant, and unstable, and failing in many things, but at any rate he is real and sincere. Ask him whether he is converted, whether he is a believer, whether he has grace, whether he is justified, whether he is sanctified, whether he is elect, whether he is a child of God – ask him any one of these questions, and he may perhaps reply that he really does not know! But ask him whether he loves Christ, and he will reply, "I do!" He may add that he does not love Him as much as he ought to do, but he will not say that he does not love Him at all. The rule will be found true with very few exceptions. Wherever there is true grace, there will be a consciousness of love towards Christ.

What, after all, is the great secret of loving Christ? It is an inward sense of having received from Him pardon and forgiveness of sins. Those love much who feel much forgiven. He who has come to Christ with his sins and tasted the blessedness of free and full absolution, he is the man whose heart will be full of love towards his Savior. The more we realize that Christ has suffered for us and paid our debt to God, and that we are washed and justified through His blood, the more we shall love Him for having loved us and given Himself for us. Our knowledge of doctrines may be defective. Our ability to defend our views in argument may be small. But we cannot be prevented feeling. And our feeling will be like that of the Apostle Peter – "Thou, Lord, who knowest all things, Thou knowest my heart; and Thou knowest that I love Thee."

We should notice, lastly, in these verses, *Christ's command to Peter.* Three times we find Him saying, "Feed" my flock. Once, "Feed my lambs;" and twice, "Feed my sheep." Can we doubt for a moment that this thrice-repeated charge was full of deep meaning?[57] It was meant

---

57   There are little nice distinctions in the original Greek of these three verses, in the words that are used, which the English language cannot convey. But they deserve notice, and are not without meaning. Two different words are used to express our one word "love." One of these two words means a higher, calmer, nobler kind of love than the other. This is the word which our Lord uses in the fifteenth and sixteenth verses, where He asks the question, "Lovest thou Me?" – The other of the two words means a more passionate and lower kind of love. This is the word which Peter always uses when he says, "I love thee!" and our Lord once uses it in the seventeenth verse. Again; two different words are employed to

to commission Peter once more to do the work of an Apostle, notwith-standing his recent fall. But this was only a small part of the meaning. It was meant to teach Peter and the whole Church the mighty lesson that usefulness to others is the grand test of love, and working for Christ the great proof of really loving Christ. It is not loud talk and high profession; it is not even impetuous, spasmodic zeal and readiness to draw the sword and fight – it is steady, patient, laborious effort to do good to Christ's sheep scattered throughout this sinful world, which is the best evidence of being a true-hearted disciple. This is the real secret of Christian greatness. It is written in another place, "Whosoever will be a great among you, let him be your minister; and whosoever will be chief among you, let him be your servant: even as the Son of man came not to be ministered unto, but to minister" (Matthew 20:26-28).

Forever let the parting charge of our blessed Master abide in our consciences and come up in the practice of our daily lives. It is not for nothing we may be sure that we find these things recorded for our learning just before He left the world. Let us aim at a loving, doing, useful, hard-working, unselfish, kind, unpretentious religion. Let it be our daily desire to think of others, care for others, do good to others, and to lessen the sorrow and increase the joy of this sinful world. This is to realize the great principle which our Lord's command to Peter was intended to teach. So living and so laboring to order our ways, we shall find it abundantly true, that "it is more blessed to give than to receive" (Acts 20:35).

John 21:18-25

Verily, verily, I say unto thee, When thou wast young, thou didst gird thyself and walk where thou wouldest, but when thou shalt be old, thou shalt stretch forth thy hands, and another shall gird thee and carry thee where thou wouldest not. This he spoke, signifying by what death he should clarify God. And when he had spoken this, he said unto him, Follow

---

express our one English word "feed." One means simply "provide food and pasture," and is used in the fifteenth and seventeenth verses. The other means not only "provide food," but "govern, lead, direct, and generally do the work of a shepherd."

me. Then Peter, turning about, saw the disciple whom Jesus loved following, who also leaned on his breast at supper, and said, Lord, which is he that betrays thee? Peter seeing him said to Jesus, Lord, and what shall this man do? Jesus said unto him, If I will that he tarry until I come, what is that to thee? follow thou me. Then this saying went abroad among the brethren that that disciple should not die; yet Jesus did not say unto him, He shall not die, but, If I will that he tarry until I come, what is that to thee? This is the disciple who testifies of these things and wrote these things, and we know that his testimony is true. And there are also many other things which Jesus did, which, if they should be written every one, I think that even the world itself could not contain the books that should be written. Amen.

These verses form the conclusion of John's Gospel, and bring to an end the most precious book in the Bible. The man is much to be pitied who can read the passage without serious and solemn feelings. It is like listening to the parting words of a friend, whom we may possibly not see again. Let us reverently consider the lessons which this Scripture contains.

We learn, for one thing, from these verses *that the future history of Christians, both in life and death, is foreknown by Christ.* The Lord tells Simon Peter, "When thou art old, thou shalt stretch forth thy hands, and another shall gird thee, and carry thee whither thou wouldest not." These words, without controversy, were a prediction of the manner of the Apostle's death. They were fulfilled in after days, it is commonly supposed, when Peter was crucified as a martyr for Christ's sake. The time, the place, the manner, the painfulness to flesh and blood of the disciple's death were all matters foreseen by the Master.

The truth before us is eminently full of comfort to a true believer. To obtain foreknowledge of things to come would, in most cases, be a sorrowful possession. To know what was going to befall us and yet not to be able to prevent it would make us simply miserable. But it is an unspeakable consolation to remember that our whole future is known and forearranged by Christ. There is no such thing as luck, chance, or accident in the journey of our life. Everything from beginning to end is foreseen – arranged by One who is too wise to err and too loving to do us harm.

Let us store up this truth in our minds and use it diligently in all the days of darkness through which we may yet have to pass. In such days we should lean back on the thought, "Christ knows this, and knew it when He called me to be His disciple." It is foolish to repine and murmur over the troubles of those whom we love. We should rather fall back on the thought that all is well done. It is useless to fret and be rebellious, when we ourselves have bitter cups to drink. We should rather say, "This also is from the Lord – He foresaw it and would have prevented it, if it had not been for my good." Happy are those who can enter into the spirit of that old saint, who said, "I have made a covenant with my Lord, that I will never take amiss anything that He does to me." We may have to walk sometimes through rough places on our way to heaven. But surely it is a comforting, soothing reflection, "Every step of my journey was foreknown by Christ."

We learn, secondly, in these verses *that a believer's death is intended to glorify God.* The Holy Spirit tells us this truth in plain language. He graciously interprets the dark saying, which fell from our Lord's lips about Peter's end. He tells us that Jesus spoke this, "signifying by what death he should glorify God."

The thing before us is probably not considered as much as it ought to be. We are so apt to regard life as the only season for honoring Christ and action as the only mode of showing our religion that we overlook death, except as a painful termination of usefulness. Yet surely this ought not so to be. We may die to the Lord, as well as live to the Lord; we may be patient sufferers as well as active workers. Like Samson, we may do more for God in our death than we ever did in our lives. It is probable that the patient deaths of our martyred Reformers had more effect on the minds of Englishmen than all the sermons they preached and all the books they wrote. One thing, at all events, is certain – the blood of the English martyrs was the seed of the English Church.

We may glorify God in death by being ready for it whenever it comes. The Christian who is found like a sentinel at his post, like a servant with his loins girded and his lamp burning, with a heart packed up and ready to go, the man to whom sudden death by the common consent of all who knew him is sudden glory – this, this is a man whose end brings glory to God. We may glorify God in death by patiently enduring its pains. The Christian whose spirit has complete victory over the flesh, who quietly feels the pins of his earthly tabernacle plucked up with great bodily agonies, and yet never murmurs or complains but silently enjoys inward peace – this, this again, is a man whose end brings glory to God. We may glorify God in death by testifying to others the comfort and support that we find in the grace of Christ. It is a great thing when a mortal man can say with David, "Though I walk through the valley of the shadow of death, I will fear no evil" (Psalm 23:4). The Christian who, like Standfast in "Pilgrim's Progress," can stand for a while in the river, and talk calmly to his companions, saying, "My foot is fixed sure – my toilsome days are ended" – this, this is a man whose end brings glory to God. Deaths like these leave a mark on the living and are not soon forgotten.

Let us pray, while we live in health, that we may glorify God in our end. Let us leave it to God to choose the where, and when, and how, and all the manner of our departing. Let us only ask that it may "glorify God." He is a wise man who takes John Bunyan's advice and keeps his last hour continually in mind, and makes it his company-keeper. It was a weighty saying of John Wesley, when one found fault with the doctrines and practices of the Methodists – "At any rate, our people die well."

We learn, thirdly, in these verses *that whatever we may think about the condition of other people, we should think first about our own.* When Peter inquired curiously and anxiously about the future of the Apostle John, he received from our Lord an answer of deep meaning – "If I will that he tarry until I come, what is that to thee? Follow thou Me." Hard to understand as some part of that sentence may be, it contains a practical lesson which cannot be mistaken. It commands every Christian to remember his own heart first and to look at home.

Of course our blessed Lord does not wish us to neglect the souls of others or to take no interest in their condition. Such a state of mind would be nothing less than uncharitable selfishness and would prove plainly that we had not the grace of God. The servant of Christ will have a wide, broad heart, like his Master, and will desire the present and eternal happiness of all around him. He will long and labor to lessen the sorrows and to increase the joys of every one within his reach and, as he has opportunity, to do good to all men. But, in all his doing, the servant of Christ must never forget his own soul. Charity and true religion must both begin at home.

It is vain to deny that our Lord's solemn caution to His impetuous disciple is greatly needed in the present day. Such is the weakness of human nature that even true Christians are continually liable to run into extremes. Some are so entirely absorbed in their own inward experience and their own heart's conflict that they forget the world outside. Others are so busy about doing good to the world that they neglect to cultivate their own souls. Both are wrong and both need to see a more excellent way; but none perhaps do so much harm to religion as those who are busybodies about others' salvation and at the same time neglecters of their own. From such a snare as this may the ringing words of our Lord deliver us! Whatever we do for others (and we never can do enough), let us not forget our own inner man. Unhappily, the Bride, in Canticles, is not the only person who has cause to complain – "They made me the keeper of the vineyards; but mine own vineyard I have not kept" (Song of Solomon 1:6).

We learn, lastly, from these verses, *the number and greatness of Christ's works during His earthly ministry.* John concludes his Gospel with these remarkable words, "There are many other things which Jesus did, the which, if they should be written every one, I suppose the world itself could not contain the books that should be written." Of course we must not torture these words, by pressing them to an excessively literal interpretation. To suppose that the Evangelist meant the world could not hold the material volumes which would be written is evidently unreasonable and absurd. The only sensible interpretation must be a spiritual and figurative one.

As much of Christ's sayings and doings is recorded as the mind of man can take in. It would not be good for the world to have more. The human mind, like the body, can only digest a certain quantity. The world could not contain more, because it would not. As many miracles, as many parables, as many sermons, as many conversions, as many words of kindness, as many deeds of mercy, as many journeys, as many prayers, as many warnings, as many promises are recorded, as the world can possibly require. If more had been recorded, they would have been only thrown away. There is enough to make every unbeliever without excuse, enough to show every inquirer the way to heaven, enough to satisfy the heart of every honest believer, enough to condemn man if he does not repent and believe, enough to glorify God. The largest vessel can only contain a certain quantity of liquid. The mind of all mankind would not appreciate more about Christ, if more had been written. There is enough and to spare. This witness is true. Let us deny it if we can.

And now let us close the Gospel of John with mingled feelings of deep humility and deep thankfulness. We may well be humble when we think how ignorant we are and how little we comprehend of the treasures which this Gospel contains. But we may well be thankful, when we reflect how clear and plain is the instruction which it gives us about the way of salvation. The man who reads this Gospel profitably is he who "believes that Jesus is the Christ, and, believing, has life through His Name." Do we so believe? Let us never rest till we can give a satisfactory answer to that question!

I have now completed my Notes on John's Gospel. I have given my last explanation . . . . The closing words of Bullinger's Commentary on the Gospels, condensed and abridged, will perhaps not be considered an inappropriate conclusion to my "Expository Thought on John."

"Reader, I have now set before thee thy Savior the Lord Jesus Christ, that very Son of God, who was begotten by the Father by an eternal. And ineffable generation, consubstantial and coequal with the Father in all things – but in these last times, according to prophetical oracles, was incarnate for us, suffered, died, rose again from the dead, and was made King and Lord of all things. This is He who is appointed and given to us by God the Father, as the fullness of all grace and truth, as the Lamb of God who taketh away the sins of the world, as the ladder and door of heaven, as the serpent lifted up to render the poison of sin harmless, as the water which refreshes the thirsty, as the bread of life, as the light of the world, as the redeemer of God's children, as the shepherd and door of the sheep, as the resurrection and the life, as the corn of wheat which springs up into much fruit, as the conqueror of the prince of this world, as the way, the truth, and the life, as the true vine, and finally, as the redemption, salvation, satisfaction, and righteousness of all the faithful in all the world, throughout all ages. Let us therefore pray God the Father, that, being taught by His Gospel, we may know Him that is true, and believe in Him in whom alone is salvation; and that, believing, we may feel God living in us in this world, and in the world to come may enjoy His eternal and most blessed fellowship." Amen and Amen.

J. C. Ryle – A Brief Biography

John Charles Ryle was born into a wealthy, affluent, socially elite family on May 10, 1816 – the firstborn son of John Ryle, a banker, and his wife Susanna (Wirksworth) Ryle. As the firstborn, John lived a privileged life and was set to inherit all of his father's estate and pursue a career in Parliament. His future promised to be planned and comfortable with no material needs.

J. C. Ryle attended a private school and then earned academic scholarships to Eton (1828) and the University of Oxford (1834), but he excelled in sports. He particularly made his mark in rowing and cricket. Though his pursuit of sports was short lived, he claimed that they gave him leadership gifts. "It gave me a power of commanding, managing, organizing and directing, seeing through men's capabilities and using every man in the post to which he was best suited, bearing and forbearing, keeping men around me in good temper, which I have found of infinite use on lots of occasions in life, though in very different matters."

In 1837, before graduation, Ryle contracted a serious chest infection, which caused him to turn to the Bible and prayer for the first time in over fourteen years. One Sunday he entered church late as Ephesians 2:8 was being read – slowly, phrase by phrase. John felt the Lord was speaking to him personally, and he claims to have been converted at that moment through the Word without any commentary or sermon.

His biographer wrote, "He came under conviction, was converted, and from that moment to the last recorded syllable of this life, no doubt ever lingered in John's mind that the Word of God was living and powerful, sharper than any two-edged sword."

After graduation from Oxford, John went to London to study law for his career in politics, but in 1841, his father's bank crashed. That was the end of the career in politics, for he had no funding to continue.

In later years, John wrote, "We got up one summer's morning with all the world before us as usual, and went to bed that same night completely and entirely ruined. The immediate consequences were bitter and painful in the extreme, and humiliating to the utmost degree."

And at another time, he said, "The plain fact was there was no one of the family whom it touched more than it did me. My father and mother were no longer young and in the downhill of life; my brothers and sisters, of course, never expected to live at Henbury (the family home) and naturally never thought of it as their house after a certain time. I, on the contrary, as the eldest son, twenty-five, with all the world before me, lost everything, and saw the whole future of my life turned upside down and thrown into confusion."

After this financial ruin from abundance, Ryle was a commoner – all in a day. For the first time in his life, he needed a job. His education qualified him for the clergy, so with his Oxford degree, he was ordained and entered the ministry of the Church of England. He proceeded in a totally different direction with his first assignment in the ministry at Exbury in Hampshire, but it was a rural area riddled with disease. His recurring lung infection made a difficult couple of years until he was transferred to St. Thomas in Winchester. With his commanding presence, passionately held principles, and warm disposition, John's congregation grew so large and strong it needed different accommodations.

Ryle accepted a position at that time in Helmington, Suffolk, where he had much time to read theologians like Wesley, Bunyan, Knox, Calvin, and Luther. He was a contemporary of Charles Spurgeon, Dwight Moody, George Mueller, and Hudson Taylor. He lived in the age of Dickens, Darwin, and the American Civil War. All of these influenced Ryle's understanding and theology.

His writing career began from the tragedy of the Great Yarmouth suspension bridge. On May 9, 1845, a large crowd gathered for the official grand opening festivities, but the bridge collapsed and more than a hundred people plunged into the water and drowned. The incident shocked the whole country but it led Ryle to write his first tract. He spoke of life's uncertainties and God's sure provision of salvation through Jesus Christ. Thousands of copies were sold.

That same year, he married Matilda Plumptre, but she died after only two years, leaving him with an infant daughter. In 1850, he married Jessie Walker, but she had a lingering sickness, which caused Ryle to care for her and their growing family (three sons and another daughter) for ten years until she died. In 1861, he was transferred to Stradbroke, Suffolk, where he married Henrietta Clowes.

Stradbroke, Suffolk, was Ryle's last parish, and he gained a reputation for his straightforward preaching and evangelism. Besides his travelling and preaching, he spent time writing. He wrote more than 300 pamphlets, tracts, and books. His books include *Expository Thoughts on the Gospels* (7 Volumes, 1856-1869), *Principles for Churchmen* (1884), *Home Truths, Knots Untied, Old Paths,* and *Holiness.*

His *Christian Leaders of the Eighteenth Century* (1869) is described as having "short, pithy sentences, compelling logic and penetrating insight into spiritual power." This seems to be the case with most of his writing as he preached and wrote with five main guidelines: (1) Have a clear view of the subject, (2) Use simple words, (3) Use a simple style of composition, (4) Be direct, and (5) Use plenty of anecdotes and illustrations.

In all of his success with writing, he used the royalties to pay his father's debts. He may have felt indebted to that financial ruin, for he said, "I have not the least doubts, it was all for the best. If I had not been ruined, I should never have been a clergyman, never preached a sermon, or written a tract or book."

In spite of all of the trials that Ryle experienced – financial ruin, loss of three wives, his own poor health – he learned several life lessons. First, care and tend to your own family. Second, swim against the tide when you need to. He was evangelical before it was popular and he held to principles of Scripture: justification by faith alone, substitutionary atonement, the Trinity, and preaching. Third, model Christian attitudes toward your opponents. Fourth, learn and understand church history. Important benefits come from past generations. Fifth, serve in old age; "die in the harness." And, sixth, persevere through your trials.

These were life principles that Ryle learned as he lived his life, as he preached, as he wrote, and as he spread the gospel. He was forever a supporter of evangelism and a critic of ritualism.

J. C. Ryle was recommended by Prime Minister Benjamin Disraeli to be Bishop of Liverpool in 1880 where he then worked to build churches and mission halls to reach the whole city. He retired in 1900 at the age of 83 and died later that year. His successor described him as "a man of granite with a heart of a child."

G. C. B. Davies said "a commanding presence and fearless advocacy of his principles were combined with a kind and understanding attitude in his personal relationships."[58]

---

58   Sources:

William P. Farley, "J. C. Ryle: A 19th-century Evangelical," *Enrichment Journal, http://enrichmentjournal.ag.org/200604/200604_120_jcryle.cfm.*

"J. C. Ryle," *The Banner of Truth, https://banneroftruth.org/us/about/banner-authors/j-c-ryle/.*

"J. C. Ryle," *Theopedia, https://www.theopedia.com/john-charles-ryle.*

David Holloway, "J. C. Ryle – The Man, The Minister and The Missionary," *Bible Bulletin Board, http://www.biblebb.com/files/ryle/j_c_ryle.htm.*

Other Similar Titles

Romans – A Commentary,
by J. Martin

A Commentary

Major highlight: The reconciliation of God's sovereignty and man's free will.

When Paul wrote the epistle of Romans, his intention was that Romans would read the whole letter in one sitting, and that they would understand what they were reading without further explanation. Sometimes we dig so deep into scripture that we lose the basic meaning of what we're reading. This is not, then, as much a commentary as it is an attempt to revitalize interest in the book of Romans itself – as it was written, and as it was meant to be understood. Attention is drawn to the words and phrases of the text, highlighting things imperative to be understood and claimed for our own.

Available where books are sold.

The Duties of Parents,
by J. C. Ryle

Training your children well and not causing them to stumble in any way ought to be one of the highest priorities of Christian parents.

In *The Duties of Parents*, J. C. Ryle presents seventeen simple and yet profound responsibilities of Christian parents. Nothing new is contained in this little volume, yet what is presented has the potential to change future generations both now and for eternity. Learn how to shepherd your children; learn how to utilize the most significant key of all – love; and learn first and foremost how to present and represent Christ to your children. As you read this book, expect to find yourself both challenged and excited to begin a wonderful, appropriate, and growing relationship with the most wonderful gift God can give us in our lifetime – our dear children.

Available where books are sold.

The Ten Commandments,
by Dwight L. Moody

The ten commandments are not popular today. Atheists want them nowhere in sight. Many Christians say they are outdated. But Dwight L. Moody challenges us to take a closer look. Which of the ten commandments can we honestly say are not good? Which of the ten commandments can we break and not suffer the consequences, both here and in eternity?

This book will challenge you to examine God's rules for life. God doesn't ask anything of us that is difficult or unreasonable, and this is certainly true with Jesus Christ as our strength and the Holy Spirit to guide us. This book is a challenging yet refreshing look at some of the oldest, most well-known words of God.

Available where books are sold.

Life in Christ,
by Charles H. Spurgeon

Volume 1

Men who were led by the hand or groped their way along the wall to reach Jesus were touched by his finger and went home without a guide, rejoicing that Jesus Christ had opened their eyes. Jesus is still able to perform such miracles. And, with the power of the Holy Spirit, his Word will be expounded and we'll watch for the signs to follow, expecting to see them at once. Why shouldn't those who read this be blessed with the light of heaven? This is my heart's inmost desire.

I can't put fine words together. I've never studied speech. In fact, my heart loathes the very thought of intentionally speaking with fine words when souls are in danger of eternal separation from God. No, I work to speak straight to your hearts and consciences, and if there is anyone with faith to receive, God will bless them with fresh revelation.

– Charles H. Spurgeon

Available where books are sold.

According to Promise,
by Charles H. Spurgeon

The first part of this book is meant to be a sieve to separate the chaff from the wheat. Use it on your own soul. It may be the most profitable and beneficial work you have ever done. He who looked into his accounts and found that his business was losing money was saved from bankruptcy. This may happen also to you. If, however, you discover that your heavenly business is prospering, it will be a great comfort to you. You cannot lose by honestly searching your own heart.

The second part of this book examines God's promises to His children. The promises of God not only exceed all precedent, but they also exceed all imitation. No one has been able to compete with God in the language of liberality. The promises of God are as much above all other promises as the heavens are above the earth.

Available where books are sold.

How to Study the Bible,
by Dwight L. Moody

There is no situation in life for which you cannot find some word of consolation in Scripture. If you are in affliction, if you are in adversity and trial, there is a promise for you. In joy and sorrow, in health and in sickness, in poverty and in riches, in every condition of life, God has a promise stored up in His Word for you.

This classic book by Dwight L. Moody brings to light the necessity of studying the Scriptures, presents methods which help stimulate excitement for the Scriptures, and offers tools to help you comprehend the difficult passages in the Scriptures. To live a victorious Christian life, you must read and understand what God is saying to you. Moody is a master of using stories to illustrate what he is saying, and you will be both inspired and convicted to pursue truth from the pages of God's Word.

Available where books are sold.

The Ministry of Intercession,
by Andrew Murray

If the answer to prayer is so positively promised in scripture, why are there so many unanswered prayers today (often misinterpreted as a "no")? Scripture teaches us that answer to prayer depends upon certain conditions. Christ spoke of faith, of perseverance, of praying in His name, of praying in the will of God. But all these conditions were summed up in the one central statement: If ye abide in me and my words abide in you, ye shall ask what ye will, and it shall be done unto you. It becomes clear that the power to pray the effectual prayer of faith depends upon the life.

Let Andrew Murray show you what it means to live in Christ, and let his challenge for genuine intercessory prayer change your life – and the lives of those you are praying for.

Available where books are sold.

Absolute Surrender,
by Andrew Murray

God waits to bless us in a way beyond what we expect. From the beginning, ear has not heard, neither has the eye seen, what God has prepared for those who wait for Him (Isaiah 64:4). God has prepared unheard of things, things you never can think of, blessings much more wonderful than you can imagine and mightier than you can conceive. They are divine blessings. Oh, come at once and say, "I give myself absolutely to God, to His will, to do only what God wants." God will enable you to carry out the surrender necessary, if you come to Him with a sincere heart.

Made in the USA
Monee, IL
25 March 2020